MYSTERIES OF THE MEXICAN PYRAMIDS

Other books by Peter Tompkins

To a Young Actress
Shaw and Molly Tompkins
The Eunuch & the Virgin
A Spy in Rome
The Murder of Admiral Darlan
Italy Betrayed
Secrets of the Great Pyramid
The Secret Life of Plants (with Christopher Bird)

MYSTERIES OF THE

Harper & Row, Publishers
New York, Hagerstown, San Francisco, London

MEXICAN PYRAMIDS

Peter Tompkins

Dimensional analysis in original drawings
by Hugh Harleston, Jr.
And historic illustrations from many sources

First Edition

Designed by Gayle Jaeger

Library of Congress Cataloging in Publication Data
Tompkins, Peter.
  Mysteries of the Mexican pyramids.

  Bibliography: p.
  Includes index.
  1. Indians of Mexico—Pyramids. 2. Mexico—An-
tiquities. 3. Occult sciences—Mexico. I. Title.
F1219.3.P9T58 1976   972   74–15857
ISBN 0–06–014324–X

For E. B. V. and H. B. T.

To the staff of the Library of Congress, guarantors of free access to the sources, without which enjoyment of the First Amendment to the Constitution could be reduced to an exercise *in vacuo.*

Contents

Acknowledgments

I am most indebted to the authors and artists whose works
are analyzed, reproduced, and credited within this volume,
and to those at Harper & Row who made the volume
possible, especially M. S. Wyeth, Jr., Gayle Jaeger,
Kathleen Hyde, Lynne McNabb, Florence Goldstein, and
Bill Janson, whose constant and invigorating collaboration
made the work a pleasure. To Nicholas Vreeland and
Edward Mitchell I wish to express my thanks for their care
in making prints for the many reproductions. Indeed to all
who gave me help, and in particular to the librarians of the
Library of Congress and of the University of Miami for the
kind use of their facilities, my gratitude.

Preface

Deep in the jungles of Mexico and Central America, in the tight embrace of root and vine, clawed by jaguar or caressed by rattler, lie the remains of perhaps thousands of ancient pyramids, pyramids on pyramids, many still undiscovered, abandoned by unknown builders at an unknown time for unknown reasons. In their secret places may lie more of the precious codices and hieroglyphic writings—celestial mathematics sculptured into geometric form—which make it possible to reconstruct the brilliance of a civilization which the Church of Rome did all in its power to obliterate. Under the axe and torch of Spanish conqueror the ancient wisdom was reduced to superstition.

For centuries this brutal story lay buried in the archives; when it surfaced it was disbelieved. Mesoamericans were described as ignorant and brutish.

Just as Egyptologists could not believe that in ancient Egypt someone had accurately measured the circumference of the earth, placing geodetic markers by astronomical observation as accurately as surveyors do today, orienting their buildings within seconds of true north, so Americanists were reluctant to recognize or admit that in their ancient glyphs and codices the Maya showed astronomical computors so sophisticated they could and still can be read by a schoolboy. The Maya, it is now clear, constructed calendars of the synodic return of the planets laced with the cyclic phenomena of solstices, equinoxes, and eclipses of the sun and moon.

Though the Aztec calendar stone has become the shopworn memento of a tour of modern Mexico, there is still reluctance in the academies to acknowledge that its superlatively aesthetic and intricate design is a perpetual cosmic clock accurately marking for the layman cycles of the visible bodies of our solar system not only in the present but deep into the future and the past.

There is no science without measure. The Maya saw their supreme deity, *Hunab Ku,* as sole dispenser of movement and measure, whose symbol, the compassed circle and the square, was identical with that of the Great Architect of modern Masonry. In the Middle East the ancients adopted the second of arc, of which they counted 1,296,000 to a circle (360 × 60 × 60), and the second of time, of which they counted 86,400 to the circuit of a day (24 × 60 × 60).

From the first second they derived their foot (of .3079 meters). One hundred such feet, they said, will be one second of arc. From the second second they derived their cubit (of .4618 meters). One thousand such cubits, they said, is the distance traveled by the earth at the Equator in one second of time.*

With these units Middle Easterners measured the cosmos and its cycles, incorporating the results, along with the mathematical constants of its structure, into their architecture—as in the proportions of the Tower of Babel and the Pyramid of Cheops. Middle Americans did likewise, as can now be extrapolated from their pyramids.

One look at the passages of the Egyptian temples was enough for astronomers Proctor and Lockyear at the end of the nineteenth century to conclude that the structures had been designed and used in antiquity for astronomical observation and for the recording of such vital data as the equinoxes and the soltices. One look at the pyramidal structures of Yucatan and Chiapas, with their corbelled walls rising to single moveable capstones (like the Grand Gallery at Ghiza, or the "tombs" of Mycenae, or of Maes-Howe), is enough to show that they were built for astronomical observation, with frets and cockscombs that could function as markers for the rising, transit, and setting of heavenly bodies.

As with the Great Pyramid of Ghiza, the Sun Pyramid at Teotihuacan was used to mark the solstices, zenith days, and equinoxes. The stelae of Guatemala, intricately carved or stuccoed, clearly served the same function as the intaglioed obelisks of Egypt, by means of which the ancients accurately measured the size of the earth, mapped it, and chronometrically ticked off the cyclic passage of the ages.

---

* Both units are truly earth-commensurate fractions of the earth's circumference in that 129,600,000 × .308 or 8,640,000 × .462 = 39,916.80 kilometers—very close to the 40,000 kilometers adopted as the circumference of the earth by the devisors of the meter in the eighteenth century.

The study of the extraordinary effects on this planet of the comings and goings of other planets in conjunction with each other and with the sun and moon, only to be monitored by constant and accurate observation and the most sophisticated coding, has been derided by moderns as "astrology"; yet, with blinding science, we treat our nursing mother earth as dirt beneath our feet, and the living cosmos as a bottomless pit for our onanistic spaceshots.

We live in a Dark Age, and have, for several thousand years. It is time for a renaissance—with the wisdom of the past.

Architecture, says architect Robert Stacy-Judd, consists of frozen symbols, which can be thawed into a palatable language, "where measures and motifs are words and sentences." Augustus Le Plongeon calls architecture an unerring standard of the degree of civilization reached by a people, "as correct a test of race as is language, and more easily understood, not being subject to change." If it is true that a nation's capital reflects its standards of architecture, we risk being judged by the phony cyclopean walls of the Office Building of the U.S. House of Representatives unless we engender architects sensitive to the cosmic values of geometry, such as R. Buckminster Fuller would envisage.

The ancient civilizations attached great importance to numbers as an exact language in which physical and spiritual ideals could be expressed and preserved; hence, they built their numbers into buildings.

As John Michell has pointed out, their monuments contain, both in their dimensions and their relative geographical positions, the whole vocabulary of the sacred language of the past. Michell believes such buildings as the Great Pyramid of Cheops were built by men who knew something of the laws which govern the intergalactic flow of living energy and their application to the development of life on earth. "The enormous task of building the Great Pyramid, the crowning achievement of prehistoric science," says Michell, "could only have been undertaken by men whose faith in the value of their labours derived from a certain knowledge of universal law. The key to every art and science may one day be rediscovered within the effortless harmony of the Pyramid's numerical scheme." To which he adds: "Written across the face of the country in letters of earth and stone the cosmic knowledge of the ancient world is now within reach."

PART II

SETTING THE STAGE

1. Return of the "Gods"

Hernan Cortes shortly after the fall of Mexico.

A freebooter who had betrayed his superiors in Havana, Cortes was 34 years old when his armada of eleven ships landed at Veracruz on the east coast of Mexico in April of 1519. Syphilitic and bowlegged from an injury acquired in a fall from a room during an amorous quest, Cortes was described by his countrymen as robust, with a deep chest and broad shoulders. His hair and beard were black and thin. Considered a good horseman, swordsman, and a great infighter with a knife, he was also renowned as licentious, gluttonous, fond of dice, and avid for women and gold. Born in the Estremadura region of Spain, Cortes had an inborn genius for treachery and could be unbelievably brutal and cruel, boasting to Charles V of Spain that he had massacred unarmed women and children in order to impose his will upon the natives.

In the Mexican highlands, in a pocket valley protected from the cold north wind by the bulk of an extinct volcano, lie the monumental remains of an ancient civilization. These weird and majestic ruins, dominated by two pyramidal mounds, lay undisturbed for centuries. First seen by Europeans when Hernan Cortes and his rabble army invaded Mexico in 1519, they have remained a source of conjecture to succeeding generations. Only now, since the beginning of the twentieth century, is the riddle of their nature beginning to unravel.

While William Prescott and others have told the story of the Conquest of Mexico in detail vivid enough to dazzle, the more sinister story of the burial, destruction, and vilification of the lore enshrined in these pyramids has largely gone untold. Intertwined, the stories reveal a struggle between two powerful forces vying for the souls of men.

Native historians described the arrival of the conquistadores as a succession of grim fatalities.

Though all the omens had foretold their coming, and an impending destruction of the Aztec empire, the actual landing of the Spaniards was so astounding to the first eyewitness that despite the loss of all his toes he climbed seven thousand feet to Mexico's highland capital of Tenochtitlan to inform King Montezuma II that towers and small mountains were floating in the sea, bearing strange beings from an unknown world with very light skin, long beards, and hair only to their ears.

Montezuma, a slender aristocratic man with a long spare face, was aware from the sacred texts of the Mexica that Quetzalcoatl, man or god, had promised to return from the East in the year 1-Reed. And this was the year 1-Reed.

3

In his fifties when Cortes landed in Mexico, Montezuma II looked more like forty and was described by the Spaniards as of good height, well proportioned, slender and spare, with a brown complexion and hair that just covered his ears. His beard was thin, black, and well shaped, giving his face an expression of both tenderness and gravity. He was considered very neat and clean and affected the Spaniards by the airs and gestures of an accomplished prince. His name was an honorary title meaning "our angry-looking lord," because an Aztec ruler was admonished "never to laugh and joke again as he had done previous to his election, and to assume the heart of an old, grave and severe man." He was considered a temporary representative and mouthpiece of an invisible, impersonal dual divinity. "You are the image of our lord god and represent his person. He reposes in you and he employs you like a flute through which he speaks, and he hears with your ears." Considered a learned astrologer and philosopher who was skilled in the arts, Montezuma succeeded to the Aztec throne in 1502 at the age of 36, elected by a Council of Six from among members of his predecessor's family, chosen because of his high attainments. Head of the army and of the church, with the official title of First Speaker, Montezuma governed through a Council of Three: the commander of the army (known by the title of "Snake Woman"), the high priest, and the governor of Tenochtitlan. Montezuma is reported to have ruled well and administered impartially and rigorously. To investigate how his ministers executed their offices he would disguise himself and move about his realm incognito. Montezuma told Cortes his forefathers had come from a land far away called Aztlan, where there was a high mountain and a garden inhabited by the gods.

As Cortes moved toward the Mexican capital with his gang of four hundred Spaniards, supported by thousands of native tribesmen happy to rebel against what they considered Montezuma's tyrannical rule, more messengers reached Tenochtitlan describing the newcomers as supernatural creatures riding on hornless deer, preceded by wild animals on leashes, dressed in iron, armed in iron, fearless as gods.

Spaniards say that when Cortes reached the city of Cholula, with its hundreds of whitewashed temples over which loomed the remnants of the largest pyramid in the Americas, his ambassador, whom he had sent ahead to seek peaceful surrender of the city, was returned with severed wrists dangling from flayed elbows. True or not, Cortes massacred six thousand Cholulans.

4

Cortes advanced on Mexico with fourteen horses and many cannon, neither of which had ever been seen by his Mexican opponents.

To reach Tenochtitlan entailed crossing two passes 10,000 feet high where hail fell and an icy wind drove down from the snowy mountains; it also meant crossing a desolate plateau of volcanic ash forty miles wide. Cortes, outnumbered thousands to one, hoped to seize the Aztec capital by guile rather than force.

The prime weapon in his arsenal, apart from the thousands of rebellious natives who supported him, was psychological. Their legends told the Mexica that white gods from the East would return to conquer Mexico, and there was no struggling against their fate.

Shocked by the news, Montezuma vacillated between defiance and surrender. Cortes and his followers were described to him as advancing in battle array, the dust rising like whirlwinds, their spears glittering in the sun, their pennons fluttering like bats, their armor rattling in the cold November wind.

At the Pass of the Eagle, by the snowcapped volcanoes of Popocatepetl and Iztaccihuatl, Montezuma's envoys knelt before the Spaniards and adored them as the Sons of the Sun, their gods. Had not the divine Quetzalcoatl dressed in black velvet as did Cortes? And, they whispered, judging from the size of the latter's stuffed codpiece he had the makings of a god.

Ahead of Cortes stretched the Valley of Mexico, a lovely plateau half filled with shallow lakes, called "Of the Moon," alive with fish and waterfowl, its clear waters mirroring the surrounding mountain forests, its shores brightened by the villages and cities of the Mexica.

5

At Cholula, Cortes was greeted by girls singing, dancing, and playing on instruments, while others brought bread and fowl. Nobles, chieftains, and common folk, "unarmed, with eager and happy faces, crowded in the great courtyard of the Temple of Quetzalcoatl to hear what the white men would say." The Spaniards then closed the entrances and at a signal fell upon the Cholulans. "Those of Cholula were caught unaware. With neither arrows nor shields did they meet the Spaniards. Just so they were slain without warning. They were killed by pure treachery; they died unaware."

Montezuma planned to recognize Cortes, by sending him—along with many fine presents—the insignia of the God Quetzalcoatl, whom he believed him to be. This way Montezuma hoped to keep Cortes from Mexico City.

The ambassadors were told to tell Cortes that the treasures were "all priestly ornaments that belonged to him." Among the presents were two circular calendars as large as cartwheels, one of gold, the other of silver, both elaborately engraved with hieroglyphs, and both of which were melted down for ingots. Some of the presents reached the Emperor Charles V and were greatly admired by Dürer.

With Montezuma's ambassadors went a group of enchanters and witchmasters to try to keep Cortes away.

In his famous speech to Cortes, which the latter carefully reported to the Emperor Charles V, Montezuma stated that: "We [the Mexican rulers] were brought here by a lord, whose vassals all of our predecessors were, and who returned from here to his native land. He afterwards came here again, after a long time, during which many of his followers who had remained, had married native women of this land, raised large families and founded towns in which they dwelt. He wished to take them away from here with him. But they did not want to go, nor would they receive or adopt him as their ruler, and so he departed. But we have always thought that his descendants would surely come to subjugate this country and claim us as their vassal."

Nahuatl pyramids usually had two stairways leading to two temples, as with the central Aztec pyramid in Tenochtitlan, dedicated to Tezcatlipoca, believed to have been built six years before Columbus rediscovered America.

Bernal Diaz said it was 54 meters high with 114 steps, and that it measured 97 meters at the base. In the interior of the top sanctuary there existed a small stepped pyramid dedicated to the sun, known as the Cuauhcalli, "House of the Eagles." Here the steps represented the heavenly planes, the highest level corresponding to the hour of zenith or midday.

The city of Tenochtitlan, divided into four quarters, each of which had five subdivisions (*calpullis*), actually consisted of two distinct parts. One of these was Tenochtitlan proper, where the Great Temple stood and where Montezuma and the lords resided; the other was Tlatelolco, where the lower classes dwelt and the merchant class prevailed.

A large temple occupied the center of Tenochtitlan, a city, according to Cortes, of five hundred palaces, well built of stone, whose walls were crowned with battlements and ornamented with serpents.

Cortes said there were "forty very high houses in the enclosure of the Great Temple" and that they were all "sepul-chres of the lords." The more substantial houses occupied the central sections of the capital, where the land was higher and firmer. Canals, bright green with water vegetables, encircled and crisscrossed the city, which an Aztec poet described as spread out in circles of jade, radiating flashes of light like quetzal plumes.

According to Bernal Diaz' eyewitness report, when the great Montezuma came forth in state to meet Cortes, he was conveyed on a sumptuous litter with a baldaquin over his head adorned with light greenish-blue feathers, gold, pearls, and jade to represent "the verdant or blue sky." He was supported by his four principal lords; and the golden soles on his sandals prevented his feet from coming into direct contact with the ground. Other lords preceded him, "sweeping the ground and spreading blankets upon it so that he should not tread upon the earth. All of these lords did not dare to think of raising their eyes to look at his face—only the four lords, his cousins, who supported him, possessed this privilege." On state occasions Montezuma, like his predecessors, was the only person privileged to sit on a throne or raised seat with a high back.

When the Spaniards first glimpsed the island capital of Tenochtitlan—glimmering like an exotic Venice at the end of a wide causeway, with stunning palaces, temples, and pyramids, stuccoed pink with volcanic ash, rising from the cerulean waters of the lake—they thought they were dreaming.

Though many had seen the splendors of Rome and Constantinople, they were amazed at a city of 300,000 inhabitants fed by fresh-water aqueducts, laced with canals and carefully paved streets, adorned by arcaded squares twice as big as Salamanca's, serviced by a market place where 70,000 Indians daily bought and sold a thousand different products, from filigreed jewelry to mountains of polychrome feathers, including those from the rare quetzal bird.

The Spaniards were enchanted by such luxuries as botanical and zoological gardens, by elegantly towered palaces, higher than the cathedral of Seville, surrounded by large and beautiful private houses with fragrant gardens shaded by bright cotton awnings where courtly nobles feasted on fruits and vegetables, sauces and soups, fish and meat, cakes and pies, varied by such delicacies as maguey grubs with hot chili, winged ants with savory herbs, and rats in chocolate sauce.

According to Aztec tradition, the city of Tenochtitlan was modeled after the lost capital of their original homeland, situated on an island in the middle of a lake surrounded by rings of canals and interconnecting dams.

Migrant Chichimecs serving in the Toltec army, who called themselves Aztecs after their mythical home in Aztlan, built the city of Tenochtitlan on a marshy island in the Lake of the Moon in A.D. 1345. The city was connected to the mainland by three causeways: north to Tepeyacac, west to Tlacopan, and south with two branches to Ixtapalapa and Coyoacan. The city, including Tlatelolco, covered some 7 1/2 square kilometers built around temples and public buildings. According to the Aztec legend, their god, Huitzilopochtli, sometimes in the guise of a hummingbird, had urged them on until they reached the island, which was said to have the same magical properties of their homeland in Aztlan.

Searching for a mote in the Mexican eye, the Spaniards claimed to be horrified by the native indulgence in unbridled sodomy, by their orgies of ritual sacrifice in which priests, each with his own penis slit to achieve pure chastity, would roast alive or rip out the pulsing hearts of an estimated 50,000 human victims a year to feed the local gentry and satisfy the theory that their solar divinity needed human blood lest it vanish from exhaustion.

On the excuse of bringing to the natives a better form of religion, the Spaniards, tough, mean, and hungry for gold, massacred without warning the unarmed cream of their hosts' warrior nobles who were innocently celebrating a feast day with a dance.

Blood-encrusted Aztec priests were accused by the Spaniards of performing 50,000 human sacrifices a year. Diaz accused them not only of human sacrifice but of cannibalism, sodomy, incest, and such drunkenness that when they could no longer stand "they lay down and did have the liquor injected by squirt into the breach." Diaz gives a description of Aztec priests half roasting a man, pulling him off the coals with grappling irons to cut out his still beating heart. He says the walls of the temple were splashed and encrusted with blood whose stench was unbearable.

Montezuma was reputed to have been fed on the little fingers of small boys as a delicacy. But Cortes stated that he never actually saw a ritual sacrifice, that the only human sacrifices he witnessed in Tenochtitlan were the normal executions of prisoners of war during the siege. Voltaire believed the Spaniards to have fabricated or grossly exaggerated the charges of Aztec human sacrifice to justify their own brutality.

Later historians have attributed subtle metaphysical motivations to Aztec sacrifices, pointing out that the Aztecs believed the earth to have already been through four cataclysmic periods, and that the only way to stave off a fifth was by human sacrifice. As "Sons of the Sun," the Aztec priests saw the earth as metaphysically nourished by a sun which in turn needed the sacrifice of human blood for its nourishment. Hence the hearts of victims—perhaps by the thousands—were ripped out to stave off cosmic disaster.

This act of infamy brought such retribution from Montezuma's braves that on what came to be known as "The Night of Sorrows" Cortes lost the better part of his army and had to flee the city. Pursued by the braves of Tenochtitlan, Cortes escaped along the river north of Lake Texcoco into a gentle valley dominated by the peak of volcanic Cerro Gordo. There, in the shadow of two pyramidal mounds, the remnants of Cortes' forces, all of them wounded, faced the greatest number of enemy warriors ever mustered for a single battle in the Indies. Tens of thousands of Indians from Otumba, Texcoco, and the cities around the lakes crowded into the valley waving shields, banners, and plumed helmets, convinced they had come to witness the death of every Spaniard.

With no hope of retreat, Cortes and a small group of horsemen charged the center of the enemy forces, where they killed their captain general, the "Snake Woman," causing such panic in the guard that it spread to the hordes of Indians, who retreated, leaving Cortes to live another day. Decimated, bedraggled, and in fear of their lives, the Spaniards paid little attention to the amazing sight around them of a great sleeping city dominated by two gigantic mounds. No one could tell them who had built the great ceremonial center, whence the builders had come, or whither they had gone. All they could learn was that two centuries earlier, when the Mexica had arrived in the valley, they had found the mysterious city already in an abandoned condition, covered with earth and vegetation. Because of the legend that the gods had used the center in antiquity, the Mexica

La Noche Triste.

On the night of June 29, Cortes and his men slipped out of Tenochtitlan along the Tacuba causeway carrying a portable bridge to cross the eight bridges destroyed by the Aztecs. Attacked by Montezuma's followers, Cortes lost half his forces, many being drowned by the weight of the gold they had looted. All would have succumbed had the Aztecs not taken time out for a ritual sacrifice of the captured Spaniards atop their sacred pyramids. In this hiatus Cortes and his surviving wounded forces managed to reach the plain of Otumba by the pyramids of Teotihuacan.

had named the spot Teotihuacan, which they interpreted as meaning either "the burial place of kings" or "the place where the lords of the people woke from the dream of life to become gods."

The greater mound, venerated by the Mexica till the arrival of the Spaniards, was called "Tonatiuh" in the native Nahuatl, meaning "House of the Sun." The smaller mound was called "Metzli Ytzaqual," or "House of the Moon." The great avenue which joined the two pyramidal mounds was called "Huicautli," or "Way of the Dead" because of the smaller mounds which flanked it, assumed by the natives to be tombs.

Claiming that only giants could have constructed the larger mounds, the Mexica said they must have been built in remote antiquity when giants and sages inhabited the earth. As evidence they showed the Spaniards the femurs of elephants or mastodons dug up in the neighborhood which they believed to be the bones of giants. But the Spaniards, intent upon their own survival, paid no heed, escaping southward to the safety of their allies, the Tlaxcalans, where they plotted a revengeful comeback.

The destruction of Tenochtitlan.

A year after *La Noche Triste* Cortes returned with 450 Spaniards, forty horses, nine field guns, and 10,000 Tlaxcalan allies. He also brought a secret weapon in the form of a dozen brigantines built in Tlaxcala, carried overland to the edge of Texcoco Lake. To capture the city, Cortes planned to advance along three of the causeways on a narrow front with bunched musketeers, cannon, crossbows and cavalry, using the ships to protect his flanks. However, just before the attack, Cortes' Mexican allies, who identified him with Quetzalcoatl, deserted because the planet Venus had gone into its yearly eight-day disappearance as the evening star. When nothing bad happened to Quetzalcoatl-Cortes during the dark of Quetzalcoatl-Venus, and the planet reappeared as the morning star, 100,000 allies flocked to Cortes' aid. On August 13, 1521, after a seventy-five-day siege, and one of the most remarkable naval operations in history, Tenochtitlan fell to the Spaniards, leaving more than 240,000 Aztecs dead from wounds or disease. The people of Tenochtitlan, in the account of Lopez de Gomara, one of the eyewitness conquistadores, were "tormented by hunger, and many starved to death. There was no fresh water to drink, only stagnant water and the brine of the lake. . . . The only food was lizards, corncobs and the salt grasses. . . . The people ate water lilies and seeds of colorin, deerhides, and even pieces of leather. . . . They ate even dirt. Almost all of the nobility perished; there remained alive only a few lords and the little children."

According to C. Harvey Gardiner, author of *Naval Power in the Conquest of Mexico,* Cortes' daring naval maneuvers on Lake Texcoco were unparalleled; no similar victorious naval engagement ever concluded a war and ended a civilization. "One sees in kaleidoscopic panorama," wrote Gardiner, "the sweep of naval history from Ancient Salamis to Korea, ships under sail and oar—ramming, boarding, fleet action, task-force operations, blockade, liaison duty, Marine-like raids by naval landing parties, close support of land operations and psychological warfare. Like Salamis, which was fought for the control of the eastern Mediterranean, the battle of Tenochtitlan also involved the mastery of a world."

The Engagem.^{nt} between y.^e Spanish Brigantines and the Canoes of the Mexicans.

2. Indian Sacrifice

When Cortes returned with enough Spaniards and native allies to defeat the Mexica, he ordered the great and beautiful city of Tenochtitlan destroyed; palaces, columns, and gods were buried in the mud. To avoid the stench of the dead, the Spaniards set up camp in the nearby village of Coyoacan. Groups of captive Indians razed every last building of the Aztec capital and filled in the canals till not a stone was standing. On the leveled ruins Cortes founded his own great capital, Mexico City, patterned on a feudal model already dying in Europe.

Mexican slaves by the thousands, many of them highly skilled as sculptors, carpenters, masons, and gardeners, hauled stone and timber from the debris of Tenochtitlan. Iron

After plundering Tenochtitlan, Cortes branded the faces of its inhabitants with hot irons and attempted to force divulgation of the location of the fabled Aztec treasure. Though $15,000,000 worth of gold was found this represented only part of what was known to exist.

For his efforts Cortes was ennobled by the King of Spain and made marquess of the Valley of Oaxaca, captain general, and given a large estate with 23,000 vassals. But Cortes became bitter at not having been appointed viceroy to the country he had conquered. He did grant Montezuma's son a quarter of Mexico City as a fief, and in Spain arranged for the marriage of Montezuma's surviving daughters to members of the Spanish nobility. Having given to one of his subordinates as wife the native mistress of his adventures, La Malinche, without whose intermediary efforts he could hardly have conquered New Spain, Cortes married Doña Juana de Zuniga, niece to the Duke of Bejar.

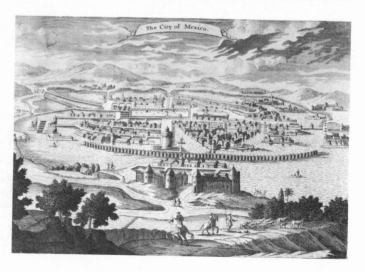

The City of Mexico.

14

chisels and iron hammers enabled them to cut the porous red stone of the valley into palatial European houses, over the doors of which the new hidalgos could place their carved escutcheons. Where Indian palaces and pyramids had stood, churches and monasteries sprang up complete with battlements, buttresses, and heavy grilled windows against the Indians who had built them.

Surviving on drinking water and a few tortillas, the Indians, at their own expense, supplied all the work and all the material. Brought up from childhood to a Spartan life, trained to endure pain, they worked long hours without showing fatigue, constantly subjected to unbelievable savagery by the Spaniards.

Individuals were torn from their families to work as slaves in gold and silver mines, branded on their faces each time they changed masters. The prettier women were raped and infected with the pox, smallpox, leprosy, and all manner of plagues. By 1545, in Tlaxcala alone, a quarter of a million Indians had died of the plague: altogether 3 million were to

The Flemish artist Theodore de Bry depicted Indians hanging themselves or taking poison in acts of mass suicide from shock at the overthrow of their culture. So great was the terror in Mexico about 1530 that Indians desisted from relations with their wives to avoid having children doomed to slavery. When asked to describe Christians, an old chief replied, "They ask for maize, for honey, for cotton, for women, for gold, for silver. Christians will not work, they are liars, gamblers, perverse, and they swear."

15

The Plague.

As a result of the Spanish Conquest, the population of Mexico was reduced to one-tenth. Indians, formerly in very good health, were weakened by hunger and fatigue and became easy prey to disease and the pox, large and small.

Fray Bernardino de Sahagun tells how he personally buried more than 10,000 victims of the plague, often in great trenches 100 at a time.

die as disease spread to Tabasco and Yucatan. Spanish apologists retorted that their presence had saved 600,000 Indian lives from being sacrificed on the altars in the first thirty years of the Conquest. They said of the Indians that "God truly did them a great service by entrusting them to the Spaniards who converted them and treated them so well."

As land was stolen from the natives, great famines ensued, yet heavy taxes were laid on Indians; those who failed to pay were tortured to death. Indians who refused to join the Catholic Church were horsewhipped, had their heads shaved, and were forbidden to hold office or title in their villages. For failing to attend mass, or for practicing any of his old rites, an Indian could receive a hundred lashes.

According to the Spaniards, Indians were supposed to know only the Our Father, Ave Maria, Credo, and Ten Commandments: reading and writing were considered as dangerous as the devil.

In Spain an eminent jurist, Juan Gines de Sepulveda, invoked the authority of Aristotle to stigmatize the Indians of the New World as natural slaves. He maintained that as inferior beings they would benefit from the labor they performed for the superior Spaniards and that war against the Indians to force them to Christianity was not only expedient

Designed for the detection and punishment of heretics, the Inquisition was used as a giant pork barrel for the enrichment of crown, Church, and Inquisitors, while cheerfully eliminating dangerous radicals: those who had been taught medicine, geography, rhetoric, chemistry, physics, mathematics, and astronomy by Moorish philosophers in universities such as Cordova, whose libraries had since been destroyed. The Inquisition was also an excuse to rid the planet of such organized mystics as Illuminati, Pantheists, Manicheans, and Albigensians. As a result no Spaniard could write, speak, or even think without taking into consideration the torture racks and fires of the Holy Office.

All the accused were presumed guilty before trial, a trial which took place in absolute secrecy. The defendant was afforded no counsel. Accuser and judge were the same person. The names of witnesses against the defendant were withheld from him. Women, children, and slaves could not be used as witnesses by the defendant, but could be used by the prosecution, who could order them tortured to obtain further accusations. There was never any case of acquittal pure and simple.

Minor penalties could be commuted for payoff. Major penalties were either the dungeon, with single or double fetters, or the secular arm for death by fire or strangling. The crown did not interfere with the operations of the Holy Office, which could, with impunity, arrest bishops and persons close to the king.

The victim's goods, subject to confiscation, were incorporated into the royal and Church domains. The Inquisitors, who paid no taxes and gave no account of confiscations effected, took their share. As a deterrent to possible opposition in New Spain thirty-four Negroes, including four women, were hanged and decapitated in Mexico City.

but lawful. Sepulveda—who never went to America and never saw an Indian in his natural habitat—considered the Indians "homúncoli, in whom you will scarcely find even vestiges of humanity, who not only possess no science but also lack letters and preserve no monument of their history except certain obscure reminiscences of some things in certain paintings."

By comparison Sepulveda considered Spaniards to be unequaled for their "frugality, sobriety, freedom from gluttony and lasciviousness," adducing as evidence their behavior during the sack of Rome, in 1527, when, as even their own historians admitted, the Spanish indulged in "the worst outburst of savagery in the annals of the period, burning monasteries and churches, violating nuns, and putting pregnant women to the sword."

In putting down the Indians, Sepulveda's ploy was to not "awaken curiosity or excite the cupidity of more scientific and enterprising nations."

17

Don Martin Cortes, the bastard son of Cortes and La Malinche, who was legitimized by the Pope, was tortured by the Inquisition with water forcibly poured down his throat for his alleged participation in the first major Creole conspiracy to make New Spain independent of Spain, with the Marques of Oaxaca, legitimate heir to Cortes, as first King of Mexico.

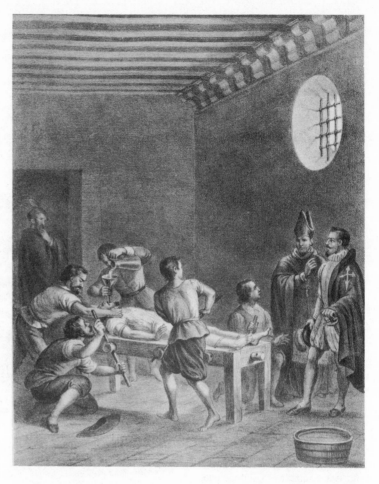

JUAN GINES DE SEPULVEDA

The Spanish jurist Juan Gines de Sepulveda said it was right to wage war against the Indians for four reasons:

1. For the gravity of the sins which the Indians had committed, especially their idolatries and sins against nature.

2. On account of the rudeness of their nature, which obliged them to serve persons having a more refined nature, such as the Spaniards.

3. In order to spread the faith, which would be more easily accomplished by the prior subjugation of the natives.

4. To protect the weak among the natives themselves.

Other ecclesiastics, opposing Sepulveda, especially the Dominican friar Bartolomé de Las Casas, who had crossed the ocean many times and spent a lifetime in America, appealed to divine and natural law to obtain better treatment for the Indians, telling succeeding Spanish kings, often to their face, of the sins committed by the conquerors of New Spain. To Charles V, Las Casas argued that the Aristotle quoted by Sepulveda was a gentile, probably burning in hell, whose philosophy should be accepted only when consistent with Christian doctrine. Las Casas believed the Indians should be Christianized without the use of soldiers or force, only by peaceful means, by the persuasion of the Gospel preached by godly men. He said the Indians were in no way inferior to the Greeks or Romans, not a whit less rational than the Egyptians; their temples, he said, were no less worthy of admiration than were the Egyptian pyramids.

Showing a healthy disregard for the orders of his ecclesiastical superiors, which forbade the baptizing of Indians

In New Spain, whereas "women of ill repute" were publicly stripped, whipped, and rubbed with honey to be bitten by insects, Jewish women had to appear naked before their judges and were put to the rack for practicing their religion.

While bands of Spaniards roamed the country destroying palaces and monuments, leveling cities, burning archives, and looting the temples of their gold and jewels, a few friars like Bartolomé de Las Casas labored for the Indian cause and tried to reconstruct the records of the past. In their villages, the Indians tried to save what artworks and manuscripts they could by burying them in their huts or taking them into the woods where they also hid and protected their medicine men.

unless instructed in the Christian religion, Las Casas was willing to baptize uninstructed children about to die disemboweled by Spanish soldiers.

To combat such unwanted opinions as those of Las Casas and to keep from the world the true story of the horrors perpetrated in New Spain, the Council of the Indies forbade possession or reading of the pamphlets published by Las Casas in Seville in 1552: they even went so far as to forbid the reprinting of the works of Cortes, Lopez de Gomara, and other conquistadores, though these were mostly apologias written to obtain favors from the crown.

The same censorship was reserved for the works of a whole series of enterprising monks who arrived early in New Spain and set about accumulating data on the history of Mesoamerica, traveling throughout the country, often at great pains, the most impressive of whom were the Franciscan friars Toribio Motolinia, Diego Duran, and Bernardino de Sahagun.

19

Franciscan friar Diego de Landa, born of the noble family of Calderones, arrived in Yucatan in 1549 at the age of twenty-five. Before becoming bishop of Yucatan, he was elected guardian of the convent of Izamal, east of the modern city of Merida. There he was told to erect a building for his monks, who had been living in houses of straw. As a site Landa chose a mound which had been used by the Maya as a "residence of the priests of the gods," in order, says Landa, "that the devil might be driven away." Vandalizing one of the greatest and oldest pyramids of Mexico, Landa eventually built for himself a fortress cathedral.

In the public square of Mani, south of Merida, Landa then amassed and burned, in the presence of the Spanish nobility resident in the country, the accumulated codices and inscribed statues of the natives.

The Jesuit Domingo Rodriguez noted that Landa destroyed 5,000 idols, 13 great stones that served as altars, 22 smaller stones, 27 rolls of hieroglyphs on deer skin, and other precious curiosities not described.

Cogolludo, in his *Historia de Yucatan,* described Landa as an "extravagant fanatic, and so hard hearted that he became cruel."

Not that it was easy for these friars to reconstruct what had actually occurred in the Valley of Mexico and surrounding Mesoamerica before the arrival of the Spaniards. The higher clergy that followed Cortes into conquered Mexico adopted his policy of destroying everything they could find of the native culture, burning whatever documents or codices fell into their hands, obliterating carefully chronicled history, myth, and legend, the worst culprits being the bishop of Mexico, Juan de Zumarraga, and the bishop of Yucatan, Diego de Landa. In the words of Landa: "We found great numbers of books written in these characters, but as they contained nothing that did not savor of superstition and lies we burnt them all, at which the natives grieved most keenly and were greatly pained."

To remedy this folly, dedicated Franciscans hit upon the device of teaching the surviving cultivated Mexicans to write in their own tongue with Latin characters, in lieu of their complex glyphs, so as to record what the natives could remember of their cultural heritage, much of which had been incorporated into songs and epic poems, passed down from generation to generation.

From such sources—including three surviving Mexican nobles, the princes Ixtlilxochitl, Tezozomoc, and Chimalpahin—the friars learned that the Mexica were members of an Aztec tribe which had only recently entered the Valley of Mexico in the middle of the thirteenth century and had established themselves on an island in the great Texcoco Lake at the beginning of the fourteenth century.

The Mexica said that around the lake they had found remnants of a high degree of civilization which they believed had existed in the area for more than a thousand years, and to which they gave the name of Toltec, meaning "artist" or "builder" in Aztec.

According to the Aztecs, the Toltecs had created a great capital city at Tollan, where, under the aegis of a divinely inspired leader, Quetzalcoatl, they had developed "superb artisans, devout worshippers, skillful tradesmen, stone masons, carpenters, bricklayers, workers in feathers and ceramics, spinners and weavers, tall, virtuous men who sang and danced, and had priests skilled in astronomy who kept an accurate count of days, years, and the movements of the stars and planets."

According to the Aztec tradition, the Toltec leader Quetzalcoatl had fallen on evil days and been obliged to depart eastward about A.D. 950 of our era. Thereafter the Valley of Mexico was invaded by less civilized Indians from the north, among the last of which were the Aztecs, who burned their own records and rewrote their history to bury their obscure

In Spain, Juan de Zumarraga had been ordered by the Emperor Charles V to exterminate the witches of Navarre, which he did by burning thousands of them at the stake. Appointed Bishop of Mexico, he boasted of having destroyed 500 Indian temples and 20,000 "idols." On Sunday, November 30, 1530, Zumarraga had Don Carlos Ometochtzin, lord of Texcoco, publicly burned at the stake in Mexico City's Plaza Mayor, accused of having worshiped the god of rain.

Familiars of the Holy Office had found two "idol" temples hidden in his palace: during the trial it developed that Indians covertly resorted to their old religious practices of inducing the powers of nature when the rain failed, much as was successfully accomplished by Dr. Wilhelm Reich in the United States in the 1950s, for which the satisfied blueberry growers of Maine paid him with money, whereas the U.S. Food and Drug Administration paid him with the public burning of his books and a prison sentence which cost him his life in the penitentiary.

In the market place of Texcoco, Zumarraga had a pyramid formed of the documents of Aztec history, knowledge, and literature, their paintings, manuscripts, and hieroglyphic writings, all of which he committed to the flames while the natives cried and prayed.

Into the holocaust went the codified laws of Texcoco's King Netzahualcoyotl (forefather of Don Fernando de Alva Ixtlilxochitl), who had reigned in Texcoco a century before the arrival of Cortes and had acquired the reputation of a Solomon distinguished for his courage, wisdom, and virtue, a refined astronomer and lover of plants and animals, who had composed sixty hymns in praise of the creator of heaven.

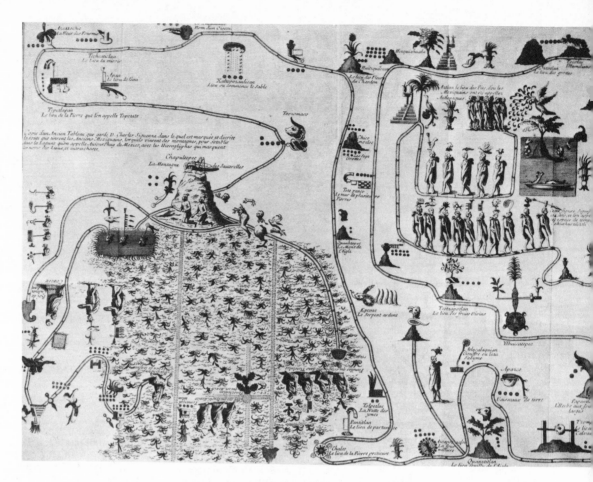

(Left) The Nahuatl word for Montezuma was written with the composite picture of a mousetrap, *montli*, for the sound *mo*, an eagle head for *quauh*, transfixed by a lance, *zo*, surmounted by a hand, *maitl* for *ma*—which came out *mo-quauh-zo-ma*.

(Above) Aztec picture writing describing the travels of their forefathers from the legendary home in Aztlan.

(Below) Tlaxcalans carrying equipment for Cortes' attack against Tenochtitlan.

origins and pass themselves off as true descendants of the indigenous noble Toltecs.

With this ready-made lineage, the Aztec Mexica—by their own saying—set about cruelly fighting for political dominance of the central plateau, stretching their power further and further afield, proclaiming their mission to be the gathering of all nations together into the service of their own god of war Huitzilopochtli.

By 1519, when the Spaniards arrived in highland Mexico, Montezuma's Aztecs ruled a polyglot colonial empire of several million people, stretching from the Pacific to the Gulf, from central Mexico to what is now Guatemala, most of whom were only waiting for an occasion such as the arrival of Cortes to rebel against their masters, and thus, inadvertently, destroy what remained of Indian civilization and turn over to the Spaniards the control of all of Central America.

Throughout the sixteenth century, by a careful sifting of the evidence obtained from Indian sources, the brighter minds among the historian friars, such as Bernardino de Sahagun, concluded that a truly great civilization had indeed existed in the Valley of Mexico, prior to the Aztecs, which had lasted over two thousand years. Sahagun also concluded that before Tollan this civilization had been centered in the great abandoned city of Teotihuacan, with its mysterious mounds, which he figured to have been destroyed almost a thousand years before the arrival of the Spaniards. It also seemed reasonable to Sahagun that so great a city must have prospered for at least a thousand years before it was abandoned or destroyed, which meant that it had been peopled five hundred years before the birth of Christ, a city as Sahagun described it, "very rich and well ordered, very wise and powerful, which suffered the adverse fortune of a Troy."

More open-minded than most of his ecclesiastical colleagues, Sahagun even managed to capture a feeling for the metaphysics of this lost civilization, establishing from the chronicles that Teotihuacan had been called the "City of the Gods" because

the Lords therein buried, after their deaths, were canonized as gods, and it was said that they did not die, but wakened out of a dream they had lived; this is the reason why the ancients say that when men died they did not perish but began to live again, waking almost out of a dream, and that they turned into spirits of gods . . . and so they said to the dead: "Lord or Lady, wake, for it begins to dawn, now comes the daylight for the yellow-feathered birds begin to sing, and the many-colored butterflies go flying"; and when anyone died, they used to say of him that he was now *teotl,* meaning to say he had died in order to become spirit or god.

23

Fray Bernardino de Sahagun.

So handsome a youth was Bernardino de Sahagun that the older monks of the Order of St. Francis secluded him to prevent temptations from the outside world. Born Bernardo Ribeira in the province of Leon in 1499, he was given the name of his home town when he joined the order.

In 1529 on a ship for New Spain with eighteen other Franciscan monks, he learned to speak Nahuatl from repatriating Mexican Indians whom Cortes had dragged to Spain to show off to the Spanish court. Having mastered the language of the Mexica, Sahagun traveled through the country acquiring a vast lore which he turned into a twelve-volume anthropological, mythological, and social history of ancient Mexico, laboriously compiled over a period of fifteen years in the Monastery of Tlalmanalco at the foot of the two volcanoes Iztaccihuatl and Popocatepetl. Realizing that the Spaniards, in their zeal to destroy a religion they considered idolatrous and barbarous, were destroying the Aztecs' whole way of life, Sahagun did much to restore to the Mexicans their rightful reputation. Brother Sahagun sought out the most learned and often the oldest natives, and asked each to paint in his Aztec picture writing as much as he could clearly remember of Aztec history, religion, and legend. He also taught the natives to transcribe their Aztec words in Latin letters. Sahagun's story of the Conquest as told to him by contemporary Indians who had witnessed the events so displeased the Spanish authorities, Sahagun was forced to revise the text to suit the victors, only salvaging his conscience by retaining the original text in Aztec. Even so, his great work never saw the light. The original manuscript was buried and is lost to this day. An incomplete copy surfaced during the French invasion of Spain in 1808, and was published by Carlos M. Bustamente in 1840, to be translated into English a century later.

Unacclaimed by his peers, "America's most remarkable historian of the sixteenth century" died in poverty and oblivion of an epidemic of catarrh at the age of 91, mourned only by a vast crowd of saddened Indians whom he had lovingly befriended and taught.

But the reports of Sahagun and other industrious friars, who conscientiously accumulated long manuscripts giving fine details of the history, customs, and religion of the Indians, might just as well not have been written. They were buried in the archives to keep from the world the shame of what the conquerors, lay and cleric, had done to the inhabitants and culture of Mesoamerica.

In the mother country, where only writings which glorified the Church and its servants were thought worthy of the press, a few works were allowed publication, all derived from highly controlled sources, most of whom had never been to America, and whose material was already superannuated before it got into print. No book could be printed except under license, nor could it be imported or exported without permit, on pain of death and confiscation of goods. All libraries, public and private, were subject to rigorous inspection, and students could not travel abroad. Access to Mexico was forbidden to foreigners in order to prevent commercial competition, espionage, and the possible contagion of Protestant heresies.

Not till the end of the seventeenth century did an observant Neapolitan traveler manage to visit Mexico and bring out detailed news. A strictly practicing Catholic with a penchant for hobnobbing with the higher clergy, considered a loyal subject of Spain because Charles II was also king of the Two Sicilies, Giovanni Gemelli Careri was able to travel freely about Mexico and bring out what amounted to the first outside report on the country and its antiquities.

Part of Sahagun's original manuscript.

25

PART III

EARLY OBSERVERS

During the century after the Conquest, when Spain was virtually sealed off from the rest of the world, one Englishman, Thomas Gage, did manage to visit Mexico as a Dominican friar. A student of the Jesuits and the Dominicans in both France and Spain, he could pass for a Spaniard, and was therefore able to do missionary work in Central America between 1627 and 1637.

Gage was most struck in Mexico City by the women, the apparel, the houses, and the streets. He noted that almost half the population of the city sported coaches, many of which exceeded in cost the best of the court of Madrid and other parts of Christendom, "for they spare no silver, nor gold, nor the best silks from China to enrich them." Gage admired the broad streets lined with goldsmiths and silversmiths, and was astounded by the freedom enjoyed by the women to gamble: "Day and night is too short for them to end a *primera*."

Gage found men and women excessive in their apparel. "The attire of this baser sort of people of blackamoors and mulattoes is so light, and their carriage so enticing, that many Spaniards even of the better sort (who are too prone to venery) disdain their wives for them." Noting that "their bare, black and tawny breasts are covered with bobs hanging from their chains of pearls," Gage concluded that "most of them have been slaves, though love has set them loose at liberty to enslave souls to sin and Satan."

In 1640 Gage renounced his Catholicism, embraced Protestantism, and, back in England, informed against a number of English Jesuits, contributing to their deaths. In *A Survey of the West Indies* he gave a broadside attack against the corruption of the Roman Catholic Church, encouraging Cromwell's government to plot invasions of the New World in order to seize Spanish territory.

THOMAS GAGE RECEIVING GIFTS FROM HIS PARISHIONERS

(Frontispiece of the First German Edition)

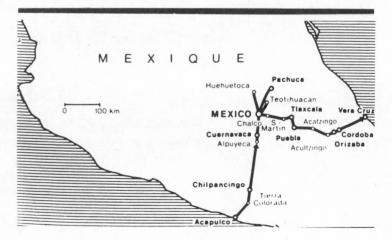

3. Reports from New Spain

On the last leg of a hazardous five-year trip around the world which had taken him to Armenia, Persia, India, and China, Careri, a jurist born in Calabria, arrived in Acapulco in January of 1697 after a gruesome five-month non-stop voyage from Manila in a small ship with two hundred passengers ravaged by scurvy.

Careri found the town of Acapulco, which he had expected to be Mexico's gateway to the East, no more than a fishing village with straw-roofed shacks inhabited, almost exclusively, by Negroes, mulattoes, and very few Indians. Only when a ship was in port would Spaniards appear from nowhere. Merchants aboard a ship from Peru brought ashore 2 million pieces of eight with which to buy silk and porcelain from China, cloth from Bengal, pearls from Persia, turning the town of Acapulco overnight into a thriving mart of free-spending Spaniards. Careri, who dabbled in commerce to help defray his traveling expenses, was quick to see that trading fortunes could easily be made in Acapulco. Even the local curate, whose yearly salary was a mere 120 pieces of eight, managed to increase his fortune to 14,000 a year by soaking the relatives of foreign merchants 2,000 pieces for a Christian burial in the local hallowed ground.

Setting off on muleback for the 14,000-foot climb over the massif to Mexico City, Careri was delighted to find the bare mountains around Acapulco alive with deer, rabbits, parrots, and turtledoves with which to improve the abominable fare at the first wayside inn, a conglomeration of straw huts where he was devoured by horseflies. Of delicate health, suffering constantly from "intestinal flux," Careri traveled in short hops and long stopovers, amazed along the way to find

Giovanni Francesco Gemelli Careri, Neapolitan jurist, at the age of 48 when he traveled to Mexico in 1699.

29

oranges, lemons, apples, peaches, and pomegranates flourishing beside exotic capulins, avocados, mameys, sapodillas, custard apples and bananas. He was even more amazed to find that oranges and lemons lay rotting on the ground because the natives, accustomed to subsisting on tortilla pancakes and kidney beans, would not bother to pick the fruit.

As he climbed, Careri found that the soil, rich in iron, yielded bountiful harvests. The woods abounded with boars, panthers, eagles, royal herons, and wild geese.

Mexico City Careri found to be a metropolis of 100,000 souls which, to his traveled eye, rivaled Italy in the beauty of its buildings and churches and outdid Italy in the beauty of its charming, well-built women, who, according to Careri, preferred men from Europe, no matter how poor, to the Mexican-born Creole Spaniards because of the latter's pronounced taste for mulatto women, a taste, so he explained, acquired as children suckling mulatto breasts.

By ten years after the Conquest, Acapulco was already a thriving port, the point of entry and departure for a vast trade, much of it based on the demand for the epicurean specialties of the New World. Spanish seamen made possible a globe-circling trade from Madrid to Havana, to Veracruz, and then overland to Acapulco for continuation across the Pacific to the Philippines and beyond.

Cacao beans, of which the Mexicans got three crops a year, were used as currency in the markets, being worth 60 or 80 to a real. A real was a quarter of a peseta.

Of the cacao bean an anonymous conquistador wrote, "These seeds which they call almonds or cacao are ground and made into powder, and some other small seeds they have are also ground, and the powder put into certain vessels that have a spout. Then they add water and stir with a spoon, and after it is well mixed, they pour it back and forth from one vessel to another until it is foamy. The foam is gathered and put in a cup and when they are ready to drink the beverage, they beat it with some small spoons made of gold or silver or wood. To drink it one must open the mouth wide, for since it has a froth it is necessary to make room for it to dissolve and go in gradually.

"This drink is the most wholesome and substantial of any drink of the world, because whoever drinks a cup of this liquor can go through the day without taking anything else even if he is on a journey, and it is better in warm than cold weather because it is a cold drink."

Another chronicler describes the care taken by the Mexicans in raising the delicate cacao tree: "It grows only in a warm climate, and before they plant it, they plant two or three other trees that have large leaves. When these are two estados high, they plant the cacao tree between them so the two can protect this delicate tree from the sun and wind and provide a covering for it. They hold this tree in great esteem because its grains are the principal money circulated in this country, each one being worth half a marchetto. It is the most commonly used coin, but very unhandy after gold or silver."

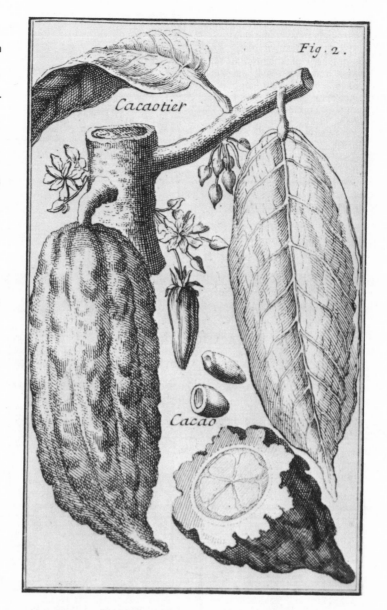

In the growing city, Careri found Mexicans largely preoccupied with the centuries-old problem of draining and lowering the level of the surrounding lakes to prevent the city from recurrently flooding, a program which involved millions of man-hours of backbreaking slave labor to dig canals and clear subterranean waterways.

The Spanish viceroy, Count of Montezuma, greeted Careri "very civilly"; and an old friend from Naples who had recently been appointed governor general of the province of New Mexico introduced him to a society which was delighted

31

The progenitors of the Meso-americans gave to the world not only cacao but maize, pumpkins, squashes, potatoes, sweet potatoes, tomatoes, lima beans, kidney beans, peppers, pineapples, strawberries, persimmons, peanuts, alligator pears, cassava, quinine, cascara, cocaine, copal, balsam, cochineal, anil, alpaca, the llama, the guinea pig, turkeys, and rubber. To have developed such produce and animals would have been the work of thousands of years.

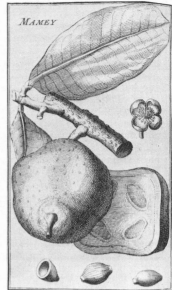

Careri's view of the porcelain tower in Nankin.

to entertain a traveler who could tell them stories of adventures in Peking, with vivid descriptions of such remote wonders as the Pyramid of Cheops and the Great Wall of China, rarely visited by Europeans.

To Careri, Mexico was a colony grossly exploited by a handful of Spanish merchants interested primarily in gold, silver, and pearls, who had managed with the support of the higher clergy to reduce the Indians to serfdom or brigandage; the penalty for which was branding of the testicles with a red-hot poker followed by two hundred lashes on the back.

On his way around the world, Careri visited the Great Pyramid of Cheops on the Gizeh plateau, where he obtained this sketch.

Careri noted that Strabo believed the Great Pyramid had originally been used as an astronomical observatory.

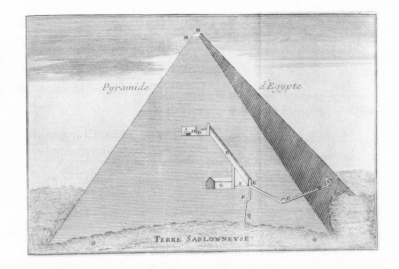

In Careri's day, in Mexico, at the beginning of the eighteenth century, religious institutions owned two-thirds of all the real estate but produced very little with their vast hoarded wealth. Twenty-nine monasteries for men and twenty-two convents for women had grown up in Mexico City, plus so many churches with sub-buildings and large gardens that it was hard to find land for new civilian houses in the lake-surrounded city.

Blacks and mulattoes, who had been forcibly added to the population, were kept strictly segregated and forbidden to wear Spanish dress, with the result, as Careri noted, that they dressed in the most bizarre fashion, "wearing a sort of skirt sideways across their shoulders."

The real owners of Mexico appeared to be the ecclesiastical authorities, who made it tough for Spaniards from Europe to get an economic stake in the country. Of an inquisitive nature that often got him into trouble, Careri discovered that the archbishop's yearly salary was a princely 60,000 pieces of eight, with access to another 200,000 income from his see. In the thirty years since the founding of the city's cathedral, 1,052,000 pieces of eight had been spent on adorning it.

When not going to mass or to the theater, Careri amused himself by searching out people of interest, and it is thanks to his rambles in seventeenth-century Mexico that the world was to get its first real glimpse of what the culture had been like before the arrival of the Spanish.

The most interesting of Careri's contacts was a long-faced lorgnetted priest, Don Carlos de Sigüenza y Gongora, then in his fifties, with a variety of duties, and a passion for probing into the historic past of the Mexicans.

Born in Mexico of noble Spanish parents, Sigüenza had been expelled from the Jesuit order, but had maintained friendly relations with his former comrades. Cultivating friendships with the native Indians, and winking at his duties for the Inquisition, Sigüenza managed to induce the Indians to bring forth manuscripts and paintings which they had carefully hidden for fear of being burned at the stake like the former King of Texcoco.

33

Don Carlos de Sigüenza y Gongora.

Professor of mathematics at the University of Mexico, General Examiner of Gunners, Corrector of the Inquisition, poet, astronomer, historian, and geographer, Don Carlos was by far the most erudite Mexican in his times, a Renaissance man who had made all of human knowledge his province, peering into dark corners to ferret out the facts.

From Sigüenza's collection of Aztec kings and warriors.

Sigüenza, on the contrary, specifically cultivated the friendship of the direct descendants of the kings of Texcoco, especially Don Juan de Alva, son of Fernando de Alva Cortes Ixtlilxochitl, author of the first history of the Mexican people written in Latin after the Conquest. In return for this friendship, Don Juan taught Sigüenza the language of the Nahua, showed him how to decipher many of the native hieroglyphs, interpreted the Indian myths, and, in the end, turned over to him an invaluable prize: the complete collection of his family papers.

Another great haul of precious original documents had come into Sigüenza's possession during the riots and ensuing fire which had swept the center of Mexico City a few years earlier. Hiring some Indians at his own expense, Sigüenza had placed ladders up to the windows of the flaming archives, smashed his way in with an axe, and thrown out all the manuscripts, codices, and capitulary books not yet consumed by the flames. With the help of his nephew, this priceless secret material was brought to the Hospital del Amor de Dios, a refuge for sufferers from the "French disease" or from bubas, where Sigüenza, as chaplain in residence, had his quarters.

There Careri paid a visit to Sigüenza and was shown remarkable writings and drawings relating to the antiquity of the Indians, including such prized items as a manuscript history of the Mexicans by Fernando de Alvarado Tezozomac, son of the successor to Montezuma; some original writings of Chimalpahin Quauhtlehuanitzin; a book, since lost, by Archbishop Zumarraga; and, most important, the works of Fernando de Alva Ixtlilxochitl.

With the help of these rare documents and a great many calculations based on eclipses of sun and moon and passages of comets as depicted in the paintings, Sigüenza was able to reconstruct an Indian chronology of Kings, tracing them back through the centuries. With his penchant for mathematics, Sigüenza was able to tackle complex calendrical problems that had baffled the earlier friars.

From Ixtlilxochitl, Sigüenza learned of an ancient Mexican calendar, which had vanished at the time of the Conquest, by means of which the Aztec priests had been able to keep an accurate chronology over very long periods of time in 52- and 104-year cycles, noting the solstices and equinoxes, the transits of Venus, and many subtle computations on the movements of heavenly bodies.

A careful study of these data enabled Sigüenza to fix certain dates with precision, such as the year 1325 for the founding of the city of Tenochtitlan and the beginning of the Aztec empire.

Portrait of Montezuma II given by Sigüenza to Careri.

From the evidence, Sigüenza concluded that a race called the Olmecs had preceded the Toltecs, coming from the East, perhaps from legendary Atlantis—as suggested by the Spanish chronicler Gonzalo Fernandez de Oviedo y Valdes —to settle on the gulf coast of Mexico. That a continent or group of islands known as Atlantis had existed, Sigüenza was convinced; he felt that they had served as stepping-stones to and from the Americas. The rest of the tribes of the

35

Western Hemisphere, he believed, had come from the north and northwest, possibly from Asia. But to Sigüenza, the similarity between Mexican and Egyptian pyramids, hieroglyphs, and calendars was too strongly indicative of the existence in the Atlantic of an intervening continent or group of islands, for which Plato's account of Atlantis fit the bill.

Pyramids, hieroglyphs, and calendars bound Sigüenza closely to the family of Ixtlilxochitl, who were still titular lords of San Juan Teotihuacan, site of the pyramid complex. This close link enabled Sigüenza to indulge in a more than superficial investigation of the ancient ruins. Whereas others attributed the construction of the great mounds to the Toltecs, Sigüenza believed them to be the work of the earlier Olmecs who had dwelt near the hills of Tlaxcala. As several sixteenth-century writers had reported the Indian tradition that the interior of the pyramids might be hollow, Sigüenza endeavored to dig into the two biggest ones, but with the limited means at his disposal was unable to uncover any passageway or chamber.

So fascinating was Sigüenza's description of these pyramids, that Careri decided he should "not miss some Indian antiquities before leaving Mexico." Rousing himself, he rode out to San Juan for a personal inspection.

On the route around Lake San Cristobal, Careri spent the night at Acolman. Inside this massive sanctuary Careri found a baroque church with a pleasant inner courtyard adorned with carvings by native Indians in the European style of the sixteenth century.

Route from Mexico City past the lake of San Cristobal to San Juan Teotihuacan. In the foreground is the monastery of Acolman. The town was famed under the Aztecs for a breed of fat little castrated dogs especially raised for the tables of the rich, and under the Spanish for its fortresslike Augustinian monastery. In the background are the hills of Sierra del Malpais.

After a night spent like the Jesuits on a pillow made of leather which could be inflated like a balloon and deflated in the morning, Careri set off at sunrise for the village of San Juan Teotihuacan, six leagues away, noting that the local Indians painted their cheeks with crushed herbs to protect them from the cold, and that they put mud in their hair to make it soft and shiny.

With an introduction from Don Carlos de Sigüenza, Careri was able to spend the night at San Juan with Pedro de Alva Ixtlilxochitl, grandson of Juan de Alva, who promised to show him the pyramids on the morrow.

At daybreak they explored first the smaller of the "mounds" called "Of the Moon," which Careri described as being a pile of stones with a slope like an Egyptian pyramid, but differing in that it was not constructed of solid stone. He found the base measured 650 palms north to south and 500 palms east to west: the height, since he had no instruments with which to measure, he estimated to be 200 palms. Taking the Aztec palm, or cemitztl, as 17.5 centimeters, this would have made the Moon Pyramid 105 meters wide at the base by 35 meters high. Its present reconstructed size is 152 meters wide by 42 high. Either Careri's palm was incorrect, or, more likely, the base of the pyramid was so covered in earth and rubble that only a smaller portion of it was visible, as was the case at that time with the Pyramid of Cheops.

From Sigüenza, Careri had heard that this pyramid had once been crowned with a "huge idol of the Moon clumsily carved from hard stone," which had been destroyed on orders from Bishop Zumarraga. That such an idol, eighteen feet tall, had once stood on the "Hill of the Moon" had been officially reported to Phillip II of Spain in 1580 by a local magistrate, Don Francisco de Castañeda, as part of the earliest-known official description of the pyramids of Teotihuacan. Castañeda also reported the presence of many more idols around the pyramid, the largest of which were "six

Aztec idol known as the God of Rain.

All over Mexico, statues of what the Spaniards called "idols" were smashed or destroyed after being stripped of their gold or jewels.

idols called the Brethren of the Moon," three large pieces of which, said Careri, still lay at the foot of the pyramid.

Two hundred paces to the south, Careri and his noble Indian guide explored the pyramid known to the Aztecs as "Tonatiuh," or "House of the Sun." Careri says that two of its sides were 1000 palms long (or 175 meters instead of about 230), whereas the other two were 650. The height he estimated to be a fourth more than the height of the Moon Pyramid. In fact it is one-half.

According to Castañeda's report, there had once stood on the summit of the Sun Pyramid, facing west, an "idol" of very hard, rough stone, all of one piece, eighteen feet high, six feet wide and six feet thick, called "Tonacatechuhtli," or "Sun God," but whether these statues formed part of the original pyramid complex or were added by later generations there was no way to tell.

Careri says he found part of this statue halfway down the pyramid; he described it as having a slot in the stomach "where one put the sun," adding that two large pieces which had formed the arms and feet still lay at the base of the pyramid. Careri was told that the statues which had once adorned the summits of the two pyramids had originally been covered in gold, which was removed by the Spaniards at the time of the Conquest.

According to Castañeda, there had also been "a small temple" at ground level at the base of the great pyramid atop which stood a smaller idol called "Mictlantecuhtli," or "God of the Underworld"; but Careri saw no sign of it. He was puzzled as to how the Indians could have cut such "idols" out of hard stone without the use of metal chisels; he also wondered how they had managed to raise such great weights to the top of the pyramids when "they had neither machines nor the wit to invent such machines."

How, asked the Italian, had the Indians been able to transport heavy stones from distant quarries when they had neither mules nor horses before the arrival of the Spaniards —a question which no one in Mexico could satisfactorily answer for him.

From the crumbling walls which he saw spread out in all directions, and the number of smaller mounds which he believed to have been erected to honor other idols, Careri had

Though Sigüenza had corresponded as far afield as with the extraordinary prelate Father Athanasius Kircher, who was determined to discover the secret lore contained or built into pyramids and obelisks, the rest of the world was not yet ready for the subject.

First page of Careri's *Voyage Around the World* published in 1719.

no doubt that a large city of Teotihuacan had once existed around the pyramids. But when it came to giving a date for the possible construction of these pyramids, Careri considered that no historian had discovered anything reliable.

Echoing the thoughts of Sigüenza, Careri attributed the construction to the Olmecs, possibly refugees from Atlantis, or to Europeans who had crossed the Atlantic, pointing out that even Aristotle had known that the Carthaginians had sailed beyond the Strait of Gibraltar to a "new world," but had been forbidden further such voyages by a senate fearful that the richness of the newly discovered lands would make the sailors forget their home. On his way back to Mexico City, it began to rain, and Careri's horse, overtired from the strenuous journey, lay down in the mud and died, a fate which was to overcome Careri's interest in the world of pyramids prospected for him by his friend Don Carlos de Sigüenza y Gongora. After eleven months in Mexico, Careri sailed for Havana and Seville, where he landed in 1698 with a handy supply of cochineal (for scarlet dye), Havana cigars, indigo, cocoa, and vanilla, discreetly hidden to avoid the duty. Because of his round-the-world trip, King Charles II of Spain received Careri but was not overly impressed.

In a six-volume opus, *Giro del Mondo,* or "Around the World in Eighty Months," which was quickly translated and condensed, Careri gave his contemporaries exotic glimpses of the Near, Middle, and Far East, plus the first and best description of Mexico to have reached the outside world. For his efforts he was quickly labeled an imposter who had never left Naples, a fiction to which historians were to cling till very recent times. Oliver Goldsmith and Adam Smith were both convinced that Careri was a fraud, and William Robertson, the eighteenth-century Scottish historian, in his monstrously inaccurate *History of America,* refused to include Careri's reports.

According to Robertson, neither the Mexicans nor the Peruvians "were entitled to rank with those nations which merit the name of civilized." He described the palaces attributed to the Indians by the Spanish conquistadores "as more fit to be the habitations of men just emerging from barbarity than the residence of a polished people. . . . Nor does the fabric of their temples and other public edifices appear to have been such as entitled them to high praise. . . . These structures convey no high idea of progress in art and ingenuity. . . . If buildings corresponding to such descriptions had ever existed in the Mexican cities, it is probable that some remains of them would still be visible. . . . It seems altogether incredible that in a period so short, every vestige of this boasted elegance and grandeur should

Calendar wheel obtained by Careri from Sigüenza. Encircled by a snake, the Mesoamerican symbol of time, the outer wheel shows a 52-year cycle divided into thirteen repetitions of the 4-year cycles of rabbit, house, cane, reed. The next circle shows the eighteen months of the Aztec year. In the center are the symbols for the four seasons.

have disappeared. . . . The Spanish accounts appear highly embellished."

And the Dutch-born historian Cornelius de Pauw, in his *Recherches Philosophiques sur les Américains,* claimed that "the so-called palace occupied by the Mexican kings was a hut."

Only a few Europeans of progressive outlook such as Giordano Bruno and Montaigne refused to believe in the inferiority and depravity of the Indians of Mesoamerica.

Sadly, as the first edition of *Giro del Mondo* came off the presses, Don Carlos de Sigüenza y Gongora, responsible for most of what Careri reported of value from Mexico, died, too poor to have had his manuscripts put into print. In line with the policy of the Inquisition to allow a man to accumulate manuscripts during his lifetime, but see to it that after his death they got no further dissemination, twenty-eight of Sigüenza's own manuscripts along with his priceless collection of books, manuscripts, and codices were quickly scattered, stolen, or destroyed. Luckily, the Jesuits salvaged the lion's share of their former novice's own manuscripts; but when their order was thrown out of Mexico in 1767 these manuscripts were also buried in some archives or lost.

Ironically, what was known of some of Sigüenza's writings was to reach the world through Careri's flimsy reports, such

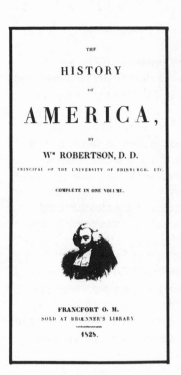

THE
HISTORY
OF
AMERICA,
BY
W⁰ ROBERTSON, D. D.
PRINCIPAL OF THE UNIVERSITY OF EDINBURGH, ETC.

COMPLETE IN ONE VOLUME.

FRANCFORT O. M.
SOLD AT BROENNER'S LIBRARY.
1825.

as his interpretation of the Mexican calendar taken from Sigüenza's lost work *Ciclografia Mexicana,* which Sigüenza had been kind enough to lend Careri when he was in Mexico City, but which the Neapolitan jurist, weak on mathematics, had poorly understood and miserably transmitted.

With venom, De Pauw attacked the reliability of the Mexican calendar found by Sigüenza and interpreted by Careri, writing that "with breathtaking impudence and ignorance Careri has followed the explanation of a certain creole professor named Congora [sic] who had not dared to publish a work he had written on the subject because his friends and relatives assured him it abounded in absurdities." De Pauw could not countenance the possibility that Mexicans had recorded the passage of centuries with the use of "calendar wheels." Such reckoning, he said, supposed a long series of astronomical observations "incompatible with the prodigious ignorance of those people." How, asked De Pauw, could they have perfected their chronology "if they did not have words enough to count to ten?"

After Careri's departure, almost a century was to pass before the veil of obscurantism was once more to be pierced by the arrival in Acapulco of another famous traveler—Baron Friedrich Heinrich Alexander von Humboldt.

4. Humboldt's Mission

When Humboldt arrived in Acapulco on March 23, 1803, aboard a frigate aptly named *Atlante,* he was in his thirty-fourth year, and one of the most popular individuals in Europe. A friend of Goethe, Schiller, Metternich, and Chateaubriand, he was almost as well known as Napoleon Bonaparte, with whom he had failed to go to Egypt during the 1799 expedition only because the ship on which Humboldt was to have sailed from Marseilles was sunk in a sudden storm, obliging him to seek adventure in the Americas.

From Guayaquil in Ecuador, Humboldt brought with him to Mexico his good friends Aimé Bonpland, the botanist, and Carlos de Montafur, a fighter for freedom in Latin America. The trio brought an enormous pile of luggage containing telescopes, surveying instruments, minerals, plants, mastodon bones, skins of jungle creatures, and specimens of birds.

In contrast to the port of Acapulco which Humboldt and his companions considered one of the prettiest in the world, they were struck by the lugubrious atmosphere and burned landscape surrounding the town, which they described as a miserable and unhealthy spot, hot and tropical, a haven for escaped convicts and rum-filled slaves.

Humboldt's original plan in coming to Acapulco had been to reverse Careri's route toward the Philippines, but because his instruments were beginning to rust he decided instead to return immediately to Europe. This plan was scotched by an outbreak of yellow fever in the gulf port of Veracruz, which determined Humboldt to stay in Mexico at least till the

43

Humboldt standing talking to Aimé Bonpland, surrounded by the equipment with which they had explored and made scientific observations across South America from the mouth of the Orinoco to the Andean highlands.

fall of the year (when the disease was less catching), or better still, the following spring so as to avoid a winter crossing of the Atlantic.

In Acapulco, Humboldt and his companions made astronomical observations to correct the misplaced coordinates of the town, and they spent some time observing the nature of earthquakes, which were frequent in the area. Finally, in a 104-degree heat wave, they set off in Careri's footsteps up the dusty mule trail toward the capital, climbing slowly because of the number of pack animals carrying their biological and mineral specimens, stopping here and there to study rocks and plants and to make astronomical and barometric observations.

During the starlit nights Humboldt obtained accurate readings of his location so that by day he could produce graphs of the geological structures he encountered, invaluable to later surveyors. He even mapped an easy way to convert the mule path into a proper roadway to the capital once traffic might warrant the endeavor.

Aimé Bonpland, aged 40.   Portrait of Alexander von Humboldt at the age of 25.

MINE

The sight of the Mexican mines led the almost radically liberal Humboldt to observe that "there can be no durable prosperity for the two Americas until this unfortunate race, humiliated but not degraded by long oppression, shall participate in all the advantages resulting from the progress of civilization and the improvement of social order."

In his own mining career in Germany, when still in his twenties, Humboldt had learned to double production of a mine by improving its working conditions and safety measures, and by providing night school for the miners, often at his own expense.

Between Chilpancingo, in the Sierra Madre del Sur, and Taxco, clinging to its hillside, Humboldt came across the great silver mines of Mexico. Indian laborers, panting by day under heavy loads of ore, blasting by night in an inferno of powder smoke and dust, were still being treated like mongrel dogs.

Leaving Taxco, the travelers wound their way through limestone mountains to Cuernavaca, where Cortes had built his first palace and planted Mexico's first sugar plantation. A day's ride took them to the crest of the continental divide, 11,000 feet above the sea, from where they could look eastward down onto the City of Mexico with its cluster of churches, palaces, and gardens, which, from their vantage point, appeared to be floating on the surrounding lake.

As a botanist, Humboldt was struck by the beauty of the cypresses at intervening Xochimilco, lovely great trees which had rooted beneath the lake to form a world of "floating gardens called *chinampas*." These gardens provided an abundance of vegetables which could be floated by the Indians along narrow waterways right to houses and convents near the viceroy's palace in the great Plaza Mayor, where the main temple of Tenochtitlan had stood.

As Humboldt and his companions approached the city, a messenger brought word of welcome from Viceroy Don José Iturrigaray, granting Humboldt passports to travel wherever he pleased in New Spain, a special treatment arranged for Humboldt in Madrid by the minister of Saxony, who had convinced the Spanish crown that such a distinguished scientist and "conservative" young nobleman would not rock the boat of state with his reports from Mesoamerica. Actually the arrangement had every earmark of being a Masonic ploy to facilitate an intelligent reconnaissance of Mexico, possibly on behalf of long-term mining interests in Europe.

Within the city, with its wide clean avenues, flanked by iron candelabra, resplendent at night with lighted palaces and churches, Humboldt was welcomed as an erudite and learned visitor. It was his charm, however, and his apparent sincerity and ease, along with his sociability and brilliance of conversation, which really opened doors to him. Wherever he went, cultivated persons gave him their confidence; in Mexico he got help from peasant and governor, missionary and bishop, savant and noble, being welcomed indiscriminately into palace or shack, workshop or hacienda. Almost everyone had heard of Baron Humboldt as either astronomer, physiologist, botanist, economist, archeologist or philologist; but seldom had any of them had occasion to frequent so distinguished a personage.

The chinampas or so-called floating gardens of the Valley of Mexico, of which Xochimilco is the most famous, date back more than 2000 years, and were the main source of foodstuff for the inhabitants of the entire valley, producing as many as seven different crops in a year, two of which were maize.

Properly maintained, they could remain fertile for centuries without having to lie fallow.

Xochimilco consisted of a network of canals of various widths laid out generally at right angles to form a grid. Rafts and water vegetation were cut from the surface of the canals and towed to strips where they were built up in layers and covered with rich mud scooped up from the canal bottom.

Many such chinampa towns surrounded by lovely canals and cultivated strips developed on the western and southern shores of the Lake of the Moon.

An added asset in the canals was an abundance of fish and axolotls, large salamanders prized for their tender meat and scarcity of hard bones.

Most amazing, the viceroy immediately opened up for Humboldt the country's classified archives. To help him with his research, Humboldt found, in circumstances that seemed more than fortuitous, a former classmate from Freiberg University, Don Andres Manuel del Rio, who had providentially become director of Mexico's school of mines. A young savant, Dr. M. Oteyza, was selected to tutor Humboldt on the history of Mexico and to show him where he could obtain rare Indian picture writings which had escaped the *autos da fe* of the Conquest, picture writings so scarce in New Spain, according to Humboldt, that the majority of educated persons had never seen one.

With access to the official files and a bent for statistics, Humboldt estimated the population of Mexico City to be 137,000 inhabitants, or twice that of contemporary New York, with the difference that in Mexico City there were only 2,500 Europeans, the rest of the population was composed of 65,000 Creoles, 33,000 Indians, 26,500 mestizos, and 10,000 mulattoes.* Like Careri, Humboldt found both town and county pullulating with priests, monks, and nuns—one priest for every sixty inhabitants, or 100,000 priests in a country of 6 million souls. To Protestant Humboldt, the higher clergy of Mexico appeared to be living in clover, some receiving incomes greater than that of the then president of the United States, Thomas Jefferson.

* Creoles were Spaniards born in Mexico; mestizos were part Spanish, part Indian; mulattoes were part Negro.

47

When Humboldt arrived in Mexico City, it was the largest city on the continent of America; he found it "undoubtedly one of the finest ever built by Europeans in either hemisphere."

After several months of studying the statistics and geography of the country, and of analyzing Mexico City as the political, commercial, industrial, and ecclesiastical capital of New Spain, Humboldt turned to the city's antiquities to observe it as an ancient center of civilization. He was shocked to discover the extent of the destruction of Tenochtitlan, as well as of ancient statues and painted codices. He also learned that since Sigüenza's death another great collection of books, manuscripts, and codices had been pillaged and dispersed, that of the eighteenth-century Milanese traveler Lorenzo Boturini Benaducci, which had been burned, stolen, or taken abroad, where part of it was seized by British pirates who destroyed it without understanding its value.

48

Perhaps the greatest collection of ancient Mesoamerican documents was accumulated by another Italian, Lorenzo Boturini Benaducci, born in the see of Como in 1702, who liked to trace his family back to the ninth century A.D. After studying in Milan and Vienna, Boturini was driven to Madrid by the war between Spain and Austria. There he found Doña Manuela de Oca Sylva y Montezuma, who convinced him to go to New Spain to collect a pension of a thousand pesos owed her as a direct descendant of Montezuma II. Armed with a papal Bull authorizing him to make a collection to provide a crown for the Virgin of Guadalupe, Boturini scoured Mexico for documentary evidence in proof of the miraculous apparition of the Virgin at Guadalupe, and in so doing came across scores of priceless ancient historical documents. Arrested as a foreigner soliciting funds for the Virgin, Boturini was jailed and his documents seized.

Deported back to Spain, he was captured by British pirates on the high seas and put ashore at Gibraltar minus clothes and belongings. Vindicated by the Spanish authorities, Boturini was given a pension and the job of writing a history of New Spain, but by that time his collection of documents in Mexico had been pilfered and wantonly destroyed. Of two hundred manuscripts only thirty-eight remained, partly destroyed by soldiers from a nearby barracks who were entertained by the exotic drawings. Of Boturini's work, all that survived of value was a booklet entitled *Idea for a New General History of North America* with a tantalizing catalogue of his unique but scattered manuscripts.

Francisco Javier Clavigero, who entered the Jesuit Order in Mexico in 1748, found in the Jesuit College Library the remaining works of Sigüenza y Gongora and what was left of Boturini's collection, which he studied and used to become what a later Jesuit historian Charles E. Ronon called "the eighteenth century's *Voice of America*."

When the Jesuits were expelled from Mexico in 1767 by Charles III, Clavigero took refuge in Bologna where he witnessed the suppression of his order in 1773. Left with little to do, he produced his *Storia Antica* (written in Italian because few in Italy could understand Spanish) largely to preserve for posterity a record of the achievements of the native civilization of Mexico and refute to the world the misinformation of such historians as De Pauw and Robertson, who had wounded his Creole feelings.

The Inquisition took objection to Clavigero's comparison of the Spanish rule in New Spain with the Turkish oppression of the Greeks, and held up publication of his work in Spanish, insisting on complex amendations. In the end they lost the manuscript. When Clavigero died in Bologna in 1778, fellow Jesuits retrieved his original manuscript, but also managed to lose it. Early in the twentieth century a dusty manuscript was identified as Clavigero's by Manuel Diaz Ramon, S.J., but it too disappeared only to reappear in the hands of a U.S. dealer. The Mexican scholar Mariano Cuevas had it published, but omitted Clavigero's dissertation on the origin of syphilis, which he attributed to Spanish conquerors rather than to native Mexicans. Modern historians, with access to wider sources, accuse Clavigero of having plagiarized material directly from Torquemada's unpublished *Monarquia Indiana*.

50

Codex from the collection accumulated in Mexico at the beginning of the eighteenth century by researcher J.M.A. Aubin.

Because of the revolutions and counterrevolutions in Mexico, and twenty-six changes of government between 1830 and 1848, Aubin was able to buy cheaply many manuscripts and paintings, including some rare items from the son of Leon y Gama, which, as an astronomer, were of great interest to him. From Mexico, Aubin managed to smuggle his collection to France by taking the manuscripts and books out of their bindings and jumbling them up to confuse the customs officials at Veracruz. He published some in Paris in 1855, but mostly kept them secret from everyone except Brasseur de Bourbourg.

In 1870, because of losses in an investment in Panama Canal shares, Aubin was obliged to sell his collection, including many of Boturini's documents, to Eugene Goupil, a Frenchman interested in Mexican documents because of his Mexican mother—and so they have survived.

Calendar Stone.

Leon y Gama recognized the great Aztec stone as a sophisticated calendar. He believed its central cloverleaf design represented the legendary Aztec epochs of four suns. In the third circle he recognized the twenty Aztec symbols for the days of the month and the hieroglyph for 4-ocelot, the day when the sun stood at the zenith over Mexico City. As for the two enormous snakes around the outer edge, Leon y Gama believed they represented the Milky Way.

From the perfection and uniformity of the circles on the great stone and the exact division of it into parts, Leon y Gama said it was clear the Indians had a fine understanding of geometry. He also pointed out the ability of artisans capable of so perfectly engraving inscriptions on the stone though they were not supposed to have had tempered chisels but only harder stones. The volume and weight of the stone, said Leon y Gama, showed the Indians' knowledge of mechanics, without which they could never have cut a stone weighing over 24 tons and brought it from its place of origin, a quarry assumed to be in the mountains near Xochimilco, thirty miles away, from which it had been dragged on greased rollers by large groups of natives to the main square of Tenochtitlan. Leon y Gama, who considered the stone an Aztec clock by which priests could tally the movements of the heavenly bodies, believed that holes found in the perimeter of the stone might have been drilled to insert gnomons, or small obelisks, to throw shadows to indicate the days of the solstice, equinox, and zenith. At the beginning of the nineteenth century Sir Norman Lockyer, the English astronomer who first recognized the astronomical function of Stonehenge and the Egyptian temples, was amazed at the brilliance of the Mesoamerican

Among the few important relics which had survived from the Aztec empire, one of paramount interest surfaced only a dozen years before the arrival of Humboldt. In 1790, when the viceroy had ordered repairs to the paving of the great Plaza Mayor to improve the drainage in front of the cathedral, workmen had struck a large stone two feet below the surface, almost in front of the viceroy's palace. The stone, a solid piece of gray-black basalt, measured twelve feet across and was almost three feet thick.

Its presence was explained by the fact that when Cortes razed the city of Tenochtitlan he had ordered all large statues and stonework too solid to be broken up to be buried so that no remnant of the great Indian capital be left to remind Indians of their former glory, or as the parvenu clergy who considered the stone a "sacrificial altar" put it, "to bury with the stone the memory of the abominable acts perpetrated on it."

With great pains the enormous relic was righted, and the underside, which had been face down in the mud for over two centuries, was seen to be covered with the most intricate and delicate carving, as incomprehensible to its discoverers as it had been to Cortes and his early followers.

But there lived in Mexico City in 1790 a historian who had spent a lifetime studying ancient Mexican documents and who, like Sigüenza, had mastered the Nahuatl language and learned to interpret some of its hieroglyphs. Antonio de stone calendar which he found recorded not only the annual rotation of circumpolar star groups but also the annual apparent course of the sun. He called it "an achievement which has never been surpassed in primitive astronomy."

At the turn of the century, archeologist Zelia Nuttall, who considered the calendar "the most precious and remarkable monument ever unearthed on the American Continent," and "one of the most admirable and perfect achievements of the human intellect," saw in the Sun Calendar not only the embodiment of longstanding primitive observations, but a calendar designed to control the actions of all the human beings of the state, bringing their communal life into accord with the periodic movements of the heavenly bodies.

As the four-branched Ollin sign divided the 52-year cycle into four 13-year periods, it also divided the day into four equal parts, consonant with the four quarters of the Aztec world named for their four elementals—fire, air, water and earth. Nuttall says there were four human lords under the Aztec king, and these governed four divisions of the population, classified by the four elements.

The earth people, says Nuttall, specialized in agriculture and pottery; the water people in providing irrigation, drinking water, fishing, etc.; the fire people worked on combustibles, lighting, cooking and metalworking; the air people were the builders, masons and artificers. As a person was given the name of the day on which he was born, this determined his position in the commonwealth, his class, his future occupation.

Seen by Nuttall, the great stone was the work of a master mind "who destined it to be the image of a plan based on the idea of a central and yet all-embracing, dual, yet quadruple force or power."

Leon y Gama, then in his fifties, recognized the stone as the famous Aztec calendar, of which Sigüenza had written, taking his information from the descendants of Ixtlilxochitl.

To Leon y Gama the discovery of the calendar proved beyond doubt the assertion of Sigüenza, cautiously reported by Careri, that the pre-Conquest Indians had possessed an advanced and remarkable knowledge of mathematics and astronomy which they had used to make accurate observations of the movement of sun, planets, and stars to produce a calendar with cycles of 52 years of 365 days, each divided in 18 months of 20 days, whereto they added 5 on regular years and 6 on leap years.

In a monograph explaining the calendar stone, Leon y Gama tried to show how falsely the ancient Mexicans had been described as "irrational and simpleminded beings." But his explanation was too embarrassing to the Spanish clergy. Without elementary notions of astronomy, they continued to insist that the "calendar stone" was a sacrificial altar, arguing that the very fact that the intertwined recurrent cycles were put together in such a complex and aesthetic manner obviously meant they were ornamental, adducing as evidence the fact that the same symbols appeared on earrings, necklaces and other purely decorative objects.

When Humboldt saw the great stone, it was propped up against the west wall of the cathedral, already wantonly disfigured by a populace exhorted by its priests to execrate anything connected with their former religion. As an astronomer, Humboldt was quick to validate Leon y Gama's interpretation of the stone, supporting him with a long essay on the significance of the Aztec calendar. Humboldt accepted Leon y Gama's interpretation that eight triangles radiating from the central sun alluded to eight divisions of the day, pointing out that the Aztecs had evidently reckoned the civil day in the same manner as the Persians, the Egyptians, the Babylonians, along with the greater part of the nations of Asia with the exception of China, dividing the day from sunrise to sunrise into eight intervals of three hours.

It was equally clear to Humboldt that the Indians had started and divided the year by the solstices, equinoxes, and days of the zenith. Humboldt pointed out that most of the names by which the Mexicans denoted the twenty days of their month were the same as those given to the signs of the zodiac in use from remotest antiquity among the nations of Eastern Asia—tiger, hare, ape, dog, serpent, and bird, heavenly asterisms that bore the same names in the Tartar and Tibetan zodiacs. From all of this Humboldt concluded that the people of the two continents might have derived their astrological ideas from a common source.

53

Humboldt's conclusion that the people of Mexico at the time of the Spanish Conquest had enjoyed a greater degree of civilization handed down from antiquity than they had been credited with, and that the American Indian in antiquity had a sophisticated understanding of astronomy, was derided by reviewers, who conceded that the Indians might have had a calendar chronology but would not admit "that a nation so barbarous as the Mexicans had any knowledge of the causes of eclipses."

Humboldt turned to other subjects. Though he traveled extensively in the country on sociological and geographical quests, he appears to have relied more on the reports of Mexican friends than on firsthand observation to fill in his knowledge of other Mexican antiquities. The Xochicalco pyramid near Cuernavaca he passed without even knowing it was there, relying on others to describe it; he did likewise for the ruins of Mitla. Though he did travel to Tula and express the opinion that it might have been the site of the Toltec capital, Tollan, he did not bother to look for archeological evidence.

Humboldt claimed that "the only ancient monuments in the Valley of Mexico imposing enough in size and grandeur for European eyes" were the ruins of the pyramids of San Juan Teotihuacan. Historians have recounted that he traveled to these pyramids by horse and coach with Bonpland and Montafur and was "immediately struck by the extraordinary geometric symmetry of the great ruined complex, marveling at what the buildings and temples must have looked like a thousand years earlier, with platforms adorned with the gilded images of gods." However it is more likely that Humboldt again relied for his description of the site on the work of Careri; and for the measurements of the Sun and Moon pyramids on the figures given him by his young friend Oteyza.

Humboldt had carefully read Careri before embarking on his exploration of Mexico; but until he arrived in Acapulco he had no way of knowing whether Careri had been telling the truth or, as his critics maintained, inventing fables. Humboldt soon discovered that Careri had indeed preceded him, and he was categorical in his defense of the authenticity of Careri's descriptions of Mexico: "Having covered a great deal of the territory so minutely described by the Italian traveler, I can affirm that there is no doubt that Careri was in Mexico. . . . Careri's descriptions have that touch of local color only found in those who have had the advantage of seeing with their own eyes."

Ironically, Humboldt's description of the Teotihuacan complex appears to have been seen through Careri's eyes.

In his *Atlas Pittoresco,* Humboldt devoted more than a hundred pages to a discussion of the Mexican calendar stone and the relationship between the mathematical and astronomical systems of Aztecs, Toltecs, Peruvians, Nootkas, and other native American peoples, with those of the Chinese, Hindus, Oigones, and other Oriental peoples.

He found a vast amount of evidence for a common origin of the cultures of the two continents, including the systems of both the solar and lunar zodiacs, with many similar animals allotted, and even similar sounds of some of the astrological terms.

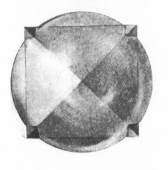

Pyramid of Cheops as model
of earth's Northern Hemisphere.

Humboldt could hardly have surveyed the Sun and Moon
pyramids at Teotihuacan as being oriented "within 52 min-
tes exactly placed from north to south and east to west," as
he describes them, when they were, and are, in fact, oriented
more than 15 full degrees (or almost 1000 minutes) east of
true north. A surveyor as preoccupied as was Humboldt with
accurate calculations of latitude and longitude (who observed an error of mere seconds of arc in the location of
Acapulco, and who calculated the latitude of the eastern
tower of the cathedral of Mexico to within 600 feet of the
modern calculation) is unlikely to have been capable of so
gross an error. Humboldt also described the slope of the Sun
Pyramid as being 52 degrees, very similar to that of the
Great Pyramid of Cheops, when in fact the Teotihuacan
slope is a much gentler 43 degrees, 35 minutes—an error of
almost 10 degrees. Humboldt also erroneously described
"a system of smaller pyramids about 10 meters high, several
hundred of them along wide avenues which follow precisely
the line of parallels and meridians leading up to the faces of
the pyramids."

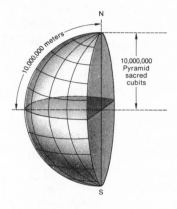

Herschel suggested that the most practical system of measures should be based on the length of the polar axis of the earth which he believed had been calculated in antiquity as 20 million Pyramid Sacred Cubits. This gave an ancient inch within one part in a thousand of an English inch. The notion first propounded by Isaac Newton was used by astronomer Charles Piazzi Smyth as the basis for his often incorrect but brilliantly intuitive conceits about the Great Pyramid and ancient units of measure.

Equally amazing is the fact that Humboldt, who was such a dedicated astronomer and geographer, should have missed the geodetic and astronomic functions of pyramids, whereas his contemporary colleague, Edmé François Jomard, with whom he was to have traveled to Egypt on Napoleon's expedition, and with whom he later corresponded, had brilliantly confirmed the scattered reports of classical Greek authors to the effect that the Pyramid of Cheops was a geodetic scale model of the Northern Hemisphere whose apex represented the North Pole and perimeter an exact fraction of the equatorial circumference of the earth—or 1/2 a minute of degree.

The only reasonable deduction is that Humboldt never visited the Teotihuacan complex, or if he did, did so in a manner so cursory that he might as well have never seen it. A careful reading of Humboldt on Teotihuacan shows him to be most circumscribed in his description, never using the first person.

For the dimensions of the pyramids he had the work of Oteyza, who had recently measured the Sun Pyramid's base at 208 meters or 665 English feet; again, because of the rubble at its base, about 8 meters or 24 feet short. To convey to Europeans an idea of what this meant, Humboldt pointed out that the northerly facade of the Hotel des Invalides in Paris, where Napoleon was eventually to be buried, was exactly 600 feet long—in French feet or *pieds du roi,* the sixth of a toise, or one French fathom. In English feet this would have been 636. Confusing, but indicative that somewhere there might be a relation between the pyramids of Egypt and those of Teotihuacan, in that 600 Egyptian feet had been found by Jomard to be one Egyptian stadium, or 1/10 of a mile, equal to 6 seconds of arc, or 1/600 of a degree of longitude.

To convey an idea of the cubic capacity of the Sun Pyramid, Humboldt relied on Oteyza's estimate of 33,743,201 cubic French feet, though actually Oteyza had measured in neither French feet nor English feet, nor even in meters, but in the Mexican *vara,* one of which consisted of 31 inches of the old *pied du roi*; all of which made it hard for anyone but a mensurational aficionado to be moved by the fact that Humboldt and Oteyza considered the height of the Sun Pyramid to be 171 French feet or 180 English—equal to 2160 English inches.

Curious as to whether the pyramids of Teotihuacan had been built entirely by man or whether the builders had taken advantage of natural hillocks to cover with stone and cement, Humboldt tended to the conclusion that they were entirely man-made, saying "their position in a plain with no

Humboldt found the Cholula Pyramid to be the largest in America, a truncated structure with four terraces, 367 feet from east to west, by 348 feet from north to south. It appeared to have been in constant use up till A.D. 1200. The interior he found to be made of mud and small stones covered by a thick wall of amygdaloid porense. On the outer layer were stones bound together by traces of mortar called *tetzontli* by the natives.

The mound could be entered through a small opening on the eastern side. Inside was a bewildering maze of passages, with here and there a frescoed wall adorned with butterflies and insects in yellow or black, and the evidence of seven superimposed constructions.

Humboldt says the pyramid had been surmounted by a jade image of Quetzalcoatl, "Lord of the Breath of Life." The Cholula Pyramid is the largest known structure in the world in terms of cubic content. Two hundred and ten feet high, it covers forty-five acres. The pre-Conquest Mexican legend about Cholula is very similar to the Biblical account of the Tower of Babel. According to the legend, after the deluge which destroyed the primeval world, seven giants survived, one of whom built the great pyramid of Cholula in order to reach heaven, but the Gods destroyed the pyramid with fire and confounded the language of the builders.

other hills makes it unlikely they were built on outcroppings." He also concluded that the Indian tradition that the structures were hollow was too vague to credit and that until the pyramids were pierced horizontally there would be no way of knowing.

Humboldt was amazed that whoever built these pyramidal structures should have done so in a manner so similar to the Ziggurat of Belus in Babylon, the remains of which he had observed. It led him to wonder whether the constructors had been allied to a Mongolian race from the East, as had first seemed plausible, or whether they were somehow linked to the Middle East, as indicated by the botanical and geological data. Again Humboldt was apparently unaware that the ziggurats of Mesopotamia had also been constructed as geodetic scale models of the Northern Hemisphere, like a stack of diminishing blocks, each facade of which gave a rectangular Mercator-like projection of the seven classic zones between the equator and the pole.

Humboldt disputed the attribution of construction of the pyramids to the Toltecs, which would have placed them in the eighth or ninth century A.D., and was inclined to favor Sigüenza, some of whose manuscript notes he had read, who attributed the pyramids to the Olmecs, the first people mentioned in the Indian chronology of New Spain, who were supposed to have come from the East, or even from Europe.

Humboldt referred to the Toltec leader Quetzalcoatl as a "Mexican Buddha," and he was amused to quote Spaniards who described him as white, bearded, and accompanied by strangers wearing black soutanes, saying they believed him to be either a Carthaginian or an Irishman, either possibility of which Humboldt was not ready to envisage.

Though Humboldt's description of the Teotihuacan complex appears to be secondhand, he devoted firsthand attention to the Great Pyramid of Cholula. After eleven months in Mexico, Humboldt decided to leave via Veracruz, stopping at

On September 16, 1810, Miguel Hidalgo y Costilla, a parish priest in the dusty little town of Dolores in the province of Michoacan, raised the cry which came to be known as the "Grito de Dolores," calling for an end to Spanish rule in Mexico. Hidalgo, who was born in Dolores, a few miles from San Miguel Allende (named for his co-insurrectionist, Captain Ignacio Allende) was a tall gaunt second-generation *criollo,* trained by the Jesuits, impressive in his black cassock and white-fringed hair.

His revolutionary ardor came from having watched government constables chop down the olive trees, vineyards, and mulberries he had taught his parishioners to grow, in contravention to the Peninsular law against the production in the colonies of olive oil, wine, or silk.

Naming himself "Captain General of America," he seized the icon of the Virgin of Guadalupe, the Morenita, most holy of all symbols to the native Indian, as banner for his army. Spaniards and officials fled before him. But at the gates of Mexico City, which the more intrepid Allende wished to attack, Hidalgo vacillated. When his forces turned to indiscriminate pillage and massacre, the *criollos,* who also longed for liberation from Spain, became afraid for their lives, especially after the example of Haiti, where native blacks had slaughtered all the native whites. The *criollos* supported the Spanish Viceroy, who ordered the summary execution of all rebels taken in arms. In recaptured towns, one man in ten chosen by lot was hanged or shot. Hidalgo's forces retaliated by garroting Spaniards. The Spanish retaliated by burying their enemies in quicklime.

Defeated and captured, Hidalgo was shorn of his vestments. Shot by a firing squad, on July 30, 1811, his skull was hung in an iron cage as a deterrent to further revolution.

Puebla to inspect the enormous pyramid, which he described as "a mountain of unbaked bricks" once dedicated to Quetzalcoatl, whom he regarded as "the most mysterious being in the whole Mexican mythology," a hero whom he now believed to have reigned much earlier, in a Golden Age of the Anuacs, "when all animals and all men lived in peace, and the earth brought forth without culture the most fruitful harvests, the air being filled with birds of marvelous song and plumage."

On his way from Puebla to Veracruz Humboldt noticed ice carriers from the snowfields of Mount Orizaba bringing ice to the sherbet makers of Veracruz, much as the Ottoman refiners of sherbet had brought it in carts to the Sublime Porte from the peaks of Mount Olympus.

Determined to visit Thomas Jefferson, a fellow naturalist, democrat, creator of an effective democracy, and brother

After Hidalgo's execution, the banner of revolt was taken up by another priest, José Maria Morelos y Pavon, who was of mixed Spanish, Amerindian, and Negro origin. Born in Michoacan, he had worked as a laborer and muleteer until he was 25. Starving himself to gain an education, he entered holy orders, where he studied under Hidalgo.

A short, squat man, Morelos was a taciturn and humble genius, ravaged by malaria and constant headaches, against which he wore a tight bandana over his balding head. Too radical for the *criollos,* who longed for Mexican independence, Morelos drove them into the royalist ranks. They feared the insurgent warfare would destroy the economy: already, commerce and agriculture were at a standstill.

Morelos was betrayed by an auburn-haired mestizo, Augustin de Iturbide, who managed to pass himself off as a *criollo* and tell all he heard about the revolutionaries to the royalists, for which service he quickly rose from lieutenant to colonel in the royalist army. When he learned that Morelos had ordered his insurgents to blacken their faces so that they could recognize each other in close combat, Iturbide, against orders, had a troop of his cavalry darken their own faces. After dark on Christmas Eve of 1813, Iturbide led a reckless mounted charge into the heart of the Morelos camp, bursting in upon the surprised insurgents. Morelos' regiments fired on each other, and the insurgent army dissolved in the face of inferior royal forces. A royalist officer, one of Morelos' old lieutenants who had changed sides, caught Morelos as he tried to remove his spurs for flight. Asked what he would do if the situation were reversed, Morelos replied he would confess the officer and shoot him. Convicted of treason and branded as a Protestant, Morelos was unfrocked and shot to death three days before Christmas 1815.

Mason, Humboldt sailed from Veracruz to New York in March of 1804, loaded with minerals, plants, sculpture, and the few ancient manuscripts he had managed to collect, all of which were to help him produce several volumes on his travels in the Americas, which, when published in expensive folio editions, opened the eyes of Europe to the astounding possibility that a civilization had existed in the Americas far more cultivated and knowledgeable than anyone had theretofore believed, scotching the general opinion that the Indians conquered by Cortes were nothing but barbarous feathered sodomites devoted to the worship of monstrous serpentine idols to whom they ghoulishly sacrificed thousands of victims.

59

Iturbide.

Having risen to the rank of general in the royalist army fighting against the insurgents, Augustin de Iturbide grew so rich on graft he overstepped himself by taking too much from a convoy of silver he was supposed to protect. Disgraced, he entered a lay retreat in the convent of La Profesa, where he plotted a revolt against the viceregal regime to detach Mexico from Spain. To subvert the army, he seized an entire pack train carrying half a million silver pesos to Acapulco. Making lavish offers of promotion, Iturbide managed to lead his army into Mexico City in September of 1821, riding on a black horse and wearing a plumed hat, surrounded by a gang of new generals decked in gold braid. As president of the council of regents, Iturbide fomented a barracks revolt to have himself proclaimed Emperor Augustin I. Of the first year's national income, 80 percent went to the army, 11 percent to Iturbide, and the rest to administer a country whose economy had been ruined by ten years of civil war. When congress complained, Emperor Augustin I disbanded it and ruled by decree in imitation of Napoleon I. But others could play the same game. One of Iturbide's lieutenants, Antonio Lopez de Santa Anna, who had risen to the rank of general, called for a republic (though he admitted candidly he did not know the meaning of the word), and Iturbide was sentenced to perpetual exile.

Humboldt's stay in Mexico caused him to be suspected of having helped foment the Mexican revolution against Spain which broke out a few years after his departure. But although he had been sought out by sensitive souls because of his philosophical and metaphysical bent, and by liberals and political actionists because of his penchant for liberal and egalitarian doctrines and his open pronouncements against the economic and social system of exploitation in New Spain, Humboldt must have considered himself too indebted to the crown of Spain, for receiving him so well and granting him such freedom, to risk writing what might have been considered subversive to his royal benefactor. But with or without his help, the revolution broke out a few years after his departure.

For a long time Humboldt dreamed of going back to Mexico.

Once the revolution, which started in 1810 and dragged on for ten years, had rid Mexico of Spanish rule, he would have liked to return to organize "a great scientific establishment for all of Free America." In October of 1822 he wrote to his brother Wilhelm from Verona that "the Emperor of Mexico, Iturbide, whom I know, is about to fall and make way for a Republican government. . . . I have the notion of ending my days in a pleasanter way and more useful for science in a part of the world where I am extraordinarily well liked, and where everything indicates I would be happy. It is a way not to die without some glory, to unite around me many educated people, and enjoy that independence from opinions and feelings which is necessary to my well being."

Humboldt wished to make a base in Mexico City from which to explore all the places he had only heard of or written about secondhand. But his expensive publications cost too much of his fortune, and though there was mention that in France 4 or 5 million francs were being collected to reorganize the mines in Mexico, nothing came of the venture, and Humboldt, growing old and depressed, was obliged to live out his life in the constricted atmosphere of the court at Potsdam without ever seeing Mexico again.

His large illustrated works, however, were to spark an unquenchable interest in a whole new breed of adventurers who set out to explore the antiquities of Mexico.

5. British Enterprise

William Bullock, a Liverpool jeweler, amateur naturalist, and antiquarian, was so impressed by Humboldt's massive volumes on Mexican antiquities that he decided to travel to Mexico and bring back specimens of his own to exhibit in London to a public whose taste for the exotic had been stimulated by the recent discoveries of Napoleon's savants in Egypt, just published in the monumental twenty-volume *Description de L'Egypte.* As a merchant, Bullock was in the *avant garde* of a whole company of English entrepreneurs who wished to profit by trading with an independent Mexico open to foreigners.

In December of 1822 Bullock sailed for Veracruz in the company of his twenty-year-old son aboard an English merchantman armed with twelve cannon for protection against ubiquitous pirates. Though he had been told to expect "the most stable government" in Mexico, Bullock found the port of Veracruz in the hands of republican insurgents under General Antonio Santa Anna, while the self-appointed Emperor Iturbide had retreated to Puebla with his royalist army.

Heading for the highlands, the Bullocks were disappointed by their first wayside inn, where they were kept awake by mosquitoes, barking dogs, and braying asses; in the morning they were obliged to "clean our persons from the deposits of the poultry that had roosted over our heads."

In Puebla, the first impressive city reached by the Bullocks, they learned that the emperor had resigned the government into the hands of the republicans and fled the country, which had installed General Santa Anna as president of the Mexican republic; so the Bullocks followed Humboldt's footsteps to Cholula, where they examined the ruins

Antonio Lopez de Santa Anna.

62

Veracruz.

Villa Rica de Vera Cruz, or the Rich Town of the True Cross, had been a mere campsite of huts until Cortes declared it a town as a device to bypass the authority of his boss Velasquez in Cuba so as to seize Mexico for the crown in his own name. By having himself elected chief magistrate of the municipality of Veracruz, Cortes became directly subordinate to Charles V and so cut Velasquez out of a fifth of the booty. Thereafter Vera Cruz became the port of entry to Mexico from Europe.

To Bullock, Veracruz had an Oriental look, with low cupolas, something like mosques without the elegance of minarets. To the south were the cemetery and the slaughter-house, to the north the flat yellow-fever marshlands inhabited by iguanas, snakes, herons, and wild duck.

Whereas Careri had complained of being devoured by field lice, Bullock found the city hot, dusty, and with filthy streets cleaned of offal by carrion vultures. Humboldt, more scientifically, had noted that all the buildings were built of stone dredged up from the sea, called *madreporicas,* there being no other stone available.

of the pyramid, which they found covered with prickly pear, tuna, copal, and other vegetation, on top of which the Spaniards had built an imposing church.

"It was here," noted Bullock, with his penchant for establishmental history, "that Cortes, on his first advance, was welcomed as a liberator and brother, but having accidentally discovered that it only arose from a deep-laid plan to assassinate him and all his followers, he, with his accustomed presence of mind and decision of character, secured the chief persons of the place; and, to strike terror in others, made a terrible example, by putting to death 70,000 of the inhabitants."

63

In the spring of 1824, Iturbide, like Napoleon returning from Elba, tried to recapture his empire, landing by boat at a port in Tamaulipas with a packet of paper money and printed proclamations, unaware that the congress had voted a bill of attainder if he ever set foot again on Mexican soil. When he did, the local authorities seized and shot him.

A good bourgeois, Bullock was as impressed by the broad streets of Puebla that were paved with large stones in checkered or diamond patterns as he was by the splendid equipages and retinues of the wealthy Pueblans, whose handsome carriages were drawn by richly caparisoned mules attended by servants in showy liveries, parading through the streets and parks.

To show the flag, and *épater* the natives, Bullock sported a walking-stick gun, a portable chair and table, a camera lucida,* "and other little specimens of English ingenuity."

Approaching Mexico City, the Bullocks came upon suburbs they considered "mean and dirty, the people covered with rags," but they were well pleased by the center of the city with its wide streets and grand houses.

* The camera lucida is an optical instrument for drawing in perspective, invented at the beginning of the nineteenth century by an Englishman, Dr. William Hyde Wollaston. By looking with one eye vertically through a strip of plain glass tilted at an angle of 45 degrees, an image is reflected onto the surface of a sheet of paper so that the outline can be accurately traced with a pencil. A helpful device for transferring architectural structures onto paper, it had the advantage of being cheap, small, and portable.

Whereas in Puebla (left) Bullock was astonished to find that the wives of mining magnates kept houses in a princely state, and would go to church escorted by hundreds of servants and twenty ladies in waiting, in Mexico City (above) Bullock was most impressed by the streets, which were two miles long, perfectly level and straight, ending in a gorgeous view of the surrounding valley with snowcapped volcanic mountains in the distance.

As snobbish as any merchant, Bullock was happy to secure the services of Count Luchese, uncle to the Duke of Monteleone, a descendant and heir of Hernan Cortes, to guide him through the city. Luchese graciously escorted his English visitors around the 700-foot-long palace of the viceroy with its 1,100 windows overlooking the Plaza Mayor, which Bullock deemed to be "the finest in the world." In the palace grounds they saw not only the mint and the prison, but a botanic garden with fountains and fragrant plants unknown to Europeans before Humboldt, aflutter with pretty, tame birds.

In the Hospital of Jesus, Bullock was even shown an iron chest in which were kept the bones of Cortes. Thirty years earlier these grisly remains of the conquistador had been removed to the hospital from the Church of St. Francis to be venerated in a crystal coffin secured by bars and plates of silver, and were only just saved by royalist "friends of the family" from a mob of republicans who wished to scatter to the winds the bones and ashes of this "detestable old Spaniard." Pensively Bullock examined the skull, which he found to be small, with some missing teeth. Later scrutinizers found evidence in the bones of degenerative symptoms corresponding to dwarfism and a condition of congenital syphilis in the osseous system.

In the city, the English merchant was most impressed by the comfort of the three-storied houses, painted in dis-

Bullock found that the sumptuous house of Emperor Iturbide had been turned into a stagecoach hotel.

Officers of the Inquisition leading "heretics" to the stake.

temper, highly decorated, with rows of wrought-iron balconies and porticoed courtyards scented by flowers and trees. He thought the climate ideal, a perennial spring, and was enraptured by the clear atmosphere, not yet contaminated by smog, a bourgeois's dream, in which even the execution of a felon appeared to be done in a "solemn and decent manner," so different from the executions he had witnessed in France after the revolution, where "the rabble behaved with the most disgusting ribaldry and obscenity." Here the victims, two Indians accused of robbery and sacrilege, were led to the public scaffold on the backs of asses, dressed in white gowns and caps with red crosses, there to be discreetly garroted "without the public witnessing the horrible contortions often seen in our executions."

As Humboldt had declared that apart from the nearby pyramids of Teotihuacan the only objects in Mexico City worthy of the notice of an antiquarian were the great calendar stone and another "sacrificial" stone found near it, Bullock decided to make large plaster casts of both to be shipped to London. With the influence of the Mexican prime minister he was able to obtain permission from the clergy to erect a scaffold by the Aztec calendar and take several separate impressions. Bullock believed the stone to have once formed part of the roof of the great temple of Tenochtitlan, much like the Zodiac of Dendera, the original of which had only just been dismantled and carried to the Louvre. Like Humboldt, he considered the Aztec stone "proof of the perfection the nation to which it belonged had attained in some of the sciences." Few persons, he maintained, even in the most enlightened cities of Europe, would have been capable in his day of executing such a work.

A hundred yards from the calendar stone the so-called sacrificial stone lay buried in the cathedral square with only

On the upper surface of this monolith there are 6 × 6 = 36 single glyphs, which yield 9 groups of 4. If these 9 × 4 are added to the 4 × 4 glyphs on which the chieftains are respectively seated, 13 groups of 4 are obtained, equivalent to the 52 years in the Mexican cycle. Each group is accompanied by the name of a tribe and its capital. Again it took a hundred years before some meaning was found for these mysterious glyphs.

its upper surface exposed, "to impress on the populace," says Bullock, "an abhorrence of the horrible and sanguinary rites that had once been performed on this very altar."

From the clergy Bullock again obtained permission to expose the sides of the stone and to make casts of the twenty-five-foot circumference on which were carved fifteen groups of figures representing the conquests by Mexican warriors of different cities. The casting performance greatly aroused the curiosity of bystanders, who, says Bullock, wondered if the English still worshiped the same gods as had the Mexicans before their enforced conversion to Christianity.

But the antique relic which most appealed to Bullock and on which he most counted to shock or titillate a London audience was reported by Humboldt to have been dug up and reburied in a gallery of the University of Mexico by Dominican priests who considered it too scandalous to be viewed by Christian students.

Bullock had great difficulty persuading the authorities to let him dig it up, but with the help of Humboldt's friend Don Manuel del Rio, who had graduated to professor of mineralogy at the university, he finally obtained permission. The burial spot was ascertained with not too much difficulty, and a few hours' digging disgorged from mother earth the Mexican goddess of earth and mother of the entire Nahuatl pantheon.

"I had the pleasure," says Bullock, "of seeing the resurrection of this horrible deity, before whom tens of thousands of human victims had been sacrificed in the religious and sanguinary fervor of its infatuated worshippers."

To Bullock it was scarcely possible that an artist "combining the ingenuity and imagination of a Brueghel and a Fuseli"

In Bullock's time, the university was a mere survival of medievalism in government and curriculum, the men of learning of the viceroyalty being dedicated to the perpetuation of a doctrinal theology that was already becoming obsolete.

could have conceived so awesome a sight. Bullock described the "colossal and horrible monster" as being hewn out of one solid block of basalt, nine feet high, its outlines giving the idea of a deformed human figure "uniting all that is horrible in the tiger and the rattle-snake." Instead of arms the figure was supplied with large serpents, its drapery was wreathed snakes, interwoven and terminating in the wings of vultures. The "idol's" feet, between which lay the head of another rattlesnake descending from its body, were those of a tiger or jaguar, claws extended in the act of

Coatlicue.

This squat, massive twelve-ton basalt statue, embodying pyramidal, cruciform, and human forms, dug at Bullock's request, and which he considered monstrous, was quickly reburied by an outraged priesthood. Only later was the statue understood to incorporate the essence of Nahuatl cosmological thought. "Nowhere in the history of art," says Professor Leo Gatz, "has a single monument achieved such a complete synthesis of human and abstract universal relations."

In the opinion of Mexico's art critic Justino Fernandez the statue represents "the embodiment of the cosmic-dynamic power which bestows life and which thrives on death in the struggle of opposites."

To Frank Waters, Coatlicue emerges as the concrete embodiment in stone of the ideas of a cosmic being who generates and sustains the universe. "It adumbrates the cruciform orientation of the quadrants of the universe, as well as the dynamic quality of time, which creates and destroys through struggle."

Author Lewis Spence points to the strong similarities between Coatlicue of Mexico and the goddess Cleito, wife of Poseidon, founder of Atlantis: each, says Spence, presided over a Sacred Hill, and each bore seven sets of twins, two of whom—Atlas and Quetzalcoatl—were mountain-born supporters of the world.

seizing a prey. A necklace, above huge deformed breasts, was composed of human hearts, skulls, and chopped-off hands fastened together by entrails. It took Bullock a week to make a cast of Coatlicue, as the goddess was called, whereupon the university authorities ordered the statue reburied "so as to hide it from the profane gaze of the vulgar."

His casting completed, Bullock was free to visit the pyramids of Teotihuacan. On Whitsunday of 1823, accompanied by his son and a co-national, Mr. Gilton, Bullock set off toward Texcoco with an Indian guide and letters of introduction furnished by the viceroy's wife, the Countess of Regla, to the principal inhabitants of this onetime capital.

Leaving the great square of Mexico City, the Bullocks passed a thousand horses and mules loaded with silver being prepared to leave for Veracruz to be shipped to Europe.

Thereafter for several miles they proceeded along the original causeway across the old lake of Texcoco, which seven weeks earlier at their arrival in the city had been covered with water and myriads of shoveler ducks but was now dry for lack of rain.

Approaching Texcoco—the Athens of America, as Bullock termed it, "residence of historians, orators, poets, artists, and the great men of every department of the sciences who existed in those days"—they crossed the "Bridge of Brigantines" from which Cortes had launched his flotilla to recapture and destroy Tenochtitlan.

In the market place of Texcoco they viewed the spot where Bishop Zumarraga had burned the Aztec heritage of manuscripts and hieroglyphic writings.

Bullock was much moved by the palace of the ancient caciques, or tributary kings of Texcoco, which extended three hundred feet, forming part of a large square built up on sloping terraces, the original walls of which were composed of huge blocks of basaltic stone, four and five feet long, two to three feet thick, cut and polished with great exactness, many of which had gone to build the nearby Catholic church.

As the sky darkened with thunder clouds, Bullock inquired about the "celebrated pyramids of the Sun and Moon, or for San Juan of Teotihuacan." But his inquiries were fruitless, so he headed for Otumba in the expectation of finding them near that place.

For a couple of hours they rode over fine country on which the number of handsome Spanish churches and haciendas exceeded those of any part of Mexico through which Bullock had yet traveled.

At one point he passed a stand of olive trees, the finest he had ever seen. "Those of Tuscany are not half the size; they

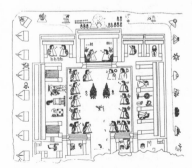

Gardens of Texcoco.

Sixteenth-century drawing of an older map of the palace court of Texcoco.

The Valley of Otumba.

must many of them be thirty feet in diameter." At the foot of some low mountains Bullock described the landscape as being soft iron-colored stone without vegetable soil or vegtation, in which the continual passing of horses had worn deep tracks up to the knees of animals.

By evening, thunder turned to torrents of rain, which filled the dry beds of the rivers, pouring muddy waters toward the great flat lakes.

On the far side of the mountain, Bullock at last caught sight of the two great pyramids on the plain before them, five or six miles away; an hour's ride brought them to Otumba just before dark, "the first place," noted Bullock, "reached by Cortes after his defeat of *La Noche Triste.*" An old lady gave them refuge in a carpenter's shop where they could dry their clothes and sleep. In the morning, after bread and hot chocolate, they queried the local padre for information about the pyramids, but he could give them none, though they were in full view of the windows of his house, about a league and a half away.

As Bullock and his party approached the shrub-covered mounds, they could see the "square and perfect form of the largest," and distinguish its terraces. Attacking the smaller pyramid first, they found it much dilapidated, but ascended to its top over masses of falling stones and ruins of masonry with less difficulty than they had expected. On the summit Bullock found the remains of "an ancient building, forty-seven feet long and fourteen wide with walls three feet thick and eight feet high, mostly of unhewn stone with three win-

70

Bullock's illustration of the Sun Pyramid on the summit of which he says he found the remains of an ancient temple.

Cortes winning the battle of Otumba by killing the "snake woman" leader of the Aztec forces.

dows on each side." The northern end of the building appeared to them to have been divided at about a third of its length.

Bullock says that he and his companions sat atop the Pyramid of the Moon, with the great Pyramid before them, "contemplating this scene of ancient wonders." His eye took in not only the greater part of the Valley of Mexico, with its surrounding mountains, but also Mexico City, some thirty miles away, a feat quite impossible now because of the smog.

Bullock was of the opinion that when Cortes came through the valley the large pyramids were in the same condition in which he found them—covered with dirt and shrubbery—and that it was on ascending one of them that Cortes was able to see the approach of the great Indian army which Francisco de Aguilar (who was with Cortes at the time) estimated at the incredible number of "five to six hundred thousand selected men." Bullock says there was no other eminence nearby which could have answered the purpose, concluding that "It was at this place that Cortes fought and defeated the innumerable army of Indians; after the horrible night of desolation he expressly says that he arrived on the plains near Otumba; he ascended an eminence, and discovered the whole district covered with armies; despair filled every breast, except the intrepid leader's." Paraphrasing Bernal Diaz' account of how a mere four hundred wounded and weary Spaniards with two score

71

Pulque is a liquor made from the fermented juice of the maguey plant, whose flower grows as high as 20 feet, with 10-foot leaves. Some yield as much as 600 liters of liquid, drawn from a hollow in the center, from which first honey then pulque is derived.

For the Aztecs, pulque was not only a nutritive drink but a medicine and a ritual intoxicant related to their complex pantheon. It was also given to conquered warriors about to be immolated.

Excessive drinking of pulque was controlled among the Aztecs, if not eliminated, by a taboo on the "fifth cup." This was reserved for priests, in whom it induced an ecstatic reaction, often causing them to dance. Even a fourth cup was frowned upon, since it might result in drunkenness, a punishable offense in Tenochtitlan except in privileged cases (the sick, the aged, or celebrants at certain festivities).

The early Spanish churchmen considered pulque detestable, the cause among Indians of "idolatry, thieving, murders, sacrilege, sodomy, incest and other abominations." But the viceregal government soon used it as a source of revenue, the tax bringing in a yearly 100,000 pieces of eight.

When the green leaves of the maguey are crushed and the fibers separated on a stone with water, hemp is produced from which cloth can be woven which takes the place of linen. Ropes are also entwined. The spines are used for needles; and the leaves, when intact, can be used to roof houses. The shoots nearest the earth, which are white and tender, can be cooked and eaten. Dry, the leaves provide fuel for a gentle smokeless fire, whose ashes are medicinal. When the root is drawn from the center of a dead plant it can be used as a rafter.

horses got out of this iron trap, Bullock pontificated romantically: "The unnumbered host of Indians arrived, and closed round the small band of Spaniards, when the dauntless Cortes, with a few horsemen, charged furiously that part of the enemy where the royal banner was carried, the bearer was killed, the banner taken, and the whole of the immense multitude fled in consternation from the field, offering no further interruption to the retreat of Cortes."

Bullock's romancing led to the conjecture that the Indians, like the Trojans in a Homeric epic, were overcome by what they considered supernatural forces, as if the Spaniards were demigods descending on them from Teotihuacan, the "home of the Gods."

At the base of the Moon Pyramid Bullock had a drink of pulque and tried to make friends with some native children, but they "seemed much terrified at our white faces and odd dress." To Bullock the smell of fresh pulque was acceptable, but very disagreeable when matured to the point it was appreciated by the Mexicans.

When Bullock asked an old woman if she could tell him who had built the pyramids, she replied, *"Si, señor. San Francisco."*

According to an old legend told to Sahagun, a woman, Mayahuel, later regarded as a goddess, and the mother of Centzon Totochtin, the patron of Tepozteco, invented pulque and knew how the maguey should be pierced in order to extract the honey. In the Borgia Codex, which originated in Puebla or possibly Tlaxcala, Mayahuel is a prominent figure dressed in white, the color of pulque. The Borgia Codex also shows another pulque god, Patecatl, who discovered how to supplement the honey from the maguey to aid in the fermentation process. His name, like that of his associate deities, was taken from the locality in which he was worshiped. Several place names survive to identify the first makers of pulque with a mountainous place called Chichinahuia. Because this drink was topped with foam, the snowcapped peak was also called Popocatepetl, meaning "Foamy Mountain."

The Codex Magliabecchiano, probably painted between 1562 and 1601, has several representations of pulque deities, including Mayahuel and Atlacoaya. Eduard Seler noted that the face of a pulque god was usually painted in two colors, one half in red and the other in black or dark brown with yellow spots. This decorative scheme also characterized representations of Tlaloc and Quetzalcoatl. Pulque deities were further distinguished by a crescent-shaped ornament worn directly under the nose.

73

Not far from the great pyramid, near a gate, they found an enormous stone with sculptured ornaments, which appeared to Bullock to be of great antiquity. A boy who had followed them beckoned Bullock's son toward a plantation where they found another great stone covered with sculpture with a hole in the top, which Bullock supposed to be a "stone of sacrifice."

The ascent of the large pyramid was less difficult than they expected. All the way up they found lime and cement mixed with fallen stone. Bullock described the terraces as clearly visible, particularly the second, which he estimated to be about thirty-eight feet wide, covered with a coat of red cement eight or ten inches thick, composed of small pebblestones and lime. But in many places, the copal trees had destroyed the regularity of the steps, though "nowhere injured the general figure of the square," which, Bullock says, "was as perfect in this respect as the great pyramid of Egypt."

Wherever they climbed, the party found broken pieces of obsidian knives, arrowheads, and spear heads. On reaching the summit, they came upon "a flat surface of considerable size, but which had been much broken and disturbed." Here they rested and again Bullock rhapsodized on the view which included the city of Mexico some thirty miles distant.

On top of the pyramid Bullock found fragments of small statues, earthenware, and, surprisingly, oyster shells, the first he had seen in Mexico. On the way down they picked up several ornamental pieces of earthenware, the relief pattern on one of which resembled those of China.

Bullock says that on the northeast side of the Sun Pyramid, about halfway down, an opening had been attempted at some remote period. He maintained that any passage should have been from south to north, on a level with the ground, or only a few feet above it, as "all the remains of similar buildings have been found to have their entrances in that direction."

In the village of San Juan Teotihuacan, Bullock and his party procured refreshment and provender for their horses. By evening they reached the town of San Cristobal, once again soaked with rain, having come by way of the long causeway built to prevent the flowing of the waters of the Lake of San Cristobal into that of Texcoco; thence they returned to Mexico City by way of Guadalupe.

Much impressed by the monumental ruins of Teotihuacan, Bullock was amazed that no one in Mexico City seemed to care the least about them or could give him any information regarding them. His three-day excursion had convinced him of the veracity of accounts of ancient Mexican splendor such as were given by Francisco Clavigero; what he had seen enabled Bullock to discount the theories of such denigrators as De Pauw and Robertson. "Had Monsieur Pauw," says Bullock, "or our better informed countryman Robertson, passed one hour in Texcoco, Tezcotzingo, or Huexotla, they would never have supposed for a moment that the palace of Montezuma in Mexico was a clay cottage or that the account of the immense population was a fiction."

Further to convince his compatriots of the splendor of ancient Mexico, Bullock had models made of the Teotihuacan pyramids to be shipped to England. He then set off on the return journey via Puebla and Veracruz, this time carried on a litter strung between two mules, taking with him a menagerie of several armadillos, deer, parrots, curassow birds, quans, and tiger cats, most of them running around loose, to the dismay of his Puebla hostess. He also took with him a variety of flowers and ornamental plants as yet unknown to European botanists. His extensive collection of preserved animals and birds astounded the natives, who could only imagine they were being taken to his homeland for medicinal purposes.

Typically, what appealed most to Bullock from his stay in Mexico were the parts of the countryside which reminded him most of Devon; fields covered with verdure, woods with

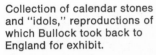

Collection of calendar stones and "idols," reproductions of which Bullock took back to England for exhibit.

Map of Tenochtitlan.

Among the mementos of manuscripts and hieroglyphic pictures brought back to England by Bullock was an original map of the ancient city of Tenochtitlan made by orders of Montezuma for Cortes to be transmitted to the King of Spain. The map shows how the city was divided into squares with chinampa gardens linked by canals and pathways.

Tenochtitlan was a chinampa city with six to eight plots to each house, each chinampa about 300 feet long and 15 to 30 feet wide. The map shows the profile of each householder and his name.

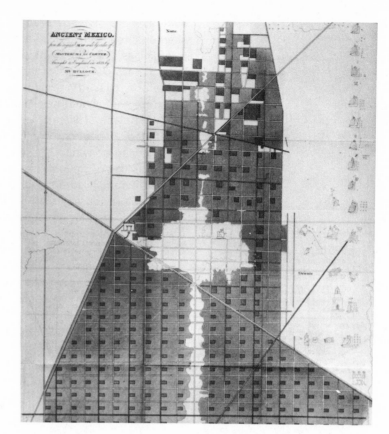

flowers and blossoms and fruits, hills smaller and more diversified than in England, "clothed with trees, shrubs and flowers in such endless variety that no part of Europe can vie with it."

What he liked least were the bullfights, with their tearing, mangling, and killing of bulls, horses trailing their entrails, and the wounded and dying matadors who gave "as exquisite delight in Mexico as Madrid."

Back in London, Bullock the impresario redecorated his "Egyptian Hall" for an exhibition of Mexican curios. Avid Piccadilly strollers could now view the "monstrous" Coatlicue and the Aztec calendar stone—which came to be known as "Montezuma's Watch." Except for a few rare Aztec manuscripts and the drawings in Humboldt's expensive folios, these were the first Mexican antiquities to reach Europe, the "first exotic peep at pre-Columbian America."

On the profits of the exhibition, Bullock acquired a silver mine in Mexico and would have dropped into oblivion except for the publication by John Murray of a booklet, *Six Months Residence and Travels in Mexico,* in which Bullock summed up his Mexican adventures.

6. Spanish Reappraisal

In their concentration on the pyramids of Teotihuacan and and the Aztec calendar stone, Humboldt and Bullock managed to miss a whole world of ancient and amazing ruins in the lower-lying jungles of Chiapas, Yucatan, and Guatemala. During the next two decades these ruins were to intrigue Europeans and North Americans as greatly as had the discoveries of Napoleon in Egypt.

The first to be discovered included a pyramid which many years later was to reveal a secret walled-up burial chamber as impressive and difficult of access as had been the so-called King's Chamber in the Great Pyramid of Cheops in the time of Caliph al Mamun.

In 1773 Friar Ramon de Ordoñez y Aguilar, canon of the cathedral town of Ciudad Real in Chiapas, then a Guatemalan province sandwiched between Yucatan and Tabasco, heard from an Indian a tale so amazing it was hard to believe. Not far from the village of Santo Domingo del Palenque, within a few miles of where Cortes was known to have passed with an escort of Indians but made no mention of the fact, there appeared to be a whole abandoned city beautifully built of stone and carved statuary, quite different from anything on the Mexican plateau, entirely smothered by the jungle. Titillated by the prospect of being the official discoverer of such an amazing relic, Brother Ordoñez had his parishioners fashion for him a palanquin to transport him sixty miles to the wattle and daub village of Santo Domingo del Palenque.

From there Ordoñez' parishioners carried him another eight miles into the jungle, where they came upon a stone complex completely overgrown with vegetation. The site was so stunning that Ordoñez was prompted to dash off an im-

Santo Domingo del Palenque.

Founded in 1564 on the grassy savannah of Tumbala by a Dominican missionary, and described as a "small Eden" shaded by huge ceiba trees, Santo Domingo received the additive Palenque, or "palisade," when the Spaniards ordered high walls built to protect themselves from the unfriendly natives resistant to conversion.

mediate *memoria* to his political superior in Guatemala City, Don José de Estacheria, which he followed with a weightier monograph entitled *A History of the Creation of Heaven and Earth,* in which he attempted to explain that the ruins—which he named the "Great City of Serpents"—must have been built in remote antiquity by a people who had appeared from the Atlantic guided by a leader called Votan, whose basic symbol was a serpent.

Ordoñez claimed to have gotten the material for his story from a book written by Votan himself in the Quiché language, asserting that the original book had been burned by Nuñez de la Vega, Bishop of Chiapas, in 1691, who before destroying it had copied parts of it which he showed to Ordoñez.

Votan was said to have set out from the land of Chivim (not specifically identified but believed to be transatlantic), and to have come to Yucatan via the "Dwelling of the Thirteen" (identified as the Canaries), with a stopover on a large Caribbean island presumed to be either Hispaniola or Cuba, but more likely the former. From there Votan is said to have crossed to the east coast of Mexico, where he made his way up the Usumacinta River to found the city now known as Palenque.

Votan is described as having arrived with a retinue dressed in long robes, of having exchanged ideas and customs with the natives, who submitted to his rule and who gave to the strangers their daughters in marriage.

Bishop Nuñez de la Vega also quoted Votan's book in a publication of his own entitled *Constituciones Diocesianos de Chiapas.* According to Nuñez de la Vega, when Votan came to America he listed the names of all the provinces and cities in the area in which he tarried. One was known as Huehueta, where Votan is claimed to have placed a treasure in a damp, dark subterranean house, appointing a woman as

Secret burial chamber in Palenque pyramid.

According to Ordoñez, Nuñez, and the native Mexican sources, the Chivim were Hivites, descendants of Heth, son of Chaanan, grandson of Noah, expelled from Geth by the Philistines a few years before the Hebrews went out of Egypt. One of their tribe, Cadmus, was believed to be the son of Ogyges who was on Mount Hermon beyond the Jordan, east of Chaanan, and was, according to Ordoñez, killed by Moses during the Exodus, which he dates as 1447 B.C. The tribe, expelled by the Hebrews, is said to have conquered Sidon and founded Tyre, from which Votan sailed for America.

chieftain of the treasure, with keepers to guard her. Nuñez de la Vega says that as bishop he carefully inspected the whole province to identify the locality where the treasure had been buried, and when he found it ordered its guardians to surrender what turned out to be nothing more than several lidded clay jars, green stones, and manuscripts. These the bishop publicly burned in the market place along with Votan's manuscripts.

Four times Votan is said to have returned to his former home across the Atlantic known as Valum Chivim, which Ordoñez eventually identified as the city of Tripoli in Phoenicia. After one of these return voyages, Votan is described as having come to a great city where a magnificent temple was under construction which was intended to reach to heaven, but was doomed by a confusion of languages. In his *Constituciones,* Nuñez de la Vega was even more specific, saying that what Votan saw was "the great wall, the Tower of Babel."

In a manuscript written in Quiché in 1554 by several Maya Indians, its Spanish translator, Padre Dionisio-José Chonay, had this to say: "It is supposed in the manuscript that the three great Quiché nations mentioned in particular are descendants of the Ten Tribes of the Kingdom of Israel, whom Shalmaneser reduced to perpetual captivity, and who, finding themselves in the confines of Assyria, decided to emigrate." The actual text ran: "These, then, were the three nations of Quichés, and they came from where the sun rises, descendants of Israel, of the same language and the same customs."

In attestation of what they had written, the Indians signed the document on September 28, 1554, saying: "We have written that which by tradition our ancestors told us, who came from the other part of the sea, from Givan-Tulan, bordering on Babylonia."

In another manuscript, Votan's arrival is dated at 1000 B.C., which led modern scholars to suggest that Votan and his "men in Petticoats" could have been Phoenicians. Constance Irwin, in her book *Fair Gods and Stone Faces,* agrees that Votan and his followers could well have been Phoenicians, but places the date somewhat later. She says the great city which Votan could have visited for trade might have been Babylon, the greatest city in the Middle East, a favorite market for Phoenician merchants, where stood the magnificent Tower of Babel rebuilt by Nobopolassar and his successor Nebuchadnezzar in the seventh and sixth centuries B.C.

After his death, Votan was associated with jade and snakes. Constance Irwin points out that two intertwined

79

Goya's portrait of his patron, King Charles III of Spain (1759–1788), who is described as one of the enlightened despots of the eighteenth century. After a long apprenticeship in Naples he came to Spain at the age of 43. During the American Revolutionary War he sided with the American colonists against the British. It was under Charles III that the Jesuits were expelled from Spain and from Spanish possessions. He also put some restraints on the hated Inquisition.

snakes formed the emblem of healing, wisdom, and fertility in Babylon, whence it spread east and west, the caduceus becoming a common object on Phoenician and Carthaginian stelae.

Ordoñez' story of Votan did not cause much of a stir in Guatemala City, but his description of the ruins of Palenque sparked his boss, Estacheria, who was president of Guatemala's Royal Audiencia, into ordering the mayor of Santo Domingo, José Antonio Calderon, to make an official survey of the ruins with the help of an Italian-born architect resident of Guatemala City, Antonio Bernasconi. Their report, forwarded to Madrid, was placed in the hands of Charles III of Spain, who, being also King of the Two Sicilies, had developed a penchant for Greek and Roman ruins. The prospect of finding similar antiquities in New Spain induced King Charles to order a systematic exploration of the architectural ruins near Palenque.

To implement the royal edict Estacheria selected a captain of artillery stationed in Guatemala City, Don Antonio del Rio. Decked in a three-cornered hat and powdered wig, "wafting" according to one account "through the jungles of Palenque an aroma of the latest fashionable scent," Del Rio set off on horseback to ascertain the age of the ruins, the extent of the population which had built the ruins, the cause of their abandonment.

Arriving on the scene, *el capitan* found the jungle so thick he couldn't distinguish a neighbor at arm's length. To clear the ruins he hired two hundred natives with axes and machetes, who soon uncovered more extraordinary buildings, palaces, temples, and pyramids, adorned with stucco sculpture and embellished with hermetic hieroglyphs in elaborate carved tableaux, all of which appeared to extend for miles into the jungle, where they had lain undisturbed for centuries. Within the buildings the captain found a maze of rooms, corridors, and subterranean passages, of which he took careful measurements.

With him, Del Rio had brought an artist, Ricardo Armendariz, who made rough sketches of the buildings and figures carved in stone or cast in stucco relief, with which to prepare a pictorial report of twenty-five plates. In his final report, Del Rio suggested the ancient Romans may have visited America, and that there had been a connection between Mexico and ancient Egypt. He quoted Father Jacinto Garriod, who visited Principe in 1638, to the effect that the northern parts of America had been visited by Greeks, English, and others. This final report, illustrated by Armendariz, was forwarded to Madrid, where Charles III had been replaced by his weak son, Charles IV. Because of systematic

Castañeda's renditions of Mayan reliefs are strikingly similar to motifs in Buddhist countries. In Buddhist tradition the Buddha's third week of meditation was spent under a Muchalinda tree, and it was during this time that Muchalinda the serpent king was said to have come forth and spread his hood as a canopy over the Buddha to protect him from the heat of the sun. It was then that the serpent became sacred. The sun, the tree, and the serpent are three of the most sacred symbols of the Buddhist; they appear in practically all decorative art, stylized or natural, throughout Mesoamerica. As with the Mesoamerican, Buddhist doctrine teaches a life after death, that the earth will be destroyed five times, that four destructions have already taken place, and the last will be by flood. Both the Buddhist and the Aztec maintained monasteries for retirement to a life of meditation and both had carvings that they worshiped, placed in niches in the walls of their sacred buildings.

opposition by the clergy, the report was buried in the archives.

Fortunately a manuscript copy made in Guatemala City was edited by an Italian, Dr. Paul Felix Cabrera, described as "a gentleman of fatuous erudition" who not only cleaned up Del Rio's "barracks language" but attached to the report a preface wherein he also ascribed to the ruins of Palenque a Near Eastern origin. In this report, Cabrera also developed the tradition of Sigüenza and Boturini, who believed the Olmecs had arrived on the east coast of Mexico from somewhere across the Atlantic with a stop on the island of Antilia or Hispaniola. Cabrera suggested that the strangers were Carthaginians, and that the first colony had been sent out from Carthage to America before the First Punic War. In the New World, said Cabrera, these Carthaginians had interbred with native women to produce the Olmecs. Cabrera's report was also buried.

81

Charles IV of Spain was a handsome, amiable near-imbecile and cuckold whose queen took a 25-year-old lover, Manuel de Godoy, to rule the kingdom first as the Duke of Alcudia, then as a prince. Godoy managed not only to disgrace and destroy the crown but to turn Spain into a pawn of revolutionary France so that the Spanish fleet was destroyed by the British. In New Spain, Godoy imposed a series of such grossly corrupt and looting viceroys that he paved the way for revolution.

Palenque Tower.

Cabrera says one of Castañeda's drawings represents Votan or a Hivite from Tripoli in Phoenicia. He says Votan was called a *culebra,* or snake, and later was "placed among the Gods." Cabrera adds that Amaguemecan was in the province of Chiapas, where the Indians carefully preserved the remembrance of their origin, and of "their ancestors' early progress from the voluntary or enforced abandonment of Palestine on the ingress of the Hebrews."

Votan is said to have declared himself "a snake," descendant of Imos of the line of Chan, and said that he came to America from a distant place by the command of God. According to Manly P. Hall, Votan founded Palenque, built a temple with many subterranean chambers called the "House of Darkness," and there deposited the records of his nation.

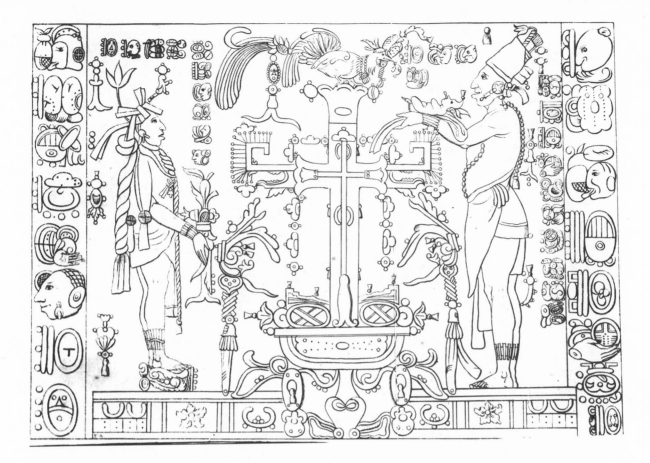

Throughout Mesoamerica a cult of the serpent existed from the most ancient times, spreading as far north as the mound builders of Ohio; it is still perpetuated today in the rituals of the Zunis in New Mexico and the Hopis in Arizona. Frank Waters points out that the plumed serpent was a primary symbol throughout Alabama, Georgia, and Oklahoma, and that the famous Hopi snake dance in which priests dance with snakes in their mouths is the most dramatic ritual still emphasizing the serpents. As for the jaguar, or Mexican *tigre,* it has been the symbol for the earth and earthbound matter since the earliest glyphs. It was so used by Teotihuacanos, Olmecs, Maya, Toltecs, Zapotecs, and Aztecs.

By this time, Humboldt was giving such wide publicity in Europe to the possibility of an impressive pre-Hispanic culture in America that Charles IV, feeling himself obliged to involve Spain in the proceedings, ordered a thorough exploration of all of Mexico for any pre-Conquest antiquities that might be located.

The job was given to Guillermo Dupaix, a retired army captain of Mexican Dragoons, evidently for no greater reason than that he had spent thirty years in the army. As a draftsman to make a record of whatever ruins they might discover, Dupaix selected a young Mexican aficionado of antiquities, José Luciano Castañeda, who had been sought out by Humboldt because of his not undistinguished collection of antiquities. Together Dupaix and Castañeda set out in 1805 to scour Mexico for remnants of pre-Columbian culture.

For three years they traveled about the country, crossing rough mountains, breaking their way through heavy jungle, delayed by sickness, bad weather, bandits, and machete-wielding natives. Their horses slipped out from under them

Archeologist Henriette Mertz points out that the fish seen eating lotus flowers in these Palenque panels, as well as the placement of the fish, resemble *makaras,* or fishlike monsters, in the lotus panel at Amaravati. In her opinion, such highly symbolic and stylized forms are unlikely to arise in two totally unrelated places, separated by thousands of miles, without some reason.

Gordon F. Eckholm, outstanding authority on Ancient Mexico, has pointed out that some of the most significant parallels between Hindu-Buddhist and late classic and post-classic Mayan art are those classifiable under the heading of lotus panels. He points out that a principal factor of the lotus panels in Buddhist art is that the rhizome of the lotus plant forms a sinuous pattern along the length of the design area, curving back and forth across the width of the panel and leaving spaces which are filled with leaves, buds, and flowers. The same pattern is followed in these temple reliefs at Palenque. The undulating path of the rhizome of the plant is apparently not a natural feature of either the Asiatic lotus or the American variety.

over steep cliffs or were swept away by turbulent currents. In the end, when Dupaix's legs became so swollen by insect bites he could no longer travel by horse, he suffered (because of his heavy French accent) the added indignity of being detained by the Mexicans as a spy for the French, Napoleon's brother Joseph having temporarily replaced his patron, Charles IV, on the throne of Spain. With all this trouble, Dupaix and Castañeda still managed on their peregrinations to visit and make sketches of the ruins of Xochicalco, Cholula, Mitla, Oaxaca, and many other areas, ending up at Palenque.

Wherever they traveled they became more and more impressed by the extraordinary achievements of the pre-Hispanic Indians. At Mitla, Dupaix found stone structures which he thought displayed "a lavish magnificence worthy of ancient Rome." He was much impressed by the symmetry and accurate measurements of the buildings. The carved stones and the arrangement of the structures gave evidence of the builders' knowledge of mathematics and geometry; artifacts indicated they had a well-formed knowledge of astronomy.

The workmanship of sculptors appeared of "singular beauty of proportion," the pottery of unusual brilliance. From finely cut and splendidly finished masonry, Dupaix was convinced that some metal had been used, though he could find no trace of any, nor of the method used to transport and

Dupaix's Discoveries.

85

hoist into position stones weighing as much as thirty tons. From the well-built aqueducts they encountered, Dupaix concluded the ancient builders had a knowledge of hydraulics; from the construction of their roads and causeways, he felt that their architects rivaled those of Rome.

In the ruins of Palenque, Dupaix was surprised to find glyphs which were like neither those of Egypt nor those of the Valley of Mexico. The work seemed quite original. Unable to compare them with anything he knew in antiquity, either Gothic, Arabic, Chinese, or Phoenician, he concluded he was dealing with a race unknown to historians, who were not necessarily the forefathers of the local Indians. In the end he favored the conclusion that the builders of Mexico's extraordinary pre-Hispanic ruins had come from legendary Atlantis.

As Dupaix was neither archeologist, historian, naturalist, nor entrepreneur, his report, with 145 of Castañeda's

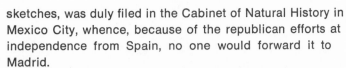

sketches, was duly filed in the Cabinet of Natural History in Mexico City, whence, because of the republican efforts at independence from Spain, no one would forward it to Madrid.

Having done his best, Dupaix disappeared, while Castañeda survived as professor of drawing and architecture at the University of Mexico. There Bullock found him early in 1823 and was so impressed by the originality of his drawings that he had twenty-five of them copied to exhibit in England, only to find on his return to London that he had been scooped by a local bookseller, Henry Berthoud, who had acquired from a British resident in Guatemala City, Dr. Thomas McQuy, a copy of Del Rio's manuscript with Cabrera's unwieldy preface, which he had translated and published as *Description of the Ancient City Discovered Near Palenque,* thus getting into print the first report on the ruins of Palenque.

Dupaix's report and Castañeda's sketches, partly consumed by fungi and cockroaches, were rescued from the Spanish archives by the French Abbé H. Baradère, and ended up in a very expensive folio edition in Paris in 1836 under the auspices of those rival but eminent ministers of state Louis Adolphe Thiers and François Guizot.

Entitled *Antiquités Mexicaines,* the edition was so limited that few could buy it. Yet those into whose hands it fell were so amazed by what they saw they could hardly be restrained from traveling to Mexico. The work was to motivate a series of French adventurers and explorers, prodded and subsidized by the state, who came to open the way for commercial, cultural, and military followers.

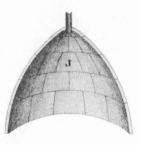

PART IIII.

ROMANTIC
EXPLORERS

7. Discovery of Mayaland

View of the tower at Palenque, seen from the northern gallery, painted as it was at the time, with vegetation growing out of the third floor. To gain sustenance the trees sent their roots some thirty feet to the ground. Waldeck recounts that these roots were stretched so tight that the wind blowing through them at night produced sounds like a harp, only deeper, which caused the Indians to travel several miles at dusk to get away from an area they believed to be haunted. The pillars on the right belong to the western galleries of the palace. The pillars on the left are decorated with stucco figures.

To illustrate Del Rio's report, the publisher Berthoud employed a romantic skirt-chasing French adventurer and former pupil of the painter Jacques Louis David, Jean-Frédéric Maximilien Waldeck, who was so smitten with the scenes he engraved from the sketches of Ricardo Armendariz that he determined, despite his fifty-six years, to explore the site himself, signing himself on as a hydraulic engineer for an English silver-mining company in Mexico in order to obtain his passage.

Boasting of his friendship with Humboldt, Lord Byron, Beau Brummell, and Marie Antoinette (whom he claimed to have visited in prison), and of having accompanied Napoleon on his expedition to Egypt, where he had become intimate with Edmé François Jomard, Waldeck soon quit the mining company and took up residence in Mexico City, no longer as Citizen Waldeck, the revolutionary vogue being momentarily over, but as the Count of Waldeck. There he supported himself painting portraits of the local gentry, soliciting right and left for a grant to explore and record the ruins of Palenque. His days he spent collecting rare books and artifacts, investigating the history of the Nahua, about whom he was to write an unpublished history. His evenings were passed at the opera, the ballet, or the theater, complaining all the time that whereas he had expected to find a lively cultivation of the arts and letters in Mexico City, he found only "an elite notorious for its neglect of cultural life."

Eventually, obtaining sufficient subsidy to take him to Palenque, Waldeck was able to spend a whole year in the village of Santo Domingo plus four months in a hut he built on the site of the ruins, shacked up with a dark-skinned,

91

Waldeck says that the two reliefs had been removed from the ruins of Palenque and were mortised into the walls of the living room in the house in the village belonging to a deputy called "Bravo," who said he would sell them only on the condition that the buyer marry one of his daughters.

This lion throne originally drawn by Armendariz was thus embellished by Waldeck. At Palenque Waldeck found wooden beams, stone pillars, and entrance posts, all carved in low relief. Everywhere were symbols and human figures, some in masks and bearded, all clothed in ornate regalia, with strange weapons and the flowing plumes of the quetzal covering their surfaces.

firm-breasted mestiza, braving the densest rainfall in the Western Hemisphere to produce ninety quite extraordinary drawings, till his legs broke out in boils and he believed he had contracted a venereal disease.

When revolution and cholera swept Tabasco, Waldeck took off for Yucatan to make more drawings. There he heard that the Mexican government, suspecting him of being a British spy, was about to seize his drawings. Carefully copying the lot, Waldeck says he allowed the Mexicans to seize the copies while he successfully smuggled the originals to England with the help of the British consul.

Making no effort to suppress his feelings about the Mexicans in general and the governor of Yucatan in particular, whom he enviously accused of keeping a harem, Waldeck took ship and followed his drawings to London. There he used them to publish a handsome folio volume of twenty-one plates accompanied by a hundred pages of text in which he concluded that the Chaldeans and the Hindus had been responsible for the construction of Palenque, a city whose collapse he dated as having occurred about A.D. 600.

93

John Lloyd Stephens aged 36.

At 3,200 francs, or several hundred dollars a copy, Waldeck's book was more of a collector's item than a popular best seller. When a copy reached John Russell Bartlett's bookstore in New York, Bartlett immediately showed it to one of his best customers, the thirty-two-year-old author of *Incidents of Travel in Egypt and Arabia Petraea,* John Lloyd Stephens, who was as amazed as he was impressed by Waldeck's drawings and the possibility of a civilization in the Western Hemisphere as advanced as that of the Egyptians. But Waldeck's reputation as a faker had accompanied his book; puzzling were his drawings of pyramids in the Egyptian style decorated with Romanesque statues in the full round. So Stephens determined to mount an expedition of his own to Central America to establish if the ruins existed in fact, or were, as suggested by many, the hoax of a romantic draftsman—a perfect possibility in that age of P. T. Barnum.

Stephens' English friend Frederick Catherwood, who had traveled widely in the Near and Middle East to make sketches of rare antiquities, was equally dubious about Waldeck, but enthusiastic about Stephens' offer to accompany him to Central America to illustrate whatever ruins they might actually encounter. In London, Catherwood had read Del Rio's book; in Paris Dupaix's; now he was anxious to check them out. But how, he wondered, were two foreigners to crash their way into an uncharted jungle through territory being fought over by revolutionaries and counterrevolutionaries?

Luckily Stephens had helped elect the Democratic President Martin Van Buren, and so was able to get himself appointed U.S. Diplomatic Agent to the government of the Republic of Central America, a flimsy appointment, in that no one at the State Department knew whether such a government existed, where its capital might be, or who might be its president or minister of foreign affairs, neither of whom had been recognized by either Spain or the Pope.

On October 3, 1839, Stephens and Catherwood sailed from New York's North River aboard the British brig *Mary Ann*

Catherwood's view of a section of the Great Hieroglyphic Stairway, overgrown by the jungle, with its two thousand glyphs mostly collapsed into rubble. In the foreground lies a Mayan head in the mouth of a great serpent which had formed part of the main staircase. At a glance, Catherwood and Stephens realized that whoever had built these ruins had indeed been part of a great culture. Huge monoliths weighing thirty tons had been carved, polished, and decorated with extraordinary art. Though Catherwood rendered the architecture and sculpture with extraordinary care, Victor von Hagen, the most readable authority on Catherwood and Stephens, says the monkeys in the view are apocryphal rhesus monkeys from Africa, whereas only Capuchins and spider monkeys are supposed to be indigenous.

Colonel Juan Galindo.

bound for Belize in Honduras. Their immediate object was to locate a mysterious city in the depths of the jungle which appeared on no map of the area: Copan.

They had chosen to search for this lost site because of an Irishman whose real name they did not know, but whose *nom de guerre* was Colonel Juan Galindo. A naturalized citizen of the Central American Confederation, Galindo had risen to be governor of Peten and had been led to Copan by an unpublished Spanish account of an extraordinary lost city. When he reached the ruins, he was so impressed that he claimed the pre-Columbian inhabitants of Central America had achieved a civilization superior to all other native cultures in the Americas.

Arriving in Belize, Stephens was supposed to accomplish his duty as a diplomat and seek out the seat of government to present his credentials, but both he and Catherwood were more anxious to get to their exploring. On the basis of Galindo's report, Stephens and Catherwood set off into the gloom of the Guatemalan jungle, "where shafts of sunlight seeped through as in a cathedral," little realizing that they would be "dragged through mudholes, squeezed in gulleys, knocked against trees, and tumbled over roots." Crossing the Mica mountain range and coping with every conceivable hurdle placed in their way by the local bigwigs, the unwary travelers finally broke through the jungle into the remains of what they realized was a whole new world, the ruins of a civilization so obscure it didn't even have a name, a great city complex whose inhabitants had vanished without a trace several centuries earlier.

Here were structures unlike anything either of them had ever seen before, pyramids studded with sculptured figures,

Copan, Honduras.

The broken stele lying by a large lava-stone tortoise was described by Catherwood as "one of the most beautiful of Maya carvings in the round." Catherwood and Stephens found the glyphs unlike anything they had ever seen in their wide travels and study of exotic architecture, quite outside the Indo-European tradition. So intricate and complicated were the designs, so entirely novel and unintelligible, that Catherwood had great difficulty accurately copying them, but a later historian was to remark · of Catherwood's drawings: "When it is taken into consideration that the Maya hieroglyphic writing was a sealed book at the time he visited Copan, and that he knew nothing about the subject matter of the glyphs he drew, such accuracy is remarkable."

Half a century after Stephens stumbled on this "altar" half buried in the jungle near Copan, his prophecy about it was corroborated by archeologists who concluded that the altar commemorated a congress of priest-astronomers who had met in Copan in A.D. 765 to make some important change in their Mayan calendar.

great plazas surrounded by stepped temples, stones carved with mysterious and quite unfamiliar hieroglyphs. Most of the buildings were so overgrown with vegetation and trees that Catherwood, standing up to his ankles in mud, his hands gloved against swarms of mosquitoes, had a hard time drawing them.

In the underbrush Stephens stumbled upon a rectangular stone altar carved with sixteen cross-legged figures, which he prophetically noted must "beyond doubt, record some event in the history of the mysterious people who once inhabited the city." A broader survey of the jungle ruins revealed a huge acropolis with five large plazas, two main courtyards, and three tall but crumbling pyramids, the whole complex laid out on a plateau a hundred feet above the river.

To facilitate his operations at Copan, Stephens had the happy thought of acquiring the whole site from its rightful native owner, which he was able to do for the sum of fifty U.S. dollars.

After weeks of exploring and drawing, Stephens and Catherwood realized they had barely scratched the surface of what lay hidden around Copan. Anxious to get to Palenque, three hundred miles to the north, they set off on muleback along ribbon trails that wound through the high pine-studded mountains of Guatemala, crisscrossed by deep barrancas and torrents—a road described by one traveler as "made only for birds."

Only the monkeys disturbed the quiet as they swung through the trees, forty or fifty at a time, with little ones in their arms, appearing to Stephens like "wandering spirits of the departed race guarding the ruins of their former habitations."

Palenque's Temple
of the Inscriptions.

A couple of Guatemala City
Englishmen, John Herbert
Caddy and Patrick Walker,
privy to the plan that Stephens
was first going to Copan,
deliberately set out to beat
him to Palenque. Though they
did so, by a matter of weeks,
Stephens was able to beat
them into print by a hundred
years.

John Herbert Caddy.

As Stephens approached the ruins of Palenque, he chose
to ignore the blanket order issued by the Mexican dictator
Santa Anna forbidding all access to foreigners. Stephens'
first sight of the ruins convinced him that Waldeck, Del Rio,
and Dupaix had not been exaggerating. Nothing in the world,
Stephens noted, "ever impressed me as forcibly as the spectacle of this once great and lovely city, overturned, desolate,
and lost . . . overgrown with trees for miles around, and without even a name to distinguish it."

On the walls of the building known as the "Palacio"
Stephens found Waldeck's name carved beside the faded
drawing of a woman and the scribbled date of 1832. He also
found the names of Captain John Herbert Caddy and Patrick
Walker.

With measuring rod Stephens laid out the floor plan of
the Palacio as a mathematical basis for Catherwood's
rendition, finding it to be 228 feet by 180, a measurement
that was to stand through the years.

Noting the similarity between the hieroglyphs of Palenque
and those of Copan, Stephens concluded that the whole
intervening area of some 60,000 square miles might have
once been inhabited by a civilization that spoke the same
language or at least used the same glyphs.

For weeks Stephens worked at uncovering the ruins
while Catherwood struggled to capture their incredible
lineaments. Soon they were groggy with malaria, their feet
swollen with nits that buried eggs beneath their toenails,
their faces swollen from the blood-sucking bites of Diptera.
When Catherwood finally collapsed, they staggered out of
the jungle and sailed for New York with the makings of what
was to become one of the great best sellers of the century.
Nicely bound and reasonably priced by Harper Brothers,
beautifully illustrated by Catherwood, *Incidents of Travel in
Central America, Chiapas, and Yucatan* brought to a wide
and fascinated public news of the mysterious and unknown
Maya, a word that up till then had not appeared in any dictionary. In three months the book went through ten printings.

General view of Uxmal seen from the upper terrace of the governor's palace, showing the Pyramid of the Dwarf, or House of the Magician, on the far right. In the center is the great "nunnery" quadrangle, so called by the Spaniards because of its ninety cell-like rooms. Catherwood and Stephens found that the ruins of the city covered an area of two square miles. The local Indians believed the buildings at Uxmal to be haunted and that all the ornaments were "animated" and would walk around at night. They believed the ornaments harmless during the day but, on the advice of their priests, constantly disfigured them with their machetes so as to quiet their potentially wandering spirits. Within less than twelve months from their first visit to Uxmal, Catherwood and Stephens found the place so overgrown with shrubs and small trees that nothing but the top of the highest pyramid and the base outlines of the other monuments could be discerned.

Labna.

Gateway to Labna, a city in the Mayapan League, between Uxmal and Chichen Itza. Stephens, in frock coat, is standing by the gate. Labna's palace with motifs of masks and columnettes is one of the largest in Yucatan, 400 feet long by 250 feet wide. Catherwood noted that the mortar with which it was built was similar to the pozzuolana found in the ancient buildings in Rome.

Uxmal.

One of two archways 20 feet high and 25 feet deep which pierce the facade 60 feet from either end of the governor's palace. The design shows repetitive patterns of the elongated snout of what was known as the "rain god."
The main body of the palace was a huge trapezoidal building 320 feet long by 40 feet wide, set on three stepped terraces. The entire length of its second story was covered by a facade of exquisitely cut stone of intricate design, a mosaic of some 20,000 sculptured stones, described by Stephens as a "mass of rich, complicated and elaborately sculptured ornaments forming a sort of arabesque," whose meaning or function entirely escaped him. Catherwood climbed a makeshift ladder to make accurate drawings of the "incomprehensible subjects sculptured on the facade." Later they discovered them to be hieroglyphs, "which from their conspicuous position," Stephens presumed to have some important meaning; but such was the limit of even his open-mindedness, he assumed they could only have dealt with some such prosaic banality as construction details of the building.

This series of pyramidal walls (which looked to Stephens like the fronts of Dutch houses), which was called the "Casa de Palomas" or "Pigeon House," had once been covered with figures and ornaments in stucco, only portions of which remained. In the center, an archway led to a courtyard overgrown with shrubbery. To Stephens, there was something mournful about this particular set of ruins. "Entering under the great archway, crossing two noble courtyards, with ruined buildings on each side, and ascending the great stair-case to the building on the top, gave a stronger impression of departed greatness than anything else in this desolate city. It commanded a view of every other building, and stood apart in lonely grandeur, seldom disturbed by human footsteps. On going up to it once Mr. Catherwood startled a deer, and at another time a wild hog."

Half a century was to pass before archeologists recognized in the frets of the "Pigeon House" a highly sophisticated astronomical observatory.

Once Catherwood had regained his health, he and Stephens returned to Yucatan to describe and draw the abandoned Mayan centers of Uxmal, Kabah, Zahil, Labna, Izamal, Chichen Itza, and Tulum, which produced an even better seller: *Incidents of Travel in Yucatan,* considered by Edgar Allan Poe "perhaps the most interesting book of travel ever published." As entertaining as its predecessor, largely because of Stephens' anecdotes and descriptions of odd personalities, it was in substance less illuminating about the mysterious Maya.

Stephens did manage to acquire in the ancient capital of Mani, where Diego de Landa had burned the Mayan codices and documents, a weathered Spanish transcription of the books of Chilam Balam, which included a chronology of ancient Yucatan as told by the natives to sixteenth-century Spanish friars, from which Stephens was able to learn something of the history and customs of the natives. From a lover of ancient lore, Don Pio Perez, who produced a work entitled *A True Exposition of the Method Used by the Indians for Computing Time,* Stephens was able to learn the dot and bar numeration system of the Maya. This gave him an understanding of their solar calendar of eighteen months of twenty days plus an extra five or six, very similar to that of the Aztecs, a system of chronology based on names and numbers for days and months which enabled the ancient Mayan to designate a particular day which could not be mistaken for any other through thousands of years.

The ruins of Kabah, south of Uxmal, another Mayan city abandoned to the jungle. When Stephens first saw this building at Kabah, called by the natives the "House of Justice," it was "so beautifully shrouded by trees that it was painful to be obliged to disturb them." To get this picture with his camera lucida, Catherwood had to stand under an umbrella held by a tranquil Indian while a tropical downpour created what appears to be a lake in the foreground.

The magnificent ruins of the ancient city of Chichen Itza, with its Castillo dedicated to Kukulcan, the Maya Quetzalcoatl, "casting a prodigious shadow" over the flat Yucatecan plain, had as great an emotional effect on Stephens as had Palenque. But he merely gilded Catherwood's lily by noting that "at the foot of the staircase, forming a bold, striking and well-conceived commencement to this lofty range, are two colossal serpents' heads, ten feet in length, with mouths wide open and tongues protruding." Unable to give a rational explanation for these extraordinary pieces of sculpture, Stephens employed the subterfuge of his age by adding, "No doubt they were emblematic of some religious belief, and in the minds of an imaginative people, passing between them to ascend the steps must have excited feelings of solemn awe."

Caracol.

Stephens was seized with the picturesque qualities of what he described as a circular building "unlike any other we had seen, except one at Mayapan, much ruined," with terraces and a winding inner staircase. Noting the novel plan of the building, he remarked that "instead of unfolding secrets, it drew closer the curtain that already shrouded with almost impenetrable folds the mysterious structures." He found the walls of both inner corridors plastered and ornamented with paintings, and noted again, without being able to explain it, a balustrade of gigantic serpents. It was not until the end of the century that archeologists realized the astronomical functions of the building.

Noting the similarities between the Aztec and the Mayan calendars, Stephens facilely concluded that both civilizations had been endemic to America, that the pyramidal structures of Yucatan had been built by neither Egyptians, Carthaginians, Greeks, Romans, nor Israelis, but by native Americans, possibly the forefathers of the natives then living in Yucatan, possibly no more than a thousand years earlier.

Stephens planned one more great work on American antiquities to contain over a hundred folio engravings by Catherwood designed to bring together in one book the works of Humboldt, Prescott, Gallatin, and Wilkinson. Stephens even traveled to Potsdam to pay his respects to an aged Humboldt. But Harper's could not raise sufficient subscriptions to produce so expensive an endeavor. In the end the idea was dropped. Though Stephens' conclusions about the origin of the Mayan civilization remained open to question, his books established him as a gifted writer, and his rediscovery of the Maya opened the way for serious archeology in the Americas.

Another monjas which Stephens found in a good state of preservation and elaborately decorated was believed by him to be the oldest building in the Chichen Itza complex. Over the doorway were twenty small cartouches of hieroglyphs in four rows, five to a row, and a circular niche with seated figure. Stephens noted the similarity between this curved projecting ornament like an elephant's trunk and those of Uxmal. These masks were said to be of Itzamna, the protean god of rain, writing, and learning. Stephens also concluded that the hieroglyphs were similar to those at Copan and Palenque.

Gymnasium.

Stephens described the ball court at Chichen Itza as a gymnasium or tennis court, pointing out that the two massive stone rings, four feet in diameter, carved with two entwined serpents mortised into the opposing walls twenty feet above the ground, probably served for the celebration of some public games. He then quoted Herrera on the diversion of Montezuma.

"The king took much delight in Seeing Sport at Ball, which the Spaniards have since prohibited, because of the mischief that often hapned at it; and was by them call'd *Tlachtli*, being like our Tennis. The Ball was made of the Gum of a Tree that grows in hot Countries, which, having Holes made in it, and moulded together, turns as black as Pitch. The balls made thereof, tho' hard and heavy to the Hand, did bound and fly as well as our Footballs, there being no need to blow them; nor did they use Chaces, but vy'd to drive the adverse Party that is to hit the Wall, the others were to make good, or strike it over."

Tulum Castillo.

Stephens and Catherwood arrived at Tulum on the east coast of Yucatan (now known as Quintana Roo) from Cozumel Island by boat and large canoe. They found the Castillo to be the main temple of the complex, which had been first spotted from the sea by the Spaniards several years before the arrival of Cortes. The site was overgrown with trees which, with their deep green foliage and mysterious buildings, presented to Stephens "an image of a grove sacred to Druidical worship." He described the surrounding scenery as the wildest he had yet found in Yucatan. Clearing a platform in front of the Castillo, whose base they measured as 100 feet long, they could look down over an immense forest on one side, and on the other could see deep in the clear water at the foot the the cliff, "gliding quietly by a great fish eight or ten feet long." No drawing, said Stephens, could convey a true idea of the solemnity of the living shroud that covered the Castillo, "or of the impression made upon us when the ring of the ax first broke the stillness that had so long prevailed around." The back or sea wall of the Castillo rises on the brink of a high, broken precipitous cliff. It commands, said Stephens, "a magnificent ocean view, and a picturesque line of coast, being visible from a great distance at sea." At night the howling of the winds, the cracking of branches in the forest, and the dashing of angry waves against the cliffs added a romantic tone to their sojourn; but Stephens lamented that "we were rather too hackneyed travellers to enjoy it, and were much annoyed by moschetoes."

With Catherwood, Stephens found some low buildings which, because of the lowness of all their doorways, were attributed by the natives to *covenbados,* or "hunchbacks."

Tulum.

The Temple of the Frescoes at Tulum was accidentally discovered when Stephens' companion Dr. Cabot went hunting for a pair of flushed oceloted turkeys. Dr. Cabot is seen off to the left. Stephens (in short coat) and Catherwood (in frock coat) are seen in front of the temple, which they reported to be 45 feet long and 26 feet deep, resting on a 6-foot terrace. The walls of the corridors of the building were found to be covered with paintings "green and mildewed from the rankness of vegetation."

(Above) Izamal.

This head, now destroyed, was seven feet wide and almost eight feet high when drawn by Catherwood. It was near what Stephens called the most stupendous mound he had seen in the country: six or seven hundred feet long and sixty feet high, built with cyclopean rocks, and containing mysterious inner chambers. In this romanticized picture, Dr. Samuel Cabot, Jr., is hunting a jaguar at the base of one of several large pyramids.

(Left) Well at Bolonchen.

Stephens and Catherwood seized torches and descended 210 feet into a dark, damp cavern, where they were taken down another 80 feet by means of a large, rudely constructed, and very slippery ladder, 12 feet wide, lashed together by withes. Beyond this another ladder descended a further 75 feet. Crawling along a low stifling passage for about 300 feet, they came upon a rocky basin full of water. By this time the two gringos were so dirty and exhausted, they not only drank of it but took off their clothes and bathed in it. The cave was called "Xtacumbi Xunan," or "hidden lady," because of some pretty girl who had been stolen from her mother and hidden in its depths by her lover. Every year when the wells went dry in the village, a festival was celebrated for the opening of the cave, and the villagers would begin their daily stint of descending 1400 feet to fetch their water. As there are no rivers in Yucatan, the only available water flows beneath the limestone shelf appearing here and there in deep cenotes. The original of this drawing by Catherwood is in the collection of Henry Schnackenberg of Newton, Connecticut.

The only known likeness of Frederick Catherwood, a self-portrait from *Views of Ancient Monuments* as he stands by the ruins of Tulum in Quintana Roo, helping Stephens measure the front of the Temple of Frescoes. Round-faced, sandy-haired, and with blue eyes, Catherwood was six years older than Stephens, taller and more solidly built. Of Scottish ancestry and a well-to-do English background, he received a classical education from Oxford. As artist, archeologist, and explorer, he had visited and drawn almost every important archeological site in the Near East, going into forbidden areas dressed as a Moslem. In Rome he was so entranced by the architectural drawings of Piranesi that he developed a brilliant technique of his own for reproducing ancient sites.

Aldous Huxley in an introduction to a monograph by Victor von Hagen wrote of Catherwood, "From dawn till dusk, day after day and for weeks at a stretch, this martyr to archaeology had exposed himself to all the winged and crawling malice of tropical nature. Ticks, ants, wasps, flies, mosquitoes; they had bitten him, stung him, drunk his blood, infected him with malaria. But the man had grimly gone on drawing. Itching, swollen, burning or shuddering with fever, he had filled whole portfolios with the measured plans and elevations of temples, with studies of Mayan sculptures so scientifically accurate that modern experts in pre-Columbian history can spell out the date of a stele from Catherwood's representations of its, to him, incomprehensible hieroglyphs."

Having failed to receive credit for his work for Stephens, even on the title page of Stephens' books, and having lost the greater part of his originals in the fire that destroyed his rotunda exhibition in New York, Catherwood sailed for England to produce in London a folio volume with twenty-five of his favorite views of Central America. For a really first-class opus, Catherwood gathered six of England's outstanding lithographers, and he had the printing executed by an intimate friend, Owen Jones, in his own studios. The resulting *Views of Ancient Monuments of Central America, Chiapas, and Yucatan* appeared on April 25, 1844. The ordinary edition sold for five guineas, and a smaller number of hand-colored sets "delicately done by an expert hand" were issued at twelve guineas.

Prince Albert, consort to Queen Victoria, bought a copy as a present to send to Humboldt in Potsdam in reciprocation for a copy of his *Kronos* which the Queen had recently received.

The edition of three hundred copies was soon exhausted; and in order to make a living, Catherwood substituted for his cherished title of architect that of civil engineer and sailed for tropical British Guiana in November of 1845 to organize the building of a railroad between Georgetown and Mahaica. When the native director was run over by the engine after the line had stretched a mere 5 1/2 miles for the exorbitant cost of £127,000, Catherwood moved to California by way of Panama.

Successful, at last, in the railway business of that booming state, Catherwood decided on a holiday in England. For the return trip to the States he boarded the S.S. *Arctic,* which sailed from Liverpool on September 20, 1854, with 385 passengers and crew. In mid-Atlantic the *Arctic* was rammed head-on by a French screw-propelled vessel, the *Vesta.* The *Arctic's* crew seized the lifeboats and pulled away from the ship, leaving the passengers—male, female, and children—to shift as best they could. By dusk the *Arctic* sank with its complement of passengers excepting the Duc de Gramont, who, determined to return to his diplomatic post in Washington, successfully jumped into the first officer's boat. Among those who sank beneath the ocean waves was Frederick Catherwood, Archt.

8. Another Champollion

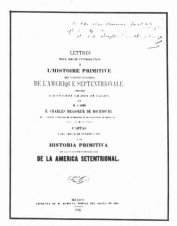

Facsimile of Brasseur de Bourbourg's letters to the Duc de Valmy designed to serve as an introduction to his *Early History of the Civilized Nations of North America.* Published in Mexico City in 1851, it is personally dedicated by the author to the Smithsonian Institute in Washington, D.C. The letters contain erudite essays on the value and veracity of Cabrera's and Nuñez de la Vega's theories about the Hittite, Carthaginian, and Phoenician origins of the people of Palenque.

While pathfinder Stephens had done a reporter's job of bringing to the world knowledge of some forty ruined cities with detailed examinations of Copan, Quiché, Palenque, and Uxmal, what was needed was a detective intellect to unravel the deeper mysteries of these ancient sites. Just looking at the buildings and illustrating them, no matter how beautifully or accurately, had not done the trick; some Champollion was needed with a Rosetta stone.

The man to make the next significant breakthrough toward explaining the origin and history of the mysterious Maya was a Fleming from near Dunkirk, who admitted that his teenage reading of Del Rio's book had "decided my archeological vocation for the future."

Encouraged by the success of Stephens' book, and anxious to resolve more riddles, Charles Etienne Brasseur de Bourbourg set off for America in 1845 at the age of thirty-one, freshly ordained to the priesthood. Tall, courtly, and strikingly handsome, he had mastered the art of journalism as a young man in Paris writing for *Le Monde* and *Le Temps;* and the art of novel writing by doing such potboilers as *Selim or the Pacha of Salonika* under the pseudonym of de Ravensburg, which developed for him as easy a literary style as Stephens'. What he needed next was academic standing. This he obtained by studying for the priesthood in Rome, sensing it would be easier to obtain access to people of substance and to the restricted archives of this planet by approaching them neither as a journalist nor as a novelist but as the Abbé Brasseur de Bourbourg, an ecclesiastical title which, along with his ecclesiastical duties, was to rest lightly on his shoulders. Not so his detective quest.

In this he became a ferreter out of rare books and valuable manuscripts, so indefatigable that he was to throw a whole new light on the origin of the natives of America.

Already in New York, on his way to Mexico, Brasseur had been able to obtain manuscript copies of the histories of New Spain by Las Casas and Duran, which had not yet appeared in print. In Mexico City, through the intercession of a friendly cabinet minister, the viceregal archives were opened to him, and Brasseur was able to read in manuscript the original history of the Aztecs written by Ixtlilxochitl. Other friends got him into other restricted libraries where he kept himself busy for a couple of years, adding to his twelve spoken languages and twenty reading ones by learning Nahuatl from a descendant of a brother of Montezuma.

To explore the country, Brasseur traveled on mule and horseback in Dupaix's footsteps, going to Tula, Queretaro, Guanajuato and the Pacific Ocean, all the time searching for rare manuscripts and artifacts. In Central America he went as far as Nicaragua, San Salvador, and Guatemala, where he found two extraordinary prizes: the *Annals of the*

Brasseur de Bourbourg.

On shipboard en route to America, Brasseur de Bourbourg met the French Minister to Mexico, Levasseur, who made him chaplain to the French Legation, a position which gave Brasseur official access to many libraries in Mexico City where he found the works of Bernardo de Lizana, one of the earliest Spanish historians of New Spain, who believed Hispaniola had been colonized by Carthaginians who spread to Cuba and Yucatan. The notion was supported by Ixtilxochitl who believed the Olmecs had come to Eastern Mexico from the Antilles via Florida.

Poking about in secret archives, Brasseur found that thirteen separate chiefs appeared to have landed in the Gulf of Mexico at different times before Cortes.

From Ordoñez' manuscript on Palenque, which he also found in Mexico City, Brasseur learned that Cabrera had plagiarized and misunderstood Ordoñez. According to Ordoñez, though Votan's forefathers had come to the Antilles from Africa via the Canaries, Votan, the sixth chief of that name, was born in Cuba, whence he sailed up the Uzamacinta to found Palenque.

Cakchiquel and the *Popol Vuh,* both important historical documents which he translated by mastering the local dialects of Cakchiquel and Quiché. The *Popol Vuh* proved to be one of the great primitive epics, a collection of myths, history, and customs of the Indians.

POPOL VUH.

LE

LIVRE SACRE

ET LES MYTHES

DE L'ANTIQUITÉ AMÉRICAINE,

AVEC LES LIVRES HÉROÏQUES ET HISTORIQUES DES QUICHES.

OUVRAGE ORIGINAL DES INDIGENES DE GUATEMALA,
TEXTE QUICHE ET TRADUCTION FRANÇAISE EN REGARD, ACCOMPAGNEE DE NOTES
PHILOLOGIQUES ET D'UN COMMENTAIRE
SUR LA MYTHOLOGIE ET LES MIGRATIONS DES PEUPLES ANCIENS DE L'AMÉRIQUE, ETC.,
COMPOSÉ SUR DES DOCUMENTS ORIGINAUX ET INÉDITS,

PAR

L'ABBÉ BRASSEUR DE BOURBOURG,

Auteur de l'Histoire des nations civilisées du Mexique et de l'Amérique centrale, Membre des
Sociétés de Géographie de Paris et de Mexico, de la Société Économique de Guatémala,
de la Société d'Ethnographie de Paris, etc., ancien administrateur ecclésiastique
des Quiches de Rabinal, des Cakchiquels de San-Juan Zacatepec,
des Mams d'Iztlahuacan, de Zipacapa, d'Ichil et de Tutnapa, etc.

PARIS,
ARTHUS BERTRAND, ÉDITEUR,
21, RUE HAUTEFEUILLE.
LONDON, TRÜBNER AND CO., 60, PATERNOSTER-ROW.

1861

The *Popul Vuh* or "common book of the people" containing national legends of the Quiche Maya was written at an unknown date in Latin script in the Quiche dialect by some native familiar with the ancient records. It was first translated into Spanish in the eighteenth century by the Spanish priest Francisco Jimenez and published in Vienna in 1857, attracting little attention. Brasseur's original text with his French translation in 175 pages of octavo was published in 1861.

Many such manuscripts survived in the wilder parts of Mayaland. On the islands of Lake Peten the Itza had brought with them many sacred books, but in 1697 they were attacked by Spaniards under General Don Martin de Vrsua, their capital was taken by storm, their books burned and twenty-one temples razed.

Back in Paris, where he published the *Popol Vuh* in a French translation, Brasseur was given access to a private collection of unique Mexican documents and manuscripts collected over the years by J. M. A. Aubin, who had previously not allowed any scholar to view them. Aubin had gone to Mexico in 1830 attached to a scientific expedition, but the loss of all his instruments and thus of his means of working had obliged him to take a job as tutor to a rich Mexican family. The job allowed him enough leisure to search for rare and ancient documents, such as a priceless ritual calendar of the Aztecs, part of Boturini's scattered collection, which he obtained from the nuns of the Convent of Tonalama for a mere eight pesos.

With access to Aubin's collection and from his own research among the Indians, Brasseur was able to produce and publish a much more impressive four-volume *Histoire des Nations Civilisées du Mexique et de l'Amérique Centrale,* which was greeted by the critics as the most comprehensive treatment of Mesoamerican history to have appeared in print. So impressed were the Spanish academicians, they immediately agreed to open their archives to Brasseur, so that in Madrid he was able to make even more significant discoveries. Buried in the archives of the Academy of History, where it had been lost for several centuries, Brasseur found Bishop Diego de Landa's manuscript *Relacion de las Cosas de Yucatan,* still today the single greatest source of information about the ancient Maya culture of Yucatan, which Brasseur immediately translated into French and published side by side with the original Spanish.

Landa's manuscript raised Brasseur's hopes of deciphering the Maya glyphs. In this he was only partially successful,

Landa's book, written in about 1566, gave a history of Yucatan from native sources, with descriptions of the Mayan calendar and ceremonies. It also included drawings of glyphs for the 20 days, 18 months, and claimed to be a key to hieroglyphic writing (right).

Brasseur published the book in French in 1864, just a year after its discovery. In his introduction, Brasseur described his Atlantean position (above).

113

Mayan glyphs for the days.

The first column on the right is from Landa's *Relaciones,* the second is from the Troano Codex. The remaining four are from the Book of Chilam Balam of Káua.

Operating on the premise that the Maya concocted composite glyphs with various meanings both symbolic and phonetic, Brasseur became overly sophisticated in the etymological nuances of meaning he attached to this or that position of a glyph. He thus got carried away by the momentum of his own notions about ancient Maya history.

Conversely, his history of Atlantis was built on a mixture of his interpretation of the Maya myths and of their hieroglyphs. Using Landa's basic interpretation of the glyphs, he read into those of the Troano Codex meanings which could substantiate the Atlantis legends.

His critics, anxious to put down Brasseur's linguistics, were equally delighted to put down his historical reconstruction of Atlantis, which did not fit their notion. Yet even Brasseur freely admitted the tenuous nature of his interpretation.

His critics, who considered him a better writer of fiction than of fact, believed his work was directed at proving preconceived ideas which they judged fanciful.

Later scholars, who discovered in the texts the most remarkable and sophisticated calendrical computers, could sympathize with Brasseur for his attempted readings in depth. He was on the scent but off the track. Brasseur believed the Troano Codex contained descriptions of part of a catastrophe which had resulted from the end of the last glacial period. He believed that the figures of the codex, though often gross in appearance and usually interpreted as the capricious efforts of superstitious genius, contain in fact the

Cod. Tro

Landa	Troano	Káua 3	Káua 4
5 Kan	12 Kan	6 Kan	13 Kan
6 Chicchan	13 Chicchan	7 Chicchan	1 Chicchan
7 Cimiy ? caloy 'no si'?	1 Cimiy	8 Cimiy	2 Cimiy
8 Manik	2 Manik	9 Manik	3 Manik
9 Lamat	3 Lamat	10 Lamat	4 Lamat
10 Muluc	4 Muluc	11 Muluc	5 Muluc
11 Oc	5 Oc	12 Oc	6 Oc
12 Chuen	6 Chuen	13 Chuen	7 Chuen
13 Eb	7 Eb	1 Eb	8 Eb
Jalta: 1 Ben	8 Ben	2 Ben	9 Ben
2 Hiix	9 Hiix	3 Hiix	10 Hiix
3 Men	10 Men	4 Men	11 Men
4 cib	11 Cib	5 Cib	12 Cib
5 Caban	12 Caban	6 Caban	13 Caban
6 Eonab	13 Eonab	7 Eonab	1 Eonab
7 Cauac	1 Cauac	8 Cauac	2 Cauac
8 Ahau	2 Ahau	9 Ahau	3 Ahau
9 Ymix	3 Ymix	10 Ymix	4 Ymix
10 Yk	4 Yk	11 Yk	5 Yk
11 Akbal	5 Akbal	12 Akbal	6 Akbal

identifying the twenty days of the month and the eighteen months of the year, as well as glyphs that personified various powers of nature, all of which was a steppingstone, but still not the Rosetta stone required for the unravelment of the mystery of the Maya glyphs.

In Madrid Brasseur became acquainted with Jean de Tro y Ortolano, a descendant of Hernan Cortes, professor of paleography at the university, who showed him a document which had been in the family for centuries, a Maya book of divination first known as the Troano Codex till sometime later another half of it turned up and it became the Codex Tro-Cortesianus. In these early documents Brasseur found support for the myths still current among the natives of Mesoamerica that a great terrestrial convulsion had sunk an island in the Atlantic extending eastward in a crescent as far as the Canary Islands.

114

Uxmal.

Catherwood and Stephens found that the quadrangular courtyard of the building called "Monjas," or "nunnery," had walls ornamented from end to end with what Stephens called the "richest and most intricate carving, presenting a scene of strange magnificence, surpassing any that is now to be seen among its ruins." The facade, which still showed signs of having been painted, displayed several masked faces with tongues hanging out, and "two colossal entwined feathered serpents running through and encompassing nearly all the ornaments throughout its whole length." Stephens was told that as recently as 1835 one of the facades had still stood intact, whereas he and Catherwood found them all badly dilapidated and overgrown with bushes alive with quail. The dilapidation enabled Stephens to note that some of the buildings had been erected over, and completely enclosed, older ones.

science of the ancient world; within the bizarre drawings he saw codified data about the geography, geology, and natural history of the ancients.

Brasseur believed that early migrations had been caused by passing comets, falling meteors, and other such calamities of extraterrestrial origin. He quoted Humboldt to the effect that primitive cultures were sometimes the debris of higher civilizations destroyed by natural catastrophes; and because he took seriously Humboldt's statement that myth could be history in disguise, Brasseur was accused of seeing history in every American myth.

Though he was derided for his method of attempting to unravel the secrets of the glyphs in this codex, he explained his reason for reading the manuscript from right to left with the sensible answer that the profiles of the figures faced in that direction. Modern experts have discovered that glyphs of the codices can be read not only up and down and left to right, but also diagonally to reveal sophisticated data.

The Codex is made up of two separate parts: the Troano, found by Brasseur in Madrid in 1864, consisting of 35 leaves or 70 pages which he chromophotoed in 1864, and the Cortesianus of 42 pages, which was found in Estremadura in 1867 and was believed to be a separate codex. The latter, refused by both the Royal Library in Paris and by the British Museum, was acquired by a private collector, José Ignacio Miro, who showed it to Leon de Rosny, discoverer of the ''Paris'' Codex. Unified into 112 pages, the full codex became the largest Mayan manuscript and was first displayed to the world in Paris in 1892.

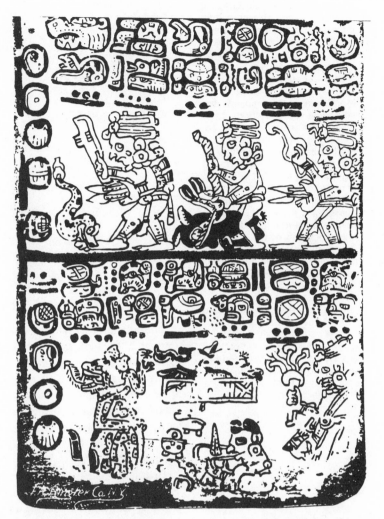

According to Brasseur, the Troano Codex placed the disappearance of this Atlantic continent in the year 9937 B.C. From this codex and from a Nahuatl manuscript purporting to be the history of the Kingdom of Calhuacan and Mexico, which Brasseur labeled the Codex Chimalpopoca, he deduced the revolutionary notion that civilization had originated not in the Middle East, as maintained by European historians, but in the West—in a large continent that stretched from America across the Atlantic, whence civilization had spread to Europe and to Egypt. Thus Brasseur explained the puzzling affinities he had found between the Mayan and the Quiché languages with Greek, Latin, French, English, and German. These languages appeared to him derivatives of Maya-Quiché.

Into the Nahuatl texts Brasseur read the story of a mighty cataclysm which had submerged the cradle of civilization

In the College of San Gregorio in Mexico City, Brasseur discovered a manuscript in Nahuatl to which he gave the name of Chimalpopoca Codex in honor of his teacher of Nahuatl, Faustino C. Galicia, who was a descendant of Montezuma's third son. Brasseur believed the codex to have been written in code so that each word had two or more meanings depending on the rhythm and cesura designed to enable the priestly scribes to conceal the history of the cataclysms and their cycles in a more banal and harmless-sounding text. From his translation of the Codex, Brasseur concluded that there had been not one cataclysm, as described by Plato, but a whole series which had shaped the world as it is today.

In his *Chronologie Historique des Mexicains,* Brasseur relied on the codex to say that in about 10,500 B.C. four periods of cataclysms had changed the world, and that each had been caused by a temporary shifting of the earth's axis.

millennia before Bishop Usher's still widely accepted Garden of Eden that dated back to 4000 B.C. From the text, Brasseur concluded that the American continent had originally occupied the Gulf of Mexico and the Caribbean Sea, extending across the Atlantic as far as the Canaries, but in some remote period it had been engulfed by a tremendous convulsion of nature. Subsequent upheavals, he believed, had restored parts of Yucatan, Honduras, and Guatemala to the surface.

Brasseur also traced the myth of Quetzalcoatl back to Plato's Atlantis and concluded that the Toltecs could have been descendants of survivors of that catastrophe.

Gradually Brasseur ascribed an increasing antiquity to the native cultures of Mesoamerica and came to believe that many of the truths of modern science had already been anticipated by the inhabitants of Mesoamerica many centuries previously. As he grew older, his cultivated notions grew out of step with those of his academic contemporaries. His penchant for seeing in the myths of antiquity explanations for what might have been actual history was too much for them. As one historian summed up the situation: "Unfortunately, as book after book appeared, his ideas grew more strange and his explanations more attenuated, so that serious leaders who had respected him increasingly lost confidence in his utterances."

Brasseur complained that no serious archeological work was being done in the Americas. That it was foolish to try to write world history leaving out one-half the world—the

Americas. He believed the Carians of Central America to have been the oldest known civilization, an industrious and commercial people who could handle metal and precious stones, great sailors and astronomers who had traveled the world, colonizing Atlantis, the Mediterranean, and ancient Egypt, whose astronomy, physics, and religious practices were similar, including a strong cult of Sirius, the Dog Star, and deification of the crocodile. From all of which Brasseur concluded that either Egypt had been a Central American colony or vice versa.

The American historian and bibliophile Hubert Howe Bancroft was to say of Brasseur that "In actual knowledge pertaining to his chosen subject no man ever equalled or approached him," but Brasseur's later writings were received by critics who were for the most part utterly incompetent to understand them; and more than a century was to pass before his prophetic intuition could be validated.

9. Reconquest of Mexico

William Hickling Prescott was born in Salem, Massachusetts, in 1796. His father was a lawyer; his grandfather, Colonel William Prescott, commanded at the Battle of Bunker Hill. Blinded in one eye by a crust of bread flung in the Harvard Commons, young Prescott was obliged to give up work in his father's law office in order to preserve his second eye, which had become paralyzed. So he devoted himself to literature, working in a darkened office with a noctograph, taking notes with an ivory stylus from what was read to him by a secretary. So proficient did Prescott's memory become that he could retain in his head the equivalent of sixty pages of printed matter, writing them and rewriting them as he walked or drove.

Meanwhile, William Hickling Prescott with his monumental *History of the Conquest of Mexico* had brought to the world the staggering story of the destruction of Montezuma's empire, making the exploits of Cortes common knowledge to the schoolboy. Using his family money to best advantage, and without ever moving from his native Boston, Prescott managed to accumulate the most extraordinary library of original data. First he gave large sums to a London bookseller to buy any book of interest that turned up on the subject of Mexico—no mean game, as Waldeck's, Del Rio's, Baradère's, and Catherwood's books each cost a fortune, and Kingsborough's nine folio volumes were coming off the presses at £150 apiece, or $3,500 the set.

Edward King, later Lord Kingsborough, an eccentric young Englishman who took seriously Humboldt's expressed desire that someone publish in book form all the known Mexican codices and manuscripts, hired an expert Italian draftsman, Agostino Aglio, and set about lithographing and hand-coloring reproductions of originals available in Europe, which had been brought back at various times since Cortes.

This was done between 1831 and 1848. Long commentaries in Greek, Hebrew, Latin, and Sanskrit, mostly in support of the theory that the Lost Tribes of Israel were the progenitors of the Maya, brought the opus to nine weighty and oversized folio volumes, one of literature's great tours de force, which no government had dared, and few individuals could have afforded or executed, but which executed its author because he too could not afford it. For failure to meet the price of the handmade paper on which the publication was printed, Kingsborough died miserably of typhus in a

Edward King, later
Lord Kingsborough.

Kingsborough took up the
notion from Las Casas that
the Lost Tribes of Israel had
peopled Yucatan. Support for
Kingsborough's version of the
Mayan origin of the Lost
Tribes of Israel also came
from the Mormon story as
told to the world by young
Joseph Smith in 1827. According to Smith, in 1820, when
he was 15 years old, a figure
appeared to him in a vision
claiming to be Moroni, son of
Mormon, "sent from the
presence of God."

During a second appearance,
when Smith was 18, Moroni
informed him where a number
of gold plates were hidden
containing writings in strange
characters which Moroni
termed as "revised" Egyptian.
According to Smith's translation of these plates, the
Israelites (progenitors of the
Nephites, who were led by
Lehi, a Jewish prophet of the
tribe of Manasseh) had landed
on the shores of Yucatan
sometime after 600 B.C.,
when the tribe was divided.

The more unusual part of
the Mormon version is that it
tells how the Israelites came
to America not via the Atlantic
but via the Pacific.

Joseph Smith

debtors' prison in Dublin, a demerit which prompted the
British Museum to omit his name from its catalogue, mentioning only Aglio the artist. But Kingsborough, for his pains,
did manage to force the world's societies of savants to
focus their attention at last on ancient Mexico.

With such powerful but little-known ammunition, Prescott
decided to corner the market and out-best-seller Stephens.
From Boston, he persuaded a Spanish scholar living in London into ransacking the libraries of England, France, and
Spain for material on Cortes. Taking advantage of a slightly
more liberal spirit in the Spanish peninsula, Prescott then
pulled his more stunning coup: he convinced the authorities
to allow him to use the vast research accumulated by the
official historiographer of the Indies, Juan Bautista Muñoz,
who had died at the beginning of the nineteenth century
before he could exploit the material. By special royal edict
Muñoz had been allowed free access to the National Archives
as well as libraries—public, private and monastic—in the
Kingdom of Spain and its colonies.

To copy this material, Prescott hired a phalanx of scribes
in Madrid under the supervision of a member of the Royal
Academy of History, the German historian Friedrich Wilhelm
Lembke. In Boston, Prescott received some eight thousand
virgin folio pages of manuscript "on which," in his words,
"the public breath had never blown."

Kingsborough's illustrations from the Codex Borgia of a strange figure representing Camaxtli, the Mexican god of fate, with the twenty day-signs attached to different parts of the body indicating different astrological effects they were believed to have on the various human organs. The interpretation is similar to Rodney Collin's thesis, detailed in his *The Theory of Celestial Influence,* that life energy is diffused from the sun through the various planets to the corresponding glands in the human body which they control.

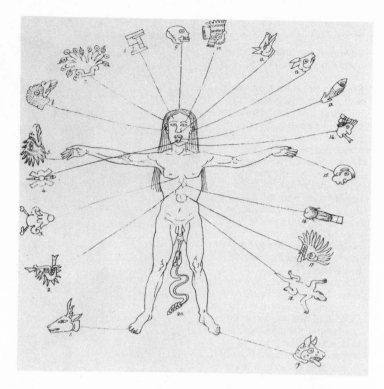

Aware that noxious effects could also come from the cosmos, the Mexicans thus depicted their Goddess of Lust.

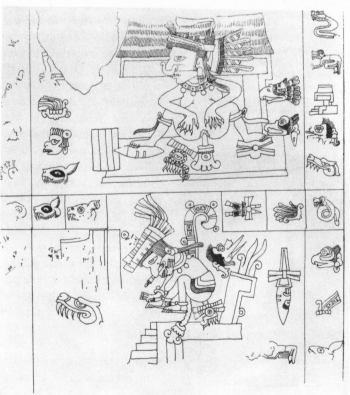

To this bonanza of unpublished material many learned historians from all over the world made contributions which helped Prescott produce his great *History of the Conquest of Mexico,* an instant success, quickly translated into scores of languages.

From the Kingdom of the Two Sicilies Prescott got more invaluable material: some from Count Camaldoli in Naples, more from the Duke of Senifalco in Sicily. In Mexico the incumbent representative of Cortes, the Duke of Monteleone, opened his family files, and the minister of foreign affairs, Don Lucas Aleman, gave Prescott his assistance both official and private, as did a man whom Prescott qualified as "a gentleman whose high and estimable qualities, even more than his station, secured him the public confidence, and gained him access to every place of interest and importance in Mexico," Don Angel Calderon de la Barca, minister plenipotentiary to Mexico from the court of Madrid.

Prescott, no longer able to read because he had nearly lost the sight of his remaining eye personally scrutinizing Stephens' four volumes on his travels in Yucatan and Central America, was obliged to produce his masterpiece from data read to him by a secretary in his Beacon Street studio, writing with a special case made for the blind which did not permit him even to see his own manuscript, the original draft of which he was never able to peruse or correct.

Knowing—as Humboldt had known from reading Careri—that descriptions of localities in Mexico only had that touch of verisimilitude when observed in person, Prescott relied for descriptions of living flora and fauna, and especially for details of such historic sites as the pyramids of Teotihuacan, on reports sent to him by Calderon de la Barca and, more especially, by Calderon's wife, Fanny. This Scottish lady had lived so long in Mexico that her book, *Life in Mexico,* based on letters to her family and friends, was used by the U.S. Army to indoctrinate the troops of "Old Fuss and Feathers" General Winfield Scott during his campaign against Mexico City in 1847, there being so little information available about the country.

Unfortunately, Fanny Calderon's description of the pyramids of Teotihuacan told more about herself and her style of living than it did about Mexico's antiquities.

As she approached San Juan Teotihuacan, the road, says Fanny Calderon, grew more picturesque and at length her attention was arrested by the sight of the two great pyramids, "which are mentioned by Humboldt and have excited the curiosity and attention of every succeeding traveler." Unfortunately, she adds, "our time was too limited to give them more than a passing observation."

General Winfield Scott.

During his shorter conquest of Mexico for the U.S. Army in 1847, General Winfield Scott, known as "Old Fuss and Feathers," was accused by the Mexicans of having removed from the University of Mexico the remaining manuscript volumes of the works of Don Carlos de Sigüenza y Gongora, and of having transported them to Washington, D.C., where they were reportedly seen by the Mexican minister. A century earlier when Francisco Clavigero had consulted the remains of Sigüenza's works bequeathed to the Jesuit College of San Pedro y Paulo, he reported that only eight of the twenty-eight known volumes were available. A careful search in Washington, D.C., at the library of the Department of State, at the Library of Congress, and in the National Archives has so far been fruitless.

Fanny Calderon de la Barca.

Fanny Calderon de la Barca and her husband, the Spanish minister to Mexico, set off at dawn on a spring day to visit the pyramids of Teotihuacan en route to a friend's hacienda. Their transport was a gilded calèche which had belonged to Charles X of France, drawn by six horses, driven by two coachmen with silver-buttoned and embroidered deerskin jackets, enormous sombreros and the high boots of a postilion, who produced wild shrieks to encourage the horses to gallop. For fear of bandits, several well-armed outriders galloped beside the calèche as it passed the cathedral of Guadalupe and crossed the marshy plain which had once been covered by the waters of Lake Texcoco. As Mexico had been for some years in the midst of a civil war, everywhere they saw the ruins of houses, whole villages crumbling, convents with broken-down walls, the abandoned country palace of a viceroy. "Robbers" living in a half-ruined house helped them with a broken wheel, while several men with guns— "sporting looking characters, but rather dirty"—observed them but did not molest them, thanks to their own tough outriders.

Instead, the Calderons changed horses at San Juan and refreshed themselves on rancid sheep's milk and biscuits so hard that Calderon asked his host if they had been made in the same year as the church! The innkeeper, says Fanny Calderon, "seemed mightily pleased, and could not stop laughing till we got into the carriage."

Mistaking Teotihuacan for Tenochtitlan, Fanny Calderon berated Cortes for his fanaticism in having ordered "the destruction of these bloodstained sanctuaries."

As a result, Prescott's description relied more on Humboldt than on Calderon, and is pleasingly atmospheric but none too correct.

There are [wrote Prescott] no remains on the top of the pyramid of the sun. But the traveler, who will take the trouble to ascend its bald summit, will be amply compensated by the glorious view it will open up to him: towards the south-east, the hills of Tlascala, surrounded by their green plantations and cultivated corn-fields, in the midst of which stands the little village, once the proud capital of the republic. Somewhat further to the south, the eye passes across the beautiful plains lying around the city of Puebla de los Angeles, founded by the old Spaniards, and still rivalling, in the splendor of its churches, the most brilliant capital of Europe; and far in the west he may behold the Valley of Mexico, spread out like a map, with its diminished lakes, its princely capital rising in still greater glory from its ruins, and its rugged hills gathering darkly around it, as in the days of Montezuma.

Romantic Prescott! To have observed such a view from the Sun Pyramid, to have seen Puebla de los Angeles sixty miles to the southeast as the eagle flies, would have required a giant such as was described to the Spaniards by the Aztecs, or an airy Quetzalcoatl.

To describe the shape and condition of the steps of the Sun Pyramid, Prescott found himself with the conflicting reports of Bullock and of Henry Tudor, a barrister at law from London, who had visited the pyramids shortly after Bullock.

122

View for Prescott of the pyramids of Teotihuacan from Fanny Calderon de la Barca's book *Life in Mexico.*

Prescott went Humboldt one step further on the question as to whether the pyramids were built from outcroppings or from a flat plain. He compared them to the North American mounds and said they were built from scratch.

Tudor maintained that "it requires a particular position united with some little faith to discover the pyramidal form at all." Whereas Bullock contended that "the general figure of the square is as perfect as the Great Pyramid of Egypt."

As Tudor and his companions consumed—along with their picnic of turkey, tongue, and cold fowl—two dozen bottles of claret and Madeira, with which they "contrived to keep famine from the door," and then "rose from our rustic table like giants refreshed with wine" to visit the pyramids, it is perhaps Bullock's report that is the more sober.

Remarking that both men had been eyewitnesses, but that Bullock "has sometimes seen what has eluded the optics of other travelers," Prescott finessed the problem by taking refuge in a French lay to the effect that he was passing on information as he read it: *"Si com je l'ai trouvé éscrité/Vos conterai la verité."*

Relying on Humboldt, Prescott described the pyramids as being constructed of clay mixed with pebbles, encrusted on the surface with the light porous stone *tetzontli,* so abundant in the neighboring quarries. Over this, he said, the builders had placed a thick coating of stucco, "resembling in its reddish color, that found in the ruins of Palenque."

For a description of the hole found by Sigüenza in the south flank of the Moon Pyramid, Prescott relied on Charles Joseph Latrobe, former governor of Australia, who visited Mexico in 1834 in the company of Washington Irving and penetrated about fifteen feet into a gallery which he said was faced with unbaked brick, terminating in two pits or wells. Prescott mistakenly assumed these pits could have been "designed to hold the ashes of some powerful chief; like the solitary apartment discovered in the great Egyptian pyramid."

Like the first explorers of the mysterious passages and wellholes in the Great Pyramid of Cheops, Latrobe and a fellow-traveler, whom he referred to as McEuen, ventured into a snake- and scorpion-infested passage, the entrance to which has since been lost. "After undergoing a partial stripping," wrote Latrobe, "I proceeded to share in the glory and danger of the enterprise. I laid myself flat upon my face

123

View of Tampico, where Charles Joseph Latrobe landed in 1834 to find everyone in the country armed to the teeth and bandits as plentiful as nopal bushes. From Mexico City, Latrobe lumbered off to San Juan Teotihuacan in a coach drawn by ten mules with faded trappings and brass-studded leather tailpieces. Looking back over Lake Texcoco, he saw the City of Mexico as a mirage, "the white edifices and colored domes of the capital appearing afloat, like a fleet of snowy sails, upon the blue surface of the water."

Between Lake Texcoco and Lake San Cristobal he noted that the 1500-foot dike and causeway, ten feet wide and four feet deep, which prevented the salty waters of one lake pouring into the other, had been built by forced labor with lassoed natives, hundreds of whom had died in the effort. He reported that in excavating for the building of the Guadalupe cathedral huge bones had turned up which he believed had belonged to mastodons used by ancient Mexicans to move great blocks for an earlier causeway.

Latrobe found Teotihuacan "emblossomed in shady groves irrigated by plenteous streams," and admired many moving pillars of dust as high as a hundred feet in the plain where "the great pyramids are perfectly distinguishable at a distance of many miles."

Climbing the Sun Pyramid, he found its surface to be a "stew of porous scoria and amygdaloid" and correctly estimated that the real base of the structure "lies below the level of the present soil, concealed by the wrecks cast down upon it."

In a hollow between two smaller pyramids at the foot of the House of the Moon, he described a large square mass with a sculptured face, saying the popular belief with regard to it was that anyone sitting down on it fainted.

John Taylor of London.

Prescott gave the length of the Sun Pyramid as 682 feet, and its height as 180, which are Humboldt's figures translated into English feet, neither figure very correct. Prescott further compounded his error by comparing the size of the Sun Pyramid to that of the Pyramid of Cheops in Egypt, using Dominique Denon's figures obtained from *Egypt Illustrated,* which appeared in England in 1825, wrong by about thirty feet when compared with the almost perfect figures obtained by Jomard in 1799, of which Prescott was evidently unaware.

and ducking into the aperture squeezed myself blindly forward, with my candle, through a passage inclining downwards for about three yards when I found myself in an open gallery, at the termination of which, not many paces distant, I found two wells which I figured to be about the center of the pyramid." There Latrobe's companion McEuen "valorously allowed himself to be lowered by rope into the aperture on the left hand, to a depth of perhaps fifteen feet, without making any further discovery."

As Latrobe had been unable to find any other evidence of internal passages, what most preoccupied Prescott was to know who had built the huge structures. "Was it," he asked, "the shadowy Olmecs, whose history, like that of the ancient Titans, is lost in the mists of fable? Or, as commonly reported, the peaceful and industrious Toltecs, of whom all that we can glean rests on traditions hardly more secure? What has become of the race who built them? Did they remain on the soil, and mingle and become incorporated with the fierce Aztecs who succeeded them? Or did they pass on to the South, and find a wider field for the expansion of their civilization, as shown by the higher character of the architectural remains in the distant regions of Central America and Yucatan?"

Unable to find an answer, Prescott concluded, "It is all a mystery,—over which Time has thrown an impenetrable veil, that no mortal hand may raise. A nation has passed away,— powerful, populous, and well advanced in refinement, as attested by their monuments,—but it has perished without a name. It has died and made no sign."

The sign, had Prescott been able to see the pyramids, might have been before his eyes, a little more hermetic perhaps than in Egypt because of more crumbled walls, but evident nonetheless. At that moment in London the π proportion in the Pyramid of Cheops—that its height is to its perimeters as the radius is to a circle—was being worked out by a bookseller, mathematician, and amateur astronomer: John Taylor. But to extrapolate anything similar from the Teotihuacan structures would have required more careful measurements and scientific reconstruction, projects for which Mexicans were as yet unready and unwilling to expend a peso. They were bankrupt from half a century of civil war.

The liberal revolt, which had overthrown the last-gasp dictatorship of General Santa Anna and ushered in a movement known as the "Reforma" whose objective was the destruction of feudalism in Mexico, had turned into another civil war between conservative royalists and liberal constitutionalists, the latter under reformer Benito Juarez. In the process both sides had become heavily indebted to foreign countries and

125

Juarez.

Benito Juarez was born a
mountain Indian. Orphaned as
a child, he was brought to
Oaxaca as a servant, where a
Franciscan lay brother sent
him to school. Quiet and
reserved, but with a powerful
logical mind, Juarez learned
his Spanish and his lessons so
well he got to law school.
Elected to congress he
became governor of the state
of Oaxaca—which he found
bankrupt and left with a
50,000-peso surplus.

As chief justice of the
supreme court, Juarez succeeded to the presidency, but
was obliged to flee the capital
as the armed struggle renewed
between the Catholic Royalists and the liberal republicans, the latter supported by
Freemasons in both the
Americas. Ironically, the
policies of Juarez had been
brought to the attention of
U.S. readers by the London
correspondent of the New
York *Tribune,* an international
exile by the name of Karl
Marx. Juarez, in exile,
received arms and supplies
from New Orleans.

Early in 1861, after the most
destructive war fought in
Mexico, Juarez was able to
enter the capital riding in a
small black carriage. Known
as "El Indio," he chose as his
slogan "Nothing by force,
everything through law and
reason." But when the new
Mexican congress narrowly
chose Juarez president, the
country was still in such tur-
moil that he was obliged to
rule by decree, one of which
expropriated all Church property and dissolved the religious corporations, leading to
renewed civil war.

In the words of Manly P. Hall,
the god of Juarez was "The
Father of Freedom, served by
a priesthood of liberation."
His rebellion was not against
God but against the theological institutions of Mexico.

The outlook of the higher
clergy, who had accumulated

and hoarded vast wealth, was
authoritarian, monarchist, and
anti-democratic, yet they felt
bound to continue to interfere in politics.

The Mexican church continued to collect the high fees
established under colonialism,
higher than in any European
Catholic country, as well as
mandatory tithes. Marriage
fees were so exorbitant that
many of the lower classes
could not afford them, and
poor people raised stable
families technically in sin
without benefit of clergy.

The clergy refused to
absolve, marry, or bury any
Mexican who stood for the
constitution of 1857. A priest,

like an army officer, could
not be tried in a civil court
for civil crime. He went before
an ecclesiastical court even
if charged with legal debts.
This infuriated Mexican jurists,
because for sixty years the
principle of equality before
the law had been established
in the advanced nations.

Vast numbers of monastics
became idle, their missions
defunct while the orders still
retained large chapter houses
and managed large estates.
These monastics, says historian T. H. Fehrenbach, who
had once been the finest,
became "probably the most
useless and corrupt of the
Mexican clergy."

Napoleon III.

Wishing to emulate his uncle's cultural, archeological, and political exploits in Egypt, so as to unify the squabbling political parties of his empire "under a mantle of imperial glory," Napoleon III decided to take action in Mexico.

Jean-Frédéric Maximilien Baron de Waldeck.

When the French government insisted on paying Waldeck by the year instead of outright, because of his advanced age, Waldeck, already in his nineties, had the last laugh. Still an avid girl chaser, he used his yearly salary to entertain the beauties of Paris at government expense, and at the age of a hundred he married a 17-year-old—attributing his virility and longevity to a diet of horse-radish consumed for six weeks every spring.

both had defaulted on their debts. Actually, Juarez had merely chosen to ignore an absurd French demand for 50 million pesos, plus 12 million in reparations, for a defaulted loan of a mere 750,000 from a Swiss banker who had subsequently assumed French citizenship. But Charles Louis Napoleon Bonaparte, as Napoleon III, was using the debt as a pretext to install by force a powerful Catholic and Latin empire in Mesoamerica under French protection.

To get a foot in the door, without upsetting either the Mexicans or his constituents in France, Napoleon capitalized on the publicity produced by Prescott, Stephens, Waldeck, and Brasseur to order his minister of public instruction, Eugène Viollet-le-Duc, to form a Commission for the Study of Mexican Antiquities, especially the pyramid complex at Teotihuacan.

Jean-Baptiste-Luis, Baron Gros, Napoleon's adviser on Mexico, who had visited the site and found a considerable analogy between the Mexican pyramids and those of Egypt, was put in charge of organizing a group of French experts to study the problem.

The French surveyors were to explore the site, establish the number of pyramids, as well as their situation and proportion, determine the nature of the blocks of which they were formed, and send some back to Paris. They were also to excavate interior galleries and ascertain whether there were any vaulted ceilings. Furthermore they were to record all the traditions preserved by the Indians in the vicinity, no matter how absurd or trivial those traditions might seem.

To produce some really prestigious works on Mexican antiquities, the French government commissioned Brasseur de Bourbourg to write a text to go with the engravings made in Yucatan by Waldeck, whom the government did not consider sufficiently founded academically to write his own text.

So Waldeck and Brasseur came together in the interest of Napoleon's grandeur.

To get more than a foot in the door of Mexico, Napoleon III overtly pressed the claim that Mexico's republican president, Benito Juarez, had defaulted on payment of the Swiss banker's loan. A military expedition was organized to collect the money, and a Catholic monarch, Archduke Maximilian of Hapsburg, brother of the Emperor Franz Joseph, was selected for enforcement on the Mexicans with the connivance of Mexico's royalist opposition to Juarez.

At noon of May 28, 1864, the Austrian warship *Novara* steamed into the harbor of Veracruz with the new thirty-two-year-old Emperor of Mexico and his twenty-five-year-old Empress Carlota, daughter to the King of Belgium.

127

Ferdinand Maximilian of Hapsburg and Carlota of Coburg.

Tall, blue-eyed, and blond-bearded, Maximilian was fundamentally a liberal interested in the arts and sciences who wanted to install in Mexico a government of honest ministers. Intelligent and hard-working, he had served well as royal governor and as head of the Imperial Austrian Navy. Carlota was an ambitious princess, daughter of Leopold I of Belgium. After the disaster that befell her in Mexico she went mad and lived in seclusion in Belgium until 1927.

Through practically deserted streets they were driven to the station of a rickety railroad that had been hastily built by the French to rush their troops out of the yellow fever area as far as Paso del Macho. There, Maximilian and Carlota transferred to old mail-coach *diligencias,* only to learn that Juarez' intrepid young republican general, Porfirio Diaz, was in the neighborhood with a body of guerrillas hoping to ambush the imperial suite. They too noted a countryside ravaged by forty years of civil war. For the steep ascent to the rocky plateau of Orizaba they transferred to horses, then back to coaches for a state entrance into Mexico City on June 12, an occasion sensibly celebrated by Maximilian with a general amnesty for all political prisoners.

10. Maximilian and Teotihuacan

Despite Maximilian's grand delusions, which included the hope of establishing a vast Hapsburg empire from the Rio Grande to the Rio Plata with the help of his younger brother, Ludwig Viktor, who was to marry one of the Brazilian princesses, Maximilian was fundamentally a liberal who honestly believed he had been called upon by the people of Mexico to end a civil war and set up an effective noncorrupt government based on "liberty and sincere love of progress."

He did not realize that in a country described by the London *Times* correspondent as "rotten to the core," where education was nonexistent, thieving and corruption general among all classes of officials, the Emperor of Mexico was no more than a prisoner of the reactionary group of clerical conservatives who had sought foreign intervention and the imposition of an autocrat on the people of Mexico solely to reverse the Juarez edicts which had secularized church property, suppressed religious houses, and abolished the privileges of the clergy. As for a mandate from the people, the situation was summed up by the British minister to Mexico, Sir Charles Wyke, who wryly observed that Maximilian might have had it in a few villages "possibly inhabited by two Indians and a monkey."

At the end of his first tour of the country Maximilian found its worst features to be the judicial functionaries, the army officers, and the greater part of the clergy. "None of them," he wrote, "are familiar with their duties, but live for money alone. The judges are corrupt, the officers have no sense of honor, and the clergy are lacking in Christian charity and morality."

To add to his problems, Maximilian promptly outraged Pope Pius IX, who had warned him in Rome that "the rights of the

Sir Charles Wyke.

129

Chapultepec Palace.

On "the hill of the grasshopper" on the outskirts of Mexico City, the palace of Chapultepec was built by Viceroy José de Galvez in the eighteenth century on the spot where the Mexica had first settled and where Montezuma had his summer quarters, surrounded by a garden enlivened by wild game under towering cypresses sixty feet round at the base. A powerful source of water which sprang from the hill had been tapped by the early Mexica and carried by aqueduct to the great city of Tenochtitlan, where its flow, according to Cortes, was as thick as a man's body.

people are great and it is necessary to satisfy them, but the rights of the church are greater and more sacred." By crossing the Pope and insisting on a separation of state and church, on freedom of religion, and on nationalization of Church property, Maximilian unwittingly signed his own death warrant.

Seeing himself as an enlightened humanitarian, he had quickly turned to improving the cultural and educational level of his adopted country and to cleaning up and beautifying its capital, wandering, like Montezuma, through the streets incognito to see that everything was progressing as it should.

With Carlota he first tried to live downtown in the Palacio Nacional, but the rooms were so small and cramped, leading from one to another like a railroad train, that he decided to move to the former viceregal palace on Montezuma's favorite spot, Chapultepec Hill.

There the young couple found the premises so filthy and in such poor repair that Maximilian had to spend his first night on the billiard table to avoid the vermin in his bed. More romantic in her outlook, Carlota was enchanted with the view over the city and the valley ringed by lakes, green fields, and the snowcapped volcanic peak of Popocatepetl in the distance, a view she considered superior to that of the Bay of Naples.

Throughout Mayaland there is evidence of a former phallic cult similar to that of the Phoenicians, and to the cult of Osiris, which was concerned with life and death and fecundity in all its forms. Almost all the ancient races worshiped the yoni and the phallus as appropriate symbols of God's creative power. According to Manly P. Hall, the Garden of Eden, the Gate of the Temple, the Veil of Mysteries, the *vesica piscis,* or oval nimbus, and the Holy Grail are all important yonic symbols. Whereas the pyramid, the obelisk, the cone, the candle, the tower, the Celtic monolith, the spire, the campanile, the Maypole, and the sacred spar are all symbolic of the phallus.

An anonymous conquistador describing phallic worship in Mexico wrote, "In other provinces, particularly Panuco, they worship the member of the body which is between a man's legs: they have it in the mosque and also set in the square, together with figures in relief showing all the kinds of pleasure that can exist between man and woman and they have these pictures with legs raised in various ways."

Childless—apparently because of a venereal disease communicated to her by Maximilian, who had contracted it from a Brazilian prostitute in his travels—the Empress had much time to devote to the affairs of state and to cultural pursuits. With her beautiful young Indian lady-in-waiting, Josefa Varela, a direct descendant of the Aztec poet king, Netzahualcoyotl, she visited many of the antiquities of Mexico, going as far as Uxmal, where she was struck by the extraordinary emblems of phallic worship, a painful reminder that her own lovemaking days were over. Whereas Maximilian, with the pick of the court at Chapultepec, was having a child by his gardener's wife at the Borda Gardens in Cuernavaca, a haunt he so favored that he had it linked to the capital by a better road, patrolled by French troops against bandits. Maximilian's taking of an Indian mistress, far from being frowned on by the Mexicans, was regarded as a token of his affection for his adopted country; but the result of the union was to have a sad consequence. Maximilian's son, named Concepcion Sedano y Lequizano, for his "legal" parents, grew up in France as somewhat of a wastrel who sported a beard like his father and took pride in being known as "the imperial bastard." On October 10, 1917, in Vincennes outside Paris he was executed by a firing squad as a convicted spy for the Germans.

To link the residence at Chapultepec with the Palacio Nacional in the Plaza Mayor, Maximilian directed the construction of one of the grandest avenues in the world, intentionally outdoing the Champs Elysées of his patron

131

Napoleon III. First called the Calzada del Emperador, it was later more democratically renamed the Paseo de la Reforma.

On the first anniversary of his acceptance of the throne, Maximilian founded the Academy of Science and Literature, negotiating with a well-known Mexican book collector, José Maria Andrade, for a magnificent 5,000-volume library of printed books and manuscripts relating to Mexican history and culture with which to form the nucleus of an imperial library for the use of the entire nation. He also established a national theater under the direction of the poet José Zorrilla, offering from his own private funds substantial prizes for the best plays written.

The National Museum was transferred from the university to the Palacio Nacional, where it stayed for exactly one whole century before it was moved to the modern Museo Antropologico. For the museum Maximilian sought to regain from abroad various relics such as Montezuma's shield and the original manuscript of a report from Cortes to Charles V, which had found their way into the imperial collection in Vienna. He also set about collecting the portraits of Mexico's former rulers, which had been scattered during the years of the civil war.

In the field of education Maximilian hoped to organize a system on such a scale that Mexico could "take its place by the side of the leading nations of the world." Of Brasseur de Bourbourg he thought so highly that he offered him the directorship of education and museums in his new government; but Brasseur, with a twinkle, declined, saying, "I never like to travel with the army."

So appalled was Maximilian by what he considered a shocking lack of interest demonstrated by Mexicans in the monuments of their own past, he organized the first genuinely scientific commission to study Mexican antiquities, with a

By careful astronomical observations the commission finally obtained more correct coordinates for both great pyramids. They set the Moon Pyramid north of the equator by 19 degrees, 41 minutes, and 52.8 seconds, and west of Paris by 6 hours, 35 minutes, and 18.32 seconds. The Sun Pyramid they placed 26 seconds of arc closer to the equator and 2 seconds of time nearer Paris. (The modern figures for the Sun Pyramid's latitude are: 19° 41' 30" north of the equator. Its longitude is 98° 50' 30" west of Greenwich.) The commission also established that the Sun Pyramid's west flank did not lie on the astronomical meridian running north-south, as Humboldt and others had suggested, but was angled about 15 degrees east of north. However, Almaraz noted that a line drawn between the vertices of the two pyramids did point very close to magnetic north, which did not particularly impress him, as magnetic north continually varies, but indicated to him that the pyramids' builders might have had a better notion of the apparent motion of the heavenly spheres, caused by the earth's rotation on its axis, than had previously been supposed.

Almaraz assumed that their error of a couple of degrees could have been due to the ignorance of the fact that the pole star is not, and was not, at the actual pole of the heavens, but circles around the pole at a varying distance, which in Almaraz' day was 1 degree 25 minutes.

particular emphasis on the ruins of Teotihuacan. The commission consisted of several eminent Mexican engineers under the direction of engineer Ramon Almaraz.

To reach the top of the Moon Pyramid, Almaraz found a stairway or zigzag ramp which started halfway up the facade, decreased proportionately, and ended in the center of the upper level; the zigzags were clearly visible on the plan he submitted. He also noted that the south facade of the Moon Pyramid had another pyramidal structure applied to it, or *adosado* as he called it, which reached a height of twenty-one meters.

At that level Almaraz found a deep excavation in the face of the pyramid, evidently Sigüenza's and Latrobe's hole, running north-south, with lateral excavations running in different directions, which he attributed to treasure seekers.

The only noteworthy feature appeared to Almaraz to be the square well which descended vertically within it, with walls formed of rows of volcanic brick held together by mud, only the southerly wall of which was slightly dilapidated.

So well preserved was this hole that Almaraz hoped to extrapolate from its measure the basic unit used by the builders of the entire complex. Very carefully he measured the well as being 1 meter 6 centimeters square.

In an intuitive flight of fancy, Almaraz suggested that as all the common units of measure in use in his time—the meter, the yard, the ana, the elle, and the vara—were more or less the same length, a similar unit might have been used at Teotihuacan. But wherever else he looked, Almaraz found

133

134

Teotihuacan pyramids with Moon Pyramid in foreground.

Almaraz described the Moon Pyramid as being on a rectangular base 156 meters long by 130 wide, covering a surface of 20,280 square meters, or 5 acres, which was within 2 percent of being accurate. He estimated its height as 42 meters, which is within a meter of the most sophisticated estimate to date.

Almaraz also saw the Moon Pyramid as originally being formed of three superimposed bodies, each about 10 meters high, only one level of which could be clearly distinguished at 21 meters from the base. He said he could see no evidence of levels on the east side, which had the aspect of an inclined plane with no break or fissure. Time, weather, and the hand of man, said Almaraz, had destroyed much of the original surfaces, causing crumbling and the obliteration of the ridges, so that the pyramids, without their original outlines, seemed at first sight to be hillocks rather than raised monuments.

To what was known of the exterior of the Sun Pyramid the commission did not add much, other than to confirm that it appeared to be divided into three stories and had a zigzag path leading to the summit, which was in better condition than the path up to the Moon Pyramid.

buildings too dilapidated and covered with rubble and earth to be accurately measured. At last in the ruins of a nearby mound, or *tlaltel,* as the Mexicans called it, Almaraz found a well-preserved piece of sculpture lying face down in the mud, which had preserved its sharp contours. Raising the statue, he found it to be a carved parallelopiped 3 meters 19 centimeters high with a square base of 1 meter 65 centimeters. This clearly gave it a height almost exactly three times the 1.06-meter width of the well, and a width 1 1/2 times that of the well.

But for some reason, instead of selecting this 1.06-meter unit, which varied no more than 6 percent from any one of the units in common usage, Almaraz chose 3/4 of that length, or 80 centimeters, which varied from all of them by more than 20 percent, on the theory that the statue was intended to be 4 units high by 2 units wide, instead of the more obvious 3 by 1 1/2 or possible 9 $\times$ 18 palms.

Almaraz also settled on the 80-centimeter unit because the distance between the Moon and the Sun pyramids was effectively 800 meters, giving a round 1000 units—a figure which pleased his francophile decimal point of view.

No attempt was made by Almaraz to compare this unit of 80 centimeters with any of the ancient units of measure found by Jomard to have been incorporated into the Great Pyramid of Cheops, presumably because Almaraz was unaware of the work of Jomard.

Because of earth and rubble around the base of the Sun Pyramid, it was difficult for Almaraz and his fellow engineers to even measure its length; but they obtained a figure of 232 meters along the west facade, very close to the 231 meters of the base of the Great Pyramid of Cheops, correctly estimated by Jomard. Though Almaraz also had no way of knowing this, as the correct length was not officially established until 1925, when the base of Cheops was cleared of a thousand years of accumulated rubble.

Scouting around the base of the Sun Pyramid, the members of the commission came upon a huge platform forty meters wide and six meters high which bordered the Sun Pyramid on the north, east, and south sides, forming a raised platform with *talud* facings.

South of the Sun Pyramid, in the area which the early Spaniards had called the Citadel, the commission found a similar platform twice as wide with walls ten meters high, except for the one facing the Way of the Dead, which was only five meters high. On these platforms were fourteen mysterious *tlalteles,* or mounds, symmetrically arranged, four each on the north and south sides, three on the east and west.

In the center of the large quadrangle formed by the platforms were the remains of another *tlaltel* with a stairway on the west face, and slightly ahead of it another smaller *tlaltel*.

Almaraz says that throughout the pyramid complex he found scores of smaller *tlalteles* that looked like hillocks, some built in a symmetrical pattern, others scattered with no apparent regularity. In the plaza before the Moon Pyramid he found a group of *tlalteles* which appeared to form a sort of circle around a central one. These had been much excavated, partly, says Almaraz, by searchers after archeological remains, but mostly by "rapacious and ignorant" persons in search of treasure. What most outraged Almaraz was the evidence that the entire area had been used as a quarry for stones for "the barbarous habitations" of the natives. In the houses of the village of San Juan he saw that many valuable carved stones had been broken up to form walls.

In one of the *tlalteles,* Almaraz found eight worked stones, also just over a meter wide, whose outer faces were carved to represent grotesque figures with the heads of serpents and tigers. The carving had apparently formed a circular monument just over five meters in radius, now chipped and broken, though one carving was sufficiently preserved for him to make a sketch. In the same *tlaltel* there were other sculptured stones in which Almaraz recognized the lineaments of a jaguar and a figure he could not make out.

Told that in an earlier excavation of one of the *tlalteles* a small stone coffer had been found containing a skull, various *cuentas,* and curious objects of beryllium, serpentine, heliotrope, and obsidian, as well as large quantities of gold dust in golden vases, Almaraz would have liked thoroughly to gut one of the *tlalteles,* and perhaps even dig a passage through the base of the two great pyramids, but was prevented from both endeavors by lack of personnel and funds. He also suggested that the entire area of ruined houses should be properly and thoroughly mapped, "as intelligent and respectable men have been suggesting for some time."

Almaraz says that at the very beginning of his efforts at Teotihuacan he decided not to draw conclusions about ancient times, but only to occupy himself with relating how he found things as they were. In the end he could not resist expressing an opinion—an opinion which only went to confirm that first impressions are inclined to be best. He said he first thought the pyramids had been intended to represent a system of planets, but in the end concluded they were merely temples and sepulchers dedicated to illustrious men. Almaraz also concluded that the ruins represented the work of several different epochs, because he had found buildings raised above the foundations and ruins of earlier buildings, as if to hide or protect the more ancient ones. It also appeared to him

Reconstructed *tlaltel* or platform temple.

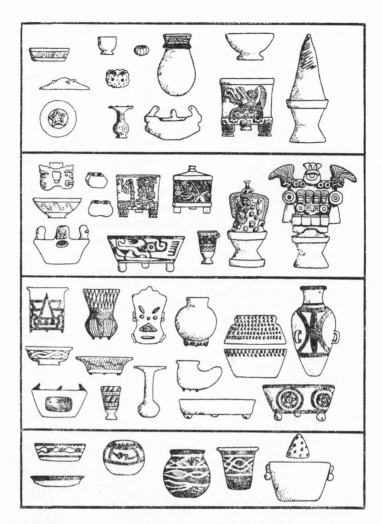

Various styles of pottery found in Teotihuacan.

that many of the houses had been abandoned by their masons because of some great catastrophe.

Almaraz was greatly puzzled by the evident antiquity of the monuments and the mystery of the people who had built them, whose history was entirely unknown.

He marveled at the enormous work involved, the quarrying and moving of such great amounts of stone over long distances, all of which, he remarked with a touch of pathos, "did not even serve to keep alive the names of the architects, gods, or potentates in whose regime the structures were built."

As a final warning, he said he had to admit that all of what he had surmised was nothing but conjecture, without fundament or sort, resting on neither historical material, "which I did not have the means to consult," nor on archeological knowledge, "to which I did not have the opportunity of dedicating myself," but mostly on what he had picked up at the table from his mess companions.

Achille Francois Bazaine, born in 1811, served in Algeria, the Crimea, and Lombardy before coming to Mexico where he was made a Marshal of France in 1864. At Maximilian's court he developed a penchant for very young girls, one of whom he married in the presence of Maximilian, and was soon distracted from his military duties. To cover up his negligence and incompetence, Bazaine double-crossed Maximilian and left him in an untenable position both militarily and politically.

Responsible for the disastrous defeat of Napoleon III at Sedan in 1870, Bazaine was found guilty of negotiating with, and capitulating to, the enemy; but his sentence of degradation and death was commuted to twenty years in jail. In 1874 he escaped to Italy and thence to Madrid where he died in 1888.

For a truly scientific and detailed exploration of Teotihuacan, Almaraz said more money and more personnel were needed. But Maximilian's coffers had been emptied; the imperial government had been required to pay the full penalty for the defaulted Swiss banker's debt, all the costs of the French intervention, plus a thousand francs for every French soldier serving on Mexican soil; and the political and military situation had so deteriorated that no further attention could be paid to cultural pastimes such as the pyramids. The United States, resolutely determined not to acknowledge the existence of Maximilian's government, had continued to accredit its representative to the rival republican government of Benito Juarez. The moment the Civil War in the States was ended and it was clear that the Monroe Doctrine could once more be enforced, Napoleon III gave up his dream of a Catholic state in Central America and decided to cut his losses, leaving Maximilian in the lurch. He ordered his military commander, Marshal François Achille Bazaine, to secretly start withdrawing French troops from Mexico. Perfidiously, Bazaine even offered to sell large quantities of French arms for cash to the opposing

Diaz as a general in the republican army fighting against French interventionists.

Maximilian, Emperor of Mexico, was fetched from his quarters to be executed on a hillside outside Queretaro, on the morning of June 19, 1867, only three years after his arrival in Mexico.

Maximilian and his two remaining generals, Miramon and Mejia, were awakened to a fanfare of bugles and drums. When Maximilian asked Miramon, "Miguel, is this for the execution?" Miramon replied, "I cannot say, señor, as I have not been shot before."

General Porfirio Diaz, who had romantically escaped from prison in Puebla by lowering himself from a window on a knotted rope. When Diaz refused, Bazaine ordered the equipment destroyed rather than give it to Maximilian's weakened forces. At the same time Bazaine, despicably, persuaded Maximilian to save himself by issuing the infamous "Black Decrees," which ordered summary execution for all republicans caught in arms. That was the end. Though Maximilian had acquired adherents by his disarming manners and personal charm, he now found himself cornered. Juarez besieged him at Queretaro with the help of Porfirio Diaz. Betrayed into their hands, Maximilian was executed by firing squad on a nearby hilltop, dying like Hidalgo, crying "Viva Mexico!"

Again there was a dismemberment and disposal of valuable books and manuscripts about Mexico and its antiquities. Maximilian's confidant, Father Augustin Fischer, a Jesuit priest who drank heavily and was rumored to have numerous illegitimate children scattered about Mexico, tried to sell several of Maximilian's private papers.

139

It was an odd twist of fate that the emperor of France caused the death of Maximilian, for Maximilian, as the natural grandson of Napoleon I, would have been closer by blood to the Imperial line of France than was his cousin Louis Napoleon III, who stood in line merely as the son of Napoleon I's brother Louis and of Josephine's daughter, Hortense. There is every indication that Maximilian's natural father was the Imperial dauphin, known as the King of Rome and more fondly as l'Aiglon, son of Napoleon I, and of the Austrian Archduchess Marie Louise. As the Duke of Reichstadt, the title by which Metternich insisted l'Aiglon be known at the Hapsburg court, he was much in love with and much loved by Maximilian's mother, the Archduchess Sophie, with whom he may also have fathered Franz Joseph, Emperor of Austro-Hungary, cuckolding his legal father, the dull-witted Archduke Francis Charles of Hapsburg.

The Andrade collection, which had not been paid for, was hastily packed up by its owner during the last days of the empire and transported on muleback to Veracruz, where it was shipped to Europe and sold at auction in Leipzig for $16,500. Many of the rare printed books and pamphlets on Mexico were acquired by the American historian Hubert Howe Bancroft and now form part of the Bancroft Library at the University of California.

Maximilian's execution put the quietus on further archeological speculation about Teotihuacan. Mexicans were more interested in the perils and possibilities of their own immediate future than in the wonders of their remoter past.

11. Foreign Intervention

The world's interest in Mexican antiquities might have withered during the next decades had it not been for the efforts of three Americanized Frenchmen, two of them adventurers, one of them a robber baron, Pierre C. Lorillard.

On vacation from teaching school in New Orleans in 1850, Claude Joseph Désiré Charnay, a young man in his early twenties, was so struck by the mysterious beauty of Mexico that he went back to France to induce Napoleon III's minister of fine arts, Eugène Viollet-le-Duc, to give him an assignment to photograph Mexico's ancient ruins with a recently developed camera obscura. Carrying the dark chamber on his

Désiré Charnay deep in the Mexican jungle with his camera obscura.

back and nursing the large glass plates on which to mix his own emulsion, Charnay got back to Mexico in 1858 for a three-year jaunt from Mitla to Monte Alban, to Chichen Itza, to Uxmal, and to Palenque. The result of these travels was a folio volume containing the first but certainly the drabbest photographs ever taken of Mexican antiquities, for which Viollet-le-Duc produced an equally drab academic text in which he came to the not surprising conclusion that an advanced civilization had once covered North, Central, and South America, well before the beginning of the Christian era, reaching its apogee several centuries before the Spanish Conquest, by which time it had broken up and fallen into decadence.

Charnay followed his folio volume with a personal memoir in octavo in which he entertainingly described the frustrations of trying to photograph Mexico under the most grueling and uncomfortable conditions. More of a vulgarizer than an academician, Charnay spiced the memoir with salacious anecdotes about the attractive Mexican maids he had encountered, telling of a sixteen-year-old who was highjacked from the coach in which they were both traveling to be raped by six tall bandits; of a sterile young wife whose Yucatecan husband, believing all foreign archeologists to be doctors, begged him to examine closely his wife's malfunctioning organ, for which Charnay successfully prescribed the dexterous use of astringent aloes and a camphorated candle; and in Mexico City of the whores who would reward a statue of the Virgin Mary with portions of their nightly earnings in return for a regular flow of clients.

In the hope that the government of Napoleon III might finance him on another trip to Mexico, Charnay unctuously dedicated his opus to "the Emperor whom nothing escapes

Charnay climbed Mount Popocatepetl, from which he was able to view simultaneously through the crystal air the shining cupolas of Mexico City and the belltower of Puebla sixty miles away.

142

of that which is useful, noble or grand, who knows how to honor merit and encourage modest work."

Unlike the Abbé Brasseur, whom he admired, Charnay was not averse to traveling with the army. As a result he got himself back to Mexico in 1864, only to be told to hurry up and wait, finally succumbing to the general debacle of Bazaine's army which followed Maximilian's execution in 1867.

Still determined to succeed, Charnay spent the next twenty years looking for a backer, until he managed to convince the Carolina tobacco tycoon Pierre Lorillard to underwrite for him, in conjunction with the French authorities, a proper research expedition to Mexico. Charnay complained, not altogether unjustly, that because most writers, especially North Americans, had taken to describing the ruins of Mexico more on the basis of what casual travelers told them than on any careful exploration of the sites, he wished to obtain permission from the Mexican government to actually dig in the soil for remnants of the past.

By the time Charnay returned to Veracruz, the port was being regularly serviced by motor sailors.

Exactly twenty-two years after his first visit to Veracruz, Charnay returned in April of 1880 to find the town much improved, houses freshly painted, steeples whitewashed, cupolas ornamented with pyramidal shapes, enameled in pink and blue.

The formerly squalid square, which had been crisscrossed by muddy watercourses, was now charmingly paved with marble and adorned by a park of shade trees in which squirrels gamboled. As much of a girl watcher as Waldeck, Charnay spent his evenings admiring the pretty women in checkered and phosphorescent *cucuyos* taking the air in the arcades with their "beautiful shops and magnificent cafes." Thanks to the influence of the French, the food had also improved. There was excellent fish, edible game birds, plenty

143

of tropical fruits; and the wines were no more expensive than in Paris. Only the ubiquitous black vultures already remarked by Bullock were the same as on Charnay's earlier visit.

Thanks to some spectacular engineering by the British, Charnay was now able to travel to Mexico City all the way by train. It was a vast relief from his previous trip, when he had been obliged to use the rough post road, being jostled in one of the "chariots" drawn by fourteen mules which moved in convoys of a dozen, each headed by a majordomo. These convoys would set off at midnight, after the wandering bell-laden mules had been recaptured with lassos by groups of picturesque muleteers.

This time the train rose from the tropics into the temperate zone in serpentine leaps across barrancas more than a thousand feet deep, at the bottom of which the vegetation still remained tropical.

On the newly built railroad, Charnay ascended from sea level through grander and grander scenery, past coffee, tobacco, and banana plantations where little houses, embowered in orange groves and creepers, peeped out from enormous shade trees. Ahead were the silhouette outlines of the Sierras, dazzlingly bright and richly colored mountains dominated by the snowcapped volcanic peak of Orizaba.

As the train left the thick forests of the temperate zone, full of songbirds, changes in the scenery were brusque and varied. After crossing an arid desert, they entered mountains with deep ravines, perfect for armed robbery.

The only feature unchanged from the previous voyage was the prevalence of bandits, which obliged the train to travel with an armed escort.

At Apam the train loaded casks overflowing with "a yellowish, thick and stringy liquid, repulsive to the smell," the best pulque in Mexico, according to Charnay, "as superior to others as Chambertin is to ordinary claret."

When the train reached the plain of Otumba, it passed close to the pyramids of Teotihuacan, still covered in grass and underbrush.

On the outskirts of Mexico City Charnay noticed many pretty villas where once there had been only marshland. Inside the city, the principal square, or Zocalo, which had

144

Mexican bandits holding up a stagecoach.

In the brand-new railroad stations, rural guards armed to the teeth and adorned with large felt sombreros trimmed with silver, ribbons, and tassels lolled about waiting for bandits, whom they were expert at tracking to their hidden lairs, as most of them were converted ex-bandits. These were the famous Rurales of President Porfirio Diaz, whose method of recruiting them was to hold five bullets in his left hand and stretch out the other for a handshake. The recruit could make his choice.

been ill paved, had become a fine garden shaded by eucalyptus trees seven feet in girth and over a hundred feet high; beneath them spread a beautiful garden with a pavilion for concerts.

But the biggest change to Charnay was the absence on the streets of any priests. Since Juarez had entered the city in 1867, all the priests had vanished, going into exile or becoming private citizens, taking up business and getting married. Even the monks had taken wives or turned Protestant to serve the Bible societies from New York and Boston which had mushroomed with the influx of foreign capital solicited by General Diaz.

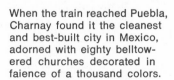

When the train reached Puebla, Charnay found it the cleanest and best-built city in Mexico, adorned with eighty belltowered churches decorated in faience of a thousand colors.

145

Operating on the theory that "two cats cannot live in the same bag," Diaz made himself supreme dictator of Mexico, a position he held for over thirty years by the simple expedient of disposing, one way or another, of any political rival.
To those who helped him, he gave jobs, on the theory that "a dog with a bone neither barks nor bites."

Manuel Romero Rubio, originator of the *cientifico* minority to fight democracy in Mexico, became Diaz' minister of interior, head of the Rurales, and strong man behind the scenes. With funds from his illegal brothels and gambling dens he organized a gang of apaches who were paid monthly to do nothing but attack enemies of the system.

José Ives Limantour. A skinny little man of French origin who considered Indians "dark, quarrelsome, lazy, thieving little men," he inherited his boss Rubio's mantle as head of the *cientificos* when Rubio died. As Minister of Finance, and power behind Diaz, he finally betrayed his new boss out of power.

Mexico's Cientificos.

While Charnay was in Mexico the *cientificos* concocted a law by which they were able to expropriate the public lands communally used by the peons so that some 50 million acres passed into private hands, often for as little as a centavo an acre. One beneficiary, Luis Terrazzas, had just become

owner of an estate of seven million acres, larger than New Jersey, on which he kept a million and a half head of cattle, while 95.5 percent of Mexico's rural families found themselves with no land. Ten million serfs were created, easily impressed into factories built by foreign investors, where the serfs were obliged to work for a pittance fourteen hours a day without even Sundays as automatic holidays. Recalcitrants, though technically free citizens, could be whipped for any infraction. Petty theft could draw two hundred lashes. Women were strung up and syringed with chili water.

If peons refused to give up the land, the Rurales and federal soldiers moved in, raping and murdering. Stubborn Yaquis, who showed title maps to their lands signed by the King of Spain, were rounded up and sold into slavery to Yucatecan sisal planters at seventy pesos a head—an ex-

tra profit for the *cientificos.* Many of the Yaqui women, like the Greek Suliotes in Byron's time, preferred to throw themselves with their babies into the sea.

Surviving Indians were left without woods, water, or any way of making a living off the land. In the United States, General U. S. Grant announced to investors that "seven million Aztecs are waiting to build railroads." Rockefellers, Aldriches, Goulds, Harrimans, Guggenheims, and McCormicks seized the opportunity to buy cheap land and hire dirt cheap labor to operate rail and mine concessions. The Creole *cientificos,* acting as middle men and legal advisers, amassed quick fortunes through large legal fees, stock manipulations, kickbacks, payoffs, and such subtle trickery as selling arms and ammunition to the Indian rebels that the government was officially exterminating.

Though millions vanished into the pockets of the *cientificos,* little of the wealth trickled down. Practically nothing was spent on schooling or education. Real wages were reduced to less than they had been a century earlier under the Spaniards.

Considering Mexicans too stupid for parliamentary democracy, the *cientificos* succeeded in making a farce of the electoral process, openly stuffing ballot boxes and

intimidating voters with bands of armed Rurales. All appointments to congress, cabinet posts, or governorships were dictated by Diaz with the connivance of the *cientificos,* yet governors and judges could be removed by a simple majority of Diaz' rubberstamp congress.

Labor organizations were outlawed, strikes put down by the army. Rebellious individuals conscripted into its ranks could be disposed of by the *ley de fuga,* "shot while trying to escape."

For opponents too much in the public eye, Diaz kept a stable of *pistoleros* who would challenge any required opponent to a duel, with usually fatal consequences. If jailed, the *pistolero* was promptly amnestied.

Judges did as they were told, and only official lawyers won their cases. The chief of police was Diaz' own nephew, Felix Diaz. Newsmen who came too close to the truth were beaten up or assassinated. One unwanted editor was sentenced to jail for material published in a fake issue of his own paper fraudulently concocted by friends of the sentencing judge. Mexican writers who sought asylum in the United States were extradited back to Mexico for punishment in return for grants to the U.S. such as the naval station at Magdalena Bay.

Foreign correspondents were subsidized to sing Diaz' praise to the world, with the result that the U.S. Secretary of State, Elihu Root, declared, "I look to Porfirio Diaz, President of Mexico, as one of the great men to be held up for the hero worship of mankind."

Here was the blueprint for a series of United States–financed dictatorships, from Mussolini to Trujillo to Franco, a system which was to pox the planet for almost a hundred years and which, though detailed by such authors as Carleton Beals, was to lead to bloodshed around the world.

Everywhere, Charnay says, he found a new spirit of initiative which had turned the governor's palace into a rendezvous for citizens, with the exception, of course, as he was quick to point out, of the vast majority of Indians. A thin veneer of progress was bandage to a running sore. In their cotton cloth and straw sombreros the peons were still not allowed on the main streets of the capital. They had to wear European trousers, which could be rented by the day from merchants on the outskirts of the city.

Considered too backward and too ignorant to govern themselves, Mexican Indians had been completely deprived of power or any say in the government by a group of Creole wheeler-dealers known as the *"cientificos,"* who thought they could "scientifically" transform Mexico into a Western state with foreign capital, operating as an elite behind the virtual dictatorship of Porfirio Diaz.

In this atmosphere of false prosperity Charnay tried unsuccessfully to rearouse the Mexicans to an interest in their historic ruins. He had developed the theory that there had once been a vast Toltec empire in central Mexico which had

Promenade of oak trees out- . side the cathedral in Mexico City's Plaza Mayor. In the evenings, "society" went there by moonlight, so the caballeros could make their conquests among beautiful women discreetly peeping out from behind their Spanish shawls.

spread its dominion from a legendary capital called Tollan as far as Teotihuacan, Toluca, Xochicalco, Cholula, and even Chichen Itza seven hundred miles to the south. From fragments of the works of Fernando de Alva Ixtlilxochitl—whom he considered every bit as trustworthy as Herodotus or Plutarch, and whose works were finally being prepared for publication by Charnay's friend, the Mexican historian Alfredo Chavero—Charnay had become convinced that the remains of the Toltec capital of Tollan were to be found in the subsoil of the modern village of Tula in the province of Hidalgo, sixteen leagues from Mexico City.

Armed with the necessary permit from a friend in the Ministry of Education, Charnay was at last able to board a train which took him past Tacuba, where he could still see the great solitary cypress under which Cortes had cried after the disaster of *La Noche Triste.* At Cuautitlan, armed with a powerful shotgun against bandits, which made his fellow passengers smile with reassurance, Charnay boarded a *diligencia* drawn by mules for a ride over a road so dusty and so rocky it caused all his fellow passengers to vomit.

At the foot of Mount Coatepetl, where the river winds through a narrow valley, the *diligencia* crossed its muddy waters at a gallop to deposit Charnay on what he believed to be the site of the once brilliant capital of the Toltecs—a quiet Indian village of 1500 souls—shaded by enormous ash trees. In the nearby fields there were only a few unpromising mounds overgrown with vegetation. But working with a gang of native diggers, Charnay soon came across large sculptured

Diligencia, or horse-drawn coach, passing Tacuba on the way from Mexico City to the town of Tula.

stones of black basalt more than two meters long and thirty centimeters in diameter, which appeared to him to be the feet of gigantic statues apparently used as caryatids (to which he gave the name "Atlanteans") designed to support a very large building.

There were also fragments of an enormous stone rattlesnake whose head had formed the base of a large column and whose tail had supported a capital much like the ones in Chichen Itza that Charnay had seen twenty years earlier. As in Chichen Itza, he also found a heavy stone ring almost two meters in diameter with a thirty-seven-centimeter hole, clearly part of a ball court.

As figures in the friezes found at Tula represented the same rulers and warriors as those at Chichen Itza, it appeared that both had been built by the same Toltecs.

Some distance away, Charnay found the remains of a large pyramid thickly covered in vegetation through which he could make out a surface with a thick coating of plaster. It was an exciting and important discovery, but even with labor so cheap that a man cost less to hire than a mule, to have tried to dig into the pyramid would have been more than Charnay could tackle with Lorillard's funds.

There was no doubt in Charnay's mind that he was on the site of ancient Tollan, and from the strong resemblance between its decorative motifs and those of faraway Chichen

View of Tula in the province of Hidalgo.

Told it was folly to look for ancient Tollan near the village of Tula, that the city was a fable which like Quetzalcoatl had never existed, Charnay was goaded into digging by the knowledge that twenty years earlier a poor shepherd boy scratching the moist ground of Tula had uncovered a vase containing five hundred ounces of gold, which he had sold for a few coppers.

In 1940 the Mexican archeologist Dr. Jimenez Moreno showed that Tula had indeed been a Toltec capital built about A.D. 900, well after the destruction and abandonment of Teotihuacan. Tula was in turn destroyed in the twelfth century by Aztec invaders who carried off much of its stonework and sculpture to build Tenochtitlan. Among the structures discovered at Tula by Charnay, the Mexican government eventually restored and reconstructed a 30-foot pyramid divided into five levels, beautifully decorated and frescoed, as well as several enormous 15-foot-high caryatids, known as "Atlanteans," armed with strange weapons.

Itza, he was convinced that a Toltec civilization had been the source of a high culture throughout Central America.

But the world of archeology, which considered Charnay unreliable and romantic, greeted his discoveries with the same reserve they greeted Heinrich Schliemann's contemporary discoveries of ancient Troy and Mycenae. They firmly denied Charnay had found Tollan.

As Charnay dug farther into the Tula fields, he found the remains of what appeared to be a whole palace, 62 feet long on one side, with an inner courtyard and garden altogether covering 2,500 square feet. On one wall was a bas-relief depicting two bearded men, which puzzled him, as they were clearly non-Indian.

On Monte del Fraile at 13,000 feet, from where he could view the Pyramid of Cholula, Charnay discovered a cemetery which he believed to be Toltec. Excavating its tombs, he came upon some chariots of terra cotta which he believed to be ancient toys that demonstrated Mesoamerican knowledge of the wheel. When told they were modern fabrications, he dropped the subject saying: "J'ai laissé tomber l'objection, qui serait une insulte à ma bonne foi." Later, more wheeled toys were found in Mesoamerica similar to the terra-cotta toy chariots modeled by the Phoenicians. The most appealing explanation for the Maya having known but not used the wheel comes from Stacy-Judd, who suggests that Yucatecan survivors from Atlantis took warning from the destruction of their former civilization engendered by over-indulgence in the wheel!

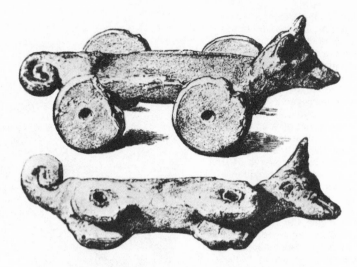

Not until the 1930s, when his excavations were finally re-examined by George C. Vaillant, who also laid the foundations for a systematic stratigraphy of central Mexico, was it realized that Charnay might have been correct. Vaillant was able to show that the artifacts at Tula placed it squarely with the Toltecs, just as Charnay had said, only at a slightly later date, between the eclipse of the great city of Teotihuacan, sometime in the eighth century A.D., and the arrival of the Aztecs in the thirteenth.

12. The First Real Digs

Charnay was surprised at the variety of human types portrayed on masks, often with considerable artistic skill: there were the features of Caucasian, Greek, Chinese, Japanese, and Negro; also Maya type heads with retreating foreheads, such as he had seen in Yucatan. They seemed to validate the theories of Viollet-le-Duc about an influx of Europeans and Asiatics, leading Charnay to comment that numerous races must have succeeded each other and amalgamated on the continent, "which, until lately, was supposed to be so new, and is in truth so old."

During fifteen years of investigation of thousands of pre-Columbian terra-cotta pottery heads and figures, art historian Alexander von Wuthenau found portraits of five different racial types: Mongoloid, Chinese, Japanese, Negroid, and all types of white people, especially Semitic types with and without beards.

Saddened by the treatment received from his contemporaries over the Tula digs, Charnay decided to attack the site of Teotihuacan to see if he could prove that it too had been a Toltec city comparable to Tula, a notion which found even less support.

Thanks to General Diaz' railway concessions, Charnay was now able to travel from Mexico City to San Juan Teotihuacan in the comfort of a railway coach in just over sixty minutes.

From San Juan, Charnay approached the pyramids on foot, his eyes falling on all kinds of fragments strewn across the fields: bits of pottery, masks, and small and large figures. There were ex-votos, idols, broken cups, stone axes, and all manner of fragments of obsidian, the volcanic glass, most often black, which could be worked into a hard cutting edge and had evidently served the ancient dwellers of the valley for cutlery, tools, and weapons. Crossing the river bed which runs through Teotihuacan, Charnay found countless obsidian pebbles of a grayish and opaque green color.

In a blistering sun Charnay climbed the larger pyramid, which he gauged to be angled at 47 degrees where the coatings of cement still adhered. It was a bright clear day, and from the summit of the pyramid Charnay was rewarded with a view of the lakes in the Valley of Mexico, the snowy peak of

Like Humboldt, Charnay found the Sun Pyramid to be divided into four stories, three of which were still visible, but his description tallies so closely with the hearsay stories repeated by Humboldt that it hardly seems original. More vivid are his descriptions of finding atop the Pyramid of the Moon a perfect obsidian earring, thin as a piece of paper, brought to the surface by ants burrowing for a nest.

Iztaccihuatl towering above the Malacinga range, and, far, far away, the faint outline of the Cordilleras.

Going Prescott one better, Charnay pictured in his imagination a great dead city as it must have once surrounded the pyramid, recreating in his mind's eye its dwellings, temples, and smaller pyramids, "coated with pink and white plaster, surrounded by verdant gardens, intersected by beautiful roads paved with red cement, the whole bathed in a flood of sunshine."

With his Indian escort, Charnay next explored the remains of the mounds known as the "Citadel," which he poetically compared to a vast tennis court whose embankment he measured as 19 feet high and 260 feet thick. Noting fifteen medium mounds and a high one in the center, he intuitively concluded that the place must have been used for public ceremonies rather than as a citadel.

Two and a half miles west of the Pyramid of the Moon, Charnay was led by his guide to some cavernous quarries, or *cuevas,* from which much of the stone to build the pyramids appeared to have been dug. There Charnay found three narrow galleries, branching off in different directions at 45-degree angles, which led to different caves, one a conglomeration of large halls supported by incredibly thin pillars, another like a rotunda, filled with human remains, which he was told were attributable to brigands who used the cave as a burial place for their victims.

154

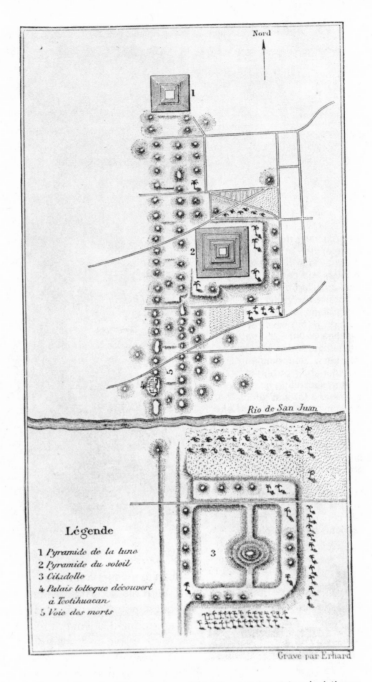

According to Charnay's guide, the caves extended three miles to the Pyramid of the Sun, and beyond, where the whole countryside was said to be undermined with caves.

As Charnay's prime interest was to dig, as he had at Tula, for remains of the ancient city of Teotihuacan, in the hope of finding remains of palaces or apartment houses to establish for the city a Toltec origin, and as diggers were needed for

Approaching the lovely baroque church at the end of a great avenue of well-watered poplars and cedars, Charnay was appalled by the way it contrasted with the hovels of the Indians, barely six feet square, within which whole families lay huddled on the beaten ground, half naked or in tatters, "suffocating in summer and freezing in winter, subsisting on a few beans and tortillas which the women ground from corn on *metate* boards kneeling in front of their hovels."

Noting in his diary that the children died mostly in their first year, and that a man earned barely a shilling a day to support a family of eight or nine, Charnay distributed a few coppers to the Indians to drink his health in pulque.

the purpose, he and his guide returned to the village of San Juan to muster volunteers.

With his accommodations in the village, Charnay was far from happy. The only place to sleep was on the floor of a bare-roomed building around a courtyard paved with brick. It was devoid of furniture, because, as he put it, "anyone who wished to, could lie beside you, and your ablutions have to be made at the well in the presence of half the village congregated in the yard."

Before the construction of the railway, Charnay remembered, the village had been a bustling relay point for mules plying to and from Mexico City, more than two thousand of them daily, when "the clapping of hands of the tortilleros was heard all day, along with copious libations of pulque." Now the village was a morgue.

Charnay attacked a terraced court fronting the Way of the Dead and found among the constructions and substructures stucco walls crisscrossing each other in all directions, over layers of ornaments, pottery, and detritus, which led him to conclude that a city had been built and rebuilt several times, and that when one building was demolished the new occupant, instead of clearing the ground of old rubbish, had simply smoothed it down and laid a new floor on the compacted detritus.

Charnay says he ate his dinner that night more to spare the feelings of his host than because he liked the menu, and also to insure by his good manners that the municipality would give him men on the morrow sufficient to start his digging.

Convinced that the village of San Juan covered part of the old city of Teotihuacan, Charnay decided to open four trenches right in the small square not far from the Plaza Mayor that was normally used for bull fighting.

The first two trenches produced no results. In the third the diggers came upon a dozen children's tombs and half a dozen adult tombs, the bones in which crumbled to dust as Charnay handled them.

The graves contained, along with a few obsidian knives, the remains of edible dogs and birds intended to feed the dead in their afterlife journey. The children were buried in circular vases with upright brims, the skeletons almost perfect, but the skulls, thin as paper, fell to pieces at a touch. From the fact that the bodies had not been cremated, Charnay deduced that he had struck a poor quarter of the ancient city.

Determined to show that Teotihuacan had been as flourishing as Tula, Charnay looked for a better spot to dig. North of the river he had noticed parts of walls, broken cement, and terraces. Settling on these, he managed in three days' digging to uncover ten rooms which formed part of a large house with inner courts, apartments on different levels, roofs supported by pillars, one chamber being 732 feet in circumference. The walls were nearly six feet seven inches thick, built of stone and mortar, incrusted with thick cement; at the

foot they sloped about three feet before becoming perpendicular.

Charnay labeled the house a "palace" because it had what appeared to be several reception rooms with stuccoed walls frescoed "like an Aubusson carpet" whose red, black, blue, yellow, and white markings were still discernible. Charnay would have liked to have unearthed a number of "sleeping accommodations" that he felt extended beyond the palace, but most of them were under an Indian's cornfield and could not be touched.

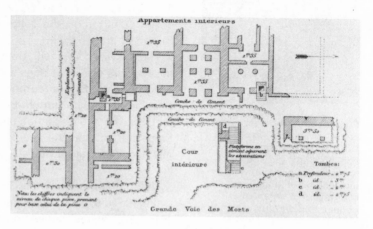

Manuel Orozco y Berra.

Convinced that he had only scratched the surface of a huge dormant city that might reveal great treasures, Charnay telegraphed messages to his friends in Mexico City, the historians Alfredo Chavero and Manuel Orozco y Berra, both professedly interested in Mexican archeology, urging them to join him to see what he had found, and to urge the Mexican government to initiate regular excavations at Teotihuacan. Neither government nor friend paid him the least heed. One friend sent word he had a headache, the other pleaded "a less poetic ailment."

As a consolation, Charnay was able to peel off some of the frescoes he had unearthed and send them to Paris, where they were put on display at the Trocadero, to arouse, in due course, enough interest among later archeologists to keep alive the prospect of further digs at Teotihuacan.

Determined also to make moldings of the stone reliefs at Palenque which he had been unable to photograph on his previous visit, Charnay finally managed to obtain the grudging approval of the Mexican government to travel elsewhere in the republic, including the rebellious areas of Yucatan, but only on condition that he take with him a colonel of artillery who was "to watch and share his labors and discoveries." Assuming, most probably correctly, that Charnay

Charnay's way of crossing the more difficult Mexican passes.

Charnay's kitchen at Palenque. Unlike Stephens and Waldeck, who had subsisted on cornmeal and iguana, one of Charnay's dinners, thanks to Mr. Lorillard, consisted of soup of purée of black beans with snail broth, Valencian olives with Arles sausage, corn-fed chicken with garlic and red peppers, fried *morne* with chives garnished with hearts of palm and asparagus tips, black bean rissoles, crêpes, American cheeses, Bordeaux and Aragon wines, coffee and Havana cigars, with Xtabentun liqueur.

was doubling as someone's agent, the government selected an amiable veteran of the war against Maximilian, Don Perez Castro. To record whatever they might discover on their travels, the Mexicans also selected a young Frenchman born in Mexico, Albert Lemaire.

At Palenque the travelers found that a stranger could still pass within a few yards of the hidden city and not see it. Much of the Temple of the Cross had given way since Charnay had first seen it twenty-two years earlier, and many of the reliefs had disappeared, the work of both scavengers and vegetation. Roots removed by previous explorers had broken up the walls and caused them further to disintegrate.

"But my admiration for this massive place, these ruined temples, these pyramids," remarked Charnay, "is profound, nay, almost overpowering."

To obtain molds of the remaining reliefs, Charnay employed a system invented by a Monsieur Lantin de Laval of France which consisted of squeezing six layers of wet paper onto the friezes and allowing the pulp to dry. With this system Charnay was able to get 325 square feet of impressions for a weight of 500 pounds instead of the 30,000 pounds it would have weighed in plaster of paris.

But the work was not easy. Almost incessant rain obliged Charnay to redo scores of the impressions. The dampness penetrated to their bones and caused vegetable mold to grow on their hats. In the mud they slithered constantly, more often on their backsides than on their feet. At night drops of water trickled down their necks from the greenish moss on the walls.

By day they were prey to swarms of insects, mostly *rodadores* and *garrapatas,* the Mexican ticks. To offset malaria they now had the benefit of quinine, made from cinchona bark, discovered in 1820 by two Frenchmen, Caventou and Pelletier, whose use had been promoted by the wife of the Spanish ambassador to Peru.

Another improvement over Charnay's first trip to Palenque —when he had survived on frightful quantities of raw cornmeal soaked in water, along with snail soup from the river— were some delicious French dinners prepared by a sophisticated cook, complete with Havana cigars, coffee, and the local liqueur called Xtabentum.

Once the paper impressions of reliefs were safely packed off to France, Charnay and the colonel set off for Chichen Itza with a guard of fifty soldiers put at their disposal by the governor of Merida to protect them against the rebellious Yucatecans, still uncontrolled since their uprising in 1847, who made forays from their safe bases in the wilder parts of eastern Yucatan and Quintana Roo.

159

The castillo Kukulkan.

This 75-foot-high pyramid has four staircases of 91 steps for a total of 364; when the upper platform is added, the sum is 365, for the days in a year. The 18 larger steps represent the 18 months of a year. The 52 panels in the large steps give a Mayan century of 52 years.

During the past decades most of the major cities of Yucatan had been burned by the rebels and half the population still lived with a weapon under one arm while the other half worked in the fields or slept.

At Chichen Itza, Charnay and his military companions climbed to the top of the Castillo, which they found still overrun with vegetation, birds, snakes, and iguanas. To avoid being ambushed by the rebels, they ensconced themselves in the main chamber and set up regular sentries.

To Charnay there was something about Chichen Itza, especially the enormous figures of idols ornamenting the frieze around the Palace of the Nuns, that reminded him of Hindu art. At Izamal, barely sixty miles away, he had been reminded by the gigantic faces built into the side of a man-made pyramid of the Sphinx in Egypt. At Uxmal he had found a Greek influence in the governor's palace; at Palenque an Assyrian motif; at Mitla Chinese motifs. Other statuary reminded him of Malaya, Cambodia, and Java, where he had traveled in the interim between his trips to Mexico. He found the storied pyramids of Yucatan much like those of Angkor Thom and Angkor Wat. All of which validated for him the theories of his first patron, Viollet-le-Duc. But to please his present patron, Pierre Lorillard, Charnay wished to do something original; he wished to rediscover and name for Lorillard what was reputed to be the greatest and least-known of Mayan ruins, Yaxchilan, on the border of Guatemala, reported by Stephens to be a phantom city.

The nunnery of Chichen Itza, much more dilapidated and overgrown than when Stephens saw it for the last time half a century earlier.

With great difficulty Charnay mounted an expedition to make his way slowly up the Usumacinta River and was within a day's journey of his goal when he discovered he had been beaten to the mark by a solitary Englishman, Alfred

The nunnery as it was seen by Stephens in 1840 (right).

Remains of a temple at
Lorillard.

Percival Maudslay, who was busy clearing the site and making remarkably beautiful drawings and photographs of its many stelae.

When Charnay finally arrived at Yaxchilan in a canoe sent down the river by Maudslay, the Englishman took one look at his expression and said with a cordial laugh, "It's all right. There is no reason why you should look so distressed. My having had the start on you was a mere chance, as it would have been mere chance had it been the other way. You need have no fear on my account, for I am only an amateur, traveling for pleasure. With you the case of course is different. But I do not intend to publish anything. Come, I have had a place got ready; and as for the ruins, I make them over to you. You can name the town, claim to have discovered it; in fact, do what you please. I shall not interfere with you in any way, and you may even dispense with mentioning my name if you so please."

After replying that he was deeply touched by the Englishman's kind manner, and "only too charmed to share with him the glory of having explored the city," Charnay proceeded to ignore his host. He named the city Lorillard "in honor of the munificent man who partly defrays the cost of the expedition," a name which hardly outlasted Charnay's stay in the Phantom City, and would have been unknown to the world except as an advertisement for tobacco had Charnay not devoted a chapter to it in *The Ancient Cities of the New World,* which he brought out on his return to France, a book more remarkable for its lithographs, mostly copies of the work of others, than for its pedestrian text. After one last

Employed by the British colonial service, Maudslay insisted he had come to Central America merely to escape the rigors of an English winter. Altogether Maudslay made seven expeditions to Central America, spending considerable periods at the ruins of Copan, Quirigua, Palenque, Yaxchilan, Tikal, and Chichen Itza. The results—in the form of casts, magnificent photographs of the ruins and particularly of the hieroglyphic texts, maps and plans, and the extremely good drawings of the glyphs, made by his companion Miss Annie Hunter—were published between 1889 and 1902, in a twenty-volume edition under the perhaps purposely vague title of *Biologia Centrali-Americana or contributions to the knowledge of the flora and fauna of Central America.*

Maudslay had struggled into Copan with a team of mules hauling tons of plaster of paris, determined to make molds of the stelae. When the molds eventually reached England they were ignominiously consigned to the basement of the South Kensington Museum.

Alfred Percival Maudslay at work.

163

At Lorillard City, Charnay found a stone lintel which he considered to be by far the most wonderful monument he had seen in America. Assuming it depicted a ceremony in honor of Quetzalcoatl, he interpreted the kneeling figure to be a priest passing a rope through his tongue. Charnay quoted Sahagun and Bishop Landa to the effect that priests did penance by running as many as four or five hundred sticks, twice as thick as a thumb, and fastened together in long cords, through their tongues, their ears, and their private parts. He also quoted Clavigero, who says the blood which flowed from these self-inflicted wounds was carefully kept on the leaves of a plant with symmetrical leaves called *acxoyatl.* The worshippers of Siva, the Hindu god of destruction, and those of his wife Kali, were wont to torture themselves by drawing a rope through their pierced tongues.

trip to Yucatan in 1886, Charnay retired to Algiers, where he wrote two romantic novels entitled *An Indian Princess* and *Across the Virgin Forest,* dealing with the beauty of the Indian and mestiza women of Mexico, whose "clear skin, beautiful flesh and thin embroidered shirts outlining their firm breasts" he could not get out of his system. One of them, "with ebony hair, a tunic of light gauze which barely disguised the beauty of her body, eyes full of timid promises," he admitted nearly having stayed to marry: "Only with great courage was I able to rouse myself in the night, saddle my mule, and make a rapid exit."

Before he died Charnay translated into French the letters of Cortes to Charles V and the *Histoire de l'Origine des Indiens* of J. F. Ramirez; but his main contribution was to have taken pick and shovel to the ruins of Mexico and shown that beneath the soil the remains of great cities were there for the digging.

164

13. Probing in Depth

On a reportorial and descriptive level, Charnay had walked in John Lloyd Stephens' footsteps. On a more philosophical and anthropological level, Brasseur de Bourbourg was followed by one of the most extraordinary and perhaps unjustly neglected of Mayaland adventurers, Augustus le Plongeon. The son of a French navy commodore who had married the daughter of the governor of Mont-Saint-Michel, Le Plongeon was neglected because his notions about the Maya and their possible connection with the lost continent of Atlantis became such anathema to academicians they were treated with the contempt reserved for the notions of his contemporary, Charles Piazzi Smyth, Astronomer Royal for Scotland, on the subject of the Great Pyramid of Cheops.

Both men, instead of propounding long-winded treatises on the available ignorance about their subjects, were bold enough to explore in the field notions outrageous to their blinkered Victorian compeers.

In New York in his middle forties, Le Plongeon married an English girl of twenty-two, then living in Brooklyn, Alice Dixon. Together they sailed for Central America in the spring of 1873 for what turned out to be twelve years in the wilds of Yucatan, most of it spent in the bush. In Merida, the capital, Le Plongeon learned to speak Maya before setting off for an intensive survey of the ruins of Chichen Itza, which had once more been engulfed by the jungle and was under attack from the Yucatan *sublevados*. When the army could no longer protect the Le Plongeons in the charred shell of the hacienda at Chichen Itza, they moved to a fortified church three miles away at Pisté. From there they walked each day to the site of the ancient ruins, where they surveyed scores of buildings,

Alice Le Plongeon.

165

Augustus Le Plongeon.

Born on the island of Jersey in 1826, the year that his idol Stephens discovered the work of Del Rio, young Le Plongeon's first adventure occurred at the age of 14 on his way to the Americas, when he became one of two survivors from a shipwreck. After a stint in South America learning Spanish, he found himself in California in time for the Gold Rush of '49. There he became county surveyor for the city of San Francisco, practiced law, and acquired the degree of doctor of medicine.

After some round-the-world traveling, he was back in Peru in the 1860s to set up a private hospital in which he applied electricity to medicinal baths for the poor and for victims of revolutions. In his spare time he studied the architectural ruins of the Incas and pre-Incas, producing a couple of religious books on Jesus and a manual on photography. His sensitivity to unorthodox but avant garde ideas was such that he concluded from the strata of oyster shells around the Bolivian ruins of Tiahuanaco that the great and mysterious city must once have been at sea level, foreshadowing by more than half a century the work of H. S. Bellamy.

took more than five hundred photographs, and made twenty careful sheets of mural drawings.

Because of his mastery of the Mayan language and his intrepid but gentle nature, Le Plongeon, who often ventured with his wife deep into the forest far from village or inhabited place, found the natives "always respectful, honest, polite unobtrusive, patient and brave." He attributed the ferocity of the *sublevados* to their reaction against a ghastly system of peonage enforced by the sisal planters of Yucatan, against which the natives had no redress but to revolt.

Gradually endearing himself to the Maya, who gave him the affectionate nickname of Great Black Beard, Le Plongeon got his new friends to confide in him much of the lore they normally kept rigorously secret from the hated Spaniards, lore for which many of their ancestors had been hanged or burned at the stake.

Like Carlos Castañeda in our day, Le Plongeon learned that the native Indians in his day still practiced magic and divination, that their wise men were able to surround themselves with clouds and even appear to make themselves invisible, materializing strange and amazing objects. Sometimes, says Le Plongeon, the place where they were operating would seem to shake as if an earthquake were occurring, or whirl around and around as if being carried away by a tornado. Sometimes they appeared to be bathed in bright and resplendent light, and flames seemed to issue from the walls only to be extinguished by invisible hands in the most profound obscurity where flashes of lightning made the dark appear darker.

Beneath the prosaic life of the Indians of his day in Yucatan, Le Plongeon concluded that there flowed "a rich living current of occult wisdom and practice, with its sources in an extremely ancient past, far beyond the purview of ordinary historical

166

Le Plongeon says that a third account of the sinking of Atlantis was written on the lintel of a door of the inner chamber at the southeastern end of the building at Uxmal called Akab-Oib, as intact in his day as when it was finished by the sculptor's chisel. The inscription, says Le Plongeon, "is a memorial commemorating the destruction of Mu, the Lands of the West, whence came the Sacred Mysteries." But his method of decipherment left much to the imagination.

Every day, all over the land, says Le Plongeon, working men in the haciendas were pitilessly and arbitrarily flogged by their overseers, then put in stocks overnight so as not to miss a day's work. Were they, says he, to lay their grievances before the owner of the hacienda, their only redress was to receive a double ration of lashes for daring to complain. If they lodged a complaint before a judge, "as by law they had the right," he, of course, "is the friend or relative of the planter. He himself may be a planter. On his own plantation he has servants who are treated in like manner."

Nor could Le Plongeon interfere on behalf of some poor man being whipped for some trifling cause, lest the victim receive a more severe punishment later.

research." He felt that occasionally the mask was lowered sufficiently for him to glimpse "a world of spiritual reality, sometimes of indescribable beauty, again of inexpressible horror."

From what he learned of the lore of the Maya it became clear to Le Plongeon that the pre-Columbian Maya had practiced mesmerism, induced clairvoyance, and used magic mirrors to predict the future. From a 150-year-old Indian, Le Plongeon learned that men still existed who could decipher meanings in the mysterious hieroglyphs scattered about the ruined cities of the Maya, which contained the history of the people who had inhabited the land.

From glyphs on the southeast wall of what Le Plongeon called the Gymnasium at Chichen Itza, he says he was able to interpret the word Chac-Mool and pinpoint a spot on which to dig for what he was lead to believe might be an effigy of this ancient character.

The undertaking seemed wildly implausible. The diggers descended painfully more than twenty-four feet, and they were about to give up when they struck a hard surface, revealing what Le Plongeon considered one of the greatest archeological discoveries of the Americas, an astonishing piece of sculpture, not in relief but in the round.

So impressed was he with his find that he wished to display it to the world at the centennial ceremonies in Philadelphia in 1876. Only how to get it there?

With nothing but his engineering ingenuity and some tree trunks and vines, Le Plongeon and his Mayan workers managed to raise the multi-ton monolith to the surface and drag it by oxcart through the jungle toward Merida. There the local authorities immediately claimed the trophy, only to be relieved of it by a warship from the central government, which decided it belonged to Mexico City, where it reclines to this day, still as

Augustus and Alice Le Plongeon with the Chac-Mool they unearthed from twenty-four feet beneath the soil at Chichen Itza, which they wished to exhibit at the 1876 Centennial.

Accused of promulgating notions on ancient America contrary to the opinion of men regarded as authorities on American archeology, Le Plongeon replied, "But who are these pretended authorities? Certainly not the doctors and professors at the head of the universities and colleges in the United States; for not only do they know absolutely nothing of ancient American Civilization, but, judging from letters in my possession, the majority of them refuse to learn anything concerning it. Can they interpret one single sentence of the books in which the learning of the Maya sages, their cosmogonic, geographical, religious and scientific attainments are recorded? From what source have they derived their pretended knowledge? Not from the writings of the Spanish chroniclers, surely. These only wrote of the natives as they found them at the time, and long after the conquest of America by their countrymen. The so-called learned men of our days are the first to oppose new ideas and the bearers of these."

enigmatic and unexplained as when it was dug up by Le Plongeon.

Disappointed, Le Plongeon sent a set of photographs and smaller artifacts to Philadelphia, but they too were waylaid and eventually fell into the hands of Stephen Salisbury, Jr., a wealthy bachelor and philanthropist from Worcester, Massachusetts, active in the American Antiquarian Society. As a result, though Le Plongeon failed to make his mark at Philadelphia, Salisbury agreed to publish reports from Le Plongeon in the society's journal. It was a pleasant association, for a while; but Le Plongeon's speculations were soon too much for his New England associates. Anyone who could speak of cycles of existence in more advanced planets and worlds than the present was likely to be in trouble with an establishment, many of whom still subscribed to a Biblical origin for the world sometime in the fifth millennium B.C.

Even Le Plongeon's notion that intimate communication had existed between the inhabitants of the Western Hemisphere and Asia, Africa, and Europe at a much earlier date than anyone else considered possible, though subscribed to by Sigüenza and by Brasseur, caused a lot of heads to shake.

168

One of several English translations of the *Ramayana,*
printed with the original
Sanskrit text.

The idea that the Phoenicians might have crisscrossed the
Atlantic long before Columbus was shocking enough; Le
Plongeon went further. He suggested as an explanation for the
extraordinary similarities between the architecture, sculpture,
and artifacts of Central America and those of Asia, Africa, and
Europe, that Mayan colonists had sailed *westward* from
Central America to develop civilizations in Polynesia, Indo-
china, Burma, India, the Persian Gulf, Babylonia, and Egypt,
all of this several millennia before Christ.

In support of this revolutionary thesis he pointed to the
Mayan legends of adepts known as Naacal, or "the exalted,"
who were reported to have set out across the world to teach
others their language, architecture, and astronomy. Le Plongeon quoted the third-century B.C. Hindu sage-historian
Valmiki's epic of *Ramayana* (in Hippolyte Fauché's translation) to describe the conquest of the southern parts of the
Indochinese peninsula in remote antiquity by a people known
as great navigators, terrible warriors, learned architects,
famous for their beautiful women and inexhaustible treasures.

Valmiki is said to have received the information from
Narana, high priest of the Rishi temple at Ayhodia, who read
to him the ancient records, but Valmiki is also accused of
having used poetic license in his own version.

Le Plongeon suggested that Valmiki's Nagas were in fact
the ancient Maya who traveled along the shore of the Indian
Ocean, reached the Indus River, and then went north to Kabul.
Others, he maintained, had continued westward across the
Indian Ocean, to the Persian Gulf, whence they had reached
Babylon, Syria, and finally Egypt. He quoted the Chaldean
historian Berosus to the effect that civilization was brought to
Mesopotamia by Oannes, who came from the Persian Gulf,
pointing out that *oaana* in Maya means "he who has his
residence in the water."

Le Plongeon added that the advent of the early Chaldeans
in Mesopotamia was historically coincident with the origins of
the art of writing, the building of cities, and the cultivation of
the sciences, especially astronomy. He also pointed out that
the Egyptians claimed their ancestors were strangers who
arrived across the Isthmus of Suez to settle on the banks of
the Nile, bringing their worship of the sun, along with the art
of writing, several thousand years before the enthronement of
Menes and the official inception of the history of Egypt. Among
the many similar words in Akkadian and Mayan, such as *ma*
for place, *naa* or *nana* for mother, and *tab* for tie, Le Plongeon pointed out that in both languages *kul* was the name
for seat or rump and *kun* for the *mulieris pudenda.*

Not content with his blockbusting reconstruction of ancient
history, Le Plongeon plunged into the even more controversial

One of the principal arguments against Le Plongeon was his apparently arbitrary interpretation of the Troano Codex. According to Le Plongeon, the author of the Troano manuscript devoted several pages at the beginning of the second part of his work to a minute description of the various phenomena attending the disastrous collapse of Atlantis, referred to in the text as the ten countries of Mu. Le Plongeon's version reads: "The year six Kan, and the eleventh Muluc, in the month of Zac there occurred terrible earthquakes which continued without intermission until the thirteenth Chuen. The country of hills and mud, the 'Land of Mu' was sacrificed. Being twice upheaved, it suddenly disappeared during the night, the basin being continually shaken by volcanic forces. Being confined, these caused the land to sink and rise several times and in various places. At last the surface gave way, and the ten countries were torn asunder and scattered in fragments: unable to withstand the force of the seismic convulsions, they sank with their sixty-four millions of inhabitants, eight thousand and sixty years before the writing of this book."

The fact that the cataclysm was said to have occurred on the thirteenth Chuen, says Le Plongeon, may account for the still lingering superstition about bad luck being attached to the number. According to Le Plongeon, it was as a result of this catastrophe that the Maya started computing their new calendar on a base thirteen with weeks of thirteen days, centuries of four times thirteen years, and a great cycle of thirteen times twenty or two hundred and sixty years. Was it chance, he asked, that the Platonic date of 9500 B.C. coincided so precisely with his date for the inception of the Maya calendar?

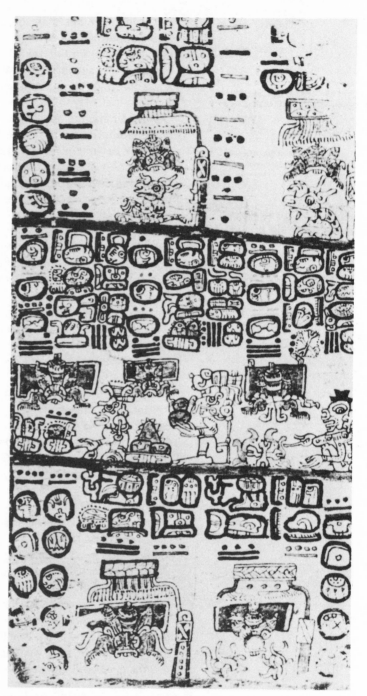

subject of Atlantis. At Chichen Itza he says he found a relief in a room sheltered from the elements which he deciphered as confirmation of Brasseur's "translation" of the Codex Tro-Cortesianus, saying it described in glyphs a cataclysm in which an island continent had sunk beneath the seas.

Later Le Plongeon claimed the discovery of a fragment of a

170

Le Plongeon quotes the Codex Cortesianus, which he calls more prolix than the Troano, to give further details on the collapse of Atlantis. "By his strong will, Homen caused the earth to tremble after sunset; and during the night, Mu, the country of hills and mud, was submerged." Homen, explains Le Plongeon, was the overturner of mountains, the god of earthquakes, the wizard who made all things move like a mass of worms, the volcanic forces anthropomorphized and then deified. "The Maya," says Le Plongeon, "deified all phenomena of nature and their causes, then represented them in the shape of human beings or animals. Their object was to keep for their initiates the secrets of their science."

Le Plongeon's translation— or, better, his interpretation— continues: "Mu, the life of the basin, was submerged by Homen during the night. The place of the dead ruler is now lifeless; it moves no more, after having twice jumped from its foundations. The king of the deep, while forcing his way out, has shaken it up and down, has killed it, has submerged it. Twice Mu jumped from its foundations. It was then shaken up and down violently by the earthquake."

According to Le Plongeon, one page of the Troano Codex depicts Queen Moo (held by the hair) falling into the hands of her enemies on the ninth day of the tenth month of the year Kan; the seventh Eb of month Yax, year Kan. He says the picture shows the queen traveling to the east across the sea. In the next panels Queen Moo is on her knees in supplication, and, symbolized as a black macaw bird, is losing hold of a Mayaland politically divided, as shown by the severed deer. Ingenious as Le Plongeon's interpretations may be, modern students dispute his identifications and suggest that the deer is more likely the symbol of a constellation.

mural painting on the walls of an apartment in one of the edifices at Kabah which to him again confirmed Brasseur's date from the Tro-Cortesianus manuscript describing the submersion of ten countries, among them the land of Mu, which to Le Plongeon might have been Plato's Atlantis. The codex, said Le Plongeon, also described the formation of a

171

According to Le Plongeon, this is a representation of Prince Coh in the heat of battle, overshadowed by the winged serpent, the genius of the Maya, who fights at his side and leads his followers to victory. Le Plongeon maintains that this is not a representation of Kukulkan, normally the image of the rulers of the country, but of the winged serpent Nonoca Can, the protective genius of the Maya, a confusion, says Le Plongeon, which authorities on the Maya were constantly falling into.

MAYA	EGYPTIAN

Comparison between Mayan and Egyptian alphabets.

strangely crooked line of islands known to the Maya as the Land of the Scorpion, and to us as the West Indies.

Later still, at Xochicalco, Le Plongeon says he deciphered another inscription which appeared to memorialize the same catastrophe.

When Americanists disputed his and Brasseur's deciphering of these glyphs, Le Plongeon pointed out that until Brasseur had found the Codex Tro-Cortesianus, and then rediscovered Bishop Landa's work in Madrid, no Americanist even knew in what language the codices were written. He complained that none of the Americanists who claimed to be authorities on American paleography could even interpret with certainty more than a dozen Mayan glyphs and none could translate an entire sentence. In his opinion the greater part of what had been published in his day on the subject of Mayan writings could only be ranked with comic literature—not very amusing at that. "Even the beautifully printed papers of the Smithsonian Institution on the subject are as meaningless as they are pretentious; and I challenge any Americanist, authorized or not authorized, to disprove this assertion."

When a member of the Société Ethnologique de Paris warned Le Plongeon not to support Brasseur, "or you will kill your own reputation and lose the fruits of your labors: all authorized Americanists will condemn you as they have Brasseur," Le Plongeon replied in the words of Themistocles: "Strike me, but hear me!"

Anyone looking carefully at Le Plongeon's analysis of a set of tableaux which he found in what he called a mausoleum at Chichen Itza can readily appreciate his imaginative flights of fancy, but also cannot help but be impressed by the originality of his interpretation. From the writings of his opponents it is clear that, as was done to Emmanuel Velikovsky a century later, they usually did not even trouble to check what he had to say, considering his notions a priori too wild to be credited.

Le Plongeon's claim that he had deciphered the totem of Queen Moo as a bird eating hearts, and that of her brother-husband Prince Aac as a turtle, and that their story could be the source of the Egyptian myth of Isis and Osiris was too much for Americanists to swallow, especially when Le Plongeon suggested that Queen Moo had traveled from Mayaland to Egypt to be welcomed and made queen again by her former co-nationals.

When Le Plongeon declared that one-third of the ancient Egyptian words he had deciphered were the same as Maya words and that the grammatical forms of the two languages were similar, he finally got some support. Pierre Lorillard gave him a subsidy with which to decipher more ancient Mayan characters.

172

Le Plongeon says that the circle divided by a cross into four parts to which wings are added symbolized "the sacred four builders," the Dyan-Chohans of the Hindu occultists which are similarly portrayed in Egypt, Assyria, and in Guatemala. He says they are the Kabiri and Titans of Hesiod's theogony, the Amshaspands of the Mazdeans, the Elohim and Seraphs of the Hebrews, the Archangels of the Christians and Mohammedans, the four Canobs of the Maya, heavenly architects emanating from the "Great Infinite One" who evolved the material universe from chaos.

GNOMON at MAYAPAN

Le Plongeon's illustration of how the Maya, like the Egyptians, computed latitude with gnomons.

Most interesting to Le Plongeon, who was evidently a Mason, was his discovery of what he called evidence of Masonic rites in Mayan sculpture, from which he deduced that "the sacred mysteries" had been practiced in ancient Mayaland as early as 11,500 years before, and that modern Masonry was but a great-grandchild of these mysteries.

He also believed that he had learned at the fountainhead the meaning of several of the symbols indicating that the old initiation rites had been similar in all countries, designed to give a better understanding of the laws that govern the material and spiritual world, thus bringing man closer into contact with the deity.

Le Plongeon appears to have been the first to realize that buildings at Chichen Itza were used as astronomical observatories. From the design of a gnomon at Mayapan he concluded that the Maya had been able to calculate both latitude and longitude.

There was no doubt in his mind that the Maya had been accomplished mathematicians, astronomers, and navigators, familiar with plane and spherical trigonometry, which enabled them to compute the size of the world, estimate the distance from pole to pole, and calculate the length of a meridian. He believed they had embodied, as did the Egyptians, their cosmogonic and religious conceptions into their sacred buildings, particularly the pyramids.

When, from the measurements he made of various Mayan buildings, Le Plongeon found that only the meter appeared to give figures in round numbers, he deduced that the Maya may have divided the circle into 400 units instead of the 360 of the Egyptians, and had taken as their unit of measure a 40-millionth of the world's circumference.

In support of Le Plongeon, it is established that the Maya described the circle by three names: *ca-an* or "two-serpent" meaning the upper arch of heaven; *ca-bala* meaning "two occult," or hidden; and *can-bak* for a full circle meaning both "circular serpent" and the number 400.

Le Plongeon further noted that many of the pyramids of Yucatan were twenty-one meters in height and that their vertical planes appeared to be inscribed in half a circumference whose diameter formed the ground line of the sacred buildings; so he figured that esoterically these buildings represented the earth. In this he was also prophetically correct.

Outraged at the vandalism that was being perpetrated in Mayaland, often in the name of science, by individuals breaking up the carvings *in situ* and transporting them for sale to European and American museums, Le Plongeon worked for years to copy, photograph, and make moldings of as many glyphs and carvings as he could manage.

173

Returning to New York in 1885 after twelve years in Yucatan, blue-eyed and with a brick-dust complexion, but balding, and with a long snowy patriarchal beard, Le Plongeon settled in Brooklyn with his wife Alice.

The many moldings he had laboriously and expensively brought back from Mayaland he offered to the Metropolitan Museum, but the director, who had eyes only for classical European art, put them in the cellar "for want of space"; and there they remained.

Complaining that he and his wife had "lifted in part at least, the veil that has hung so long over the history of mankind in America in remote ages," Le Plongeon asked if it was to be allowed to fall again. "Will no efforts be made by men of wealth and leisure in the United States, to remove it altogether?"

The answer, for the moment, was no.

To arouse further interest in exploration in Mayaland, Le Plongeon hinted at the existence of old Maya books, the writings of the H'Menes, or wise men, of Yucatan, which he said had been buried long before the advent of the Spaniards lest they fall into the hands of the Nahuatl conquerors from Tula. He said he would see to their disinterment, but only on condition the U.S. government agreed to protect such treasures against arbitrary seizure by the Mexicans, something the Department of State was unwilling to consider.

The only real friend and supporter Le Plongeon acquired in New York was a young Englishman, James Churchward, whose ideas on the antiquity of civilization on this planet coincided remarkably with his own, except that Churchward's lost continent of Moo, or Mu, was in the Pacific, different from Plato's continent of Atlantis in the Atlantic. Like Le Plongeon, Churchward based his information on the decipherment of some very ancient tablets which he said had been written by the same Naacal priesthood mentioned by Le Plongeon but which Churchward said originated not in Yucatan, but in the

In Le Plongeon's analysis, this panel represents Queen Moo as a child seated on the back of a peccary, or wild American boar, under a royal umbrella of feathers which Le Plongeon says was the emblem of royalty in Chaldea, India, and Egypt, as well as in Mayaland. Queen Moo, says Le Plongeon, is consulting a H'Men, or wise man, who is revealing her fate by reading the tints of vapors rising from an armadillo shell that is being slowly cracked by the fire of a brazier.

Le Plongeon says that facing the Queen sits the soothsayer, whom he judges by the blue and yellow feathers of his ceremonial mantle to be a priest of high rank. The scroll issuing from the seer's mouth is seen as representing his prognosis, and the position of his hand is said to have a special significance for occultists. The winged serpent represents the protective genius of the Mayan Empire. Behind the priests, says Le Plongeon, are the Queen's ladies in waiting.

Here, says Le Plongeon, Queen Moo is no longer a child but a comely young woman seated under the royal umbrella accompanied by a suitor; she is consulting a priest, or H'Men, whose face is concealed by an owl's head. According to custom, says Le Plongeon, an old lady acting as spokeswoman tells the priest the young man sitting on the stool wishes to marry the queen. But the young queen refuses, as is indicated, according to Le Plongeon, by the reversed direction of the scroll issuing from her mouth.

Le Plongeon adds that it was the custom among the Maya, as among the Egyptians, Chaldeans, and Greeks, for girls of royal blood to marry their brothers, hence the impossibility of the present marriage.

Le Plongeon's reconstruction of Chichen Itza building, from Stacy-Judd.

It was said of Le Plongeon that his "carefully detailed analyses and conclusions were founded upon conditions in the facade which never existed." It was a problem of restoration and reconstruction. According to Stacy-Judd, Le Plongeon mis-reconstructed the "Temple of the Tigers" at Chichen Itza and made several mistakes.

lost Pacific continent of Mu, mother country of colonists who had later developed Mayaland.

Churchward described having come across the Naacal tablets as a civil servant working for famine relief in India—though transparently an agent of British Intelligence. Churchward described entering a monastery in a valley near the headwaters of the Brahmaputra, where he was befriended by a high priest who eventually began to teach him to decipher inscriptions in a language the priest believed to have been the original language of mankind. Finally the old priest, then in his seventies, whom Churchward described as a "great master," last survivor of the Naacal priesthood, brought forth some sun-baked old tablets, written in the language of the Naacal priests, very dusty, which he said were records of the geology, history, and religion of Mu as well as of the cataclysmic disaster which had overcome that continent.

Le Plongeon's regard for his fellow Mason Churchward became such that he showed him much of his unpublished work on Yucatan and in the end bequeathed him his literary estate. As birds of a feather, Le Plongeon and Churchward became fair game for any academic with a shotgun.

In 1908, at the age of eighty-three, Le Plongeon died without anything having been done about the "hidden books" and without having been able to return to Yucatan. Twelve years later, in 1920, when his wife, Alice, realized her own death was imminent, she entrusted to a Mrs. Henry Blackwell the notes, photographs, and floor plans of the location of the Maya books in the ruins of Uxmal and Chichen Itza. But nothing was done with this tenuous lead, at least not for another twenty years; meanwhile the spiritual and intellectual achievements of the Mayas were once more ignored, and the archeological quest in Mayaland reverted to a materialist search for loot to adorn the world's museums.

Le Plongeon's chronology, which filled the gap between Plato's destruction of Atlantis in about 9500 B.C. and the historical record of Babylon and Egypt some five thousand years later, was too outrageous for his contemporaries, as was his

175

Stephen Salisbury, one of the founders of the American Antiquarian Society.

Edward H. Thompson after he had been in Yucatan for almost a quarter of a century.

overtly expressed distaste for the endless bloodshed perpetrated on the planet by the Church in the name of Christ.

Disappointed in Le Plongeon, Stephen Salisbury, Jr., contrived with Charles P. Bowditch, the guiding light of the Peabody Museum of Anthropology in Cambridge, to send a more controllable young man to Yucatan to be their eyes and ears in Mayaland. To pay his way and insure him a free hand to explore, they hit upon the stratagem of having him appointed U.S. Consul to Yucatan and Campeche, using the influence of their fellow member, the senator from Massachusetts, George F. Hoar, to get the President to make the appointment.

Ironically, the young man, Edward H. Thompson, a jovial blue-eyed six-footer, also from Worcester, Massachusetts, came to the attention of Salisbury because of an article he had written for *Popular Science Monthly* while still a student at Worcester Polytechnic Institute, pointedly entitled "Atlantis Not a Myth," in which Thompson suggested that the mysterious civilization of the Maya on the peninsula of Yucatan might have been a broken branch of the civilization that had once existed on the lost continent of Atlantis.

Fired by Brasseur's books, Thompson argued that although there was no proof of the Atlantis theory, a tradition so widespread and a legend so persistent must have some basis in history, which made it legitimate "to hold as probable the notion that at some time in the remote past a group of people representing a civilization of which we have lost all trace, made their influence felt upon the races indigenous to Mexico and Yucatan."

Thompson pointed to the traditions of widely separate peoples concerning a mysterious appearance on the shores of the Gulf of Mexico of the People of the Serpent, or Chanes. According to the legends, light-skinned beings, tall and blue-eyed, had landed at Tamoanchan, near Tuxpan in the Tampico district, wearing strange garments and emblems like entwined serpents on their foreheads. The sides of their vessels were said to have shone like the scales of serpents' skins. Thompson pointed out that the leaders of the "Ulmecas" were known as Chanes, or among the Mayas, as Canob, "Serpents' Wise Men," or Ah Tzai, "People of the Rattlesnake."

As the article appeared three years before Ignatius Donnelly brought out his best seller on Atlantis, Thompson's article attracted enough attention to get him the job as the youngest U.S. consul ever to be sent to Mexico.

With his bride and baby daughter, Thompson arrived in Yucatan in 1885, the year that Le Plongeon left for good.

Like Le Plongeon, Thompson threw himself into the job with enthusiasm, learned to speak fluent Mayan, and took off

into the bush to hear from the natives firsthand their legends as they macheted their way along jungle trails, surveyed ruined cities, or squatted at night around campfires. Traveling light and living on the food of the Indians, Thompson soon visited over a hundred ancient cities and temple centers. In his own words he became "almost a Maya in the belief that a close study of the descendants of the ancient builders and cabinet makers might be of aid in reconstructing the ideas and methods of times long past."

But somehow Thompson either lacked the spark of Le Plongeon or did not make the proper contacts. He says he soon numbered among his friends members of the H'Menes, or wise men, of the modern Maya, and that he became an initiate of the Sh'Tol Brothers, one of the dominant secret societies of the Maya; but it was evident, even to him, that the society was no more "than a fading remembrance of some body among the ancients comparable to the Masons."

Unlike Le Plongeon, to whom the Maya had given one of the nicknames they reserved for those they admired, Ahmeexnal, "he of the long beard," Thompson was always respectfully referred to as Don Eduardo.

With neither the knowledge of Mayan glyphs nor the imaginative curiosity of Le Plongeon, Thompson had little basis from which to interpret the carved figures on the buildings he discovered. Yet the dry descriptions of the ruins he found and forwarded to Cambridge were evidently more satisfactory to his patrons than Le Plongeon's fanciful and potentially boat-rocking conceits.

Thompson was most adept at satisfying his patrons with the enormous efforts he expended on producing for them molds of the facades of buildings such as those at Labna, which measured more than a thousand square feet, the arrival

Atlantean figure of a painted stone from Chichen Itza's upper Temple of the Jaguars.

177

One of the intricate facades Thompson was requested to reproduce for exhibition in the United States.

of which in Boston only prompted them to ask for even bigger examples from Uxmal. This next job cost Thompson fourteen horrendous months in a fever-stricken area where one by one his forty workers turned into "yellow-skinned caricatures of their former selves." Delirious at the end, Thompson nevertheless managed to deliver to Chicago the enormous molds for their 1890 World's Fair. His reward was to be befriended by the meat magnate Allison V. Armour, who provided him with sufficient funds to achieve his life's ambition: to become the owner of the ruins of Chichen Itza. For the equivalent of about seventy-five dollars Thompson bought himself almost a hundred square miles of jungle and untold acres of prime Mayan ruins, the whole parcel accessible only by jungle footpath, along which on the night he took possession Thompson stumbled over the bones of the last inhabitant of the burned-down hacienda, murdered by the *sublevados*.

The ancient ruins were familiar to Thompson from having acted as Maudslay's assistant there two years earlier, surveying, measuring, and photographing, though no digging had

The Chichen Itza Cenote, alive with iguanas, is an oval-shaped opening in the rocky crust with a diameter of 180 feet, and craggy sides, which fall perpendicularly 60 feet to the rim of the water. Forty feet below the dark green surface is a layer of mud. One of the legends that spurred Thompson to submerge himself into this mud was contained in a report to Charles V from the mayor of the nearby Yucatan town of Valladolid written in 1579: "The Lords and principal personages of the land had the custom, after sixty days of abstinence and fasting, of arriving by daybreak at the mouth of the Cenote and throwing into it Indian women belonging to each of these lords and personages, at the same time telling these women to ask for their masters a year favorable to his particular needs and desires. The women being thrown in, unbound, fell into the water with great force and noise. At high noon, those that could, cried out loudly and ropes were let down to them. After the women came up, half dead, fires were built around them and copal was burned before them. When they recovered their senses, they said that below, there were many people of their nation, men and women, and that they had received them. When they tried to raise their heads to look at them, heavy blows were given them, and when their heads were inclined downward beneath the water, they seemed to see many deeps and hollows, and they, the people, responded to their queries concerning the good or the bad year that was in store for their masters."

179

been done other than what had been accomplished by Le Plongeon.

During the nearly three decades Thompson spent in Chichen Itza from 1885 to 1910 he somehow did not manage to produce as much data as had Le Plongeon in three months. He did, however, find a lintel with a date deciphered as A.D. 618, which was considered a coup. But most of his reports still lie unpublished in the vaults of the Worcester archeological library.

Thompson's main claim to fame was to end in his undoing: the dredging of the Sacred Cenote at Chichen Itza. Having read in Landa that the well was used for sacrificial offerings, both human and precious, Thompson was determined to produce from it artifacts to adorn the Peabody Museum in Cambridge. The prospect of descending sixty feet below the surface of the water into forty feet of pitch black mud meant getting some efficient diving gear and a certain expertise, both of which he obtained on Boston's Long Wharf from a Captain Ephraim Nickerson.

After years of dredging, and several almost fatal dives during which he ruptured his eardrums, Thompson eventually

180

came up with enough gold, jade, and pretty artifacts to satisfy his Boston sponsors, to whom the artifacts were clandestinely smuggled and discreetly kept from public notice. Only when Thompson rashly publicized the results of his dives in the New York *Times* was the Mexican government aroused to sue him for the return of its chattels, placing a lien on Thompson's Chichen Itza property for a million pesos.

To collect back rent from his peasant tenants Thompson meanly threatened them with sterner measures and received in return a burned-down hacienda along with the destruction of his entire library and archeological collection. Obliged to return to Boston penniless, Thompson was kept alive by a subsidy from the Carnegie Foundation. Eventually, years after his death, the Peabody Museum obliged the Mexicans by returning them their artifacts, having kept them half a century.

Gradually, as archeology became a science, and the sale of *Kultur* became a means of feeding the academies, interest in the inherent meaning and value of the artifacts began to dwindle, giving place to an increasing appetite and market for looted artifacts around the world.

RAISING THE SHROUD

PART IV

MONOGRAFIAS DE ARQUEOLOGIA MEXICANA

IV TLALPILLI
CICLO O PERIODO
DE 13 AÑOS.

PIEDRA DEL AGUA

Descifrada por

LEOPOLDO BATRES

14. Batres' Archeological Pork Barrel

Leopoldo Batres

The first native Mexican to be impressed by Charnay's and Le Plongeon's approach to digging beneath the earth to discover the extent of Mexico's antiquities and treasures was one of General Diaz' ex-militiamen, Leopoldo Batres, who was able to approach such an offbeat and potentially expensive pastime because of his particular pull with the dictator, to whom he was illegitimately related. His natural father was Manuel Romero Rubio, who had become Diaz' top henchman by giving the fifty-year-old dictator his teenage daughter Carmen in marriage.

As a natural son of the leader of the all-powerful *cientificos,* Batres' venture into archeology was not such a wild idea; furthermore, he was astute enough to combine his interest in Mexico's hidden treasures with a wholesale and retail dealership in antiquities.

Struck by Ramon Almaraz' report on Teotihuacan that the smaller mounds paralleling the Way of the Dead contained treasure and gold dust which discreetly handled might prove of more than archeological interest, Batres got Diaz—whom he considered a brother-in-law—to appoint him "Inspector and Protector of the Archeological Monuments of Mexico," a sinecure which enabled Batres to poke about for treasure and have digs made wherever the fancy struck him—all at government expense.

To legitimize his efforts, Batres told the world he believed Teotihuacan to be "one of the most interesting cities in the world of archeology."

185

Expedicion cientifica à las Ruinas de San Juan Teotihuacan por el Inspector y Conservador de monumentos arqueologicos de la Republica Mexicana
Leopoldo Batres.
1884 á 86.

Perspectiva de las ruinas de Teotihuacan.

The Way of the Dead as seen by Batres from the top of the Moon Pyramid in 1884. Digging into a mound on the western side of the Way of the Dead, only a year after Charnay had been in the same area, Batres unearthed a perfectly preserved "temple" with a stairway facing west. Because its walls were decorated with mythological scenes, Batres argued that the building was neither a tomb nor a private dwelling, as had been assumed by his predecessors, but a religious center. Uncovering one mound after the other along the Way of the Dead, Batres showed them to be all "temples" built on platforms of adobe, or sun-baked brick, in groups of five or six around plazas with smaller temples in the center, none of which contained tombs or bodies. He therefore suggested that the entire forty-meter-wide esplanade between the terraces might have once been used for some sort of religious ceremony, and that the Way of the Dead should be renamed "La Via Sacra," or "Holy Way."

Whatever treasures or artifacts Batres may have found in these digs at Teotihuacan, little was heard of them publicly; yet his appetite for digging did not flag and he began to put out monographs to validate his endeavors.

In the rubbish near the Pyramid of the Moon, Batres found the monolithic statue of a woman of "colossal dimensions" known as the "sacrificial stone"; but he argued that the name had been inappropriately applied by the Spaniards, who were overly preoccupied with Aztec sacrifices. The earlier Toltecs, whose work Batres believed Teotihuacan to be, were reputed to have made sacrifices only of flowers, fruits, seeds, butterflies, and occasionally birds.

From the vestiges of pottery and artifacts he unearthed, and from the fact that nowhere did he find objects of war or fortifications, Batres concluded, like Charnay, that the city of Teotihuacan had been built by Toltecs, whom he believed to have been an eminently artistic and religious people, not the least warlike—deductions that turned out to be both facile and wrong.

Near the southeast corner of the Pyramid of the Moon, in the level plaza which fronts it, Batres came across a large mound of earth covered with underbrush. Digging into it, he uncovered a building with striking mural paintings depicting historical and religious personages, animals, butterflies, owls, beetles, human jaw bones, geometric forms, and concentric red and green circles with black outlines. The paintings were in various tones of red, or with green, yellow, blue, black, white, and gray pigment. As understood by Batres, the re-

186

Teotihuacan wall painting from the Temple of Agriculture.

Large jaguar heads carved in stone, with open jaws and large fangs, painted red, yellow, and blue, appeared to him to be symbolic of some power he could not identify.

A curious sculptured relief of lassos, coiled hawsers, and lambent flames, painted red, green, and blue, was interpreted by Batres as symbolizing the knot of years and the feast of the renewal of the sacred flame every fifty-two years.

ligion of the Toltecs was a "zoological mythology" in which the butterfly represented the soul's immortality, an idealized beetle called Pinahuiztli represented their astronomical system, and the owl, or Tecototl, was the demon of evil.

As well as temples, Batres found many more buildings such as had been unearthed by Charnay, evidently designed as dwellings, with large pillared halls connected by passages to smaller rooms, the main entrance being through a lobby supported by square pillars, the bases of which were painted red. On each side of the inner doorways, forty centimeters from the floor, Batres found holes which he assumed to have been used for leather thongs to tie back curtains.

These dwellings, all one-storied, had walls made of lava fragments held together with clay and mortar, faced with coatings of stucco, highly polished and painted red and white. Roofs were made of the same material, supported by wooden rafters ten or fifteen centimeters thick, so durable that they still resisted the blows of a crowbar.

Thousands of shards which came to the surface exemplified a great variety of pottery with or without feet—square, cylindrical, smooth, engraved, pierced, in monochrome or polychrome, on a fine white stucco base. But the great stylistic variety of these shards, found at different levels, and the fact that many of the buildings in and under which they were found appeared to have been built on the foundations of the previous ones, often many times, convinced Batres, as it had Almaraz, that reconstruction of the city's history would not be an easy job.

The dwellings appeared windowless, but each had a central patio thirty centimeters below the level of the main floor which could gather rainwater from the inward-sloping roofs, where it could either be held in a cistern or taken away through a central drain.

Everywhere Batres excavated he found a network of aqueducts covered by a layer of perfectly polished mortar through which water could flow, and still did flow from the many springs that gushed up from under Cerro Gordo.

He also found what he called an "underground" part of the city with rooms on different levels, the purpose of which he could not fathom, which he reinforced with steel beams in the hope that later archeologists might decipher their purpose.

Looking at the plain which stretched around the large pyramids, Batres found a great many more mounds, ten to fifteen feet high, whose arrangement led him to deduce that the ancient city must have once covered an area of some twelve square kilometers, four running north-south, three running east-west. On the south side of the city he considered the perimeter to be limited by the ruined edifices on the two low terraces known as the "Citadel."

The Way of the Dead and the north and east sides of the Sun Pyramid before Batres began his excavations.

Batres concluded that within the great city there had not been a single square meter not artificially paved with layers of small stones held together by mortar to a depth of ten to a hundred centimeters.

The most striking discovery made by Batres convinced him that some holocaust must have hit the city. Wherever he dug he found evidence of a great fire which had destroyed buildings "like a terrible Troy." He found that the upper parts of walls where they joined the flat roofs were charred, and that many rafters had fallen to the floor, where they lay carbonized.

Inside the dwellings he found the skeletons of men, women, and children in different positions, some still wearing necklaces of small stones which had withstood the heat.

It was hard for Batres to believe that anything but an earthquake followed by a fire could have so thoroughly destroyed a city; yet he kept encountering an extraordinary anomaly. In the excavations which he made he occasionally found roofs of houses perfectly preserved, the interiors filled with stones neatly fitted into place, joined one with another by claylike cement, forming a compact mass which he had

189

to remove, piece by piece, with great care so as to avoid injuring the mural decorations. The anomaly set him to wondering: could the inhabitants of the great city have purposely destroyed it themselves? "Could those who had built it, fleeing before the invasion of barbarous tribes from the north, and with the hope of returning someday, jealous of the respect and veneration due their gods, have covered their sanctuaries with rubbish to protect them from the profanation of the sacrilegious?"

The conceit was stunning; it meant that the work of burying the city, along with all its temples, would have been as great as that of constructing it, a truly gigantic task, and one that required some pretty sophisticated explanation.

Batres would have liked to continue to dig at Teotihuacan to establish the truth of what had occurred, even hoping to unearth the whole city and its potential treasures, but his department ran out of funds. By 1890 it was clear to Batres it would take a million or more pesos to continue the job.

Skull of a grown man found by Batres in the House of the Priests, and skull of a sacrificial child found by Batres at the corner of the Sun Pyramid.

His benefactor, Diaz, at the end of his third term as president, was not yet sure of re-election. The country was in a financial crisis, the treasury empty, and bankruptcy threatened. Among the peons there was starvation, with epidemics of typhoid and smallpox, as well as insurrection among the Yaquis.

So Batres abandoned Teotihuacan and went off to look for greener sites in Mexico, potentially more profitable—also less of a burden on the national exchequer.

To justify his efforts and improve an unsavory image with the public, Batres produced—at government expense—a series of slick-looking illustrated booklets in which he said little of interest or value in very large print, mostly taking issue with opponents who attacked him in the press and accused him of purloining mountains of illicit gold from his digs.

Batres then had a row with Mexico City's Department of Sewers. They were digging new drains so stinking that no one else would go near them, but Batres insisted on spending long days underground with no one but his son Salvador, ostensibly, in Batres' words, to protect "treasure of inestimable value which would otherwise fall into the possession of negotiators who consider nothing but than their own pecuniary interest, destroying, like the horse of Attila, all that obstructs their way."

Each year Batres turned to a new site to exploit.

In 1902 he explored the ruins of Monte Alban, in 1903 the Valley of Mexico and "La Quemada," in 1904 Texcoco and El Garciclan, where he disinterred an enormous monolith. Of Monte Alban he wrote an inane book that attacked all other points of view but substituted nothing. His major complaint was against having had to supply sufficient water for all the diggers, which cost him two dollars for each barrel carried to the site by donkey.

La Quemada.

For the fifteen years between 1890 and 1905, virtually nothing was done at Teotihuacan except for the destructive efforts of an engineer called Antonio Garcia Cubas, who dug into the southern face of the Pyramid of the Moon on the theory that he would find an entrance to passages and chambers in approximately the same spots they had been found in the Great Pyramid of Cheops. He found no entrance, but seriously marred the structure.

191

Then, in 1904, better times appeared. Porfirio Diaz got himself re-elected president, this time for an extended term of six years. As he drove about the capital in his new Mercedes motorcar over well-paved, well-lighted and well-drained streets, the peons doffed their hats. As T. R. Fehrenbach put it in his spirited history of Mexico, *Blood and Fire,* "The first decade of the twentieth century appeared to be another of those calm, golden late-afternoons in which history seemed to pause."

But outward appearances were deceiving. "In the burning fields of Morelos and Yucatan, for men on their knees with bleeding fingers, and in the dismal mines and shops and airless factories, it was the worst of eras. Almost in hearing of the capital *pelados* still screamed and begged under the overseer's lash."

No sooner was Diaz inaugurated than Batres approached him with the idea that if Teotihuacan were made into a great national monument it might add to Mexico's national image, and that if the Pyramid of the Sun could be unearthed and restored to its former shape in time to commemorate the centennial of Mexico's liberation from Spanish rule, due in September of 1910, coincident with Diaz' eightieth birthday, it might cause enough of a splash to perpetuate the dictator in office.

The idea—which would assure Batres six uninterrupted years of well-funded digging—appealed to Diaz' vanity. Funds were provided, and on March 20, 1905, under the

North and east slopes of the Sun Pyramid before Batres began his excavations.

Northeast corner of the Sun Pyramid where Batres decided to search for the arris line.

Batres discovers an arris line on the northeast corner of the Sun Pyramid.

auspices of the Secretariat of Instruction and Fine Arts, as part of the program to celebrate the centennial of liberation from Spain, Batres began a large-scale dig at Teotihuacan, with enough money, men, and authority to make a noticeable dent. To facilitate his work he took up residence on the spot in a small two-story fort with narrow slotlike windows. His commission was simply to uncover buildings and restore and consolidate their exposed surfaces; but political considerations indicated he concentrate on the Pyramid of the Sun in order to accomplish his ploy for Diaz and justify the money he was spending by uncovering and restoring a really grandiose monument.

To see if an architectural structure actually existed beneath the rough mound of earth, and thus to try to determine the purpose for which it might have originally been built, Batres realized that he would either have to peel off the entire mantle of dirt and rubble from the Pyramid of the Sun, or leave it as it was, a mute and dormant monster. No halfway measure was possible.

Batres assumed that under the dirt and rubble the Sun Pyramid would consist of a five-terraced structure diminishing in size as it rose to a height of sixty-three meters, half as high as the Pyramid of Cheops in Egypt, but on the same-sized base, with a staircase two meters wide zigzagging up one side to a sanctuary on top. Batres suspected that the outer faces might reveal surfaces plastered with mortar and lime, suitable for frescoes. He also suspected, with some justification, that such a pyramid would have been built little by little, beginning with a small central core, growing with successive layers of rock and earthwork to its final dimensions.

Batres' next problem was to figure out at what point to start peeling away the mantle of earth and debris in order to reach a recognizable surface of the shrouded architectural structure which could only vaguely be discerned as a quadrangular stepped pyramid with four apparent levels. After careful scrutiny of the whole mound he found a likely spot near the base on the northeast corner.

Probing to a depth of four meters, Batres exposed a wall made of stone and mortar; the wall had a perfectly defined edge which he believed to be the profile of the northeast arris. Using this wall as a starting point—though he admitted it would have seemed more sensible to start from the top— Batres launched upon his monumental job.

Wheelbarrows and dump wagons were brought to the scene, and eventually even a steam locomotive, whose tracks were laid right to the base of the pyramid. Batres' workers began to remove dirt at the rate of eighty to a hundred tons an hour. Even so, progress was slow. The entire operation

Batres' mule train.

(Facing page)
Batres' 25-cent-a-day
laborers working to uncover
the southeast corner of the
Sun Pyramid. With
wheelbarrows they could
remove a thousand tons a day,
which was then carted away
on specially built train tracks.

required the removal of several hundred thousand tons before the dormant giant could begin to be liberated.

Critics promptly raised complaints at the unheard-of waste
of government funds to remove one mountain of earth simply
to reveal another, especially when hungry Mexican mouths
needed feeding, which they did. Wags in Mexico City joked
that "Señor Batres, excavating in the pyramid, has already
gotten out of it two automobiles!" Batres, secure in the head
man's approval, continued unperturbed. By modern standards,
his operations were remarkably economical. His stonemasons
received the equivalent of twenty-five U.S. cents a day; a
donkey cost him two cents a day. For his own services, because they were so special, Batres received an expense of
seventy-five cents per diem. He did employ what seemed to
be an excessive number of guards to police the area day and
night, but this was ostensibly to secure all kinds of recovered
objects—pottery, ceramics, and sculpture—from the greedy
hands of outside scavengers and souvenir hunters.

As the outermost layer of dirt began to be removed from
the pyramid, Batres was happy to show that it was not just a
pile of rocks and earth, but "a temple, perfectly constructed
and planned." He even found surfaces plastered over with
mortar and lime, hard and smooth, decorated with polychrome frescoes. To Batres it looked as if the pyramid
might have originally been covered with cut stone, fashioned
in the *talud tablero* style, that is, with sunken panels and
entablatures enclosed in projecting slab cornices, built on
sloping sides, anchored by projecting stones. Yet it was
clear to Batres—if not to everyone else—that most of the
original surface of the pyramid had been broken up, either
purposely by some human hand, or by time and vegetation.

194

195

Southwest corner of the Sun Pyramid as the first two levels were exposed by Batres.

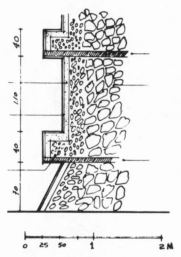

Again Batres even suspected that the whole structure might have been purposely hacked about and covered with earth to hide it from human eyes.

Then came trouble. The surface he was uncovering, clearly not the *original* outer surface, was made of adobe brick held together by mud. In heavy rain the mud began to dissolve, exhibiting plastic flow which threatened to destroy the whole edifice. Had it not been for the viscosity of the dissolving clay, which rendered disintegration slow enough to be arrested by hurried remedial measures, the whole surface of the pyramid might have been dissolved.

"As rainwater coursed downward from the heights of the pyramid in a veritable waterfall," wrote Batres, "it would have carried away completely the covering if I had not restrained the damage by establishing drains of wood to collect the water precipitated from the higher bodies which had not yet been uncovered, and, channeling this water with canals of wood, guided it away from the construction."

To prevent further damage, and to save the outlines of the structure as he uncovered it, Batres hit upon a method of

It was evident to Batres that the builders of Teotihuacan had everywhere employed the *talud-tablero* architectural motif of rectangular panels inset into sloping batters. Adobe bricks, measuring 40 by 30 by 10 centimeters, were laid horizontally for vertical stress and vertically for lateral stress. Over the adobe was laid a thick covering of crushed rock mixed with mud; on top of this was a layer of volcanic rock, four to six meters thick, followed by mixed concrete and mud, then the *tablero* or carved stonework, such as the colossal jaguars or hieroglyphs.

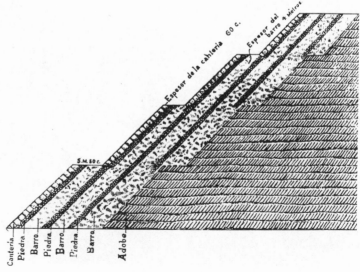

immediately introducing a mixture of lime and cement between the claybound bricks, reinforcing the mortar with fragments of volcanic stone. To this end he organized a group of skillful masons who dug with small spoons into the spaces separating the bricks to a depth of ten centimeters, removed the old mud, and, without moving the bricks from their position, rejoined them with the mixture of mortar and lava fragments.

During the excavation of the southeast corner, Batres found stone walls extending out from the surface like fins; these he assumed had been intended to hold the original surface in place; also there were some buttresses of stone and adobe, evidently intended to provide stability for the structure. This stonework was laid in diagonal rows, each series forming a braid of different widths.

As Batres continued to work upward on the pyramid, but at a slower pace because of the consolidating process, he decided to set other groups of men to digging around the base of the pyramid. At the foot of the west face they uncovered an immense mound fastened to the first level, whose outlines had been visible in the plan published by Maximilian's commission.

After removing a great deal of earth and rubble from a mound attached to the west side of the Sun Pyramid, Batres found atop the first level three temples, an enclosed room, and three stairways leading up to the next level. The central temple was like a three-stepped ziggurat, rising in shorter steps with angled faces. On the south side of the central temple, on its upper plane, Batres found a white and perfectly polished pavement, as well as a shallow cavity, oval in shape, which he believed had been a receptacle for some religious service. In the central temple, Batres found a carved stone with symbols in relief that seemed to be examples of a writing "more advanced than Mexican."

197

Northeast corner of the "House of the Priests" near the Sun Pyramid at Teotihuacan.

Meanwhile another gang began to explore the far western end of the platform surrounding the pyramid. Under a field of corn they discovered a large group of dwellings which, because it was only twenty meters from the corner of the Sun Pyramid, Batres named "House of the Priests."

Batres was amazed at the beauty of the walls which were uncovered, with massive carvings and polychrome frescoes, realizing they must have been striking when the colors were fresh.

Under a meter-thick layer of debris Batres found that the platform around the pyramid was 39.2 meters wide and 6 meters high, with sides in *talud tablero*. He believed this platform was designed to give stability to the pyramid and to prevent slippage at the base.

Batres' work had been in progress for a little over a year when money began to run out. To prime the pump, he decided to invite President Diaz to view the scene and see for himself that more funds were needed for what might be an imposing result.

At seven A.M. of April 6, 1906, General Porfirio Diaz took the train from Mexico City for the hour's ride to the San Juan station. There he and his company of ministers got into horse-drawn carriages and set off to see the sights under a riveting spring sun, raising great clouds of dust.

They were shown various frescoes and carved *tableros,* recently uncovered temples, and the platform around the base of the pyramid; then the party was invited to make a hot, sweaty climb to the top of the Pyramid of the Sun to admire the view. The retinue of ministers, impressed by Batres' work, were even more impressed by the "virile resistance" of their seventy-six-year-old "first magistrate," who climbed without

198

President Porfirio Diaz and members of his cabinet visit the pyramids at San Juan Teotihuacan in April of 1906.

visible effort to the top, perhaps because of the Zapotec blood from the Monte Alban hills which ran in his veins.

In the heat of the day the party descended from the pyramid and took refuge in one of the sixty-foot caves visited by Charnay, where they were served a typical Mexican meal. The guests were reported to be in very good spirits, exchanging historical anecdotes. At three-thirty the president took the train back to Mexico, "very gay and satisfied."

The next day newspapers gave details of the president's visit, noting that the caves in which he had lunched had been renamed the "Cuevas de Diaz." Controlled by the *cientificos,*

The older residents of San Martin recall how their grandfathers spoke of the times when the bandits who robbed the silver cargoes from coaches traveling south from Pachuca to Mexico City would disappear underground at Teotihuacan and emerge long after at Amecameca, sixty-five kilometers southeast.

Geologists report that the volcanic activity which took place in the Valley of Teotihuacan millions of years ago left tubular holes and bubble-shaped caves throughout the area. To the north of Cerro Gordo, lava flowed 6 million years ago. One of the giant underground bubbles left by the volcanic flow still lies to the east behind the Sun Pyramid, and is now called "La Gruta." Behind the Moon Pyramid a cave entrance leads to a tubular tunnel that was explored in 1964 and found to almost circle the pyramid.

the papers pointed out that in one year of work the two lower levels of the pyramid had been uncovered and consolidated, suggesting editorially that it would be very worthwhile if in a few years this extraordinary monument could be cleaned up and reconstructed in its original form.

To accelerate the work, and get it finished in time for the centennial of Mexico's independence, Batres said he would need to hire 400 more men and receive another 100,000 pesos. When the money was not forthcoming, Batres resigned in a huff and went off to explore the Mayan ruins in Yucatan.

15. Americans Good and Bad

The second level of the pyramid as uncovered by Batres was 16 meters high, sloping at an angle of 47 degrees, with a broad staircase 7 meters wide which provided access to a 3-meter-wide walkway on the next level which widened to 9 meters on the western facade.

A third body nearly 14 meters higher had a split staircase 5 meters wide either side of the center line. It also had more vertical fins held together by mud. A fourth body rose 6 meters higher, with a staircase on the center level, but at a steeper incline.

At Chichen Itza, Batres found Edward H. Thompson busy diving for artifacts in the Cenote. Batres, though official Protector of Mexican Antiquities, made no objection to what Thompson was doing, indicating a certain honor among thieves.

By October, Batres had won his point in the capital: work could once more be resumed at Teotihuacan on the Sun Pyramid. In a few months the outlines of the structure began to be clearly discernible. While removing the debris, Batres found more strange artifacts and curios. From the south face he removed a whistle in the shape of a bird. Whistling into it and moving his fingers over four small holes cut into the back of the bird, he was able to produce seven notes of a scale different from that of our "well-tempered clavichord."

A more macabre discovery was made in the form of the skeletons of several six-year-old children, crouching, and purportedly buried alive, one at each corner of each level of the pyramid. Like the skeletons found by Charnay, they fell

into dust as soon as they were uncovered, with the exception of one which Batres was able to preserve by immediately varnishing it.

On top of the pyramid, Batres found a horizontal platform with "the remains of a central temple," something no one else had noted since the eighteenth century. Three meters under the rubble he found a large number of clay figures carved out of jade, jasper, alabaster, and even out of human bone, as well as many shells of different sizes, also worked, and snakes of serpentine and obsidian. From these digs Batres deduced that what had been called the Pyramid of the Sun must, at an earlier time, have been dedicated to Quetzalcoatl, the plumed serpent, god of the air.

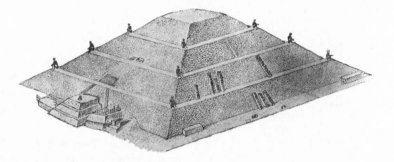

Batres' reconstruction of the Sun Pyramid with western *adosado,* and the skeletons of children on the various corners where he found them.

An unpublished find on the fifth level has never been adequately explained. While the Sun Pyramid was first being probed by Batres in 1906, an archeologist working with him reported a thick sheet of mica covering the top of the fifth body. This material was apparently carried away during the course of the restoration.

Coincidentally, a "Temple of Mica" was also found to the south of the Sun Pyramid about 350 meters down the Way of the Dead, where the local guard will still let one peek through a glass panel at the floor covered with mica slabs. Mica has two outstanding characteristics: high electrical resistance and opaqueness to fast neutrons. Hence it acts as an insulator or nuclear reaction moderator, which raises the question as to why two separate areas of Teotihuacan were covered with mica. By Batres the question was not even raised; the commercial value of mica was apparently sufficient to his purpose.

To complete the unveiling of the pyramid in time for the approaching celebration of the centenary of the war of independence, due on September 16, Batres pushed his workers to the utmost. His patron, General Diaz, about to celebrate his eightieth birthday on September 15, now allowed himself to believe he had become indispensable and should run for another six-year term. On his successful election depended further funds for Teotihuacan. By September of 1910 Batres had spent 566,798.06 pesos, or $45,000, to uncover the pyramid; more funds were essential to make the result grandiose enough to justify the expense.

In Batres' nearly completed reconstruction of the pyramid, none of its original covering remained, only the anchor stones of the central mass. Batres figured that altogether he had removed a mantle of 7 meters north-to-south and 4 meters east-to-west, leaving a pyramid that measured 225 meters north-south at the base and 219 meters east-west, with a height of 62 meters, 4 meters more than was found by Maximilian's commission in 1864. To finish the job, Batres had to await the re-election of his patron.

But Diaz, because of his own foolhardy gesture of saying he would allow the formation of an opposition to his regime, no longer faced a totally unopposed re-election. Opposition had concentrated around a rich landowner from the north, Francisco I. Madero, who although he had been trained at the University of California, was not taken very seriously by Diaz. Barely five feet tall, with a birdlike high-pitched voice, Madero seemed hardly *macho* enough for Diaz, who laughed at his penchant for vegetarianism and spiritualism.

However, when large crowds began to gather around Madero, Diaz quickly had him arrested, with 60,000 of his supporters, on a charge of inciting to riot. Madero, disguised as a mechanic, managed to escape across the border to San Antonio, Texas; elections were held without him.

On September 16 celebrations for the centennial of liberation from Spain and for Diaz' birthday commenced as scheduled, with grandiose festivities which cost the government 20 million pesos, or more than it spent in a whole year for social services. Pageants, viewed by half a million standees, depicted great moments in Mexican history, such as Cortes' confrontation with Montezuma. At Chapultepec Park 50,000 citizens attended a garden party. At the Palacio Nacional, under 30,000 electric stars, 2000 dignitaries banqueted on gold plate, consuming ten boxcars of French champagne served by 500 picturesquely costumed lackeys.

In the course of the festivities Diaz casually announced to the throng the results of the election—99 percent in his favor.

In a cheap hotel room in San Antonio, Francisco Madero and a few fellow conspirators declared, with some justice, that the election was fraudulent; they called for an uprising against Diaz to make him respect the will of the nation. Madero and his followers demanded effective suffrage, expulsion of the *cientificos,* and a law against a president following himself in office.

Francisco Madero.

Educated at the University of California, Francisco Madero was 32 years old when he tried unsuccessfully to oppose Diaz in the election of 1905. In 1908 Madero published a book—*La Succession Presidencial en 1910*—that was immediately suppressed by Diaz because of its reasoned statement of the problems of Mexico and its criticism of the Diaz regime for its unconstitutional method of ruling. After leading an armed rebellion against Diaz, Madero showed such notable generosity for the vanquished that he won the esteem of the people. After a six-month rule as provisional president he was elected by a large majority.

203

Diaz' rougher edges had been rubbed off by his wife, Doña Carmelita, who put him in white tie for ceremonies and taught him to use gold plate and bread instead of tortillas to scoop up his beans. In Chapultepec Palace they lived more regally than had Maximilian and Carlota.

To Diaz' surprise, all over the country disaffected citizens rose in rebellion. In various areas armed groups formed around such leaders as Doroteo Arango, better known as Pancho Villa, or Emiliano Zapata, a tall robust peasant with a big black mustache who had long complained about the misappropriation of peasant lands.

Diaz, who had systematically downgraded his army, weeding out officers of ambition and ability in favor of corrupt and docile servers, now found himself with gouty, rheumatic generals over eighty, colonels over seventy, lieutenants over sixty, and a roster half filled with straw men, paid, uniformed, and fed at regular rates, but in fact nonexistent. Even his

204

When Emiliano Zapata raised the cry of "Land and Liberty," he was quickly supported by an army of small dark *campesinos* in white pants and conical sombreros, armed with sharp machetes and icons of the Virgin of Guadalupe, ready to fight for the return of their stolen lands.

After the civil war, Zapata hoped independently to restore economic well-being to the ravaged state of Morelos but the newly elected president, Carranza, attacked him with federal troops. When the attack failed, Carranza fell back on treachery. A federal colonel, Jesus Guajardo, pretended to defect to the Zapatistas with 600 men. Although warned of the treachery, Zapata agreed to meet the colonel, each with only thirty men. The colonel showed up with 600, and when Zapata entered the hacienda there was a bugle call: the unarmed Zapata was shot to death.

vaunted Rurales (like the later militia of Mussolini's fascism) turned out to be better at gang-beating individual citizens than fighting as an organized group; they soon went down before the rebels.

When a mob gathered outside the palace on the Zocalo shouting for Diaz' resignation, the dictator ordered the presidential guard to open fire, machine-gunning two hundred demonstrators to death. Popular outcry could no longer be stemmed. The leader of the *cientificos,* José Limantour, who had inherited the mantle from Batres' father, deserted Diaz and made a deal with Madero, who was eventually installed as president. Half delirious with pain from a rotting tooth, Diaz

205

Batres replied to his critics that he had taken all the necessary precautions to preserve the Sun Pyramid while removing the rubble and earth which incrusted it, that "all structures in Teotihuacan" were formed of layers of construction, whether stone, adobe, or volcanic dust and mortar, and that even mural paintings were to be found, one beneath the other, like "colossal palimpsests." He argued that he had been obliged to peel off the outer layer of the pyramid so as to reveal its true shape. He dismissed the accusations against him as being political, leveled at him by revolutionary enemies for having been a close friend and faithful servant of General Diaz. "Nothing," wrote Batres, "is easier than criticism when one does not have the noble proposition of illustrating, teaching or correcting, and such criticism is reduced to the venomous desire to damage another man personally, as in my case, without it mattering to the accusers the damage done to science and to history by attributing imaginary defects to our archeological monuments."

was hustled under guard to a train for Veracruz, where he was put on a ship for France, never to return to Mexico.

Diaz' exile, despite Limantour's efforts, brought to an end the reign of the *cientificos,* and with it, that of Batres. Deprived of his title of Inspector General of Monuments, Batres was quickly attacked for having gone about his work with more vigor and enthusiasm than care, of having peeled the Pyramid of the Sun "like an onion," for fear of not being able to reveal it in time for Diaz's birthday.

He was accused of having removed all the remains of the original covering of cut stone and of having left nothing but a disfigured core with a few projecting anchoring stones. He was further castigated for having cruelly mangled the pyramid by giving it five platforms instead of the "archeologically correct four," and of having grossly reduced its size, disfiguring its faces with irregular edges.

Bitter and disappointed, Batres retired from public view, leaving the field open to a young rival who had been groomed for the job by his opponents ever since 1906.

Batres' most determined antagonist in Mexico for over a decade had been an American lady, Zelia Nuttall, an amateur archeologist whom Batres had managed to outrage. Mrs. Nuttall, who was as well endowed intellectually as she was financially, had made some interesting discoveries on the Island of Sacrifices off Veracruz, for which Batres stole the credit. He also blocked Zelia Nuttall's friend Alfred P. Maudslay from excavating at Monte Alban, and took for himself the credit for work at Mitla done by Marshall H.

Archeologist Zelia Nuttall.

Gamio.

In 1917 Manuel Gamio, excavating off the main road from Mexico City to Cuernavaca, found an overgrown hill called Cuicuilco enveloped by prehistoric lava streams. It turned out to be an enormous ancient pyramid or truncated cone with four galleries and a central staircase.

Saville, even going so far as to have his own name carved in letters of gold on a lintel of the finest palace.

Savoring her revenge, Mrs. Nuttall now put into print what was common knowledge about Batres, that as a wholesale and retail merchant in antiquities he had rifled the nation of its archeological treasures, consistently smuggling antiquities from sites he was supposed to be guarding in order to sell them for export. At the same time Mrs. Nuttall exposed, with devastating particularity, the arbitrary and misleading nature of Batres' classification of archeological objects. In trenchant terms she showed that archeology in Diaz' dictatorship had been just another pork barrel at which the same old cronies could feed.

Batres was publicly accused of having grafted in illegal permits to take art objects out of the country, of having blown up an arch at Uxmal to steal a statue, of having faked many of the important pieces in the Mexican museum in order to sell the originals abroad, and of covering up his misdeeds by writing a pseudo-scientific book exposing the forgeries.

Zelia Nuttall pointed out that when the famous Codex Sanchez passed to the German minister to Mexico, Batres was shortly thereafter decorated with the high German order of the Red Eagle.

Batres' downfall, for which Mrs. Nuttall had been planning for years, was as complete as was her triumph.

For years she had been grooming as a successor to Batres a young Mexican named Manuel Gamio, for whom she had maneuvered a scholarship at Columbia University in New York, with the help of the head of the Department of Ethnology and Anthropology, Professor Franz Boas, an authority on Mexican antiquities, on the ground that what Mexican archeology most needed was a museum director thoroughly trained in the most modern methods of archeological research. By repeated intercession with high Mexican authorities Mrs. Nuttall had gotten young Gamio a leave of absence from his job in charge of historic items at the Museo Nacional to study at Columbia, expressing the hope that someday he would be made director of the archeological section of the National Museum and inspector of monuments instead of her *bête noire* Batres.

With the revolution of 1910 all of this came to pass, and the International School of American Archeology, subsidized by various U.S. academic institutions, got off to a start in Mexico with Gamio following Boas as director.

Unfortunately, not all United States efforts in Mexico were as beneficial as those of Mrs. Nuttall. The U.S. ambassador, Henry Lane Wilson, virtually a Guggenheim employee, considering his paramount concern to be the protection of the

207

billion-dollar investment by North American capitalists in Mexico, decided to be rid of Madero.

Falsely reporting to Washington Madero's supposed addiction to radicalism, Wilson did his best to make Madero appear to be a Bolshevik. Madero, a good-hearted nineteenth-century liberal, more accurately described by historians as "a do-gooder whose honesty and charity were unassailable," merely urged compromise and reconciliation among all parties, insisting that all change must come through the legal process.

Exaggerating the destruction of foreign property during Madero's revolt against the Diaz regime and falsely arousing alarm in the United States that in Mexico "every north American citizen's life and property are in jeopardy," Ambassador Wilson conspired to replace Madero with a military figure, General Victoriano Huerta, described by one historian as "an immoral drunkard, devoid of loyalty or honor, supported by the Church and the Army."

U.S. Ambassador Henry Lane Wilson seated stage right of Porfirio Diaz and his thoroughly unpopular vice president, of whom Diaz said, "Ramon Corral is a faithful lad who does what I want him to without discussion."

Huerta falsely lured Madero's brother into a restaurant to a parley, where he had him savagely tortured to death. He then arrested Madero and had him brutally murdered. The same night Huerta met with Ambassador Wilson at the U.S. Embassy to receive his official support.

Surrounded by cronies, Huerta tried to run the country from a bar, until Pancho Villa and Zapata and other insurgents marched on the capital to avenge Madero. The result of Ambassador Wilson's intervention was a bloody civil war which lasted seven years, during which unbelievable atrocities were committed, often on both sides. Huerta's federalists refused to take prisoners; they hurled the Chihuahua governor under the wheels of a running train, and staked out men in anthills to be eaten alive.

208

Pancho Villa.

Oregon-born and Harvard-educated correspondent John Reed (whose body is buried in the Kremlin wall because of his *Ten Days That Shook the World*) became intimate with Pancho Villa during his coverage of the Mexican revolution. Reed described Villa as representing the peasant soul of a whole continent which had brooded over its bitter condition since the Spanish Conquest and since the Diaz sequestration of land.

Before he became governor of Chihuahua, Villa was a bandit for twenty-two years. At sixteen he murdered a government official, reputedly for the violation of his sister. Outside the law, Villa became a Robin Hood, stealing from the rich to feed the poor. In time of famine he drove off thousands of head of cattle from the Terrazzas' vast ranges, feeding whole districts and taking care of entire villages evicted by the Diaz soldiers in their land grabs.

Reed reported that Villa's great passion was schools, because he believed that land for the people and schools for their children would settle every problem in the country. When he came to power in Chihuahua, Villa established over fifty schools and would have liked to send his son to school in the U.S. but could not afford it.

When he took over the government of Chihuahua, Villa also ordered every Spaniard caught within the boundaries of the state in the next five days to be escorted to the nearest wall by a firing squad. When the U.S. consul reproached him, Villa replied, "Señor Consul, we Mexicans have had three hundred years of the Spaniards. They have not changed in character since the conquistadores. They disrupted the Indian empire and enslaved the people. We did not ask them to mingle their blood with ours. Twice we drove them out of Mexico and

allowed them to return with the same rights as Mexicans, and they used these rights to steal our land, to make the people slaves, and to take up arms against the cause of liberty. They supported Porfirio Diaz. They were perniciously active in politics. It was the Spanish who framed the plot that put Huerta in the palace. When Madero was murdered, the Spanish in every state in the Republic held banquets of rejoicing. They thrust on us the greatest superstition the world has ever known—the Catholic Church. They ought to be killed for that alone. I consider we are being generous with them."

When asked by Reed why he did not aspire to the presidency, Villa replied, "I am a fighter not a statesman. I am not educated enough to be president. How could I, who never went to school, hope to be able to talk to foreign ambassadors and to cultivated gentlemen of the Congress."

He believed that armies were the greatest support of tyranny. "There can be no dictator without an army." He suggested instead the resettling of veterans on the land, where they could farm and teach citizens the basics of soldiering so that "if the patria is invaded, we will just have to telephone from the Palace in Mexico City, and in half a day, all the Mexican people will rise from their fields and factories, fully armed, equipped and organized to defend their children and their home. It would be fine," said Villa, "to help make Mexico a happy place."

209

General Porfirio Diaz at the age of 81 at Veracruz about to go into permanent exile in Paris, where he was joined by Batres. Unwanted at home, Diaz managed one last fame-making action by diving into Lac Leman to save a girl from drowning.

It was a dismal period for archeology, one when most of the digging was done not for artifacts but to bury bodies. Manuel Gamio, one of a few determined spirits, continued working quietly through the years of the revolution. Applying the stratigraphic techniques he had learned at Columbia, he managed to establish by digging into layers of refuse around Mexico City, and carefully noting each stratum of residue, a record of human habitation in central Mexico going back over 1400 years. Working backwards from the top, Gamio found layers of Aztec and Toltec and then traces of an earlier civilization which he labeled "Archaic." It was a whole new field to be explored.

16. Mexicans for Mexico

Not until 1917, and the establishment of a representative democratic federal republic, was sufficient peace restored in Mexico to resume the search into its past. A new liberal constitution opened the way for the renaissance of native talent; such artists as Diego Rivera, José Orozco, and David Siqueiros appeared on the scene. Interest was aroused not only in Mexico's history but in its ethnic development and its general educational advancement.

With Manuel Gamio as head of the Department of Anthropology at the Museo Nacional, a thorough study was decided upon not only of the ruins of Teotihuacan, but of the entire Valley of Teotihuacan, from a historical, geological, anthropological, and sociological point of view. For the first time in Mexican history teams of young Mexican scientists went out to make studies on the spot for a long-term investigation of Mexican antiquities. It was hoped that they would be able to reconstruct in detail the various cultures that had inhabited the Valley of Teotihuacan from remotest antiquity.

The earliest vestiges of human habitation found in the lava beds of San Angel were some adobe walls, given the name of Otomi. Gamio's students established that the earliest "archaic" metropolis at Teotihuacan had been built on a gently sloping plain irrigated by a network of crystalline springs which had their source in the volcanic mound of Cerro Gordo. Lava, abundant in the immediate surroundings, had been the main building material for this metropolis. The soil, known locally as *tepetate,* was heavily compacted and impermeable, which made it unnecessary to dig foundations for buildings; walls were not subject to deterioration from humidity.

211

Large deposits of hard, glassy volcanic obsidian, found in the northeast end of the valley, furnished the raw material for ancient arrowpoints, knives, and other weapons; also for jewelry and ornaments.

By February of 1918, Manuel Gamio was authorized by the secretary of agriculture to resume exploration of the ruins of Teotihuacan. In sixteen separate excavations he attempted to determine by stratigraphical studies the chronological development of the architecture he uncovered. Gamio believed the buildings of Teotihuacan antedated those of the lowland Mayas, which he believed to be two thousand years old; he assumed the earliest ruins of Teotihuacan might be five hundred or a thousand years older than that.

With the end of World War I, and renewed foreign interest in Teotihuacan, Gamio decided to attack an area of the city which he believed would reveal one of the most imposing ceremonial plazas in Mexico, the area known as the "Citadel."

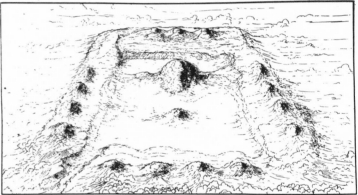

When Gamio first attacked the area of the Citadel, he found it entirely covered with a sheet of earth from under which its lineaments could only just be discerned. Setting aside the question of who could have covered it and why, Gamio decided to excavate what he could.

As with the Pyramid of the Sun—before Batres uncovered it—the Citadel's mounds and embankments, with one exception, were completely shrouded in earth on which flourished indigenous flora and many *pirul* (Peru) trees. The exception was a mound on the east side which had been partially unearthed by Batres to reveal a well-proportioned temple with the usual pyramidal base and *tablero* cornices.

As had been the case with Batres, Gamio realized that as soon as he uncovered a structure it would have to be protected or it would rapidly be disintegrated by rain or the germination of fresh vegetation in the clay mortar; it was also clear to Gamio that no one would be able to appreciate the original beauty of these ancient monuments unless they were restored into clear geometric lines.

Yet Gamio did not wish to incur the heavy criticism which had been heaped on Batres when he had lost the political support of Diaz.

The whole Citadel turned out to consist of a huge quadrangle, 1 mile in perimeter, or 400 meters on each side, covering an area of 36 acres. Facing the Way of the Dead, it had a 40-meter-wide platform 7 meters above the ground; on the other three sides similar platforms were 80 meters wide, around a central patio of almost 40 acres. Atop these platforms, symmetrically arranged, were fifteen mounds indicating the presence of temples. Within the patio were two more small mounds and one very large one. It was misnamed the "Citadel" by the Spaniards because of its high embankments, which they assumed were for military protection, but the true purpose of the complex remained a mystery.

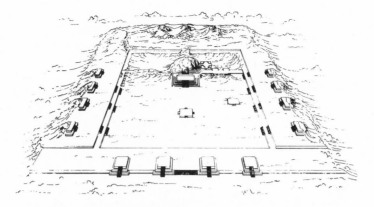

To avoid a similar treatment, Gamio availed himself of the talents of an architectural draftsman of high repute, Ignacio Marquina, who made extremely careful renderings from the fragments of the walls, cornices, and stairways that came to light, recreating each monument as it might have looked in its original state. On the basis of these drawings Gamio concentrated on anchoring any parts of the original building that were found in place, or any part of the original concrete, immediately replacing the fallen rubble with fresh cement. Like Batres, he replaced weak mortar with cement, studded with volcanic fragments, but maintained that his method was more advanced than the primitive technique employed by Batres.

To limit the enormous amount of work such a project entailed, Gamio decided to uncover only the inward facing sides of the Citadel's embankments and temples, leaving the exteriors on the north, south, and east sides safely covered by their centennial or millennial coat of dirt.

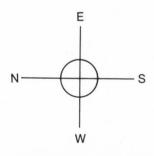

Digging into the embankment around the central patio, Gamio found it to be a two-tiered affair with the usual *tablero* cornice, broken at regular intervals by stone stairways which led seven meters up to the flat platforms on which the fifteen temples were arranged. Those on the north and south sides faced inward, those on the east and west sides faced west, toward the Way of the Dead. Each temple had its own staircase leading to a flat top.

213

Mound in the center of the Citadel before Gamio attacked it.

In the spring of 1919 the first soundings were made in the large central mound of the Citadel. By June it was excitedly reported to Gamio that huge sculptured serpents' heads were appearing from the mound, along with indications of other monoliths carved in the shape of curiously stylized animals which at first could not be identified. Unfortunately the rainy season had just begun, and it wasn't till September that Gamio was able to proceed with the excavations.

By carefully probing into the side of the mound, the diggers discovered they were dealing with two pyramids, one built up against the other, partly overlaying it. Gamio considered this to be corroborative evidence of two successive epochs having flourished at Teotihuacan. In order to reveal both pyramids it was necessary to make a passage between them. In the process part of the front pyramid had to be destroyed in order to reveal the facade of the back one, which Gamio found to be artistically finer and of an earlier period than the front pyramid; it appeared to have been superimposed during a later and more decadent era.

As earth was removed, an extraordinary sight was revealed; the rear pyramid, built on a base of some 25,000 square meters, rose in six stages to a height of 22 meters, each stage consisting of heavy stone cornices with polychromed sculpture of huge undulating serpents carved in relief with heads protruding from petaled collars to represent Quetzalcoatl. Each snake bore in the center of its body a large humanoid head with fanged jawbone, straight bar mustache, and circular orbs over its eyes, which, because of the sea shells and conchs that accompanied it, were interpreted to symbolize the rain god Tlaloc, though it could just as well have been interpreted as a jaguar representing Tezcatlipoca, the "smoking-mirror god of the rain of fire."

214

An imposing stairway, from which protruded the heads of plumed serpents, led to the uppermost terrace, where six graves were found by six deep wells containing large wooden pillars. Sculpture and stairway, which had been covered by the front pyramid, were in excellent preservation, considered to be the most successful integration of architecture and sculpture so far found at Teotihuacan. But the front pyramid,

Jutting from the facade of the Pyramid of Quetzalcoatl at regular intervals are great carved heads of feathered serpents, the symbols of Quetzalcoatl. Some of the eyes still glitter with polished obsidian insets. Alternating with the serpent is the symbol attributed to Tlaloc, the rain god, with circles inscribed around his eyes, more likely a representation of the jaguar Tezcatlipoca. Carved in low relief is an undulating design suggestive of waves. The intervening space is filled with carvings of seashells of Caribbean varieties.

Batres contended that on the west side of the Citadel there had originally been three temple mounds atop the platform facing the Way of the Dead, but that Gamio and his department had leveled the mounds and the structures within them, arbitrarily replacing them—for symmetrical, or aesthetic, or whatever reason—with four "invented" mounds. Batres insisted he knew whereof he spoke, because several years earlier he had uncovered one of these temple mounds and had taken a photograph of it; and on the original survey made by Maximilian's commission only three mounds appeared. Batres accused Gamio and the Department of Anthropology of destroying large parts of the Citadel, literally razing them in order to build entirely arbitrary new buildings, which he called fantastic. Batres said he had devoted his life to the preservation of these monuments, and that now they were being destroyed beyond any hope of repair, to be replaced by "grotesque" reconstructions.

Ignacio Marquina's reconstruction of the Pyramid of Quetzalcoatl before the second pyramid was superimposed.

like most of the other mounds, had been largely despoiled of its stonework since colonial times, when the Citadel had been used as a quarry for stone to build churches and bridges.

In his attempt to remedy this vast spoilage Gamio got himself attacked by the man he had replaced. Batres, now old and crotchety, labeled Gamio's work a "savage destruction" of the Citadel, "done by men without understanding or conscience."

It was a serious accusation, but one that went largely unnoticed, as did the more fundamental issue of *arbitrarily* rebuilding ancient monuments. Both Batres' and Gamio's approach to their work had been more anthropological than scientific; they were looking for pretty temples to strange gods rather than to the possibility that the very dimensions of the buildings they were uncovering might contain scientific data.

The argument, often futile, which had been going on for several hundred years as to whether or not the base of the Great Pyramid of Cheops had been intentionally designed as

216

a scientific device for recording a fraction of the earth's circumference, thus to serve as a standard unit of measure, was not to be resolved until 1925, when the base of the pyramid was finally cleared of rubble and the British engineer J. H. Cole was able to pinpoint the length of the four sides to within millimeters. The answer, as classical writers had been saying for over two thousand years, was, of course, that the base of the Great Pyramid was an earth-commensurate eighth of a minute of arc, exactly 750 ancient geographic feet, or 500 cubits to the millimeter.

Unfortunately the difference in the length of the base of Mexico's Pyramid of the Sun, as found by Gamio and Batres, was still being disputed in meters rather than millimeters, so that as yet no rational system could be extrapolated from its measure.

If anything but an aesthetic thrill was to be derived from further unearthing of buildings at Teotihuacan, it would have to be done with a more scientific approach.

Ironically, whatever scientific shortcomings Gamio may have had, it was he who was credited with having initiated a new era of "scientific" inquiry at Teotihuacan. Soon the idea spread that the entire city might have to be explored.

But funds were lacking. North America's contribution to Mexican archeology came mostly through such foundations as the Carnegie Institute, whose new director in the field, Sylvanus G. Morley, was more interested in deciphering Mayan stelae in Yucatan than in any reconstruction of Teotihuacan.

He did gasp in wonder when Gamio showed him the freshly uncovered pyramid of Quetzalcoatl, and then took him to lunch in Diaz' grotto. Told that Batres had tried to disparage the accuracy of the work done on the Citadel, Morley gave an impassioned interview to the press in which he attacked Batres and praised the work of Gamio, saying that nothing in the New or Old World matched the ruins of Teotihuacan.

Gamio ond Morley at the Sun Pyramid of Teotihuacan.

217

Sylvanus G. Morley, a very short, slender Philadelphian, was known throughout Yucatan for the high and voluminous straw hat he sported. Described as a nearsighted bundle of energy, both lovable and exasperating, he had a high-pitched nasal voice and an odd Pennsylvania accent. His Spanish, though he had an extensive vocabulary, was considered atrocious, with mixed-up genders and tenses.

Inappropriately named Sylvanus, he loathed the jungle, especially the jogging on muleback over parched trails or through the smothering atmosphere of the rain forest. "Only liars and damn fools like the jungle," he said; but he stuck it out for twenty years to bring home what he called, "the epigraphic bacon." He was determined to find and decipher every possible dated stele with the long-term object of plotting the rise and fall of Mayan civilization, about which little or nothing was known.

At times only half conscious and afraid he would fall from the saddle, Van, as he was called by his friends, would tie his feet beneath the animal and plunge on despite sunburn, thirst, saddle sores, rock bruises, and cactus stabs. J. E. Thompson, who was to become England's leading expert on the Maya, describes Morley "squatting before a new-found stela to draw the glyphs, often with handkerchiefs around each wrist to keep the sweat from running down his arms onto the paper."

Eventually he learned to travel in greater comfort with a baggage train consisting of forty boxes, twelve kyacks, and over a dozen bundles of chairs, cots, and other luggage to make life along the trail as bearable as possible. In the bush he required thirty-four mules, two thirds of them for baggage and the remainder for personnel, who included a guide, four muleteers, and a Chinese cook.

Had it not been that the world was just then engulfed in a major depression, funds might have been forthcoming for further research at Teotihuacan. As it was, the site was allowed to languish until the economically solvent Swedes, who in the depths of the 1930s depression could still permit themselves the luxury of archeological exploration, financed Sigwald Linne to take up the spade at Teotihuacan.

In a short time Linne showed a truly urban side to what had theretofore been considered primarily a ceremonial center. East of the Pyramid of the Sun, Linne discovered a large complex of small houses, interspersed with palatial residences. In one complex, encompassing a total of 4000 square yards, Linne uncovered a conglomeration of 175 rooms built around a network of corridors with twenty-one patios and five large plazas. Here, jammed between the more important religious edifices, were narrow alleylike streets leading off into residential areas where people had lived in crowded quarters separated by small courtyards and alleyways.

Along with the monumental religious structures there appeared the remains of public baths, theaters, and ball courts.

Linne found inner courts to houses with spacious basins for water complete with finely polished stone plugs to stop the drains, still *in situ*. Beneath the floors of these houses were graves replete with domestic utensils, jewelry, pottery, and

obsidian artifacts. From the kitchen utensils, it was clear to Linne that the buildings had been used as dwellings.

A second group of houses had forty-five dwellings around a rectangular patio surrounded on four sides by platforms, with an altar in the center. Some of the houses appeared to be designed like hotels, indicating the possibility of pilgrim quarters for thousands of visitors.

Linne was followed by Pedro Armillas, who, with money from a foundation called the "Viking Group," uncovered more buildings with frescoes which provided surprising information about the religious customs of the Teotihuacanos. Murals revealed the gods of Teotihuacan in impressive scenes.

Other paintings, made with mineral colors mixed with unfermented maguey sap painted on lime mortar, mixed with quartz dust to make the colors stand out, indicated to archeologists a civilization more of king-priests than of warriorprinces.

Still more gods, some of whom had also appeared in Tenochtitlan, were found on murals by Laurette Sejourné, a Mexican archeologist born in France. Digging into a bean field at Teotihuacan, she uncovered the ruins of a palace called Zacuala, covering 5000 square yards.

Yet all of this was desultory work. The mystery of when, how and why Teotihuacan had been built remained as deep as ever. To open up the ancient city a real financial shot in the arm was needed. It came in 1960 after the election to the presidency of Adolfo Lopez Mateos. A sharp economist, Lopez Mateos realized that a major effort at uncovering and restoring at least the ceremonial center of Teotihuacan might provide an attraction for both domestic and foreign tourists; they in turn might refill the state coffers.

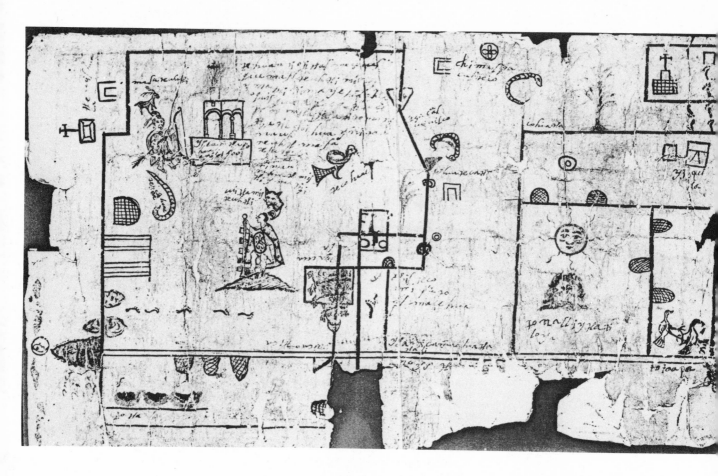

At Teotihuacan, Batres had found in a stone chest two manuscripts, one of which he gave to Marshall H. Saville, who presented it to New York's Museum of Natural History (where it is now stored on the shelves of Gordon Eckholm). The other, which he gave to Edward Ayres, is now in Chicago's Newberry Library.

Both maps, apparently made shortly after the conquest, contain unusual data and symbols not found elsewhere. Recent restoration of the Ayres manuscript revealed a backing paper with writing and the seal of Pope Urban VIII whose pontificate was from 1623 to 1644.

On the Ayres manuscript the Moon Pyramid is marked as "the moon house" and further down the Way of the Dead is "the place of the brilliant serpents." The Pyramid of the Sun, which is drawn in its proper position and correctly proportioned to the Pyramid of the Moon, is labeled "shining house."

Stansbury Hagar, Secretary of the Department of Ethnology at the Brooklyn Institute of Arts and Sciences, one of the first to realize the astronomical nature of Mexican monuments, suggested the smaller mounds could represent the planets or other stars.

Hagar believed the Way of the Dead, which was also known as the Way of the Stars, might represent the Milky Way; he pointed out that to Indians in the United States, the Milky

Way was known as the Path of the Dead because spirits were believed to pass to and from it, between earth and the land of the souls amid the stars.

Hagar suggests that Mixcoatla, the Mexican Cloud Serpent, might represent the Milky Way.

To Hagar, it appeared that Teotihuacan had been a sacred city because it reproduced on earth a supposed celestial plan of the sky-world "where dwelt the deities and spirits of the dead."

He believes the Citadel to have been a solar temple with two enclosures devoted to the solstices and equinoxes, and that its principal mound pertained to the sun and the summer solstice in distinction

to the Pyramid of the Sun which was dedicated to the Sun as a celestial body. Hagar suggested that the great size of this zodiacal enclosure probably indicated a predominance of the cult of the stars over that of the Sun at Teotihuacan.

Hagar pointed out that footprints appearing on the maps could indicate the constellation of Capricorn at the moment of the December solstice. He interpreted the red and circular object outside the lower right-hand corner of the Citadel in both manuscripts as probably a tortoise, symbol of the summer solstice.

The word *itzquitla* in the margin he interpreted as a corruption of Dog, name of the day sign attached to the

winter solstice.

The third enclosure of the Citadel containing two small mounds and two birds of equal size, one black and one white, Hagar interpreted as symbolizing the vernal equinox, which falls between the day sign Quauhtli, for eagle, and Cozcaquauhtli, for vulture. "Evidently," wrote Hagar, "we have not realised either the importance or the refinement, or the widespread distribution through ancient America of the astronomical cult of which the celestial plan was a feature, and of which Teotihuacan was at least one of the principal centers." But some time was yet to pass before further evidence was forthcoming on the astronomical functions of Teotihuacan.

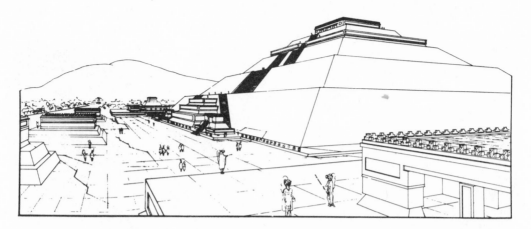

Impressive but improbable reconstruction of the pyramids of Teotihuacan by Mexican architect J. A. Gomez Rubio.

Seventeen million pesos were appropriated for a two-year campaign. Scores of archeologists were hired to supervise some six hundred spade diggers. It was hoped that dozens of the temples buried along the Way of the Dead might be excavated and restored so as to give visitors a more vivid sense of the ancient city's splendor.

Under the direction of Jorge Acosta, a Mexican archeologist born in Peking in 1904, whose digging at Tula had been responsible for confirming Charnay's contention that the ancient city had once been the seat of a prosperous Toltec kingdom, the area around the Pyramid of the Moon was first attacked. In a few months the plaza before the pyramid and three surrounding hectares were completely cleared of rubble. So was a large part of the Way of the Dead. The plaza in front of the Pyramid of the Sun could only be partially restored because of the damage done by previous excavators, including Batres' pet railway.

In the course of operations around the Moon Plaza, the remains were unearthed of a building with another large stairway with enormous snake heads leading to a patio with square sculptured columns, where Acosta found rooms with some of Teotihuacan's finest murals. This was the beautiful place of Quetzalpapalotl, the butterfly god.

Palace of the Butterfly God.

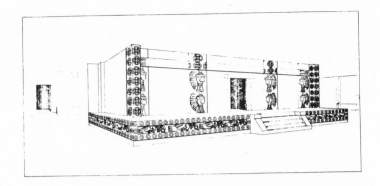

Substructure of the Palace of the plumed shells.

To analyze the enormous quantity of pottery, sculpture, tools, and ornaments dug up in these vast operations, a special scientific lab was created under the supervision of fifty-year-old Florencia Muller, a Mexican specialist in ceramics who had done her early schooling in St. Louis, Missouri.

At which point another fifty-year-old Mexican archeologist, Ignacio Bernal, joined Jorge Acosta in the decision to embark on the major project of uncovering and reconstructing the remaining major monument at Teotihuacan, the Pyramid of the Moon.

Gamio had found it a mound covered with earth and vegetation, and so he had left it. Only a few portions of the external structure of the Moon Pyramid had been uncovered, showing the remains of a staircase, fifteen meters wide, on the south side, looking down the Way of the Dead, but largely destroyed by Garcia Cubas, who had left a hole of several thousand cubic meters in its center.

As Bernal and Acosta went about carefully uncovering the rest of the south face, four stages came to light, plus sufficient remains of a fifth stage for them to risk undertaking its reconstruction, in no way an easy job, even for twentieth-century archeologists, especially as no one could be sure that the building had not already been reconstructed two millennia previously. Not only had external stones subsided from their "original" positions and angles, but underneath the outer surface of the Moon Pyramid the archeologists found traces of two more "original" structures which might at one time have been external.

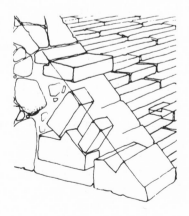

Thanks to some careful exploration by archeologist Ponciano Salazar, 565 original stones to the staircase were recovered from rubble around the plaza. One stone was still in its original position—luckily a cornerstone. From this stone it was possible to reconstruct the entire angle of ascent. As the whole staircase had been ingeniously designed with odd-shaped interlocking stones to prevent slippage, forty-eight courses could be reconstructed, which brought the top of the

Pyramid of the Moon as Bernal and Acosta began to uncover and restore it.

staircase to a third of the way up the south face of the Moon Pyramid. Later reconstruction added three more staircases to the top of a fourth level.

As the workmen proceeded to clean up the rest of the ceremonial area, Bernal and Acosta were faced with the difficult choice of deciding whether to reconstruct buildings in the later, and to them inferior, Teotihuacan period, or to dismantle these remains in order to reconstruct the earlier, and more impressive, buildings beneath them. Mostly they decided to concentrate on rebuilding the city as it had been at what they considered the height of its glory. At the same time they left standing a number of buildings of the later, more decadent, period, when the city had apparently lost its role as a great capital and had become inhabited by peoples of "a lower cultural level," incapable, according to Acosta, of understanding the grandeur of the past.

Once the east and west sides of the Moon Pyramid had been cleared (leaving the north side in its original earth-covered state), visitors were afforded a spectacular sight of the great reconstructed pyramids joined by a temple-lined avenue prolonged to include the resurrected Citadel.

Theoretical reconstruction of the Pyramid of the Moon from Jorge Acosta's guide to Teotihuacan.

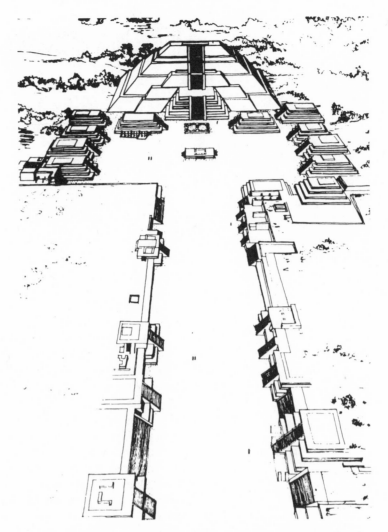

As had been expected, the lavish reconstruction of Teotihuacan caused an influx of tourists, both Mexican and foreign, which soon replenished the state coffers, to the delight of a government which still did not realize it had barely scratched the surface of the great city of Teotihuacan.

17. Imperial City

The person who was to spark the discovery of the true proportions of Teotihuacan turned out to be a young American of French origin, René Millon, who arrived in Mexico City in 1950, fresh from Columbia University. At the age of twenty-nine, Millon was so fascinated by what he saw and by how such a city as Teotihuacan could have risen in the Valley of Mexico that he came to devote his career to finding out its true dimensions.

After years of exploratory work at Teotihuacan and its surrounding valley he was able, in 1962, as a professor of anthropology at the University of Rochester, to obtain sufficient funds from the National Science Foundation in Washington, D.C., to start the preparation of a photogrammetric map of the entire area of Teotihuacan as a base for a comprehensive archeological survey to establish the exact dimensions of the ancient city.

Until 1922 the only topographical map of the ceremonial center and heart of Teotihuacan had been the one prepared in 1865 by Maximilian's commission. In 1922 Gamio made a more detailed map of the same area, but did not even take it as far north as had Ramon Almaraz.

Millon decided that a proper map would have to show the full extent of the ancient urban zone so as to verify for density of construction and establish the way in which buildings had been disposed and related to each other.

To limit the area to be photographed, Millon and his colleagues first made a field survey to establish a neutral band, at least 300 meters wide, with no trace of a building in it. He first estimated that this would give him a city area of some 25 square kilometers. In the end he had to

Irregular boundary of Teotihuacan is shown as a solid
line that approaches the edges
of a grid, composed of 500-
meter squares, surveyed by
Millon's team. The grid drawn
by Millon parallels the north-
south direction of the Way of
the Dead, the city's main
avenue.

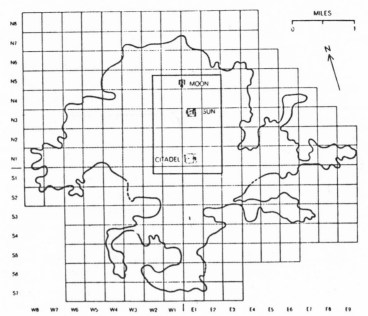

Teotihuacan was strategically
located on the best route
between the Valley of Mexico
and the Valley of Puebla leading to the Gulf of Mexico.

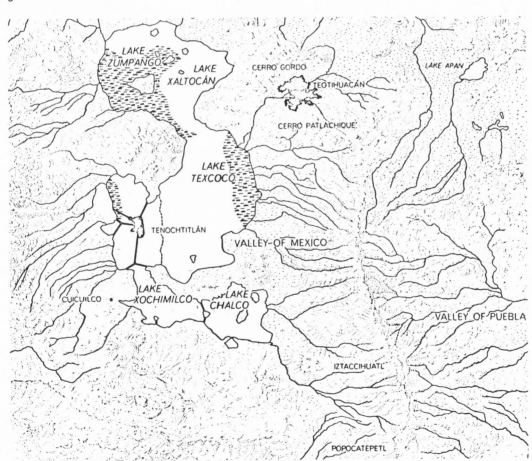

227

cover 38 square kilometers, which caused a hiatus in his operations while more funds were sought to handle the enlarged project.

Once the funds were found, the job was to be carried out under the aegis of the Mexican Institute of Anthropology and History, whose new director was Ignacio Bernal.

The map was to represent the most detailed surface study of so large a prehistoric urban area ever attempted. Photography took place in April of 1962, when the cloud-less conditions prevailed that are essential for aerial shots from 4000 feet. Concurrently, a comprehensive archeo-logical survey on the ground was undertaken to transform the raw photographic manuscript into a finished map con-taining all possible structural information of archeological interest. This was completed five years later, after various interruptions, in 1967. Overlay sheets would present a hypothetical reconstruction of what the city had looked like at the height of its development.

When the job was done, the results were staggering. From the jigsaw overlapping of photographs and the drawings made there appeared a fantastic view. At last it was clear to Millon that Teotihuacan had been an immense and well-planned city, laid out on a grandiose scale, teeming with life as early as 2000 years ago. There could no longer be any question about its having been only a ceremonial center. It appeared to be the first and most important urban center of the American continent, vaster than the area within the walls of imperial Rome of the Caesars, housing at the height of its development as many as 200,000 inhabitants organized into a most complexly stratified society. Teotihuacan had clearly been a religious, cultural, economic, and political capital, as well as the greatest known market center in Mesoamerica.

Millon realized that as a holy city, with thousands attached to its temples, Teotihuacan must also have been the seat of a religion with a wide appeal, possibly headed by a supreme pontiff, a city with the qualities of a Rome, Mecca, or Benares.

Economically it was clearly one of the largest pre-industrial cities in the world, with tens of thousands employed in crafts, and perhaps a hundred thousand involved in great markets at fixed intervals, a great attraction to visitors and traders, who had their own enclaves within the city.

Politically, Teotihuacan had evidently been the most influ-ential center in Mesoamerica during the major part of the first millennium A.D., astride the major trade and access routes into and out of the Valley of Mexico, the seat of an increas-ingly powerful state that appeared to have extended its dominion over wider and wider areas.

228

Reconstruction of the great city of Teotihuacan as imagined by Feliciano Peña of the National Museum of Anthropology.

Aerial photos revealed broad avenues to the east and west of the Citadel which had not been suspected, but which were quickly confirmed by surface reconnaissance. Other street patterns and clusterings of buildings into larger complexes, hypothesized through examination of the map, were also confirmed by field crews.

More than 2600 apartment compounds showed up, as well as other types of compounds, temples, platforms, and major structures. Of these larger stone-walled structures, more than 1200 manifested walls, floors, or other structural evidence *in situ.* In the course of surveying the city, more than 1800 floors and 1900 walls were recorded.

The outer walls of the apartment compounds turned out to be massive battered masonry or *taludes,* much thicker than interior walls, which made them easier to locate. High walls were on the exterior, without windows, giving onto narrow streets.

Millon estimated that sixty persons could have lived in one apartment compound of 3600 square meters, that thirty could live in a compound of 1600 square meters, and twelve in a compound of 600 square meters. Extrapolating from these figures, he obtained a possible population of 200,000.

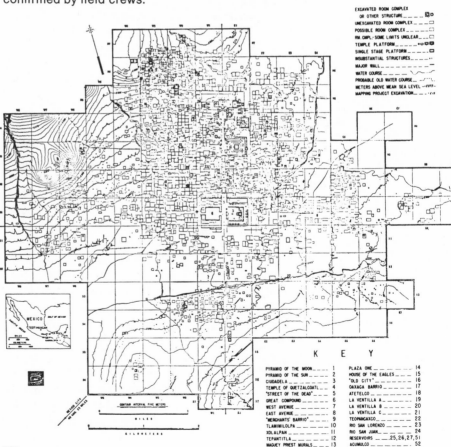

LEGEND

EXCAVATED ROOM COMPLEX
OR OTHER STRUCTURE
UNEXCAVATED ROOM COMPLEX
POSSIBLE ROOM COMPLEX
RM. CMPL- SOME LIMITS UNCLEAR
TEMPLE PLATFORM
SINGLE STAGE PLATFORM
INSUBSTANTIAL STRUCTURES
MAJOR WALL
WATER COURSE
PROBABLE OLD WATER COURSE
METERS ABOVE MEAN SEA LEVEL
MAPPING PROJECT EXCAVATION

K E Y

PYRAMID OF THE MOON _ _ _ _ 1
PYRAMID OF THE SUN _ _ _ _ _ 2
CIUDADELA _ _ _ _ _ _ _ _ 3
TEMPLE OF QUETZALCOATL _ _ 4
"STREET OF THE DEAD" _ _ _ _ 5
GREAT COMPOUND _ _ _ _ _ 6
WEST AVENUE _ _ _ _ _ _ _ 7
EAST AVENUE _ _ _ _ _ _ _ 8
"MERCHANTS' BARRIO" _ _ _ _ 9
TLAMIMILOLPA _ _ _ _ _ _ 10
XOLALPAN _ _ _ _ _ _ _ 11
TEPANTITLA _ _ _ _ _ _ _ 12
MAGUEY PRIEST MURALS _ _ _ 13

PLAZA ONE _ _ _ _ _ _ _ 14
HOUSE OF THE EAGLES _ _ _ 15
"OLD CITY" _ _ _ _ _ _ _ 16
OAXACA BARRIO _ _ _ _ _ 17
ATETELCO _ _ _ _ _ _ _ 18
LA VENTILLA A _ _ _ _ _ 19
LA VENTILLA B _ _ _ _ _ 20
LA VENTILLA C _ _ _ _ _ 21
TEOPANCAXCO _ _ _ _ _ _ 22
RIO SAN LORENZO _ _ _ _ 23
RIO SAN JUAN _ _ _ _ _ 24
RESERVOIRS _ _ _ 25,26,27,51
ACUMULCO _ _ _ _ _ _ _ 52

229

Development of the great city of Teotihuacan from its inception in about 100 B.C. to its collapse in 800 A.D.

Between A.D. 450 and 650 the city, though it did not extend over twenty square kilometers, or twelve square miles, was, according to Millon's map, most densely populated, with more than 2000 apartment complexes. The city's peak of power and influence may have been reached about A.D. 500, and most of what is visible in Teotihuacan today is attributed by archeologists to this epoch.

By 650, some form of degeneration appears to have set in, and many inhabitants seem to have moved to the east side of the city. Yet the city still flourished, despite a slight drop in population.

The maps of Teotihuacan from 100 B.C. to A.D. 800 were prepared by Millon in 1967. Since 1966 additional data have significantly modified some of the areas shown. The maps are published with the permission of Professor René Millon, courtesy of the Sociedad Mexicana de Antropologia.

Ceremonial and/or administrative buildings along the Way of the Dead could now be clearly differentiated from residential areas on both sides of them. Surface survey and excavation indicated that Teotihuacan had been divided into neighborhoods or *barrios,* groups of buildings clearly set off from surrounding structures, forming easily definable units.

Inspection of the map showed the city to have been divided into quadrants. The north-south axis was formed by the Way of the Dead; the east-west axis, subordinate to it, was formed by two great avenues that determined the city's center, interrupted by the Citadel.

A striking feature of the northern and northwestern part of the city was its many walls and great precincts. Most of these massive long free-standing walls were identified in the field by locating ruined stretches of their two sides exposed on the surface, though excavation was often needed to reveal them.

Though Millon estimated that most of the inhabitants probably lived from cultivating the land outside the city, it was clear that a very significant part of the population was engaged in craft activities within the city, the vast majority being obsidian workers in some five hundred workshops.

Millon and his principal colleagues, Bruce Drewitt of the University of Toronto and George L. Cowgill of Brandeis University, also found evidence of over a hundred other types of workshops—for ceramic, figurine, lapidary, shell, basalt, slate, and ground-stone work. They infer that different crafts lived in separate neighborhoods and believe that many were employed in the building crafts, such as masons, plasterers, and carpenters.

From aerial photos, examined stereoscopically, Millon made another surprising discovery: a part of an immense platform opposite the Citadel, with a counterpart to the south of equal size. These two great platforms formed an enormous compound around a plaza that appeared to be larger than the main plaza of the Citadel. It seemed extraordinary to Millon that so large a structure could have existed and never have been observed. The next day he and his associates went into the field and easily found outlines of the two enormous platforms with remains of apartment compounds on them, "though no prominent structures."

Millon put forward the hypothesis that this great compound had once been the city's principal market place, a bureaucratic center with compounds built on the immense platforms. With the Citadel, these compounds evidently formed the religious and commercial center of the ancient city, a megacomplex surrounded by broad avenues and plazas, with more open space than in any other part of the city, a sort of island in its center. Millon considered the plan

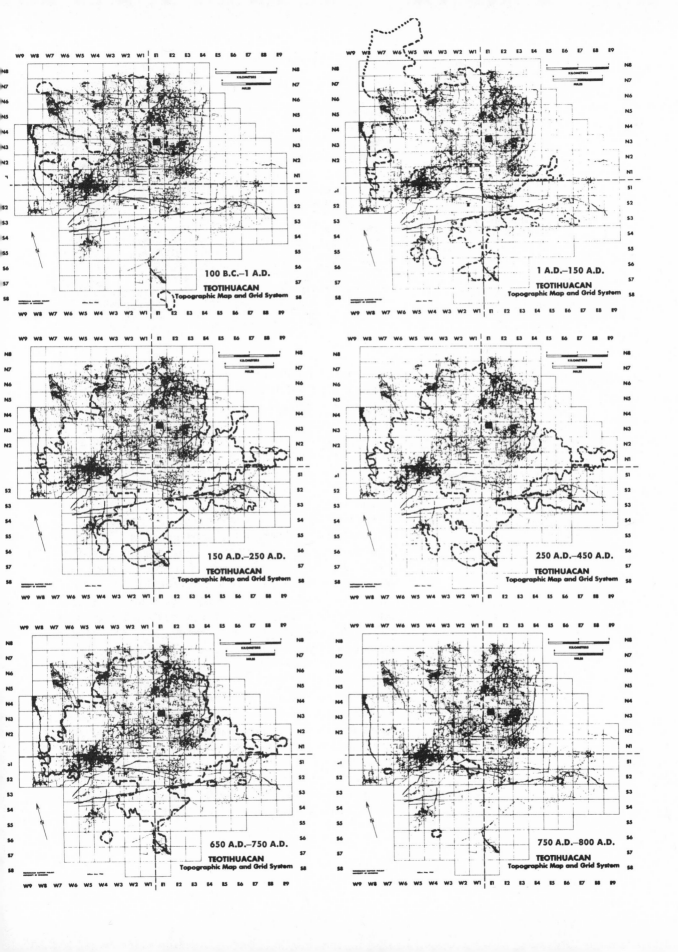

100 B.C.–1 A.D.

TEOTIHUACAN
Topographic Map and Grid System

1 A.D.–150 A.D.

TEOTIHUACAN
Topographic Map and Grid System

150 A.D.–250 A.D.

TEOTIHUACAN
Topographic Map and Grid System

250 A.D.–450 A.D.

TEOTIHUACAN
Topographic Map and Grid System

650 A.D.–750 A.D.

TEOTIHUACAN
Topographic Map and Grid System

750 A.D.–800 A.D.

TEOTIHUACAN
Topographic Map and Grid System

In the course of his explorations, Millon found that Teotihuacan had many carefully laid out canals and systems of branching waterways artificially dredged into straightened portions of a river fed by eighty permanent springs and its tributary streams, which altogether formed a network within the city and ran all the way to the lake, now ten miles away, but perhaps closer in antiquity. With these lakes and waterworks the ancient Teotihuacanos appear to have been able to feed a vast population with their system of chinampas, or so-called floating gardens, on which they could produce several crops a year.

Richard Ford of the University of Michigan analyzed plant remains of more than thirty superimposed kitchen floors and hearths in a "high status" apartment compound at Teotihuacan. He believes practically everything edible was consumed, including beans, squash, chili peppers, as well as an ample selection of wild plants such as sumac seeds. He found at least two varieties of goosefoot and portulaca leaves. He also found evidence of fish, deer, rabbits, and other game having been consumed.

one of the most majestic architectural achievements in the history of the pre-Columbian people of the New World.

Several more compounds revealed by the map, one west of the Moon Pyramid, and another immediately north of the Citadel, demonstrated that a great deal of planning had gone into the city. Millon concluded that the Way of the Dead must have been decided on very early in the history of the city, possibly before the construction of any permanent buildings other than the pyramids.

With the help of Millon's map it was now possible to re-create a tentative history of the development of Teotihuacan. Because the systems of scientific nomenclature devised by different archeologists to specify each historic period of Teotihuacan development are as confusing to the layman as they are unsatisfactory to scientists, the simplest way to date the development is by means of the Christian calendar.

From Millon's map and the shards that were excavated, it appeared that the Teotihuacan area had first been settled in the latter part of the first millennium B.C. when a handful of villages sprang up. The archeologists involved mostly agreed that it was during the period between 150 B.C. and the birth of Christ that Teotihuacan grew into a large settlement covering an area of more than six square kilometers, mostly in what was to become the northwest quadrant of the later city. In this area Millon found remnants of public buildings with stone walls and hard earth floors, the orientation of which was quite unlike that of the later city, an area that was to continue to be the most crowded throughout the city's later history.

The map survey revealed far more extensive residential areas covered with pottery fragments from the first century A.D. than previously believed. Since the same pottery was found on the Pyramid of the Sun, Millon concluded that the pyramids of the Sun and of the Moon probably were built in the earliest phase of the occupation of Teotihuacan, A.D. 1–150, rather than several centuries later, as had been assumed by Gamio and others. Early carbon dates were inconsistent, but later ones argued that the Sun Pyramid, or the greater part of it, had been built by A.D. 150.

Other archeologists hold that the city was flourishing as early as 1500 B.C., and a small group maintains that the construction of Teotihuacan goes back to an era before the eruption of the volcano Xitli, perhaps 6000 years ago.

Historians and anthropologists maintain that the cooperation of vast numbers of people would have been needed to build the two pyramids, and that this indicates the pre-existence of a great metropolis with a stable society and strongly centralized authority. These experts envisage Teotihuacan as a planned city laid out by priest-architects.

Between the first and second centuries A.D., Millon sees the city as growing rapidly to a predominant position in the Valley of Mexico, covering an area of more than twenty square kilometers. During this period Millon found evidence of the construction of more than twenty temple complexes, mostly on either side of the Way of the Dead, which had grown so long it made it impossible for travelers or traders to pass through the valley without passing through the city.

Between A.D. 150 and 200 there is evidence that the city shifted to the south and east, partially abandoning the northwest. From Millon's mapping, it is clear that by A.D. 200 the city had been split into four squares or quadrants centered on a point along the Way of the Dead opposite the entrance to the Citadel. Based on excavations carried out as part of the mapping project, Millon believes it was in this period that the Citadel was first built in its present form and that the uppermost part of the Sun Pyramid was completed. He believes that the Citadel, which was developed over the next two hundred years, along with the Great Compound, formed the symbolic as well as the geographic, political, and religious center of the city, and that nothing approaching them in scale of conception is known anywhere else in the prehistoric New World.

Between 200 and 450, the evidence shows an enormous amount of building activity, and a revolutionary change in the settlement pattern. Permanent stone-walled residential compounds, mostly consisting of a number of apartments, appear to have been built in all parts of the city, replacing most

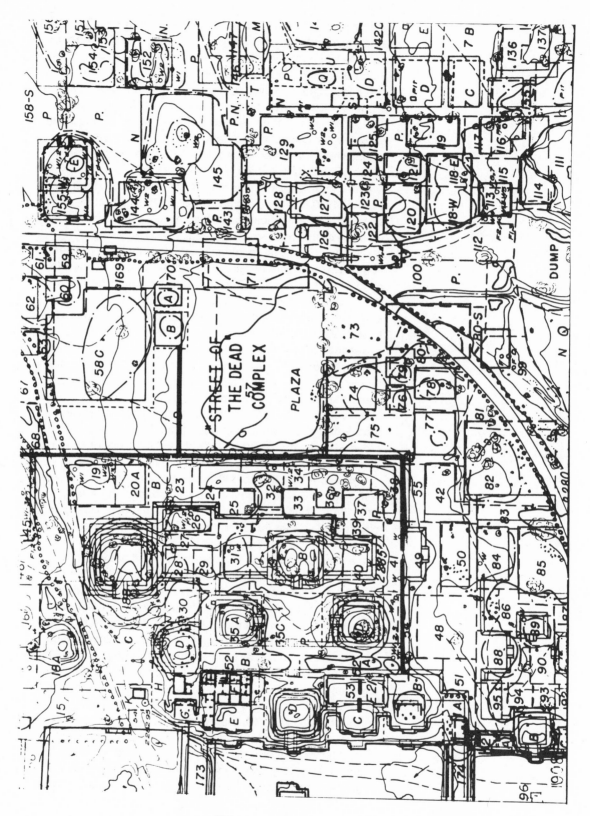

234

René Millon's chart showing current views on the chronological placement of Teotihuacan, including periods prior to its known existence as a major center and periods between its fall and the arrival of the Spaniards.

VALLEY OF TEOTIHUACAN CHRONOLOGY
Table of Concordances

		Phase Names [1]		Phase Numbers [2]		
A.D. 1500		Teocalco		Aztec IV		
1400		Chimalpa		Aztec III	POS⁻
1300				Aztec II	CLASSIC
1200		Zocango		Mazapa	
1100		Mazapan			PERIOD
1000					
900		Xometla		Coyotlatelco	900 A.D.
800		Oxtoticpac		Proto-Coyotlatelco	
				Teotihuacán IV	CLASSIC
700	T	METEPEC			
600	E		Late	Teotihuacán IIIA	
500	O	XOLALPAN	Early	Teotihuacán III	PERIOD
400	T		Late	Teotihuacán IIA-III	300 A.D.
300	I	TLAMIMILOLPA	Early	Teotihuacán IIA	
200	H			Teotihuacán II	TERMINAL
	U	MICCAOTLI		Teotihuacán IA	PRE-CLASSIC
100	A		Late	Teotihuacán I	
A.D.	C	TZACUALLI	Early		
B.C.	A				PERIOD
100	N	PATLACHIQUE	Chimalhuacán *		
				Proto-Teotihuacán I	LATE
200		Terminal Cuanalan; Tezoyuca	Cuicuilco *		PRE-CLASSIC
300		Lete Cuanalan	Ticoman III *		
400		Middle Cuanalan	Ticoman II *		PERIOD
500		Early Cuanalan	Ticoman I *		MIDDLE
600			Middle		PRE-CLASSIC
700		Chiconauhtla	Zacatenco *		PERIOD
B.C. 800					

[1] Phase names used by personnel of Teotihuacán Mapping Project (Millon and others) and by personnel of Valley of Teotihuacán Project (Sanders and others).

[2] Phase numbers used by personnel of the Proyecto Teotihuacán, of the Instituto Nacional de Antropologia e Historia (see Acosta 1964: 58-59).

* Pre-classic phases elsewhere in the Valley of Mexico.

NOTE: The absolute chronology shown is that used by the Teotihuacán Mapping Project. Terminology for the Teotihuacán phases is based on the Armillas classification (1950) with modifications.

TEOTIHUACAN MAPPING PROJECT
UNIVERSITY OF ROCHESTER

J A Cerda

RENÉ MILLON 9/64
REVISED 7/71

of the earlier structures built of relatively impermanent materials. High faceless walls and narrow streets, says Millon, became the rule in most of central and north central Teotihuacan, and the city assumed the form it was to hold till its fall. From this era date such beautiful temples as that of the Plumed Shells with its monumental deeply carved stone columns.

During the latter part of this period, or from around 350–400, the influence of Teotihuacan appears to have spread to all other parts of civilized Mesoamerica; for four hundred years, says Millon, its political and religious dominance went unchallenged. This period also saw the culmination of its architects' dreams: the city grew into a great religious center with palaces for the clergy and the aristocracy, and large apartment compounds with communal dwelling areas for farmers, craftsmen and specialists.

Between 450 and 650, the city, though it did not extend more than twenty square kilometers, or twelve square miles, was, according to Millon's map, most densely populated, with over two thousand apartment compounds. The city's peak of power and influence may have been reached about A.D. 500, and most of what is visible of Teotihuacan today is ascribed by archeologists to this epoch.

By 650, some form of degeneration appears to have set in and some inhabitants seem to have moved to the east side of the city. Yet the city still flourished, despite a slight drop in population. Sometime around 750, some great holocaust hit the city. Charred areas around all or most of the city's temples and public buildings suggest to Millon that they were deliberately burned. Millon and others found considerable evidence that the city's center, after burning and collapsing, was never thereafter rebuilt.

But whether the city was sacked by invaders or destroyed by a great fire of accidental origin remained the unanswered question. The only evidence on which all agreed was that the collapse was sudden and catastrophic.

After 750, Teotihuacan was a ghost town. As Millon reconstructs the evidence, only a few people lived in what amounted to a village one square kilometer in area. Some refugees, fleeing the traumatic experience, appear to have settled closer to Lake Texcoco and at nearby Azcapotzalco, but what happened to the rest of the population remains a deep mystery.

To account for the sudden end of Teotihuacan, other than through the agency of some unknown cataclysm, major earthquake, or violent invasion, several theories have been propounded, including a drastic change in climate, sudden soil exhaustion, massive crop failure, dreadful epidemics of malaria, yellow fever, or typhoid, or the rebellion of the agricultural populace against too demanding rulers. On the fringes of science fiction, it has been suggested that the inhabitants were removed by spacecraft from elsewhere in the universe, during which operation the city and its pyramids were discreetly covered with earth to hide their whereabouts from other travelers from space.

Climatologists maintain that a gradual decline in annual rainfall brought the city to a semi-arid climate in the latter half of the first millennium A.D., that deforestation of the hills caused erosion and a decrease in soil moisture for crops. Certainly the valley around Teotihuacan had once been humid, with vast forests in which game was abundant, with lakes teeming with fish and aquatic birds. One archeologist suggests that the destruction of the surrounding forests was caused by the burning lime that was used to carry out the great building programs in the city. Others suggest that there were repeated invasions of barbarous nomads from the north, one horde of which overwhelmed the city.

Whether or not Toltec tribes could have destroyed the great city, by A.D. 850 they were settling in the area. Millon says that, although at a relatively late date the Citadel underwent architectural modifications which could have been defensive, there is no evidence, except for the slaughtered inhabitants found by Batres in the House of the Priests, of attackers, foreign or otherwise.

Millon and others have wondered whether tensions, antagonisms, and conflicts within apartment compounds—or among people in different compounds, neighborhoods, states, classes, or sectors of the Teotihuacan society—could have posed insoluble problems for the hierarchy in the city and played a significant role in the dissolution of Teotihuacan society. He points out that great clusters of apartment compounds in an urban setting did not survive the fall of Teotihuacan and never again were the basis for a continuing tradition of urban living in central Mexico.

Was it coincidence, archeologists ask, that toward the end of the ninth century some mighty crisis appears to have overcome all the classic civilizations of Mesoamerica, at which time the many gigantic ceremonial centers that were scattered throughout the area, such as Tikal, Uaxactun, Copan, and Palenque, were suddenly abandoned for no known reason, to be devoured by the jungle?

The ninth century has been described by historians as a period in Mesoamerica of degeneration, migrations, mass warfare, long and brutal invasions, followed by terrific confusion.

Toward the end of the century, Toltec tribes appeared in the Valley of Mexico to build on the remains of the Teotihuacan empire, only to vanish three centuries later and be replaced by the Aztecs, leaving the mystery of who the Teotihuacanos may have been and what may have become of them as shrouded today as when their great monuments were sighted by Cortes fleeing Tenochtitlan after the Night of Sorrows.

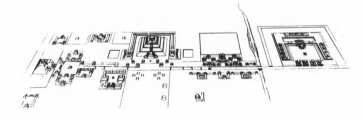

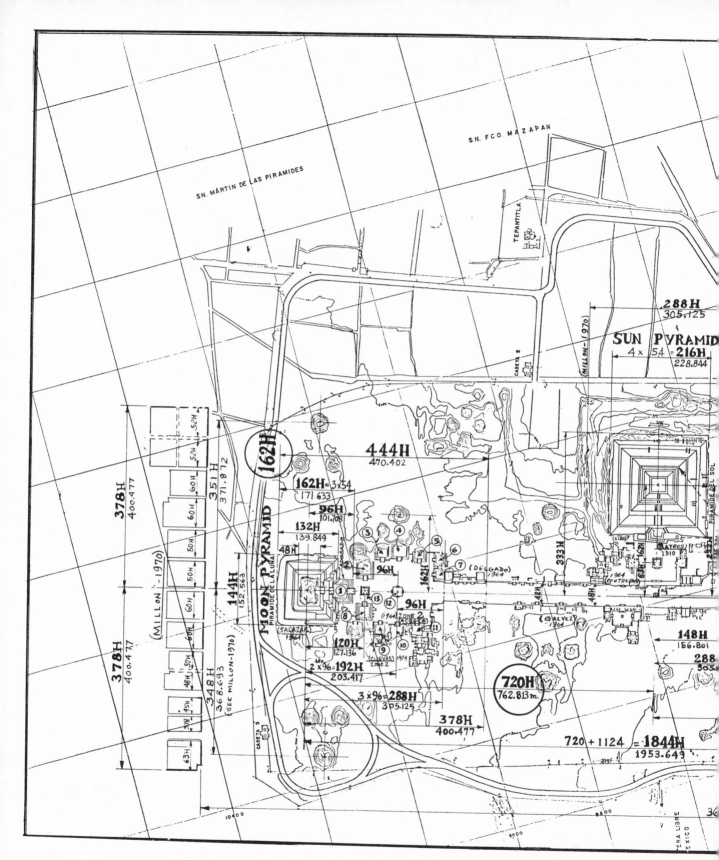

SN. FCO. MAZAPAN

SN. MARTIN DE LAS PIRAMIDES

TEPANTITLA

.288H
305.125

SUN PYRAMID
4 × 54 = **216H**
228.844

(MILLON-1970)

CASETA 2

PIRAMIDE DEL SOL

162H

444H
470.402

162H = 3×54
171.633

96H
101.708

132H
139.849

48H

333H

MOON PYRAMID
PIRAMIDE DE LA LUNA

96H

162H

(DELGADO)
1964

BATRES
1910

222H

(CONTRERAS)
1964
63H

48H

48H

148H
156.801

96H

ZONE 2

(GALVEZ)
1964

288
305

(SALAZAR)
1964

120H
127.136

(CUEVAS) 1974
ZONE 2

720H
762.813 m.

2×96=**192H**
203.417

3×96=**288H**
305.125

378H
400.477

720 + 1124 = **1844H**
1953.649

378H
400.477

352H

351.872

60H 60H 50H 50H 60H 60H 52H 48H 45H 37H 63H

144H
152.563

348H
368.693
(SEE MILLON-1970)

(MILLON-1970)

378H
400.477

CASETA 3

10400

9000

9500

CARRETERA LIBRE
MEXICO

36

PART V

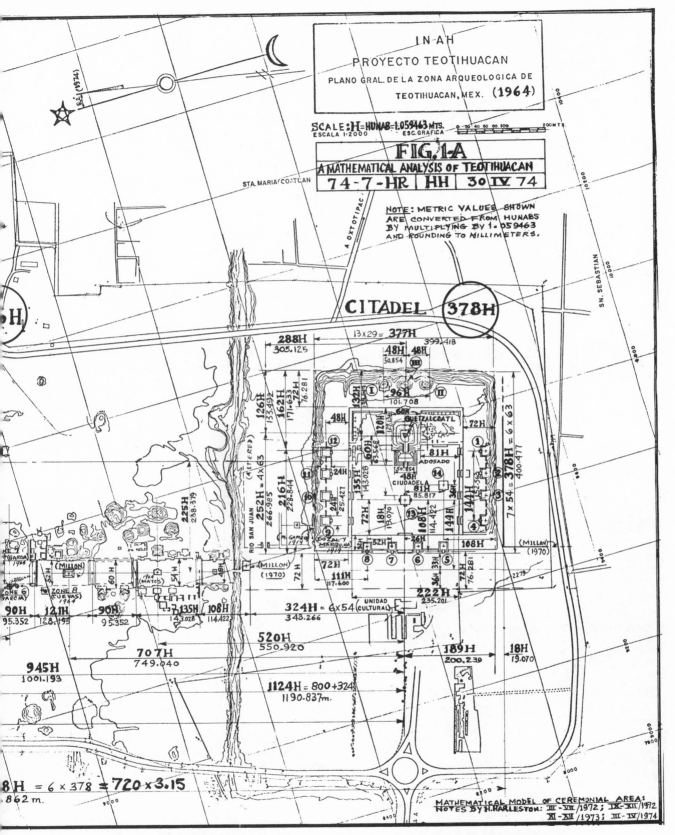

SCIENTIFIC ANALYSIS

87°☆FROM SUN PYRAMID
27.9 KM. TO UAC-KAN 13

90°☆FROM SUN PYRAMID
27.5 KM. TO UAC-KAN 14

66°☆ TO SUNRISE
ON SUMMER SOLSTICE

ASTRONOMER'S CHAIR

18. Mathematical Extrapolations

From Millon's map it was clear that the great city of Teotihuacan had been built by master builders according to a thought-out plan. The question remained as to whether such a vast complex with its massive temples might also have served a more special purpose, like Stonehenge, Cheops, or the Tower of Babel. Could Teotihuacan, like other great temples of antiquity, have served as a geodetic and astronomical marker to locate man in space and time, to fit him in the cosmos?

Unlike the Pyramid of Cheops, which has been measured to the millimeter, or the ziggurats of Babylon, for which cuneiform texts give the precise dimensions, no sound dimensional pattern had so far surfaced at Teotihuacan. Yet it was obvious that whoever laid out the city must have used some unit of measure as a yardstick, whether or not it was earth-commensurate as with the Pyramid of Cheops, whose base line of 500 cubits (or 750 Egyptian geographic feet) is exactly the distance traveled by the earth at the equator in half a second of time, there being precisely 86,400 seconds in one 24-hour day and 86,400,000 cubits in the circumference of the earth.

With the exception of Le Plongeon, none of the early diggers and reconstructors of Mexican antiquities since Almaraz —most of whom were intent on finding treasure and uncovering idols—appear to have been aware of the work of Edmé François Jomard, John Taylor, and Charles Piazzi Smyth, or of the controversy over the earth-commensurate dimensions of the Egyptian pyramids.

Unlike Cheops, with its chiseled corner sockets and trigonometrically reconstructable lines, the overgrown and dilapidated stone work at Teotihuacan made it difficult for archeologists to be sure exactly from what spot a piece of stone had been tumbled by vandals, crumbled by rain, bumped by an earthquake, or, indeed, replaced by some builder in remote antiquity.

Though the photogrammetric work of Millon's University of Rochester mapping project supplied a wealth of overall measurements, especially on a very large scale—distances of one to three kilometers—details were better shown in the drawings of Ignacio Marquina's *Prehispanic Architecture,* based on a careful survey of the Citadel area by Pedro Dozal, made with civil-engineering methods in the second and third decade of the century. Marquina considered this earlier data more reliable than the 1960 to 1964 information provided by maps in the files of the Mexican Institute of Anthropology, or even by the 1970 Rochester project.

Marquina, who had directed much of the rebuilding of the Citadel, pointed out that many of the dimensions, especially the longer ones of 150 to 200 meters, could only be considered accurate to within about 1 percent, which meant variations of over a meter.

With such margins of error, it seemed unlikely that a common unit of measure would emerge from Teotihuacan until in 1972 an American engineer, Hugh Harleston, Jr., who had lived a quarter of a century in Mexico and become obsessed with the beauty and challenge of Teotihuacan, hit upon a stratagem. Harleston decided to create a "mathematical model" to superimpose on the field measurement diagrams obtained by Millon and Marquina, on the theory that when and if a large percentage of points coincided with only a small margin of adjustment, a deliberate pattern of relationships might emerge.

To Harleston the key to resolving the problem lay in the *proportions of large measurements;* that is, if he divided the distance between the center of the Sun Pyramid and the center of the Moon Pyramid (almost 800 meters or over 2600 feet) by the overall length of the whole ceremonial zone from north to south (which is a little more than 2400 meters) the result, 2400/800, gives a ratio three to one, which changes very little if either of the distances is wrong by a few meters. Harleston reasoned that a comparison of *proportions* would show significant relationships despite any errors made in the reconstruction, especially if taken over large areas.

The first 3:1 relationship indicated to him to look for a system which might be organized in multiples of three. Taking as a supposition that errors of reconstruction or movements by earthquakes (though the geologists assured him that this had not happened) had shifted the centers between the two main pyramids by no more than 5 or 6 meters, which would make the distance between the top centers 806, instead of 800, and that if one side of the citadel were 402 meters instead of 400, the proportion of 806 to 402 would be 2.005 instead of 2.000, the result would be a proportion that varied by a mere 2/10 of 1 percent, a parameter within which Harleston could obtain valid results.

Already Millon had found what appeared to be a large recurring measure in both residential and semiresidential buildings with walled compounds which ran 57 meters to a side, twice that dimension, or a fraction of it. Longer streets also appeared to be measured off in multiples of 57 meters.

With a draftsman's compass, a pair of dividers, and all the maps he could find, Harleston set his dividers at 57 meters and began a search for further coincidences.

Almost immediately he saw that the north-south base line of the Moon Pyramid was 171 meters, or exactly 3 times 57. The base of the Sun Pyramid, marked on the map as 228 meters, was 4 times 57. The Citadel's wall of 399 meters was 7 times 57. Along the Way of the Dead, Harleston found markers at 114 and 342 meters, which is to say 2 and 6 times 57.

As 57 was clearly a recurrent measure, Harleston looked to see what fraction of it might give him a smaller proportionate measure. As 57 is only divisible by 3, he took the resulting 19 meters and searched with his dividers for any-

Harleston's view from the east of the Way of the Dead with the three major pyramids indicated in round-number distances marked by the center lines of the structures which produced such key numbers as:

162 for the Moon base
216 for the Sun Pyramid
378 for the Citadel.

The overall ceremonial zone of 2268, says Harleston, is equal to 6 Citadels, or 14 times the base of the Moon Pyramid. Individual walls along the way also show factors of 2268 including 2268/720 which is the line from the center of the Sun to the center of the Moon Pyramid from north to south or 3.15, evidently an easy figure for π, or the constant relation of diameter to circumference.

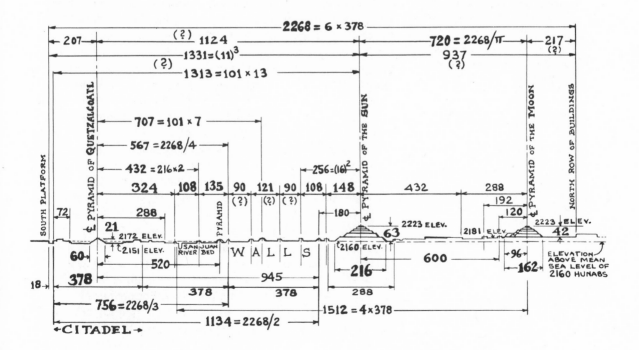

243

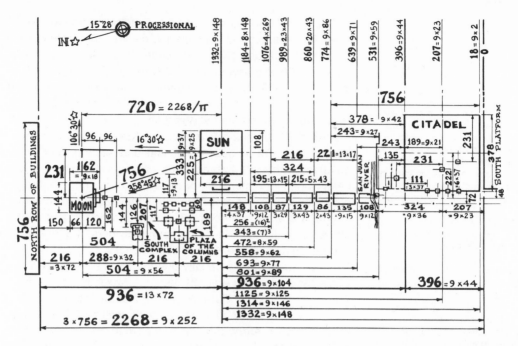

Sun Pyramid.

Harleston found that if he started at the Sun Pyramid and went south measuring walls, he got a significant set of numbers as far as the north face of the last big platform found and shown by Millon on his first map, which Harleston recognized as a clearly marked Ceremonial Avenue, 18 units beyond the Citadel wall. Measuring back from this point, Harleston was surprised to get a series of multiples of 9. This indicated to him some purposeful meaning which was only to become clear to him later. Meanwhile he noticed that most of the prime dimensional numbers in the Teotihuacan complex added up to 9: 162, 207, 216, 225, 369, 504, 531, 639, 720, 801, 936, 1125, 1314, 1332, etc.

thing that matched. In the Citadel and around the Moon Plaza he quickly found several platforms that were exactly 19 meters square. Assuming he might be on the right track, Harleston looked for a yet smaller measure. Dividing 19 by 3, the resulting 6.333 was at first sight unrewarding, until it struck him as being very close to the 6356-kilometer polar radius of the earth deduced by Sir John Herschel and Piazzi Smyth in their study of the geodetic values of the Great Pyramid of Cheops. Could the Teotihuacanos, Harleston wondered, have used as a basic unit of measure a fraction of the polar radius such as Herschel's and Newton's "sacred cubit" of .6356 meters, 10 million of which make a polar radius? The idea was intriguing, except for the fact that there seemed to be no other indication of a decimal system in the Teotihuacan figures: only 3s, 6s, and 9s.

Looking for a shorter unit, Harleston divided 6.356 meters by 6 and obtained a figure of 1.059, again a surprising result, for this was a very significant quantity in the realm of the mathematician, virtually the twelfth root of 2—a number which multiplied by itself 12 times gives a product of 2. Harleston wondered if the ancient builders of Teotihuacan might have arrived at such a basic unit by dividing the polar diameter of the earth not into 20 million parts as postulated by Herschel and Smyth for a unit of .6356 meters, but into 12 million parts for a unit of 1.059 meters. For neither one of these units was knowledge of the meter required; but Harleston had to use some conventional unit to work with

244

Moon Pyramid.

Harleston found that the edge lengths of the Moon Pyramid, from south to north, using the third *adosado*'s southern edge as a base zero point, repeated the same modules used at the Citadel and the Sun Pyramid: 30, 48, 60, 72, 81, 128, 132, and 162 STU. He found that the dimension 132 STU duplicates the distance from the center of the Quetzalcoatl Pyramid to the east edge of the Citadel, and can be factored into 11 × 12, 2 × 66, and 3 × 44.

and choose to translate what he found in terms of the meter instead of the foot or the cubit, both of which are more inspired units, because the world has largely and unfortunately adopted the meter as its basic unit of measure.

To check his theory that the Teotihuacanos had used a unit equivalent to 1.059 meters, Harleston set about measuring lengths of buildings, walls, and platforms on the basis of such a unit. Immediately he obtained modules of 18, 24, 54, 72, 108, 144, 162, 216, and 378, all in round numbers.

The Moon Pyramid, as carefully reconstructed by Salazar, gave Harleston lengths of 30, 48, 60, 63, 72, 81, 96, and 144 units, with a major north-south base of 162 units.

In the plaza at the foot of the Moon Pyramid, various temples each measured 18 by 18, for an area of 324 square units.

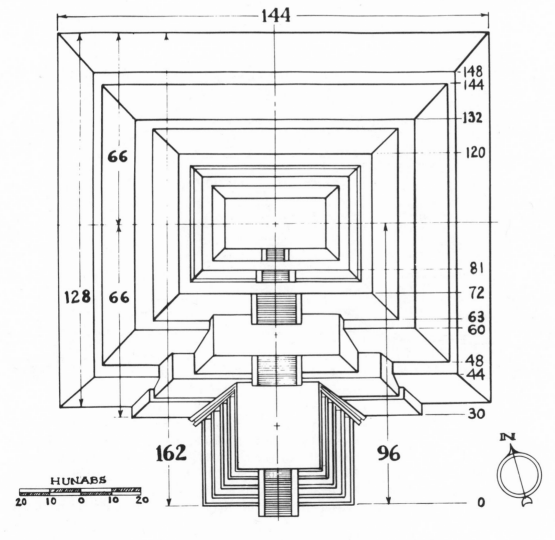

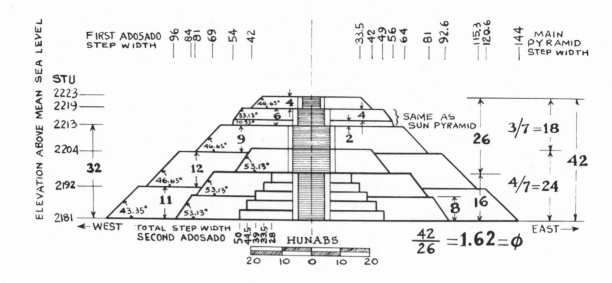

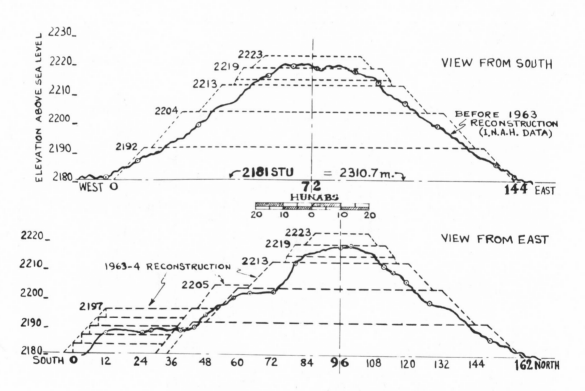

At the Sun Pyramid, measurements of the base and upper levels of each body duplicated measurements at the Citadel and the Moon Pyramid, indicating a logical series of 9, 12, 18, 27, 36, 54, 81 and 108, all multiples of 3. Lengths of 162 and 216 repeated lengths at the Moon Pyramid and the Citadel, adding up to 378, the overall length of the walls of the Citadel.

In his mathematical reconstruction of the Moon Pyramid, Harleston followed the basic principles of restoration outlined by Mexican archeologist Ponciano Salazar, who rebuilt the Moon Pyramid in 1964, maintaining the same lengths, heights, and original angles. But composite data yielded a more probable configuration with the top of the reconstructed Moon Pyramid at the same elevation above sea level as the Sun Pyramid, its base being higher than that of the Sun Pyramid. The Moon Pyramid is thus formed of thirteen basic components: the main pyramidal mass consisting of five bodies, the first *adosado* on the south side made up of three bodies, followed by a secondary *adosado* of five more bodies.

In Harleston's reconstruction, the first *adosado*'s height divides the Moon Pyramid vertically into 3/7 and 4/7, proportions shown horizontally by the west base line of the Quetzalcoatl Pyramid that cuts the Citadel into 162 STU to the east and 216 STU to the west. The north-to-south base of the Moon Pyramid, including the *adosados*, measures 162 STU and the base line of the Sun Pyramid is 216 STU, again giving the same proportions of 162/378 and 216/378 or 3/7 and 4/7.

The face angles of the Moon's first body are sloped at 43.35 degrees, the same as the Sun Pyramid. In Harleston's reconstruction, the projection of the sides to an overhead intersection point shows a triangular height of 68 STU. This means that the proportion of the 42-*hunab* truncated height becomes 68/42, again 1.62, the golden mean.

Combination of the heights of the Moon Pyramid's thirteen bodies gave Harleston values that cover a range of numbers from 2 to 42, reflecting major modules that appeared as significant factors throughout Teotihuacan matching other cosmic correlations.

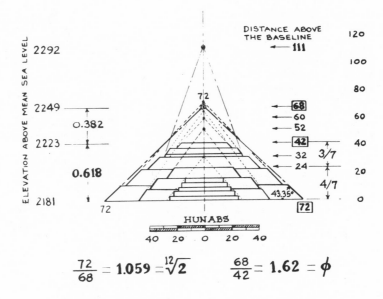

$$\frac{72}{68} = 1.059 = \sqrt[12]{2} \qquad \frac{68}{42} = 1.62 = \phi$$

Along the Way of the Dead, boundary markers appeared at 378 and at twice 378, or 756 units. The overall length of the ceremonial zone was 6 times 378, or 36 times 63, the height of the Sun Pyramid.

The north-south length of the Moon Pyramid, the familiar 162, multiplied by 14 was also 2268, the length of the ceremonial area.

Behind the Moon Pyramid a row of buildings, almost perpendicular to the main north-south avenue, ran east and west. Harleston found that these boundary buildings ran 378 units both ways, totaling 756 units, twice the width of the Citadel, equal to the distance from the center of the Sun Pyramid to the center of the Moon Pyramid.

Convinced now that he had hit upon a possible Standard Unit of Measure or STU of the builders of Teotihuacan, Harleston named the unit a *hunab,* the Mayan word for "unified measure."

Studying the figures obtained from the Citadel, Harleston noticed that 378 times his basic unit multiplied by 100,000 gave a very accurate figure for the circumference of the planet, whose average spherical circumference is 40,049,589.35 meters. Harleston then found that the 60-unit base of the Quetzalcoatl Pyramid multiplied by 100,000 gave the polar radius of the earth. This led him to wonder whether the Pyramid of Quetzalcoatl, like the Pyramid of Cheops and the stepped ziggurats of Mesopotamia, could have been designed as a scale model of the earth, part of a citadel designed to incorporate mathematical, geodetic, astronomical, and possibly cosmic data.

247

Harleston decided the Citadel might include an earth-commensurate unit when he figured that the 378 *hunab* length of the Citadel divided by the 60 *hunabs* of the Quetzalcoatl Pyramid could represent the circumference of the earth divided by twice its radius, or 378 ÷ 120, which gives a value for π of 3.15.

But he overlooked the fact that the length of the Citadel wall is also 1296 Egyptian feet, or 864 cubits, lengths used by the Egyptians and Mesopotamians to compute the circumference of the earth.

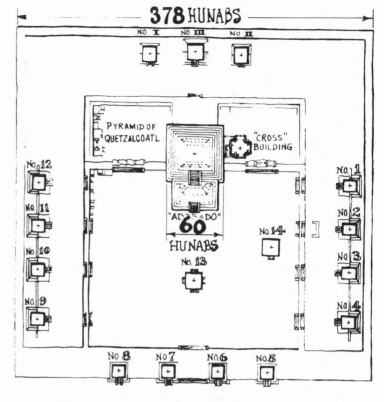

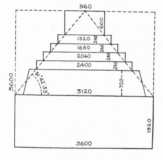

Smith's Tower of Babel.

As with the ziggurats of Babylon, the square base of the Quetzalcoatl Pyramid covers exactly 3600 square units of Harleston's measure, equal to 43,482 square English feet, which is virtually an English acre. It also compares with the Mesopotamian land measure of 60 double cubits, as shown in the Babylonian ziggurats documented in the Smith cuneiform tablet.

As the Babylonians used each face of a stepped pyramid to represent a 90-degree quadrant or hemisphere of the earth, dividing the area between the equator and the North Pole into seven bands or zones, each diminishing in width to correspond to the shrinking degree of longitude, Harleston decided to check the reconstruction of the Quetzalcoatl Pyramid to see if the same system might apply.

The elevation plans of the Quetzalcoatl Pyramid made by the Mexican Institute of Anthropology show a structure rising in six tiers to 17 meters, on top of which rests a seventh structure of 5 meters, for a total of 22 meters, or 21 of Harleston's units. However, as the precise corners of the lower six levels have not been restored, it was necessary for Harleston to use the east-west values of the rebuilt horizontal face widths to arrive at a probable original length for each step.

248

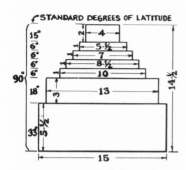

BABYLONIAN ZIGGURAT
(RELATIVE PROPORTIONS)

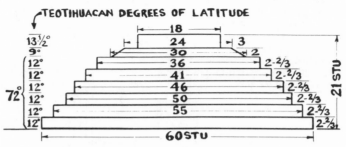

PYRAMID OF QUETZALCOATL
(ACTUAL DIMENSIONS)

Temple of Jupiter Belus. The lengths of the seven stages of this Babylonian ziggurat were found inscribed on a palette by George Smith, F.R.G.S., according to which the area of the lowest section was 3600 × 3600 inches, or 12,960,000 inches.

The Quetzalcoatl Pyramid, as reconstructed by the Mexican architect and archeologist Ignacio Marquina in the 1920s, was also made in seven stages. The ziggurats at Ur, Uruk, and Babylon were as high as 300 feet (91 meters), equivalent to a 25-story building. This compares to Teotihuacan's Sun Pyramid at 18 stories. As Livio Stecchini has shown, the stepped pyramid, or ziggurat, transfers curved data to a flat surface in order to make a projection of an earth hemisphere with a minimum of distortion. Each main step face represents a 90-degree quadrant, and the levels can represent the zone between two parallels of latitude, in a series of mercator projections.

The Babylonians divided the area between the equator and the North Pole into seven bands, or zones, each diminishing in width to correspond to the shrinking degree of longitude. The base line corresponded to the equator, and the first step to the 30th

parallel. The ziggurat in Mesopotamia raised the first step to a height corresponding to 33 degrees of latitude instead of 30 degrees, since 33 degrees was the location of Babylon. Thereafter each step rose in units of 6 degrees of latitude. By dividing the length of the step by 2/3, an easily remembered calculation of the cosine value of the latitude is obtained.

The Babylonian ziggurats incorporated a series of map projections several thousand years before modern cartography was refined in Europe during the eighteenth century. The Naba ziggurat at Barsipki was made in seven stages, and was said to have been painted with seven "planetary colors."

The Babylonians preferred counting in sixes, and their mathematical systems were hexagesimal and heptagesimal; that is sixes and sevens. This preference was apparently

also characteristic of the Egyptians. Livio Stecchini shows how the degrees of latitude of a parallel represented by each ziggurat step can be obtained by multiplying the step height by 6. Thus 6 × 5 1/2 becomes 33 degrees of latitude for the first step.

A similar system emerges at the Pyramid of Quetzalcoatl in Mexico. The elevation and plan views of the Mexican Institute of Anthropology allow converted measurements that show the height of the known steps in six tiers to total 17 meters, with a seventh structure of somewhat more than 5 meters on top. In Harleston's units each main vertical step becomes 2 2/3 *hunabs,* and the upper structure of 5 *hunabs* makes the pyramid 21 *hunabs* high, or 7 × 3. Since 21 *hunabs* represent 90 degrees of latitude, each step becomes 11 3/7 degrees of latitude.

Step No.	Step Length	Cosine	Latitude Angle, Std Degrees	Denotes
1	15	1.0000	00.00	Equator
2	13	0.8667	29.93	Thirtieth Parallel
3	10	0.6667	48.19	
4	8½	0.5667	55.48	°Lat. = °Long. (Equator)
5	7	0.4667	62.18	
6	5½	0.3667	68.49	
7	4	0.2667	74.53	Magnetic Pole

Harleston's reconstructed plan of the Pyramid of Quetzal-coatl with measurements in *hunabs*. However, when measured in Egyptian units, the width becomes a very interesting 204 feet, or 136 cubits, and its height 72 feet, or 48 cubits.

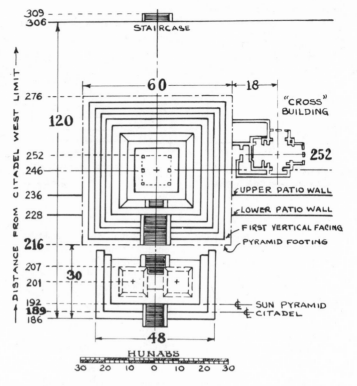

Harleston's reconstruction shows that the steps of the Quetzalcoatl Pyramid may have been designed to rise in lengths which indicated various important latitudes on the planet. When measured in *hunabs* the steps rise in increments of 2 1/3. But when measured in palms, they rise evenly in units of 24 from a base of 360 palms.

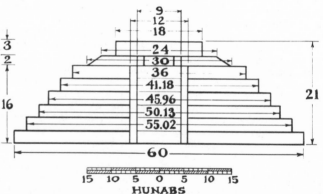

From the various figures given by the Mexican Institute, Harleston made several mathematical reconstructions until he arrived at one which seemed closest to what the original might have looked like.

To find the angle, or latitude, represented by the various steps, Harleston divided the length of each step by 60 to obtain the cosine of the angle of that latitude. The first step produced a result of 23.449 degrees, which corresponds to the latitude of the Tropic of Cancer. Other steps gave the latitude of the Arctic Circle, and the magnetic pole. The system appeared to be the same as that of the Babylonians.

250

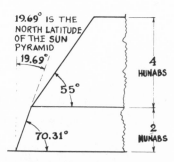

19.69° IS THE
NORTH LATITUDE
OF THE SUN
PYRAMID

19.69°

55°

70.31°

4
HUNABS

2
HUNABS

55° IS THE LATITUDE AT
WHICH ONE DEGREE OF LONGI-
TUDE EQUALS ONE DEGREE
OF LATITUDE.

Sun Pyramid's fourth body.

Conversion of the Sun Pyramid's metric measurements to
hunabs is shown by Harleston's theoretical reconstruction. The solid lines indicate
the restoration by Batres in
1906 to 1910, and by the
Mexican Institute of Anthropology and History in 1963
to 1964. The dotted lines use
the Citadel logic and are
based on refilling almost
exactly the parts left off. The
flying buttresses formed retaining walls for the missing
material that would have cost
too much money and time to
have restored in 1910. The
mathematically sequenced
lengths of the pyramidal
bodies follow a series of
increasing sums. The individual heights and also the
elevations above sea level are
factors of the number 3.

This still did not necessarily prove that Harleston's unit
of 1.059 was the unit actually used by the builders of Teotihuacan; if the proportions were correct, the results would
check out with whatever unit of measure had been used. But
it did indicate that the Quetzalcoatl Pyramid had the measurements of an earth-commensurate model, like the ziggurats
and pyramids of the Middle East.

To see what information might be keyed into the Sun
and Moon pyramids, Harleston made composite reconstructions of them using minor deviations from the res-
torations made by the Mexican Institute of Anthropology. On
the Sun Pyramid he replaced the amounts of missing material
which the literature indicated had been removed by Batres
from the first, second, and third levels.

Immediately he noted a 1-2-3 relation between the Quetzalcoatl, Moon, and Sun pyramids, which turned out to be respectively 21, 42, and 63 units high, measured in his *hunabs*.

But it did not occur to Harleston that these same figures
also gave 48, 96 and 144 of the ancient Egyptian cubit of
.462 meters on which the great Pyramid of Cheops is built.

On the fourth body, Harleston felt that Batres had actually
conserved practically the "original" positions of the stones (as
he stoutly affirmed to his critics) and that the original design
was close to what is seen today.

Noting that the lower portion of the fourth level was slightly
convex and that it formed a triangle with an angle of almost
19.69 degrees to the vertical, it struck Harleston that this was
also the latitude of Teotihuacan. This meant that when the sun
crossed the pyramid at the equinox its rays would fall onto the
north face of the fourth body at the same angle of 19.69
degrees to the vertical.

To observe what would actually happen at the equinox,

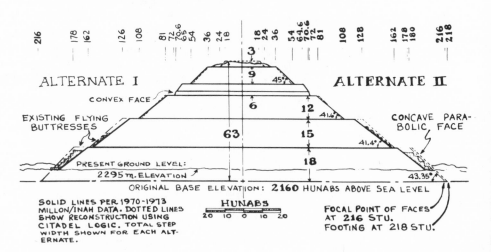

251

12:35'30"

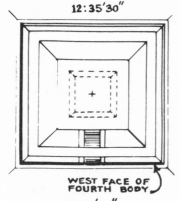

WEST FACE OF
FOURTH BODY

12:36'03"

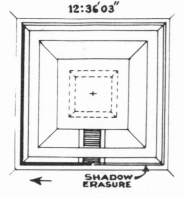

SHADOW
ERASURE

12:36'37"

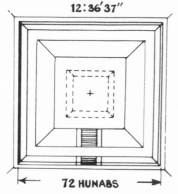

← 72 HUNABS →

Manner in which the shadow
on the lower part of the fourth
body of the Sun Pyramid—
a constant and boldly outlined
feature of the structure—is
eliminated at the equinox.

Hugh Harleston, Jr., showing lower fourth level in shadow. The only two shadows on the Sun Pyramid at midday on the equinoxes (March 21 and September 23) are on the western and northern faces, as seen in the above photograph of Hugh Harleston, Jr. The shadows appear only on the lower part of the fourth body. The shadow on the west face is removed by the advancing sunlight within a time lapse that suggested to Harleston that the designers divided a minute into 63 of their seconds (67 Newtonian seconds), the same number as the height of the Sun Pyramid itself in *hunabs*. The shadow on the north face is not removed until two days after the equinox, when it "flashes" on and off at midday, signaling the event and providing a calendar count correction twice a year, making of the Pyramid a living clock.

Harleston noted that the phenomenon in fact took place two days after the equinox. As the shadow did not wipe on the actual day, it meant the angle of the slope was 19.5 instead of 19.7, which could have been an error in reconstruction, or the angle was intended to convey some other meaning. However, observing the west face of the pyramid at the equinox, Harleston was able to witness a unique effect. As the sun crossed the zenith at 12:35' 30" (local noon at the longitude of Teotihuacan), the lower west part of the fourth face of the pyramid, which is in shadow during the morning, became illuminated as the sun's rays moved from south to north. The whole effect occurred in 66.6 seconds, a phenomenon which makes the Sun Pyramid a perennial clock, still transmitting its silent message, exactly as does the Great Pyramid of Cheops, or as does the south corner of the Castillo at Chichen Itza, each equinoctial day of the year. All these structures would have had to be designed by architects aware of the considerable astronomical and geodetic data required to achieve such effects—*before* the buildings were begun.

Harleston's analysis, interesting as it might be, remained

Harleston measuring Citadel.

circumstantial. There was no valid substantiation of his notion that the builders of Teotihuacan used the twelfth root of 2 as their constant, and it seemed hardly possible that they could have arrived at it as he had by means of the meter—or 1.059 thereof. Furthermore, as there appears to have been a great deal of intercourse between the Middle East and Mesoamerica, with a flow of technicians as well as religious and philosophical notions, it seemed reasonable to assume that any earth-commensurate unit used in Mesoamerica be related to the unit used in the building of the Great Pyramid of Cheops, or at least to have been derived from some common source. By applying to the Teotihuacan complex the ancient Egyptian geographic foot, of which there are 750 built into the base of the Pyramid of Cheops, the results were surprising. The most definite measure in the Teotihuacan complex is the width of the Citadel, given by Marquina as 399.48 meters (and by Harleston as 378 of his *hunabs*). Measured in the geographic feet of the Great Pyramid (or of the entire ancient world) 399.48 meters is 1296 feet or 864 cubits.

Here were the figures used by the ancients to define the circumference of the earth in both seconds of arc and seconds of time, the numbers from which they derived both their foot and their cubit. These two numbers, 1296 and 864, are basic to the entire ancient system of measures. Elsewhere in the Teotihuacan complex the foot and the cubit appear in easy and significant numbers. Harleston and Marquina's 800.6-meter distance between the Sun and the Moon Pyramids is 2600 ancient geographic feet.

The Quetzalcoatl Pyramid as measured by Harleston (on the basis of INAH's data) gives a width of 204 feet or 136 cubits. Its height comes to 72 feet or 48 cubits, figures that are every bit as significant as Harleston's. By his reconstructed measures, translated into geographic feet and cubits, the Moon Pyramid's height would be 144 feet or 96 cubits. Its reconstructed width, which is arbitrary, would be 558 feet or 372 cubits. The Sun Pyramid comes out to be 216 feet high or 144 cubits, all figures which Harleston considers significant. As there is still no known way of accurately measuring the base of the Sun Pyramid, of which only the northwest corner has so far been found, it may be idle to speculate on its length, but *if* it were to be the 218 *hunabs* postulated by Harleston, it would be almost to the millimeter the length of the Great Pyramid of Cheops: 750 feet or 500 cubits.

Even more startling is a transfer to feet and cubits of Harleston's reconstruction of the Palenque Temple of the Inscriptions. Whereas his measurements in *hunabs* come out to a mostly uneven 26, 21, 17 5/6, 14 1/2, 12 1/3, 11 1/2,

253

Temple of the Inscriptions at Palenque showing measurements made by Harleston in *hunabs* of 1.059 meters, which come out in random fractions. Computed in Egyptian feet and cubits the same measures give an extraordinary progression of even numbers from 12 to 90.

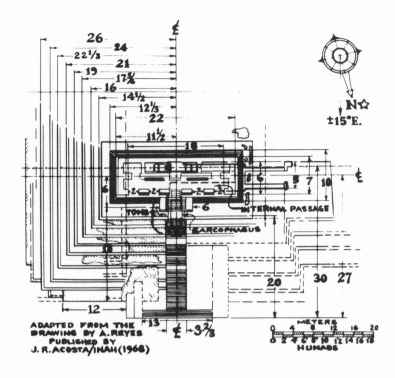

ADAPTED FROM THE
DRAWING BY A. REYES
PUBLISHED BY
J. R. ACOSTA/INAH(1968)

3 2/3, when measured in the geographic feet of the Egyptians, these same numbers come out to a round 90, 72, 60, 50, 42, 40, and 12.

As the ancient foot and cubit were divided into palms and fingers and the Aztecs also had palms and fingers, the same divisions may have been used by the Teotihuacanos: if measured in palms all Teotihuacan measurement numbers would simply be increased by a factor of six, or by a factor of 24 if measured in fingers. The ancient Middle Eastern finger of .01925 of a meter is one of the most indelible measures: 96 fingers equal their fathom, 9600 fingers their stadium, and 96,000 fingers their mile; 21,600 of these miles, or 60 × 360, will take you around the world. The Arabs also divided their finger into 6 grains of barley or 36 hairs of a camel; thus their cubit was equal to 864 hairs of a camel, whereas the circumference of the earth was 86,400,000 cubits, or 100,000 times the Teotihuacan width of the Citadel in cubits.

Evidence for the use of finger, palm, foot, cubit, and fathom in Mesoamerica is solid as a pyramid.

Dr. Daniel G. Brinton, head of the Archeology Department of the University of Pennsylvania, in his *Essays of an Americanist,* published in 1890, is unequivocal about the unit of the Aztecs: "the foot measure was adopted as the official and obligatory standard both in commerce and architecture." To which he adds that there is ample evidence that it was "widely recognised, very exact, and officially defined and protected." Quoting Herrera, he shows that, just as in the Hebraic world, anyone in the Aztec world who falsified units of measure was considered a public thief, an enemy of the community, and severely punished.

After a long and careful study of the subject, Brinton concluded that the foot and the cubit (of a foot-and-a-half) had been the basic units of measure not only of the Aztecs but of the Maya and the Cakchiquels (among whom he includes the Quiche and the Tzutahil). To this he added that "the Aztec terms for lineal standard being apparently of Maya origin, suggests that their standard was derived from that nation."

The Mayan foot was the *oc*. Their cubit was the *cuc* or *noch cuc*, which Brinton describes as being about 18 inches, or a foot-and-a-half. Their fathom of six feet was a *zap* or *zapoul*; half a fathom or *betan* was their three-foot yard.

A *kaan* was 36 fathoms square, and 20 *kaan* made a *vinic*, the area of land needed by a man to support one family in corn. According to Brinton, the smallest Maya units of lineal measure were the finger breadth or *u nü kab*, and the thumb breadth *u na kab*, our inch or French *pouce*. The Maya also had three different spans of which the most used was the *nab*, from tip of thumb to tip of index; but they also had the *chi nab*, from thumb tip to little finger tip, and the *kok*: closed finger palm with extended thumb.

Father Thomas Coto expressly states that the cubit or *chumay* was the customary building measure among the Cakchiquels. "When they build their houses they use this cubit to measure the length of the logs. They also measure ropes in the same manner." Cakchiquel fields were marked off in fathoms of four cubits, and a three-fathom unit was a circle around a man with outstretched arms. The Aztecs also had the finger, span, and foot, as well as the cubit which they called *cemmolicipitl*, from *ce* = one and *molicipitl* = elbow. Their fathom was the *cemmatl*, and a half-fathom or yard the *cenyollatli*. For measuring longer lengths they used the *octacatl*, and though the unit has not been identified, Brinton believed that because *oc* is the Mayan for foot, it may have been a ten-foot length, a unit of which he found considerable evidence in the Americas.

Father Duran reports that along the Aztec highways, there were posts or stones erected with marks upon them showing how many of these stops there were to the next market town, a system employed throughout the Middle East. Unfortunately Duran did not measure or find out the distance between two such markers.

If it seems astounding that no one quickly established just what the Aztec unit of measure might have been, as related to European or any other measure, it must be remembered that it is a perennial and fundamental rule among conquerors to obliterate their victim's system of measures and place on the ruins of their sacred temples new structures built with an imposed system of measures.

It would have been pleasant to leave the matter there, but a possible complication may eventually lead to even further clarity. The Egyptians, or Middle Easterners, had a unit of 40 fingers called a *bema* whose length was .77 of a meter, 300 of which fit exactly into the base of the Great Pyramid; it was widely employed as a measure equal to ten palms.

If Harleston's *hunab* is divided into 60 fingers, a unit of .01765 meters is obtained, which is virtually the Aztec finger, as reported by V. M. Castillo in his *Unidades Nohuas de Medida,* forty of which make an Aztec *bema* of .706 meter. When applied to both the Teotihuacan and Palenque complexes, Aztec fingers, palms and *bemas* give even more significant results than Harleston's *hunab.*

The Quetzalcoatl Pyramid base, instead of being 60 *hunabs* becomes a more rational 90 *bemas* or 360 palms, and its steps rise in increments of 4 *bemas* instead of 2 1/3 *hunabs.* The perimeter of the Sun Pyramid becomes 12,960 *bemas* and its base length 1296 fingers. As the numbers 1296 and 864 were the key to unraveling the astronomical and geodetic secrets of the Great Pyramid, they may in due course resolve the mysteries of the Mesoamerican Pyramids.

Is it a coincidence that a circle of 1,296,000 units has a radius of 2,06,265 units and that 20.6264 is the length of both an English and Egyptian cubit, that the Hebrew shekel weighs 129.6 grams, and the English guinea 129.6 grains, and the measure of the Most Holy in Solomon's Temple is 1296 inches?

Not only was the number 129600 the numeric basis for astronomical measurements as far back as the records are traceable, it was also the favorite number in Plato's mystic symbolism. W. H. Wood, in his *Ideal Metrology,* says the multiples and submultiples of 12960, which are easily memorized—1728, 864, 720, 432, 360, 216, 180, 90, 40, 36, 20, 16, 10, 8, 5, 4, 2—were everywhere used as sacred numbers in the building of temples. The Babylonian tablet Igi-Gal-Bi contains all of them, plus 144, 162, and 810, which appear at Teotihuacan in both *hunabs* and cubits.

Wood points out that in the law of the Yoga, all periodic

actions developed under the inspiration of the Invisible are measured by ideal cycles, expressed in geometric form by the number 1296 in thousands or thousands of thousands. The third stage of Yoga is represented by the third of 1296 or 432, which is considered the symbol of consecration, or standing in harmony with nature's beauty and order. The exalted life of a disciple of Buddha called for a cycle of 4320 million years.

Alan Watts in his *The Book* points to the Hindu myth which says that as time goes on, life in the world gets worse and worse, until at last the destructive aspect of the Self, the god Shiva, dances a terrible dance which consumes everything in fire—shades of Tezcatlipoca! There follows, says the myth, 4,320,000 years of total peace during which the Self is just itself and does not play or hide. And then the game begins again, starting off as a universe of perfect splendor which begins to deteriorate only after 1,728,000 years, and every round of the game is so designed that the forces of darkness present themselves for only one third of the time, enjoying at the end a brief but quite illusory triumph.

Charles Muses, writing on the origin of certain Babylonian numbers in a note in *Ancient Cultural Anthropology,* says the Chaldean priesthood of the ancient Sumero-Babylonian civilization was convinced, as were the later Pythagoreans, and indeed many physicists and cosmologists today, that embedded in cosmic structures lies a comparatively small "alphabet" of deeply fundamental numbers. As Muses put it, rephrasing Plato, "God not only geometricizes, but profoundly arithmetricizes."

Among those numbers still in great use today, Muses lists 360 degrees for a circle, 60 minutes for an hour, 60 seconds for a minute, and 24 hours for a day. He also notes our 7 days of the week, 12 months of the year. Taking the 4 states of matter, plus a quintessence, and adding to them unity and trinity, Muses makes a list of 1, 3, 4, 5, 7, 12, 24, 60, and 360; he proceeds to show how all of these numbers are simply and uniquely related to patterns of *circular arrangement.*

Using as an example a hostess with a round table of guests to be seated, Muses shows how the number of arrangements she can choose from jumps from 12 for 5 guests to 60 for 6 guests and to 360 for 7 guests. The seven guests, says Muses, represent the heavenly bodies of Babylon. Babylonian astronomy, which existed overwhelmingly for astrological purposes, was developed upon the 5 visible planets plus the Sun and the Moon.

These all appeared to revolve against the background of the stars in a comparatively narrow belt, changing the pattern of their place arrangement about what Muses calls "the great round table of the sky," overtaking each other because of their observably varying speeds. With 7 bodies, the number of arrangements was just 360. With 6 bodies, obtained by placing the sun in the center—the system standardly used for the interpretation of horoscopes—the number becomes 60. With 5 bodies, setting aside both sun and moon, the number is reduced to 12, or a division of the sky into the 12 zodiacal signs, or the twelve months of the year.

According to Muses, a twofold twelveness, or 24, comes from uniting the 12 signs of the zodiac with 12 hours of the day. Thus from 360, 60, and 24 came a circle for time of $24 \times 60 \times 60$, or 86,400 seconds; and a circle for space of $360 \times 60 \times 60$, or 1,296,000 seconds.

When a fellow engineer from Louisiana, Alfred E. Schlemmer, suggested to Harleston that he scan the Citadel for indications that it might have been used as a vast calendrical complex built around the numbers 13 and 52, Harleston realized that the four temples on the north, south, and west platforms of the Citadel, all the same size, plus one more, oddly placed within the patio, added to thirteen; all of them had thirteen steps on each of four sides for a total of fifty-two—the length of the Aztec century. Harleston noted that the distance between the centers of the western temples when measured in his units was 3 times 52, or 156.

This led him to conjecture that the builders of Teotihuacan could have celebrated ceremonies on various temples specially designed and arranged to incorporate the mathematics of their calendars.

He figured that if the Teotihuacanos had added one day to their calendar every 4 years, repeating the exercise thirteen times for a cycle of 52 years (perhaps using the four faces of their thirteen temples for a yearly ceremony), and then added another day at the end of three 52-year cycles (perhaps using the three larger temples on the east side of the Citadel for this 156-year cycle), they could have spread their calendrical ceremonies over a span of five human generations to obtain a calendar far more accurate than the Gregorian, correct to within 9/10 of a second per year, which would have needed no further correction for another 97,500 years.

For this the Teotihuacanos would, of course, have had to use a sidereal year, observing when a star reappeared in the same position in the sky at the end of 365.2564 days. With such a fraction of a day, just over the quarter, or .25, they would eventually have had to add another whole day over and above the leap years in order to keep their calendar correct; once every 156 years, to be exact.

258

The four western platforms of the Citadel mark 156 *hunabs,* a distance that could represent a tricentennial time period of three 52-year "centuries."

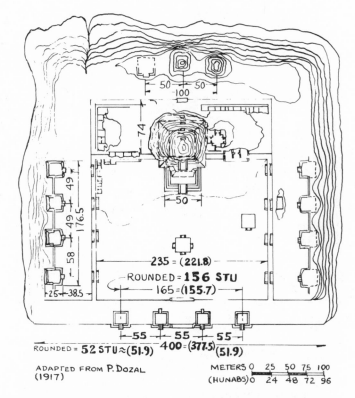

50 — 50
—100—

74

—50—

49

49

176.5

58

235 = (221.8)
ROUNDED = **156 STU**
165 = (155.7)

25 — 38.5

—55— —55— —55—
ROUNDED = **52 STU** ≈ (51.9)   400 = (377.5) (51.9)

ADAPTED FROM P. DOZAL
(1917)

METERS 0   25   50   75   100
(HUNABS) 0   24   48   72   96

Spurred by the results of his hypothetical reconstruction, Harleston looked to see if there were other measurements in the Citadel to indicate a calendrical system. Starting at the entrance and moving clockwise around the perimeter of the patio, Harleston was surprised to obtain three counts of 365 and one of 366 units—clear indications of a yearly cycle—for a total of 1461 days, or units, identical with the Sothic cycle of the Egyptians.

Already in 1962 a similar notion had been advanced by George Kubler, author of *The Art and Architecture of Ancient America,* who suggested that the Citadel was "probably used for rituals of a calendrical nature." It struck Kubler that the three groups of four platforms round the Citadel plaza added to the Quetzalcoatl pyramid made thirteen ritual locations which could have been used for ceremonies dividing the calendrical cycle of fifty-two years into four parts of thirteen years each.

Kubler's idea was sustained and elaborated by David R. Drucker in a doctoral thesis for the University of Rochester. Drucker, who had worked on the Citadel as an assistant to Millon, suggested that the Teotihuacanos, fully conversant with the Maya technique of day counts in intermeshed calendars of 260, 360, and 365 days, could have used succeeding platforms in the Citadel to celebrate a constantly

259

A. FIRST COUNT

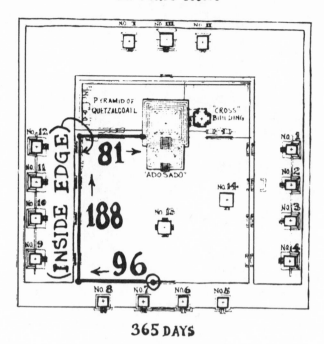

365 DAYS

B. SECOND COUNT

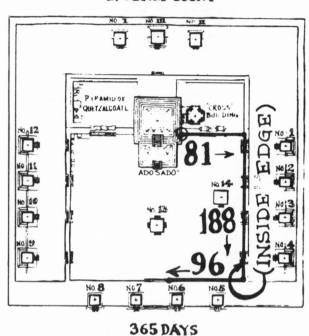

365 DAYS

C. THIRD COUNT

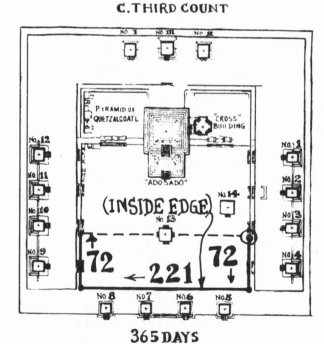

365 DAYS

D. FOURTH COUNT

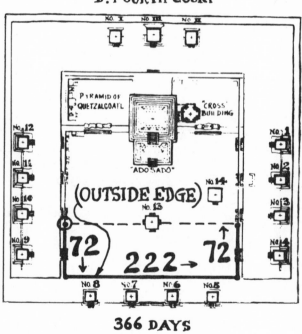

366 DAYS

Harleston's four-year calendar count.

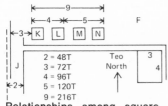

Relationships among square platforms on F J and the Palace area expressed as simple whole numbers.

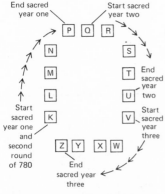

Drucker's calendar count in the Citadel.

Drucker took Platform Q as his starting point because it was the largest, and proceeded clockwise counting by twenties. He suggests there was a ceremony every 52 years on the Temple of Quetzalcoatl, and that each mound may have been surmounted by a temple with a flag or insignia on its roof to signify its role. Drucker says the system would have been perfect for recording a *tun,* or 360 days, as the last day would end on the main pyramid and start again.

unfolding day count for each of these rounds, plus the 584-day synodic return of Venus.

If, says Drucker, each Venus year were celebrated counterclockwise on the next platform immediately to the right, after 104 calendar years of 365 days (equal to 146 sacred years) a conjunction of the vague and Venus years would occur on the Quetzalcoatl platform where the ritual could be witnessed from the plaza.

Drucker furthermore believes that the Teotihuacanos laid out their whole city on the basis of a calendrical system that was most likely a heritage of the Olmecs (though it now appears that the Maya may have preceded the Olmecs). Drucker points out that the bearing of sunset at the beginning and end of the 105-days interval after the day of zenith was perpendicular to the Way of the Dead at the latitude of Teotihuacan, or 19° 42′.

Harleston concluded it might be worth investigating whether other geodetic, astronomic, or physical data could have been displayed in the actual geometry of the Citadel's buildings; if, for instance, there were triangles whose sides contained information deliberately encoded by the builders.

To eliminate the possibility of irrational or chance occurrences obtained from using any desired dimension to force answers, he put some elementary restrictions on his search. Any lines used had to fall on integral numbers defined by marker limits in the Citadel, such as walls, edges of platforms, centers of platforms, centers of pyramids, edges of staircases, and so on. Triangles had to be right-angled, and had to run north-south and east-west.

Within these parameters, Harleston soon found a score of Pythagorean right-angle triangles, and it was clear to him that the designers had a knowledge with exceptional accuracy not only of π, but of ϕ and ϕ^2—numbers which have a mathematically abstract relationship, and which appear to be basic to the construction of this universe.

In the case of π, Harleston found nine integral triangles, all of whose sides included principal Citadelic dimensions such as 189, 222, 246, 147, 165, and 216 units.

Surprisingly, the triangle with the sides 216 and 165 units produced a hypotenuse of 271.810596, extremely close to the constant *e,* the natural logarithmic base 2.718281828 for Napierian logarithms. Twelve more triangles gave *e* with exceptional accuracy.

Harleston found that the probability of multiple reiterations of such numbers being strictly chance approached zero as the number of repetitive displays increased.

When Harleston saw that the Citadel's message might contain such "modern concepts" as the value for a logarith-

Harleston found the φ proportion in the Citadel, starting from the center of the Quetzalcoatl Pyramid. 207/127.9 = 1.618 = φ, and 144/89 = 1.618. As with many classic and Renaissance structures, these φ relationships are aesthetically satisfying and account for the Citadel's extraordinary air of elegance.

The constant, known to the ancients and designated by the Greek letter φ, is the proportion called "the golden mean." It has been found to be related in nature to the spiral growth in sea shells and other organisms. Mathematically the number is obtained in two ways: as the limit of a series of numerical divisions called the Fibonacci series (after the Italian mathematician), or simply taking the square root of 5, adding 1, and dividing the sum by 2:

$$\phi = \frac{\sqrt{5}+1}{2} = \frac{2.236068 + 1}{2} = \frac{3.236068}{2} = 1.6180339885\ldots$$

The number is usually shortened to 1.618, or further to simply *1.62*.

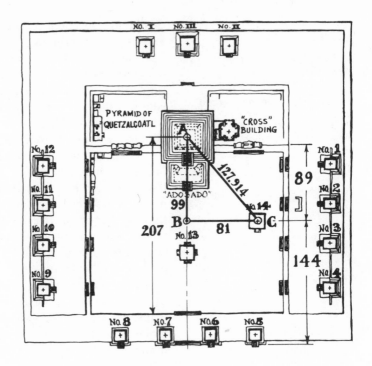

In the Citadel Harleston found several 3:4:5 Pythagorean triangles.

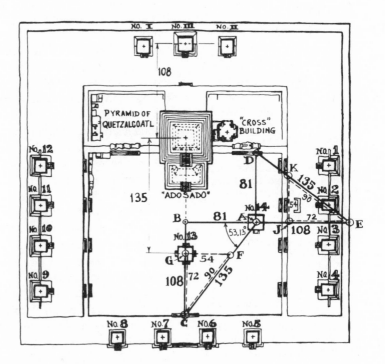

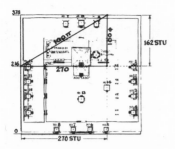

π and ϕ triangle in the Citadel.

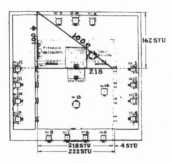

e and ϕ triangle in the Citadel.

mic hyperbolic function, he wondered if there might not also be triangles which would give values for the other basic Einsteinian constant, the speed of light, which would have to be expressed as one-millionth of its value, namely 299.7925.

Harleston found that a triangle with sides 144 and 262 (which are 12^2 and $100\phi^2$) gave the speed of light within —1.0028, and another, with sides 162 and 252, gave a diagonal within 99.93 percent.

To Harleston, the correlative triangular information defined by the design of the Citadel's walls, platforms, and other delimiting structures was of such a complexity and interwoven exactness that he could only compare it to that of a computer program readout.

Here, said Harleston, was a design whose dimensional configurations provided accurately universal mathematical and other constants with a minimum of shared points. It was as if punch cards had been supplied for a four-dimensional advanced computer with the request to display an ideal architectural design that would incorporate major universal constants, geodetic, atomic, astrophysical, and other cosmic information in the minimum number of structures, all of which had to conform to right-angle Cartesian coordinates on an optimum scale model of the earth.

As the chances of the designers and builders of Teotihuacan having deliberately laid out such triangles to incorporate the values of π, ϕ, e, and the speed of light seemed remote, the more acceptable conclusion appeared to be that the designers could have been operating from some higher state of consciousness with the benefit of more cosmic and therefore simpler mathematics by means of which they could intuitively sense valid relations which would automatically include the basic constants of our three-dimensional math, which we, like blind men touching the elephant, can only describe with the squaredom of Cartesian coordinates.

Perhaps the pyramid complex was an intended hint to latecomers to expand their consciousness for a clearer view of the cosmos and of man's relation to the whole.

19. Cosmic University

Like a dog with a bone, Harleston continued to worry his *hu-nab* length and growl at any scoffers. If the Sun Pyramid had served its designers as a geodetic clock, and the Citadel as a gigantic calendar and repository of triangular data, what, Harleston wondered, was the function of the great north-south axis of Teotihuacan, misnamed the Way of the Dead? As he pursued his research, he began to get indications that it might have served as an enormous planetarium, a scale model of our solar system.

If one side of the base of the Pyramid of Quetzalcoatl of 60 units had been used by the Teotihuacanos to represent the radius of the earth, the radius of the sun would have been proportionately 6500 units, with a diameter of 13,000 units. Searching for such a demarcation, Harleston saw that this was roughly the distance across the Valley of Teotihuacan.

Rolled up and gathering dust in the vertical bins of the third-floor map and record room of the Mexican Institute of Anthropology, Harleston came across some old material considered to be strictly obsolete and only of academic interest, some of it still in the form of pencil drafts on squared graph paper, depicting the Way of the Dead.

Analyzing this material, Harleston saw that lengths between the walls with respect to the Sun Pyramid's center line provided integral proportions similar to the magnitudes already displayed by the Citadel and the Sun and Moon pyramids: lengths of 108, 144, 135, and 324 units. Already Millon had found a regular spacing of north-south streets, with definitely placed structures at fixed intervals not only along the Way of the Dead but along its prolongation north of the Moon Pyramid, and had suggested as a zero point for the ceremonial

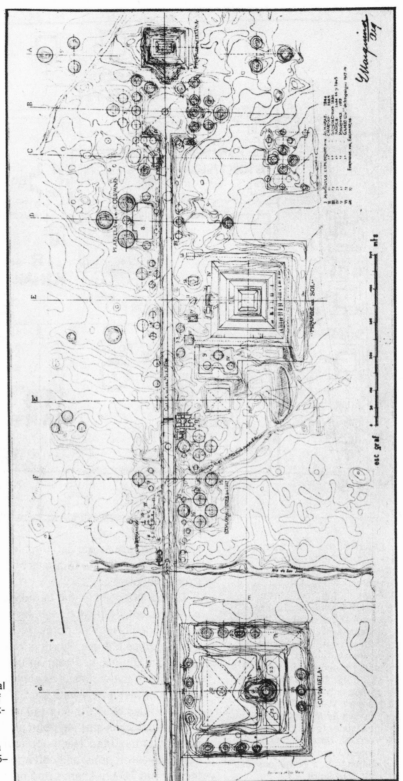

Ignacio Marquina's early aerial map of the ceremonial area of Teotihuacan done while working with Gamio shows the areas explored by Almaraz in 1864, Charnay in 1885, Garcia Cubas in 1895, Batres in 1885–1905, Rodrigues in 1912, and Gamio in 1917–1919.

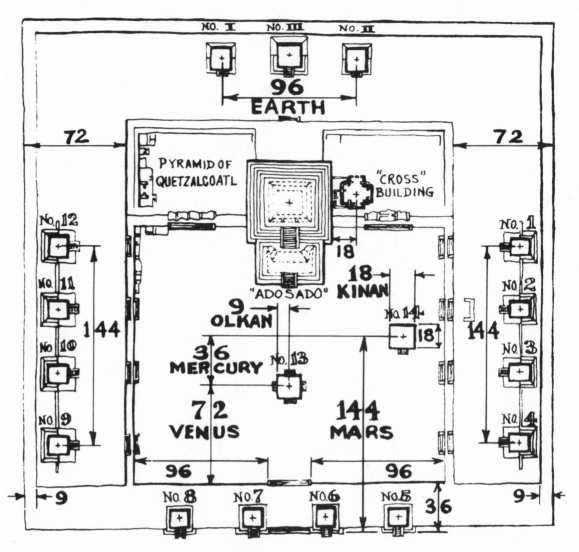

NO. I   NO. III   NO. II

96
EARTH

72   72

PYRAMID OF
QUETZALCOATL   "CROSS"
BUILDING

18

No. 12   No. 1

18
KINAN
No. 11   No. 2

No. 14
144   18   144
9
OLKAN
No. 10   No. 3

36   No. 13
MERCURY

72   144
VENUS   MARS

No. 9   No. 4

"ADOSADO"

9   9

96   96

36
No. 8   No. 7   No. 6   No. 5

Orbits of the inner planets.

Harleston measured from the center of the Citadel to the edge of Platform 13 for a total of 9 units. He then realized that the values of the distances of the inner planets from the sun were displayed by the various walls and platform centers giving 9, 18, 36, 72, 96, and 144, which correspond to the orbits of Mercury, Venus, Earth, Mars, plus two additional possibilities closer to the sun than Mercury. These Harleston named Olkan and Kinan meaning "Sun Consciousness" and "Sun Spirit."

zone and approximate geographical center of the ancient city the intersection of the Citadel's center line with the axis of the Processional.

Taking this point as the center for a scale model of the solar system, Harleston was able to find markers along the Processional which to him gave values for the orbits of the various planets. Starting from the exact center line of the Pyramid of Quetzalcoatl in the Citadel, and arbitrarily assigning to the earth's orbit a value of 96 *hunabs,* the inner planets of Mercury, Venus, and Mars fell on their correct orbital values of 36, 72, and 144 units.

From the same starting point and traveling northward up the Way of the Dead, Harleston found that the canal of the San Juan River, apparently diverted from its original course by the ancient Teotihuacanos and made to flow under the Processional parallel to the Citadel, gave the average maximum orbital distance of the asteroids at 288 *hunabs,* or twice the orbit of Mars. This was only a vague indication. But still further, at 520 units, the remains of a pyramid corresponded to the average proportional distance of the orbit of Jupiter, as found by our astronomers, some 3 percent out of line from an ideally stable orbital shell.

Excited, but still doubtful, Harleston paced his way on up the Way of the Dead with a steel tape measure. At 1000 meters, or 945 *hunabs,* north of the Citadel's center line there is a spot where there had once been a platform, now obliterated. During the work of reconstruction carried out between 1962 and 1964 this section of the Way of the Dead had been paved over with asphalt to allow rubber-wheeled tourist trains to transit through the zone. By Harleston's calculations the spot could have been the demarcation for the average orbital distance of Saturn, which is now 9.55 astronomical units, about 2 percent further out than the ideal symmetrical orbital shell.

CERRO GORDO

7628 ——— 7200 ———— ●   PLANET "X" (XIKNALKAN)

Outer planetary orbital distances

Starting with the center of the Quetzalcoatl Pyramid as a mark for the sun, and measuring northward up the Processional, Harleston found that all the known planets, plus another potential one, fell on definite markers which were symmetrically spaced in what appeared to be a binary progression beginning with the number 9: i.e., 9, 18, 36, 72, 144, 288. This is illustrated by the actual distances of Mercury, Venus, Mars, and the asteroids (9 × 4, 9 × 8, 9 × 16 and 9 × 32 units when the earth's orbit is assigned a value of 96, a number which is clearly displayed in the Citadel). It was here that Harleston concluded that the earlier indications of multiples of 9 appearing throughout the ceremonial area could have been intentional.

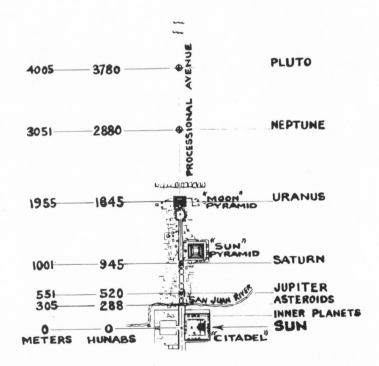

Starting from the premise that the law of angular momentum is valid for all the known universe, a Soviet named Schmidt, for whom the Institute of Geophysics in Moscow was named, formulated a theory of the harmony of the distances between planets by which the square root of the distance of planets from the sun increases from planet to planet by a constant amount. Schmidt's theory has now been verified not only for the planets of our solar system but also for the satellites of the larger planets.

In 1963 Lloyd Motz, then associate professor of astronomy at Columbia University, stated the view that planetary systems must appear and develop around stars of a given type as uniformly as the formation of salt crystals, which are always the same, whether they are formed on earth, Mars, or a planet millions of light-years away.

Until late in the eighteenth century, only five planets were known: Mercury, Mars, Venus, Jupiter, and Saturn. However, at the beginning of the seventeenth century when Johannes Kepler discovered that the orbits of the planets were slightly elliptical rather than truly circular, and that even these ellipses were irregular, the aberrations were attributed to some other as yet undiscovered planet or planets.

In mid-eighteenth century an astrologer, Johann David Titius of Wittenberg, noted a deep numerical connection between the planetary orbital distances of our solar system. His discovery, publicized by the German astronomer Johann Elert Bode in the following century, became known as Bode's Law. The formulation derives the mean distances of the planetary orbits by multiplying a series of numbers by 3 and adding 4 to each result, obtaining the numbers 4, 7, 10, 16, 28, 52, 100, 196, 388, which correspond roughly to the positions of the planets. Recent refinements, such as those of Alfred Schlemmer

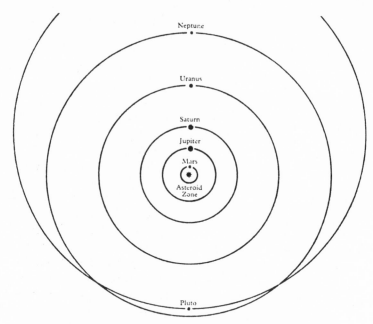

Next came the center point of the Moon Pyramid, corresponding to 19.2 astronomical units, or the precise orbital distance of the planet Uranus.

Encouraged by what he considered the extraordinary consonance of these processional markers, Harleston took off behind the Moon Pyramid and climbed the flank of Cerro Gordo to see what more he could find. At 2880 and 3780 *hunabs* from the Citadel, he came upon two typical temple mounds not yet reconstructed by the Mexican Institute of Anthropology and History. The first mound marked the correct orbital distance of Neptune at 30 astronomical units from the sun. Neptune was discovered in 1846. The second mound marked the distance of Pluto at 39 astronomical units. Pluto was discovered in 1930. Further up Cerro Gordo, at 7200 *hunabs* north of the Moon Pyramid's center line, Harleston came across the remains of an ancient temple known to the native residents as the Temple of Xochitl (or "Flower"), remains that were barely visible because treasure hunters had thrown most of the structure over the side of the ravine to cover up the traces of their pilfering.

Extrapolating from the previous Teotihuacan data, Harleston theorized characteristics at this location for an unknown planet "X," almost twice as far from the sun as Pluto. Naming it Xiknalkan (Mayan for "Flying Serpent"), Harleston attributed to it a mean orbit of 11,212,800 kilometers, or 75 astronomical units from the sun, a diameter approximately three times that of the earth, or 37,000 kilometers, and an inclination to the plane of the ecliptic of 4.74 degrees, compared with Pluto's 17 degrees.

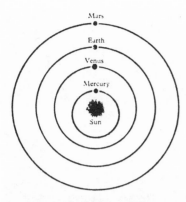

and Charles Muses, show a more complex law is at work.

In 1787 Sir William Herschel, Astronomer Royal at the Greenwich Observatory, realized that what was thought to be a star was actually a planet. First named for him, it was later called Uranus.

In 1845 a bright young Englishman, John Couch Adams, figured out where to look for a second new planet, but the local observatory paid him no no heed until a local Frenchman, Urbain Leverrier, reached the same conclusion by independent calculation and the planet Neptune was discovered during the night of the autumn equinox of 1846.

In 1930, at the observatory built in Flagstaff, Arizona, by wealthy Bostonian Percival Lowell, a young man, Clyde Tombaugh, got a picture of a new planet which turned out to be Pluto, a planet so eccentric in its orbit that in 1976 it moved in closer to the sun than Neptune.

Because such evidence indicates an overall system operating from the macrocosmic to the microcosmic, occultists have based their number systems on the time periods of the planets which are a direct function of their distance from the sun. To occultists the fact that twelve earth years is equal to one year of Saturn, leads them to conclude that 12 times 30, or 260, must be a significant number in the system.

There is, of course, considerable mention in occult literature of undiscovered planets in the icy regions of space beyond Pluto, and the Russian philosopher Georges Ivanovitch Gurdjieff maintained that we experience the influence from two such undiscovered planets beyond Pluto.

Physicists, philosophers, and psychics have all adduced data on the possibility of intra-Mercurial and extra-Plutonic planets as yet unofficially discovered. Several leading astronomers, including J. J. See, W. Peck, T. Gugril, and G. Forbes, have predicted planets with varying periods of orbit. But the weight of academic thought on their putative postions does not correspond with Harleston's locations. Dr. William H. Pickering, working out of his private observatory in Jamaica in the 1930s, postulated, on the basis of an exhaustive study of the perturbations of both Uranus and Neptune and of the period comets, the existence of two more planets beyond Pluto and predicted that the first of these, which he called "S," would have a sidereal period of 333 to 336 years, at a mean distance from the sun of 48.04 astronomical units, or half of Harleston's distance.

Pickering's figures agree remarkably well with those obtained by Dr. Charles Muses, a mathematician, physicist and cyberneticist who placed such a planet—which he suggested calling Pan—at 48.4 astronomical units from the sun with a period of 342 years. Dr. Muses obtained his data from two different approaches: by a refinement of the Bode-Titius law into a threefold law whose parts are related and mutually overlapping at their successive limits of application, and by a theory of cylindrical wave formation whereby the planetary orbits appear as rings formed by the comparatively dense matter of the planets in contrast with the light-filled bands of interorbital space in the solar system, as explained in his paper published by the National Research Council of Italy in 1965, and in a more popular version as "Why Do Celestial Bodies Rotate and Revolve?" in the *Journal for the Study of Consciousness*.

One other mathematician, Joseph L. Brady of Livermore, California, in an effort to explain the major irregularities in the orbit of Halley's Comet, has proposed a planet closer to Harleston's location, one that would orbit retrogradely in a period of 512 years, with a mass 300 times that of the earth, and tilt of 60 degrees to the ecliptic.

Within the Citadel's boundaries, where he believes the dimensions may indicate the orbits of the inner planets Mercury, Mars, and Venus, Harleston thinks that the dimensional system may indicate two more planets closer to the sun than Mercury, to which he has given the names of Olkan and Kinan, "Sun Consciousness" and "Sun Spirit."

269

Harleston's drawing represents his and Alfred Schlemmer's "far-out" notion derived from Aztec mythology of a flayed planet—the twin to Mars—called Quetzalcoatl or "Sumer," whose outer surface is conceived to have been deliberately "peeled off like an orange" by space people and deposited into the oceans of Terra in the form of the present continents, leaving the moon as a sterile core.

According to this reading, the damaged twin companion, Xipe Xolotl, the flayed Red God of the East, or Mars, retreated to a new position at a distance of 228,000,000 kilometers from the sun, its face cratered with the evidence of celestial bombardment confirmed by the Ranger space probes of 1976.

In this Velikovskian heavenly drama, Venus, the former twin companion of Earth, would have plunged into a nearly circular orbit at a symmetrical position of 108,000,000 kilometers from the sun, three-quarters the distance to her sister Earth. According to Harleston, the "arrow," that the Aztec said Venus launched, returned to her as a gravitational field, and she bounced sunward, stopped her clockwise spinning, and began to revolve backwards in retrograde rotation. Thereafter a dead planet, her incandescent atmosphere slowly cooled enough to have a temperature of boiling oil.

In this legend, Terra, the planet with the iron heart, was not light-headed like Quetzalcoatl, the hollow moon that arrived from the *west* (an orbit farther away from the sun), so she now deviated in her orbital circling only six percent. As Schlemmer reconstructs the tale, rotational rates may have varied, along with polar inclination, as the differences caused climatic changes, worldwide macroearthquakes, rains of meteorites, floods, and general havoc that remained engraved in the subconscious memories of the survivors.

Geoffrey Hodson, the psychic Theosophist, using what he calls "etheric vision," was able to spot an intra-Mercurial planet postulated under the name of Vulcan by astronomer Urbain Leverrier, who successfully predicted the discovery of Neptune. Using Hodson's and Leverrier's data, another astronomer, George Sutcliffe, was able to determine an orbital period for Vulcan. According to Sutcliffe, Vulcan can only be seen on very rare occasions of its transit as a small black disk over the sun's face because it radiates and reflects only deep infrared radiation.

In Dr. Muses' analysis there is room for just one such planet orbiting between Mercury and the sun, with a period of 42.9 days, but there has been little systematic search for Vulcan because of observational difficulties due to its proximity to the sun.

Surprisingly corroborative evidence for Harleston's figures then came from his friend Alfred Schlemmer, who for years had been analyzing the recurrence of large-scale earthquakes around the globe, keeping records of where they occurred and how big they were. From this accumulated data Schlemmer established to his own satisfaction that tornadoes and earthquakes repeat in cycles in a broad band around the world, cycles which he says are conditioned by the effect on the earth of the several motions of the other bodies in our solar system, motions called torsional because of the twisting effect they have on the earth as it rotates on its axis and revolves around the sun. When the moon, for instance, is at perigee (closest to the earth) every 27 1/3 days, its pull on the earth increases by 6 percent. The constantly differing patterns of planetary movements cause great torsional pull on the earth's crust, as does the sun's varying gravitational field, all of which cause earthquakes.

Curious to see if the periodicity of the earthquakes had anything to do with the length of the earth's rotation on its axis, measured in either tropical or sidereal years, Schlemmer came up with a list of thirty-eight numbers which appeared to be constants. By using a tropical year of 365.242189 days and dividing it by 1440, the number of minutes in a day, Schlemmer obtained the number 0.2536404097, by means of which he was able accurately to extrapolate orbital distances for the planets; he was also able to conjecture the theoretical existence of six additional planetary shells between Mercury and the sun, which may or may not be occupied by condensations called "planets" or merely by rotating fields, with the first three either non-condensed or burned out.

To Harleston and Schlemmer's surprise, nineteen of Schlemmer's constants coincided with numbers obtained by Harleston along the Processional at Teotihuacan. They found this so remarkable, as might any reader of Arthur Koestler's *The Roots of Coincidence,* that they concluded that if anything they had underestimated the scientific capacity of the Teotihuacanos and the reach of their overall mathematical display. It looked to them as if their Teotihuacan constant of 1.059 might provide an index of orbital distance, while ϕ, or 1.618, might be an index of time, both incorporated into the laws of celestial mechanics.

If repeating shell data could be validated by further outer space probes, Harleston figured there might be not one but two more planets beyond Planet "X," the first, Planet "Y," at 100 astronomical units, orbiting at an inclination of 2.09 degrees to the ecliptic, and Planet "Z" at 150 astronomical units, or 22 1/2 billion kilometers from the sun, at an inclination of 0.44 degrees.

A further clue to the possible layout of the Way of the Dead came to Schlemmer from watching a pan of oil on a tractor in which standing waves of a very particular shape were being engendered by the simultaneous spinning and vibrating motion of the tractor.

Schlemmer figured that if an earthquake in one part of our spinning globe can cause standing waves to form on a liquid surface right across the planet, then the several walled-off levels of the Processional, whose lengths coincided with his torsional constants, could have been used as a series of reflecting pools, falling down from the foot of the Moon Pyramid to the area in front of the Citadel, like the pools at the Royal Palace of Caserta, near Naples, harmoniously designed to enable Teotihuacanos to read from the standing waves formed on them the location and strength of earthquakes around the globe, enabling them to predict such an occurrence in their own area. Harleston then figured that at a time when earthquakes appear to have been more frequent and more devastating, knowledge of the characteristics of resonant vibration could have permitted the Teotihuacanos to use the several pools as long-range seismic monitors. It could also be an indication that the modern penchant for laying out reflecting pools, like the raising of obelisks, may be just a hangover from an ancient science no longer understood. Certainly a series of reflecting pools with the Moon Pyramid in the background would have been as impressive a sight as the Taj Mahal; and in support of Schlemmer's theory, one can still see sluices at the foot of each of the partitioning walls along the Processional.

Spurred by this conceit Harleston could no longer be restrained. He suddenly saw the Teotihuacan layout as possibly containing clues not only to the planetary orbits and telluric convulsions, but to much more hermetic data. It occurred to

Harleston's romantic reconstruction of how pools of water could have cascaded from one to another down the Way of the Dead, fed by springs from Cerro Gordo. When sluiced from below and used as reflecting pools, Harleston and Schlemmer believe that standing waves generated in the variously sized pools by distant earthquakes could have served the Teotihuacanos as a form of seismograph.

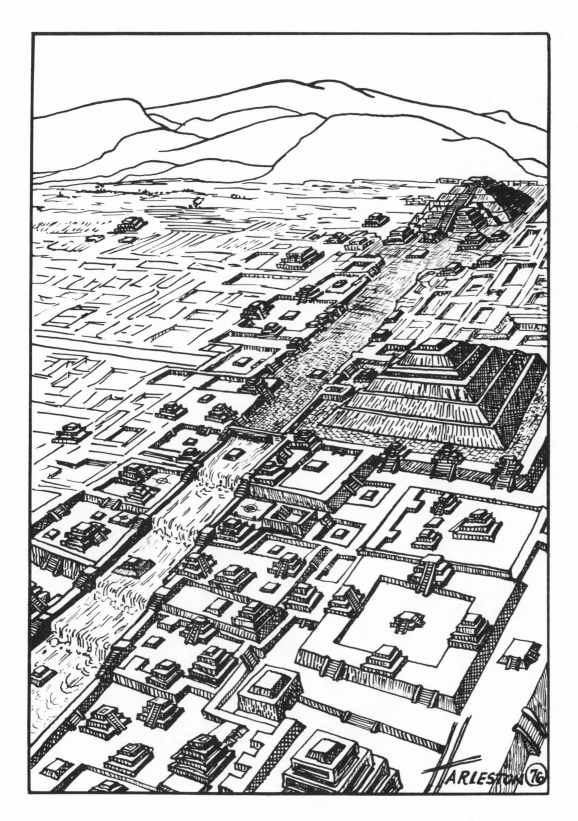

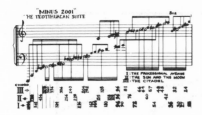

Harleston says the modular lengths of Teotihuacan can be compared with musical octaves. If the distance from north to south between the Sun and Moon pyramids were a huge guitar string 763 meters long, it can be imagined to sound a fundamental vibration, like a bass violin or the lowest note on the piano. He arbitrarily calls this tone C (or do). To sound the tone G (or sol) the guitarist would place a finger one-third of the way up the string 254 meters from the Moon Pyramid, and leave two-thirds free to vibrate. The string will oscillate one and a half times as fast as before.

Harleston found that the three chords overlap at one wavelength: 96 units, which he calls the relative orbital distance of the earth on the Teotihuacan planetarium. The orbital proportion of Mercury would then become what he calls the note B (or si) and one octave below it is Venus, while two octaves below represents Mars. To Harleston these are three base chords that might form the structure of a Teotihuacan suite.

When the proportional "notes" which corresponded to steps, walls, and buildings of the Processional, Citadel, and the Sun and Moon pyramids were converted to "chords" and diagrammed on paper, three great chords appeared, which, to Harleston's surprise, were just like the opening bars of Richard Strauss's *Thus Spake Zarathustra,* used by Stanley Kubrick as background for the opening of his motion picture *2001.*

Harleston that the Way of the Dead, as seen from the bird's-eye view of Acosta's mapping, might give the appearance of an enormous guitar whose frets were the walls of Schlemmer's reflecting pools. Could the Teotihuacanos, Harleston asked himself, have incorporated in their design of the great Processional an eight-note musical scale? Looking for "musical relationships" in the distance between the wall "frets," Harleston arbitrarily took as his note B (or *si*) the marker he had found for the relative orbital distance of Mercury. In this way an octave below it came Venus, and two octaves lower, Mars. But the distance of the markers did not quite work out, at least so long as he went by the frequencies of our "well-tempered clavichord," a scale worked out by Johann Sebastian Bach in which the mathematical frequencies are slightly corrected for the pleasure of Western ears and the convenience of orchestral scoring. Some of the notes were as much as four cycles lower than the mathematical frequencies displayed in the Teotihuacan measures. Then Harleston remembered that when he had first arrived in Mexico in the late 1940s he had been taken to the house of the Mexican composer Julian Carillo, who composed music in a different scale, one which he called "sound 13" because it divided an octave mathematically by means of the twelfth root of two, or what

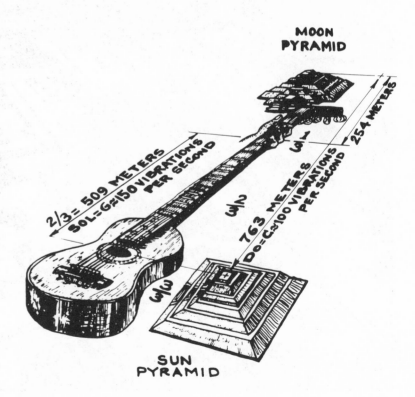

Mexico's composer Julian Carillo.

Harleston says that as Teotihuacan yielded its secrets, one by one, he began to sense the sweep of its creator's vision. "At the lower level of the vibration, three major chordal sequences merge at a common note that symbolizes our planet's orbit: 96. At the intermediate range of the visible spectrum six balanced colors of light point toward the invisible vibrations beyond the range of our normal optical capabilities. And beyond this the sounds of our spiral universe are heard, as the evolution of an open-ended wave that becomes four-dimensional radial space and three-dimensional expanding time, the tetrahedron, and the sphere."

Harleston considered was the Teotihuacan constant, into thirteen equally spaced notes (or twelve intervals) with seven white keys and five black keys. In this system, each frequency multiplied by 1.059 gave the next half note, which, multiplied by itself, gave the next whole note.

Harleston found that Carillo's musical proportions, which produced a weird and exotic effect on the listener, turned out to be the closest approximations to the relationships of the measurements at the area of the Teotihuacan monuments.

Creation is certainly mathematical and harmonic, with physical relations such as the orbit of a planet, the pentagonal divisions of a fruit, the spiral growth of a vine, or the shape of a honey bee's cell, all expressible in mathematical terms: even the structure of bones, nerves, muscles, cells, molecules, and atoms, all appear to be governed by mathematical law.

Light, music, color, and even the table of chemical elements appear to be harmonically linked. Were the human ear capable of discerning sounds produced by chemical action, we might perceive a musical harmony, or better a symphony, in all forms of living. In the past, certain members of society may have had just such abilities.

According to Michael Heleus, an astrologer from St. Petersburg, Florida, who has developed a theory called "astrosonics," the actual motion of the planets as they orbit the sun makes sounds, or creates wavelengths, which affect a human being in different ways, more especially as they harmonize, or not, with the person's own birth chart.

By reproducing the various wavelengths of orbiting planets and raising these sounds sufficient octaves to be audible, Heleus claims to be able to produce in people astrological effects at will.

Like Orpheus, who was supposed to be able to charm any creature with his lyre tuned to the motions of the planets, Heleus says he can produce painful or pleasant sensations in humans. Gurdjieff also describes a broad gamut of musical effects, including the raising of boils on bodies with a tune.

Citing the stock example of a glass shattered by a singer's voice because it can only absorb so much energy on that wavelength, Heleus suggests that objects and especially buildings on this planet absorb and retransmit only if their proportions are earth-commensurate or harmonize with wavelengths from the cosmos. He believes the yard, the foot, and the inch are more in tune with telluric and cosmic forces than the inadequate meter.

There may even be wavelengths and receptive shapes which together generate natural growth and reproduction—effects attributed to the ϕ proportion—as opposed to other wavelengths and shapes which restrict or enchain.

275

Harleston next saw the Teotihuacan layout as possibly giving clues not only to wavelengths of the structure of the immediate world of sound, heat, color, smell, and touch in which we live, but also to the wavelengths of light, the microuniverse of atoms, and the macrouniverse of galaxies.

Whether it was known or not to the designers of Teotihuacan, Harleston realized that the constant of 1.059 controls not only the frequencies of sound but those of light. If visible light is divided into six basic colors from ultraviolet to infrared, omitting the arbitrary indigo, the frequency of each succeeding color is obtained by multiplying by 1.059 or its square. The seventh frequency at either end of the band of light remains invisible. Harleston found other phenomena such as the fact that when the color orange is multiplied by 1.059 it gives the wavelength of the helium-neon laser.

Schlemmer's symmetrical series for the orbiting distances of planets, says Harleston, can be reduced proportionately all the way down through the interior of the sun and finally to atomic configurations, indicating that Teotihuacan may also have been a display of cosmic data.

Of the whole numbers which Harleston considers to be deliberately displayed along the Processional, he was puzzled by 148 till he divided it by 4 for 37. Closer inspection of the

The Hydrogen Constant.

When a physicist tries to calculate the optical properties of a material or the way an object will behave in the presence of light, the hydrogen constant, or 1.37037037, enables him to make his experimental results fit theories which may be largely based on incorrect assumption. The constant, says Harleston, should be particularly useful when humans will have to cope with very large amounts of energy.

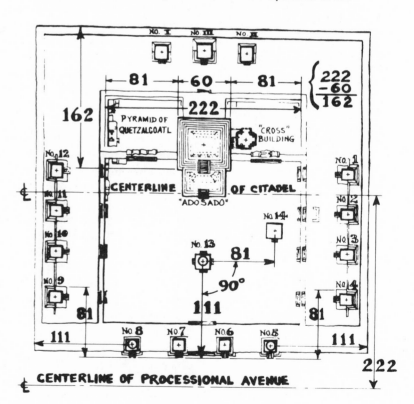

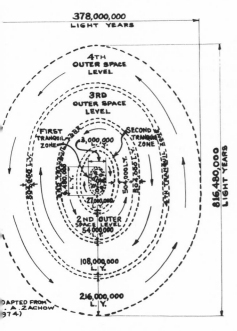

Harleston's adaptation of
A. A. Zachow's logarithmic
plan of the Grand Universe.

Zachow's transverse section of
the Grand Universe.

Citadel showed Harleston that the west platforms were located 111 *hunabs* from the north-south ends—that is 3 × 37—and the Citadel's central patio was 222 units or 6 × 37. Searching for some meaning to this apparently intentional indication, it was some time before the relationship of 37 to 27 came to him. In twentieth-century physics, 37/27 or 1.370370370, with the 037 continuing indefinitely, is the physical constant which forms the connection to the level of the atom. Multiplied by 100, this number is the average fine constant for hydrogen and deuterium, published in 1972 by the Bureau of Standards in Washington, D.C., a basic datum, says Harleston, for eventual macroenergy management.

Such a built-in datum appeared to him to be another indication that seen from another dimensional point of view the Teotihuacan complex contained vital physical data about the energetic and geometric makeup of the cosmos.

Harleston quotes the cosmology of A. A. Zachow, who postulates seven superuniverses that follow an elliptical path around dark gravity bodies, known as "black holes" by today's astronomers, to show that the Teotihuacan parameters could also relate to the structure of the *macro* universe. The cosmology of Zachow implies that the proper motions of nearby suns seem to indicate centroid positions that are "intelligently directed," and that this would suggest that stars, as well as star groups and galaxies, may be found to be located on symmetrically repeating orbital shells when future analyses permit the comparisons to be made. As each of Zachow's superuniverses contains seventy-two galaxies,

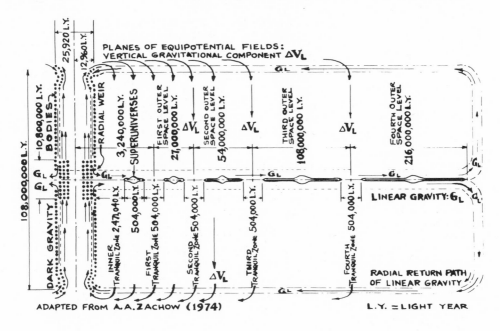

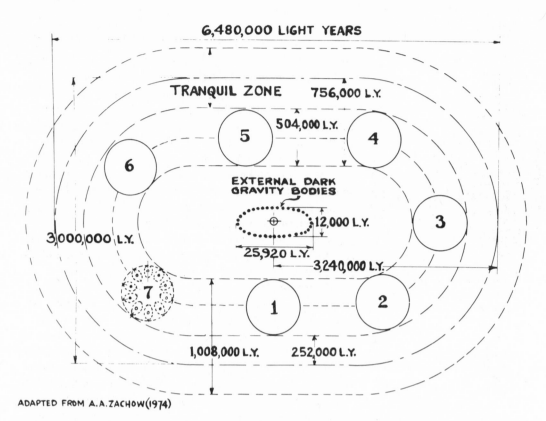

6,480,000 LIGHT YEARS

TRANQUIL ZONE   756,000 L.Y.

504,000 L.Y.

5   4

6

EXTERNAL DARK
GRAVITY BODIES

12,000 L.Y.

3

25,920 L.Y.

3,000,000 L.Y.

3,240,000 L.Y.

7

1   2

1,008,000 L.Y.   252,000 L.Y.

ADAPTED FROM A.A. ZACHOW (1974)

Zachow's plan of the Super
Universes.

which cause our sun to experience seven distinct directions
of motion through the superuniverse, Harleston surmises that
the Teotihuacan standard unit of measure, or *hunab,* may be
a natural unit of space-time. The selection of a measure that
unifies space and time taken from a stable planetary dimension (such as its polar diameter), says Harleston, gives the
advantage of enabling one to see cosmic relationships such as
orbital symmetry in a simplified manner. He believes it most
likely that the same proportion would exist on all planets,
and suggests that one 12-millionth of the diameter would
give a unit of measure appropriate for that orbit, correctly
relating it to the unit and diameter of all other planets.

The angles and perspectives in the Teotihuacan layout
appear to Harleston to show the framework of an integrated
earth and heaven—along with the megaspace of the heavens
above—as being the work of a master mathematician. To
Harleston the messages of Teotihuacan point to a new way of
looking at time and space, and to some new source of energy
from the cosmos, some new field fabric that our science has
not yet isolated. He believes that if Teotihuacan could express
knowledge of cosmic relationships erected in the form of a
ceremonial center, the whole complex could have served as a
university. The ceremonial center, whose architecture exhibits

Zachow's view of our Super Universe.

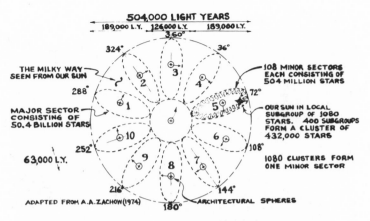

504,000 LIGHT YEARS
189,000 L.Y. 126,000 L.Y. 189,000 L.Y.

360°

324°   36°

THE MILKY WAY
SEEN FROM OUR SUN

288°

MAJOR SECTOR
CONSISTING OF
50.4 BILLION STARS

252°

63,000 L.Y.

216°   144°

180°

108 MINOR SECTORS
EACH CONSISTING OF
504 MILLION STARS

72°

OUR SUN IN LOCAL
SUBGROUP OF 1080
STARS. 400 SUBGROUPS
FORM A CLUSTER OF
432,000 STARS

108°

1080 CLUSTERS FORM
ONE MINOR SECTOR

ADAPTED FROM A.A. ZACHOW (1974)   ARCHITECTURAL SPHERES

information such as the rotational distance moved at the equator in a given time, plus positional latitudes and longitudinal distances of rotation, could have been used as an educational center for geodesy and navigation.

To Harleston the Teotihuacan messages are timeless concepts which could teach the student to reach beyond himself to a larger vision of the relationship of man to the cosmos and of man to himself as knower and perceiver. He says the overall information of Teotihuacan presents logical relationships so simple that the basic principles can be learned in a day; from these principles cosmic information can be deduced. "It is as if the Teotihuacanos," says Harleston, "had wanted to provide a method of teaching cosmic truths so simple that, once learned, the survivors of some unforeseen cataclysm could rebuild the knowledge from memory."

Harleston says that once the student at Teotihuacan learned the important values of thirds, sevenths, and ninths, and that squares and square roots were basic mathematical tools, the next step was to understand the relationship in space of two simple geometric solids: the sphere and the tetrahedron.

It was some time before Harleston found the clue to a tetrahedral geometry incorporated into the Teotihuacan complex, but he finally found it in the dimensions of the Pyramid of the Sun. Unlike the Pyramid of Cheops, which is a very exact scale model of the Northern Hemisphere (with the apex as the North Pole, the base as the equator, and its perimeter equal to one-half minute of arc), the Sun Pyramid does not fit such a system; it does, however, very accurately give the entire surface of the earth.

Harleston divided this surface into four great circles, making four great spherical triangles, each of which corresponded to the area of one face of the Sun Pyramid. This solution brought with it the question of how and why the Teotihuacanos should have chosen such an apparently complex system. That is where the tetrahedron came in.

279

Harleston finds it significant that if you stand a tetrahedron on its nose at the South Pole it will form three triangles above the equator splitting the world into four equilateral great-circle triangles which will exactly divide into areas of 1/3 above and 2/3 below the equator.

A Teotihuacan sphere whose diameter is 12 will give an area of 144 π, a quarter of which is an easily reckoned 36 π, and so forth. Again all the numbers run in a 3, 6, 9, 12, 24 series, unique with a sphere of diameter 12.

The tetrahedron, simplest of the five Platonic solids, is a perfect pyramid, a geometrical figure that represents the smallest number of points that will form a solid in three-dimensional space. It is constructed by uniting four identical equilateral triangles at their edges to form a body with four nodes, four faces, and six edges.

Harleston points out that the abstract properties of such a six-edged tetrahedron involve functions of 3, 6, thirds, square roots, and the number 1.06, all emphasized by the Teotihuacan displays.

When he inserts the tetrahedron into a sphere of diameter 12 some extraordinary relations develop. When the diameter of the circle is 12 (and therefore its radius 6), the ratio of the area of the sphere to the tetrahedron is 2.72 to 1. This is the only case in which this significant correlation occurs.

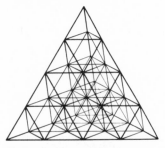

R. Buckminster Fuller's isotropic vector matrix.

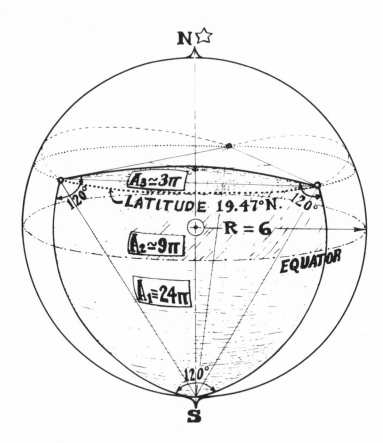

The four points at which the great circles meet form the nodes of a tetrahedron inscribed in a sphere. This apparently casual relation showed on closer inspection that an extraordinary and unique relation exists between a tetrahedron and a sphere whose diameter is twelve, one from which cosmic data ensues.

Oddly, or coincidentally, the relation between a tetrahedron and a sphere constitutes the thrust of the work of Buckminster Fuller, who, in his book *Synergetics,* maintains that the tetrahedron gives the basic mathematical blueprint for the universe.

From what he calls his "isotropic vector matrix" Fuller obtains a constant of $\sqrt{9/8}$, which comes to 1.06066, so close to Harleston's 1.059 constant that it fits the Teotihuacan complex virtually as well.

The difference between them—a mere one part in a thousand—produces a difference in length of less than 1 meter in the 800-meter overall distance between the Sun and the Moon pyramids, and less than 10 meters on the overall length of the entire Valley of Teotihuacan, differences easily absorbed by Harleston's own postulated margins of error.

The regular tetrahedron.

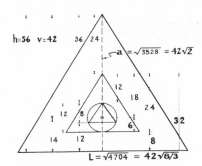

$h=56$ $v=42$ $36/24$

$a=\sqrt{3528}=42\sqrt{2}$

12
18
24
12 8
6
32
14 12 8

$L=\sqrt{4704}=42\sqrt{6/3}$

A tetrahedron whose height is 12 is demonstrated by Harleston to have a side that equals the square root of 216, the length of the base of the Sun Pyramid, which is 6 × 6 ×6 or 6 cubed.

The height of an equilateral triangle of 216 base will be the square root of 3 × 6 × 9, or 162, the length of the Moon Pyramid.

If a larger tetrahedron is selected so that the sphere exactly fits inside it with the surfaces of the sphere touching the centers of the four faces of the tetrahedron, then the characteristics of the superscribed tetrahedron will be exactly three times the values for the one inscribed within the sphere, and its height twice the diameter of the sphere.

Harleston is impressed by the fact that the side of the tetrahedron's apothem, or slant height, as well as its area and its volume, are all multiples of 216—the side of the Sun Pyramid in *hunabs*. The ratio of the volume to area of this tetrahedron equals 2 to 1, the same as for the sphere of radius 6 it encloses. All the above numbers are major Teotihuacan dimensions. Harleston considers the tetrahedron to be fundamental to the message of Teotihuacan. A tetrahedron inside a sphere will have linear properties that are 1/3 of the tetrahedron surrounding the sphere.

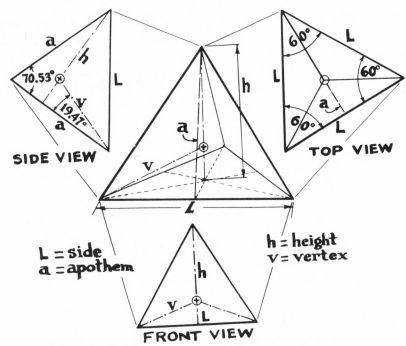

SIDE VIEW

$70.53°$ ⊗

$19.47°$

TOP VIEW

$60°$ $60°$ $60°$

L = side
a = apothem

h = height
v = vertex

FRONT VIEW

Pointing out that the carbon atom—which is the basic building block from which the material bodies of all living organisms are made—is a regular tetrahedron, and that the water molecule has characteristics that conform to the tetrahedral structure, Harleston concludes that the fundamental message conveyed by the Teotihuacanos is that the physical universe is tetrahedral from the microscopic level of the atom all the way up to the macroscopic level of the galaxies on a scale of vibrations in which man stands about the center. Man would thus have built into him, as suggested by Pythagoras and Plato, the tool for unlocking the geometry of the cosmos and recovering the knowledge of his role in the scheme.

What evidence is there that the ancient inhabitants of Mesoamerica had sufficient physics, mathematics, and knowledge of the cosmos to leave such a message?

20. Wisdom of the Ancients

The most explicit Mesoamerican text on the origin and mechanics of their universe is the Quiche manuscript of Chichicastenango, better known as the *Popol Vuh,* which slips gently from a description of the physical world of men to a description of the spiritual entities and elementals which produced it.

In a carefully reasoned analysis of its text (which translates from the Spanish as *The Popol Vuh Is Right!*) the distinguished Maya linguist and philologist Domingo Martinez Paredes concludes that a very old and very highly developed culture existed on the American continents whose cosmogony agrees very closely with modern hypotheses about the origin of the universe and of its evolution.

According to Martinez the Maya came to the mathematical certainty of the existence of a cosmic consciousness which they named "Hunab Ku," sole dispenser of measurement and movement, to whom they attributed the mathematical structuring of the universe. This divinity they represented by a circle in which was inscribed a square, just as did Pythagoras.

Hunab Ku, sole source of movement and measure, symbolized the universe for the Maya in the form of a circle with an inscribed square. The circle was the symbol of the infinite, the spiritual; the square of the material. Hunab Ku was thus a universal dynamism or that which motivates and stimulates life in its total manifestation as spirit and matter, the all in one. Martinez points out the similarity between the Mayan Hunab Ku symbol of a square in a circle and the Masonic symbol of the Great Architect of the Universe: the compass and the square. Martinez says *Hun* means sole or single in Mayan, *Naab* means measure, and *Ku* means giver.

 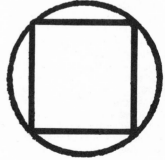

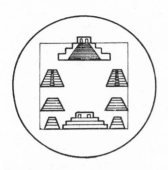

According to Martinez, the central ceremonial area of a Mesoamerican pyramid complex was made in the form of a square circumscribed by a circle, symbol of Hunab Ku.

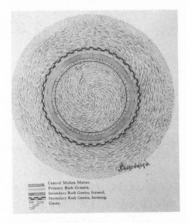

Central Molten Matter.
Primary Rock Granite.
Secondary Rock Gneiss, formed.
Secondary Rock Gneiss, forming.
Gases.

The Maya believed the world had been formed from a condensing nebula, here seen in Churchward's rendering.

The Maya believed that their supreme divinity functioned through a principle of dynamic dualism, or polarity, active and passive, positive and negative, masculine and feminine, by which, through the agency of four prime elements, air, fire, water, and earth (symbolizing space, energy, time, and matter) the whole material world was engendered.

The Maya conceived of the earth as having been formed from a nebula through the combination of fire, water, and gases which produced "solid" matter. Their name for the lesser deity of creative energy was Can or Kan; and Huracan was the rotary vortex which made possible the condensation of primordial elements by incorporating them into a nucleus, thus reintegrating elements disintegrated by Chaos. Gucumatz was water, Tepeu was fire, and the four elements symbolized by a square also represented matter in its four states: plasmic, gaseous, liquid, and solid.

The Maya considered every element in nature to be a co-operator in cosmic harmony, bound by its own vibrations into geometric form, a form which changed in type and quality as the vibrations changed. Modern science, Martinez points out, has found that no cell, no molecule, whether animal, vegetable, or mineral, escapes geometric form.

To the Maya the earth was not a corpse, it was neither dead nor inert, but a living entity intimately tied to the existence of man both physically and psychically; they knew that by laying their naked bodies on the earth they could revitalize their forces. They saw that trees and water constantly purified and revitalized man, as part of the cosmic order.

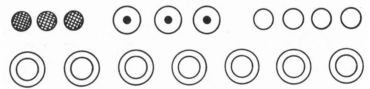

The Mexican mathematician Hector M. Calderon says that a people as sophisticated mathematically as the Maya would have had to incorporate its theogonic concepts into actual numbers, using the latter to express their ideas about the universe. He gives as examples Tzacol, the creator, as 1; Kukulcan as 2; Bitol, the fashioner, as 3; Alom, the female cosmic progenitor, as 4; Cajalon, the male progenitor, as 5; and Tepeu, the governor, as 6. All, were considered part of Hunab Ku, the primordial source of movement and measure.

Tzacol as 1, the creator, was considered a supernatural originator of energy, time, space, and matter. Creation, says Calderon, was considered foreign to the law of the conservation of energy, and nothing could be created or destroyed, only changed.

The Maya symbolized 1 by a point which, depending on its position, could increase in value to the infinite.

Number 2 was Quetzalcoatl, the airy plumed serpent symbol, the feathered part of which represented the spiritual and abstract, whereas the snake was the earthly and palpable. It represented the spirit-matter duality of the universe.

Number 3 was Bitol, the Maya formulator, modeler of the clay of creation into countless evolutionary patterns of ever greater complexity. Its symbol was the wave, the basic giver of shape to the universe, a wave half evolution and half involution as it was represented by the Maya in their architectural designs. It symbolized the polarity or motor principle of the cosmos, which, from atom to star, is positive-negative—the latter not necessarily worse, just opposite, as gravity is to levity. Numerically, the 3 was derived from 1 plus 2.

Number 4 was Alom, mother of life, whose symbol was the flower, which receives the fecundating pollen; it is mother earth, which receives the grain of corn and the fertilizing rays of the sun. Its symbol is fourfold or a square. Cajalom, 5, is the father of life, or ⦂·⦂ the sun at its zenith, bathing the earth with fecundating energy. Its symbol is the celestial cosmic cross, four points with a central sun, which becomes ⦂·⦂, or 7, with the addition of East and West and the enlivening rain. For the Maya, 13 was the sun amidst the 12 constellations of the zodiac.

In all of nature the Maya saw countless combinations and manifestations of primordial forces which they incorporated into their architecture as geometric designs and represented by a host of nature spirits; yet they did not violate the basic notion of a single creative principle, a ubiquitous supreme dual god who created itself and all that exists.

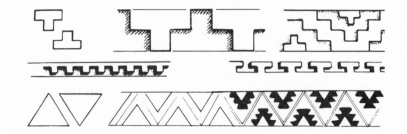

Calderon shows how Tepeu, the governor, who puts order into the furthest reaches of creation, was represented by the Maya as the number 6 or 3 and 3, a series of interlocked Taus, "as above so below," "synthesis and antithesis."

To the Mesoamerican everything was possessed by a "respected spirit." Not only the mineral, plant, bird, animal, and human kingdoms, but the mountains, clouds, and stars—all were possessed by invisible forces of life, the spiritual components of outer physical forms. These forces, or primordial images, were represented by men wearing strange anthropomorphic masks.

Itzamna, head of the Maya pantheon.

Kukulcan, the wind god.

Chac, the rain god.

The god of sacrifice.

Like the Hindus, the Maya postulated rhythmic astronomical cycles as a result of which great civilizations appeared and disappeared, cycles that the priests maintained they were aware of and could understand through their mathematics, astronomy, and astrology.

285

The basic Mesoamerican chronology envisaged four great eras or world periods before the present or fifth world in which they lived. They believed that each of the previous worlds had been destroyed—the first by jaguars representing earth, the second by air, the third by fire, the fourth by a great flood. The fifth, they prophesied, would be destroyed by a cataclysm of earthquakes.

Ixtlilxochitl, writing in the sixteenth century, concluded from his study of Nahuatl sources that the creation of the Fifth Sun occurred in 3245 B.C. But the preponderance of modern experts on Maya chronology, following Herbert Joseph Spinden's correlation, project the beginning of the Great Maya Cycle back to August 12, 3113 B.C.; they interpret the Maya prophecies to indicate the end of this fifth world will come on December 24, 2011 A.D., when the earth is supposed to be destroyed by catastrophic earthquakes.

At the end of his remarkably erudite and sensitive book *Mexico Mystique, or The Coming of the Sixth World Consciousness,* Frank Waters has attached an appendix by an astrologer, Mrs. Roberta S. Sklower, who has computed the probability of the particular arrangement of the planets which occurred in 3113 B.C. taking place only every 4500 years. As for the arrangement in A.D. 2011, she estimates it can occur once in 45,200 years, which led Waters to remark, "From this extraordinary pattern we might well expect an extraordinary effect."

The notion that the earth is periodically destroyed was not restricted to Mesoamerica. Heraclitus and Aristarchus both concurred, as did Hesiod, who recounted the destruction of previous worlds; Hindus, Tibetan Buddhists, and Persian Zoroastrians all shared the notion.

Convinced that nature was governed by cyclical laws, the Maya believed that everything could be foreseen—providing you understood the numbers which lay beneath the manifestations.

Nor were they mean mathematicians. Thanks to a checkerboard system, the Maya were able to handle very high numbers with little effort. Their system was so simple a child of four could multiply, divide, and obtain square roots without having to memorize a multiplication table; yet so versatile was the system that a housewife could manage her budget, and an astronomer could plot the centennial motion of the stars so as to calculate the arrival of a new eclipse.

The Maya knew our $+$, $-$, $=$, $\div$, and $\times$, but their zero was not a symbol for nothing: it represented completion and the seed from which all could be derived.

In his *La Ciencia Matematica de los Mayas,* Hector M. Calderon, a Mexican engineer who carefully analyzed the

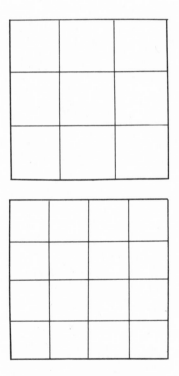

Calderon shows how the Mayans used a checkerboard or mat, lined in nine or sixteen squares, to perform the mathematical operations of addition, subtraction, multiplication, division, and the finding of square roots with a minimum of effort and without having to memorize a complex multiplication table.

To add the following Maya columns of numbers:

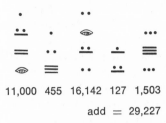

| 11,000 | 455 | 16,142 | 127 | 1,503 |

add = 29,227

The Maya moved them all together by adding each column from the left, properly adding each square and moving upward any excess over 20.

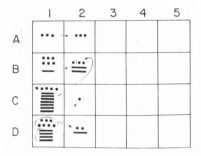

The result

$$\bullet\bullet\bullet = 3 \times 8000 = 24,000$$
$$= 13 \times 400 = 5,200$$
$$\bullet = 1 \times 20 = 20$$
$$\bullet\bullet = 7 \times 1 = 7$$

29,227

Aztec numbers.

Maya numbers.

Mayan system of mathematics, says the Maya were able to resolve complex mathematical problems, perhaps several millennia before Christ, by means of a very simple system of grains of two colors to represent the numbers 1 and 5, placed in various positions on a checkerboard which they could draw on any flat surface. By means of these boards—represented on their monuments, paintings, clothes, and mats—the Maya were able to handle their chronology, astronomy, engineering, and architecture.

Calderon points out that what the Maya were using was a technique of metrical calculation only redeveloped in the middle of the past century, a system which for centuries was lost to humanity when the use of the checkerboard degenerated into sorcery, augury, and a simple game. He also points out that the universality of abstract numbers, a concept expressed with such insistence by the Maya in their ornamental boards, has only been repostulated in our century with dimensional analysis and the laws of similarity.

It is easier to picture numbers and their interrelationships with groups or sets of points than it is to do so with our symbolic figures.

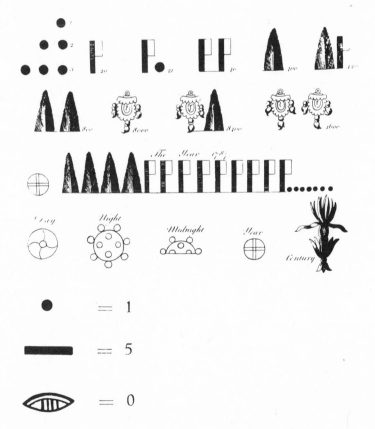

$$\bullet = 1$$

$$\rule{1cm}{2mm} = 5$$

$$= 0$$

287

Science, says Calderon, has now recognized that in the internal mechanisms of all phenomena there are certain mathematical relations which are independent of space, time, and the mass in which they are manifested. The recent rediscovery of this principle has made possible the deduction of several fundamental equations in every order of human knowledge. Thanks to these equations, says Calderon, there now exist hydraulic modules and constructional analogical computers for the rational compilation of statistical data. Now, for instance, it is possible to use a flow of water through an arrangement of levers and pivots to arrive at the results of a mathematical computation.

Calderon says the Maya identified man with the cosmos and created a school of philosophy based on the symbolism of numbers many centuries before Hermes Trismegistus or Pythagoras. Martinez says the Porrua Codex depicts the integration of man into the cosmos with symbols for one and zero to his right, left, and below him, in a square composed of calendrical hieroglyphs and numbers. The man holds a female serpent in his right hand and a male symbol in his left, interpreted by Martinez as man, time, and space.

Martinez points out how this "peregrination" from the Porrua Codex perfectly interprets the serpentine movement and the circle over the square, admirably depicting man and the cosmos. All took place within two geometric forms, the circle and the square.

Quipus, or knotted cords, used by Indians, Aztecs, pre-Incas, Mexicans, Egyptians, and Chinese as mnemonic devices like the rosary of the Catholic Church for recording and remembering long periods of history. The mathematical board with black and white pieces was used to make advanced mathematical calculations. Calderon says that throughout the Americas a similar if not identical system of mathematics, using colored beans or stones on a checkerboard, was employed before the Spanish conquest; he also points to the coincidence that our word for calculate comes from the Latin *calculi,* meaning little stones.

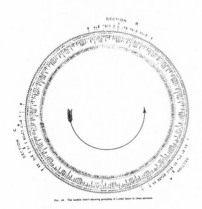

The great 260-day *tzolkin* calendar of the Maya known as *tonalamatl* by the Aztecs, showing grouping of lunar dates in three sections.

Intuitively considering the earth to be part of a whole, affected by the cyclical movements of the sun, moon, planets, and stars, the ancient Mesoamericans searched for the laws inherent in their recurring positions.

Well aware, long before the birth of Christ, that the foundations of chronology lay in the daily rotation of the earth on its axis and in its yearly revolution around the sun, Mesoamericans divided their year into 360 days plus 5 extra on regular years and 6 on leap years or 13 every 52 years.

On this point there is some discussion. Michael D. Coe of Yale University is categoric in his assertion that "there is no evidence that the Mesoamericans ever intercalated days or leap years." According to Coe, because the tropical year is 365.2422 days, the 365-day "vague" year simply gained on the seasons by a factor of 13 days every 52 "vague" years. But the fact remains that whatever system the Mesoamericans used, the result was a calendar more accurate than ours.

Calculating the orbit of the earth about the sun as 365.2420 days, the Maya marked the close of a year by the erection of a stone they called a *tun.* They did likewise for a twenty-year cycle or *katun,* a period they considered to be governed by the conjunction of Jupiter and Saturn.

Furthermore, they marked the passage of years by means of four distinct systems which acted as checks on all the others. Along with the year of 365 days and the more accurate tropical year of 365.2420 days there was a year of 365.25 days (the Egyptian Sothic year, whose .25 fraction was useful for the calculation of equinoxes, solstices, zenith passages, eclipses, and Metonic cycles), a lunar year of 354 days, and a very special "sacred" year of 260 days called *tzolkin* by the Maya, and *tonalamatl* by the Aztecs.

This special 260-day calendar, which has been called "one of the greatest jewels of human talent of all ages," was divided into 13 months of 20 days, and the multiples of 13 and 20 became the heart of a chronological computation "stunning in its simplicity and exactness."

On a monthly basis, twenty day names of the month were linked to the numbers from 1 to 13 to produce 260 different arrangements, such as 1-alligator, 2-wind, 3-house, 4-lizard.

A day with the same name and number could therefore recur only once every 260 days, forming a cycle which could repeat endlessly without regard to the actual movements of the sun and planets, which marked the natural time periods.

A greater cycle of 260 years was 13 consecutive Jupiter-Saturn cycles of 20 years, each one of which was considered to have a different quality depending on the series of angles formed between Jupiter and Saturn during each *katun.*

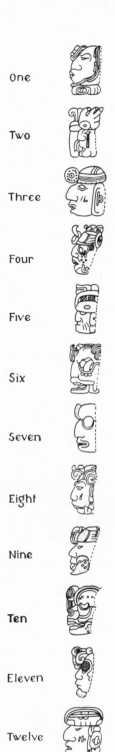

One

Two

Three

Four

Five

Six

Seven

Eight

Nine

Ten

Eleven

Twelve

Thirteen

This sacred calendar was used as a divinatory almanac or *Book of the Good and Bad Days,* a *Book of Fate* rather than a calendar dependent on the seasons.

Each day of the *tzolkin* was governed by a deity who was thought to influence that day for good or evil, each separate day being regarded by the Maya as an individual god, whose glyph was a stylized portrait of his attributes. The numbers 1 to 13 were also personalized as the heads of the gods they represented.

A baby was given the name of the day on which he was born. The name of Cortes' mistress, La Malinche, for instance, was a corruption of Ce Malinalli, or "1-grass."

The imposition of this 260-day calendar was in no way arbitrary. The Mesoamericans had figured out correctly that 260×18 is the same as 360×13, that 260×7 is the same as 364×5, that 260×73 is the same as 365×52 and that 260×1461 (the Egyptian Sothic cycle) is the same as 365.25×1040.

To these calendars, which all fell into the 260-day pattern, were added more refinements for calculating the synodic returns of the moon and the planets.

In the latitudes of Mesoamerica the planet Venus looms in the dawn sky with extraordinary brilliance, and the astronomers of both the Nahua and Maya devoted particular attention to the planet, and especially to its heliacal rising.

Venus revolves around the sun every 224.7 days; but because the earth is moving along its own orbit, the planet appears at the same place in the sky in a little less than 584 days. As 5×584 is equal to 8×365, the Maya considered eight Venus years equal to five solar years. And as 365×104 is equal to both 146×260 and 65×584, the solar, sacred, and Venus calendars become coincident every 37,960 days, or 104 years, which was two Mesoamerican centuries of 52 years.

Actually the Maya knew the Venus cycle to be 583.92 instead of a round 584 days, so they dropped 4 days every sixty-one Venus years in order to compensate for the discrepancy and make a round number divisible by 260.

As astronomers are quick to point out, such an accurate knowledge of the cycle of Venus, whose revolutions are by no means regular, points to long and sustained observation.

The Mesoamericans furthermore devised a lunar calendar that would fit with the others. Calculating that 405 lunations or 11,960 days was exactly divisible by 260 (or 260×46), they obtained a lunar period of 29.53 days with a mere discrepancy of .112 of a day from what we know today. This would give them a lunar calendar accurate to within a day over a period of 300 years.

Hieroglyphic representation of an eclipse of the sun.

	= 16
	= 0.5
	= 5
	= 8
	29.5

Noriega's decipherment of the 295 days in the Aztec lunar cycle.

Raul Noriega's analysis of the Aztec Sun calendar of a 243-year period between passages of Venus before the sun.
121.5 + 8 + 105.5 + 5 = 243

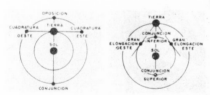

The phenomenon, first calculated in modern times by Kepler in 1631, and first observed in 1639 by two Englishmen, William Horrox and Benjamin Crabtree, was seen in Mexico City in 1882.

The same phenomenon is recorded in the Tizoc stone in a slightly different manner.

They also realized, as had the Athenian astronomer Meton in the fifth century B.C., that 19 Sothic years of 365.25 days were equal to 235 lunations, or 6940 days, which the Maya correctly figured to be one *katun* of 7200 days less one *tzolkin* of 260.

As a simple way to cope with the fraction slightly more than half a day over 29 for a lunar cycle, the Mayans reckoned their moons in groups of five or six, alternating between periods of 29 and 30 days. They could thus accurately state how many days after a new moon a date in question might be, how many moons of the group had been completed, and whether the actual moon, then running its course, was on a 29- or 30-day cycle.

From a glyph they could tell how many days the date was after the full moon, which moon it was, and how long the previous moon had run.

As for eclipses of both the sun and the moon, instead of being terrified by them as were their contemporary Europeans, the Mesoamericans calculated them accurately to use as a further check on the interrelation of returns of the planets.

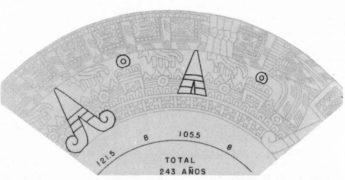

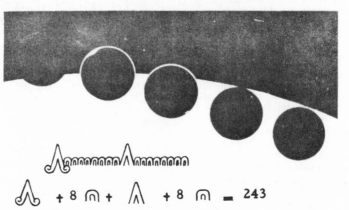

291

In the early 1930s J. Antonio Villacorta, a Guatemalan lawyer, put together a set of books in which he reproduced the three main Maya codices—known for convenience as the Madrid, the Dresden, and the Paris—giving descriptions of their various glyphs and figures with whatever meaning for them he was able to glean from various sources. For the finely drawn copies of all the pages of the codices he enlisted his nephew, Carlos.

The effort itself did not bring much that was new to the art of decipherment, but the care with which the figures are reproduced, and the orderly manner in which they are annotated on opposite pages, made available to other researchers copies of the codices at a reasonable price to which they could apply their own talents of decipherment.

In the early 1950s a Soviet enthusiast, Yuri Knorosov, suggested that the Maya might have used two or three phonetic syllabic signs joined together to make a word. It was as radical an approach as Landa's, and met with as much opposition. Over the years, Knorosov produced a long book on the Maya and their hieroglyphs. He translated the *Chilam Balam* and other chronicles into Russian and added a short Maya dictionary along with reproductions of many of the glyphs—much as Thompson had done. Knorosov also reproduced Villacorta's drawings of the codices.

In the 1960s three Soviet mathematicians working in the Soviet Academy of Sciences Institute in Novosibirsk on the development of computer sys-

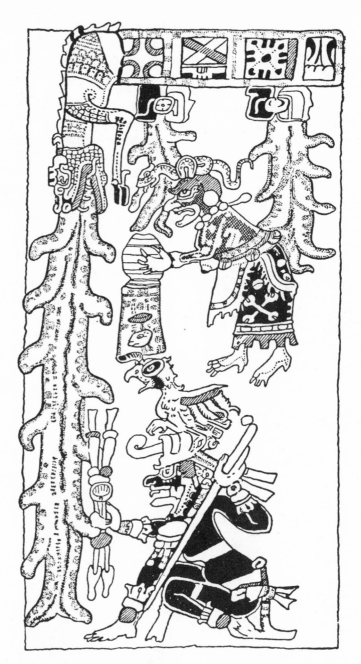

Villacorta describes the body of a large crocodile issuing from glyphs recognized as those of the planets Venus, Mars, Mercury, and Jupiter, from which hang all the glyphs representing the Sun and the Moon. From the crocodile's jaws pours a torrent of water which floods the earth, while a black god destroys humanity with a fistful of arrows.

Villacorta says that quite probably the Mayan priests wished to represent in this realistic scene the destruction of the world either in some distant future or possibly in the cataclysm produced by the flooding of the oceans as told in the *Popul Vuh,* when the gods wished to destroy humanity.

tems fell for the idea of using Knorosov's material in an attempt to decipher the Maya glyphs as a test project for a new large-scale computer they were designing. On the advice of Russia's most eminent mathematician—Soboliev, head of the Institute's mathematics department—the three Soviet computer experts, E. V. Evreinov, Yuri G. Kosarev, and V. A. Ustinov, fed into the computer all the known Maya glyphs, half glyphs, affixes, and prefixes they could find in the apprehensive expectation they might at last decipher the Maya texts. When all the data had been fed by number into the computer, the results filled four thick volumes with thousands of random phrases made up of Mayan words and syllables; but it did not do much toward an understanding of the Mayan writings.

J. Eric S. Thompson, the Polonius of Mayan hieroglyphics, accused Knorosov of doing violence to the language with his "disregard for all that is known of context and subject matter." Thompson was scathing in his criticism. "These numerous attempts to make silk purses out of Landa's sow's ear ended in disaster; the extravagances of the decipherers, growing with each failure, shrouded in clouds of fantasy the three or four reasonable decipherments."

In 1976 Knorosov brought out a new volume which was heralded by Reuters as a breakthrough; but Knorosov appears to have merely translated into Russian the random phrases put together by Villacorta, which were computerized by the mathematicians at Novosibirsk. Knorosov has promised a deeper analysis in a future publication. But the fact that the Russians have suddenly taken a distinct interest in the solution of the Mayan glyphs may indicate they suspect there is data of interest to be derived from them, or, indeed, may have already obtained such data.

The boldest glyph recognized by Villacorta on page 12 of the Tro-Cortesianus Codex is that of the Sun surrounded by clouds producing tropical rainstorms. Immediately below, in four squares, are the glyphs for Mercury, Mars, Venus, and Jupiter. Villacorta says the large figure falling from under the four planets is the rain god painted in blue. Around his neck is a bag of copal painted red, yellow, and blue. Copal was burned as incense by the Maya with their prayers for rain. The large serpent entwined down the page has four Chicchan glyphs on his body each of which is interpreted as signifying "serpent." According to Villacorta the page is a prologue to the scenes depicted on the next seven pages (one of which is missing), where five large snakes (and possibly a missing sixth) represent time.

Page 60 of the Dresden Codex is interpreted by Förstemann as representing a "Battle of the Planets" including the Sun, Moon, Mars, Venus, Mercury, Jupiter, and Saturn, plus glyphs for an eclipse. In the top panel, according to Förstemann, the Sun is being threatened by the moon at an eclipse—symbolized by what he calls a dog under the platform about to devour the hieroglyph day-sign for *Lamat.* He believes the figure behind the moon to be Mars.

At the bottom of the page, Förstemann says the scene represents another struggle between the planets in their cyclical appearances, disappearances, and overtaking of each other. In this case, Sun, Moon, Mars, Venus, Mercury, and Saturn are shown.

Villacorta says the figure at the top left riding the snake represents Venus overcoming Mercury, whose eyes are bandaged—planets that alternate as "morning and evening stars."

Opposite them Jupiter is overcoming Saturn (with the black eye) and relegating it to a far corner of the sky.

293

In Vienna in 1739 the librarian of the Royal Dresden Library, Johann Christian Gotze, was given a mysterious 12 foot by 8 inch codex folded up like a fan into 39 sheets which he filed away with the notation, "A Mexican book with unknown characters and hieroglyphic figures written on both sides and painted in colors."

In 1813, Humboldt published a few pages of the codex in his *Vues des Cordilleras,* and Agostino Aglio copied it for Kingsborough's *Antiquities of Mexico,* which appeared in 1831. Yet little or nothing was understood of its 74 fig-bark paper pages illustrated with white, red, yellow, blue, and brown figures until they were chromophotographed by Naumann in 1880. With a working copy of the codex, Ernst Förstemann, director of the Dresden library and son of a Danzig mathematician, was able to study it more carefully and see in its glyphs an astronomical treatise. Over a period of fourteen years Förstemann was able to piece together the Maya long-count calendar determining the positions of five numerical signs with relative values of 1, 20, 360, 7,200, and 144,000. He then noted the appearance of zero in almost all the computations, established a Venus cycle of 584 days, and found the base date for a lunar calendar.

The next major step in deciphering the Dresden Codex was made by John Teeple, an American chemical engineer, who took up the study of Mayan codices to divert himself on long train trips.

Teeple saw how the Mayans had computed the synodic returns of Venus, which vary between 580 and 588 days, averaging 583.92. To offset the discrepancy between the rounded figure of 584 days, they added 24 days every 301 revolutions, reducing the error to one day in 6,000.

During World War I another German, Martin Meinshauser, was able to decipher in the

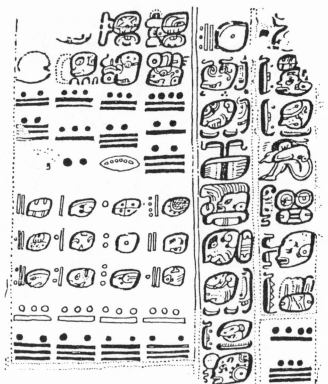

codex a calendar of eclipses, and during World War II an attorney friend of Förstemann's, Paul Schellhaus, who was killed by the Nazis in 1944, described fifteen Maya deities who appear throughout the codex. The manuscript, kept in a wine cellar for safety during the bombing of Dresden, narrowly escaped being destroyed by fire and was somewhat damaged by water.

Subjected to tense scrutiny in the middle 1970s by the hieroglyphic section of the Institute of Maya Studies of the Miami Museum of Science, the codex can now be described as a highly sophisticated astronomical computer.

Pages 57 and 58 of the Dresden Codex provide a perpetual lunar calendar of 11,960 days consisting of 405 months divided into 69 groups of 177, 178, or 148 days. It is a very accurate lunar calendar, with a table for new moons for prediction of solar eclipses. 11,960 divided by 405 gave the Maya 29.5308 for the lunar cycle. Modern astronomers

compute it at 29.5309. In the Dresden Calendar 11,960 divided by 69 gave the Maya 173.3333 as an average period between eclipses. 69 groups give the days when solar eclipses can occur as the new moons pass between the earth and sun.

Another calendrical device in the Dresden Codex is made by the serpentine pattern found by moving from one space up two rows and over one, then down two rows and over one. This produces an unending count of 91 days between each day-sign for a total of 20 cycles or 1,820 days. As each season of the year is divided from the next by the 91-day interval between the solstices and equinoxes, the calendar makes it possible to plot the sequence of equinoxes and solstices on the pattern beginning at any particular point of the 260-day sacred calendar, returning to that point to begin again in a perpetual cycle. To account for the discrepancy of 4.968 days every four years, the Maya added five days.

Courtesy of *The New York Times*.

Newly Discovered Codex.

During 1971 a fourth Mayan codex surfaced in New York, where it was exhibited in June at the Grolier Club. As its anonymous owner did not wish to divulge its origin, the manuscript has become known as the Grolier Codex. It is now safely back in a Mexican museum. According to Dr. Michael D. Coe of Yale University, who helped prepare the exhibit, the codex, which is a painting on "bark cloth," dates from between A.D. 1400 and 1500. The manuscript consists of an eleven-page fragment of an original book of twenty pages, but unlike the other codices it does not have a profusion of complex hieroglyphs. On each page are columns of thirteen day-glyphs with relevant illustrative glyphs, each of which can now be read.

Like the Dresden Codex, which is a 104-year Venus calendar, the Grolier Codex is clearly a calendar of the phases of Venus, but displays a much more sophisticated system. Though it appears on the surface to be simply a 104-year calendar, it is described as "the world's first and only known perpetual calendar of Venus ever produced by any civilization." According to Charles H. Lacombe, "this ancient Mayan document must rank among the supreme intellectual achievements of human history."

The codex predicts the appearance and disappearance of Venus in a great cycle of 845 revolutions equal to 1352 years; and after completion, the cycle repeats itself endlessly by means of a shift in the order of the lines and the way they are to be read.

Viewed horizontally, each line of figures represents an 8-year cycle of the revolutions of Venus, and as there are 13 lines of figures, the chart represents 13 × 5, or 65 revolutions, equal to 104 years. But as each line moves up one place every 104 years and the top line goes to the bottom, every line is back in place at the end of 1352 years, at which point the process is repeated in an endless cycle for a perpetual calendar.

Curious as to why there appeared to be an extra 104 years in the calendar, Lacombe realized this was an essential correction built into the system to make it perpetual.

According to Dr. Douglas Duke, professor of astronomy at the University of Miami, Venus actually takes just 780 synodical revolutions, or 1247 years, to return to the exact spot at the exact time it started the cycle.

The Grolier Codex also supports the evidence for the Spinden and Makemson correlations, which place the date of the origin of the Mayan system in 3374 B.C.

To those who have suggested that this newly found codex could have been a fake, Lacombe replies that no forger could have been clever enough to fake such data for which there is no other source among Mayan scripts.

295

Tro-Cortesianus Codex.

Detailed analysis by the hieroglyphic section of the Institute of Maya Studies of the Miami Museum of Science, revealed that the illustrations function admirably as a computer for astronomical data.

In the words of Charles H. Lacombe, director of the hieroglyphic section, and Samuel S. Block, a Miami architect who has made several breakthroughs in deciphering the astronomical functions of Mayan hieroglyphs, this part of the codex is "unbelievable in its perfection and simplicity, instantly performing the incredible combination of mathematical functions required to program and retrieve the mathematical data."

The Mayan day-signs which run in columns of four from page to page of the codex are entwined with five serpents and a possible sixth which appears to have been on a page now missing. Read vertically, these day-signs provide a solar calendar of 365 days; as the sequences repeat themselves they provide a perpetual calendar of 4 times 13, or 52 years. The same day-signs read horizontally in groups of 5 times 13, or 65, give a Venus calendar (each of which takes 584 days), the equivalent of 104 years of 365 days, or two 52-year cycles.

Read diagonally in a succession of M's across the pages, or in what Block calls "a curious but fascinating economy of programming," the mechanism shows Venus appearing as the morning star, as the evening star, and in its superior and inferior conjunctions.

To identify two points on the diagonal separated by a Venus year, or 584 days, the computer shifts 65 spaces to the right, nine times, and one space to the left, for a total of 65 × 9 − 1 or 584.

The five looped serpents entwined into the solar and Venus calendars are also arranged in such an exact manner, mathematically and geometrically, that they also function as a mechanism of the computer: they give the synodic cycles not only of Venus but of Mercury, Mars, and Jupiter. Explanatory panels across the top and bottom of the codex carry glyphs representing these planets as well as the long-nosed rain god Chac-Mool suspended over a serpent.

The first two serpent heads face left, the second two face right, and the fifth faces left, only in a reverse fashion, and each serpent intersects at four points. The total number of days covered in the intersections of all six serpents is 2600 days, or ten Mayan sacred *tzolkins*.

Lacombe and Block point out that the system is especially flexible in that the day-signs appear on the chart without the required numeral coefficient and can therefore be read up, down, or diagonally, producing readouts for different calendars, giving equinoxes, solstices, solar eclipses, and the days on which two or more celestial events can coincide.

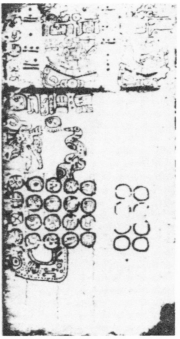

After a great deal of careful observation, astronomer Marian Popenoe Hatch recently discovered that the various snake positions correlated exactly with the path of the constellation Draco as it would have appeared in the evening sky two thousand years ago.

Dr. Hatch noted that the star Eta of the constellation Draco was unique in that it alone among all the stars remained virtually unchanged in right ascension for the 2300 years between 1800 B.C. and A.D. 500, regularly transiting across the meridian at midnight of May 23rd and November 22nd with a variation of less than one degree. Thus the star Eta Draconis provided the Maya with an accurate measure of the sidereal year, and a yardstick for comparison between the tropical and the sidereal years, as well as an indication of the processional lag in the other stars.

Hatch found that the path of Eta Draconis, as it moved through the celestial orb in the course of the year, corre-

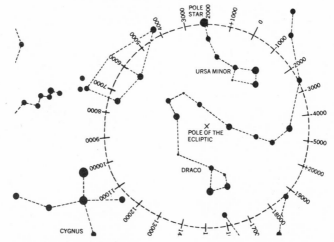

lated perfectly with the pictures of the serpents on the pages of the Madrid Codex, each of which astronomically represents a rotation in the sky of 45 degrees per page. When Draco is visible in the western part of the sky, the appropriate serpent looks to the left, when Draco is in the eastern sky the serpent faces to the right.

Noting that the word *Tzab* in modern Yucatec Maya means both the rattle of a rattlesnake and the constellation Pleiades, Hatch was pleased to find that the rattle on the snakes also correlated with various positions of the Pleiades in the sky.

The glyph with crossed bands which appears in the Codex was interpreted by Hatch as representing the constellation Cygnus whose star Gamma, when it transited at midnight, used to announce to Meso-americans the advent of the summer solstice.

297

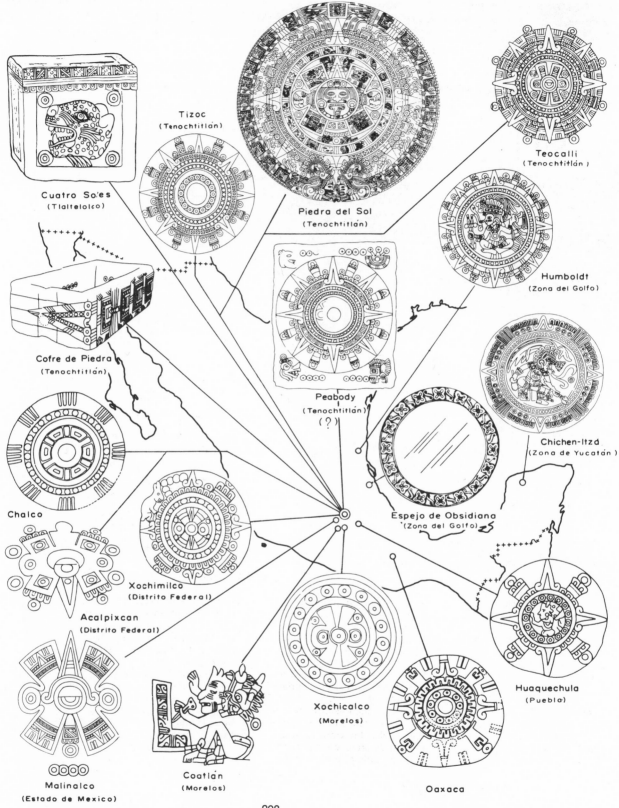

Cuatro Soles
(Tlaltelolco)

Tizoc
(Tenochtitlán)

Piedra del Sol
(Tenochtitlán)

Teocalli
(Tenochtitlán)

Cofre de Piedra
(Tenochtitlán)

Peabody
(Tenochtitlán)
(?)

Humboldt
(Zona del Golfo)

Chichen-Itzá
(Zona de Yucatán)

Espejo de Obsidiana
(Zona del Golfo)

Chalco

Xochimilco
(Distrito Federal)

Acalpixcan
(Distrito Federal)

Huaquechula
(Puebla)

Malinalco
(Estado de México)

Coatlán
(Morelos)

Xochicalco
(Morelos)

Oaxaca

298

Raul Noriega was able to achieve what Leon y Gama and Humboldt suspected but could not adequately accomplish: he demonstrated that the great Aztec monolith was a cosmic clock of extreme sophistication.

Noriega realized that with the exception of the obviously mythical figures, such as the twenty day-glyphs in the circle, and the four ages glyphs in the second circle, most of the other symbols carved into the great stone were purely mathematical, with algebraic functions, which could describe a great variety of calculations, harmonized into an aesthetic whole. With very few glyphs and some multiplication signs, the ancient Mexicans had been able to express at will either very small or very large astronomical-calendrical cycles, in days, weeks, months, years, and centuries.

Noriega found astronomical computations that showed an exact knowledge of the cyclical movement of the planets, calculated in their synodic (or apparent as opposed to sidereal, or actual) returns with an accuracy equal to our modern astronomers' five points of decimal.

The calendar enabled its priests to compute the rhythmic cycle of solar and lunar eclipses, the passages of the sun at zenith, equinox and solstice, the furthest points reached on the horizon by the rising and setting sun and moon at different seasons, the phases of the moon, the heliacal rising of Venus, and the passage of Venus across the face of the sun (four times in 243 years), probably observed through fine sheets of obsidian or mica.

The third cycle of the calendar, says Noriega, will show a modern high school student how to determine the recurrence of planetary conjunctions going into the past or the future for thousands of years.

By locating in Oppolzer the 454 eclipses of the sun ob-

Noriega found a system of multiplication signs in the Sun calendar which he deciphered as follows:

servable in the mid part of the North American continent from 1207 B.C. to A.D. 2161, Noriega was able to show the accuracy of recurrent periods of eclipses noted by the Ancient Mexicans in time lapses of 52, 104, 156, 208, 260, 416, 780, and 1248 years, all multiples of the Mexican century of 52 years.

The 1248-years cycle is quite remarkable. It is 12 centuries of 104 years each of 365 days. In that period the planet Venus makes as many synodic returns as there are days in a Mars revolution (780), and Mars makes as many revolu-

tions as there are days in a Venus revolution (584). There are also exactly 1,752 calendars of 260 days in 1248 years.

Realizing that the earth was affected by the relative movements of the sun, moon, and planets, the ancient Mexicans, says Noriega, sought to master these cycles, by counting days, weeks, lunations, years, centuries, and synodic returns of the planets with the long-term object of being able to find the repetitive pattern in cataclysms, cyclones, tornados, earthquakes, floods, pestilence, and periods of relative serenity.

299

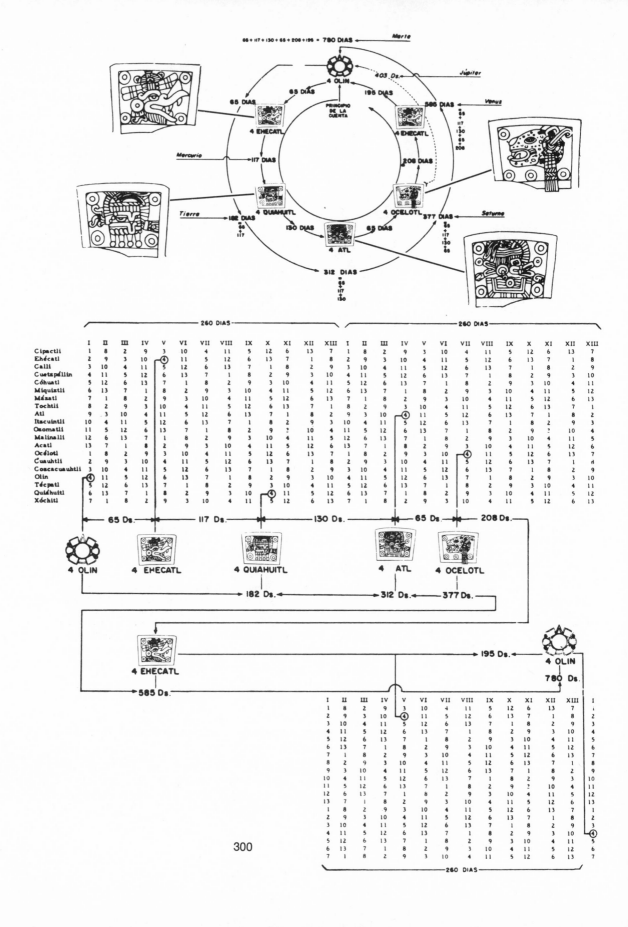

Noriega realized the four boxes around the central face of the calendar stone—4 Ehecatl, 4 Quihuitl, 4 Atl, 4 Ocelotl—together with the basic 4 Olin glyphs signalled the lapses of synodic revolutions of the planets.

Noriega deciphered the second ring of the calendar stone as an indicator of the synodic returns of the planets. Computed from 4 *Sun* to 4 *Hurricane* to 4 *Cyclone* to 4 *Water* to 4 *Ocelot,* all fit into a 260-day calendar, which gives the following time periods.

From 4 *Sun* to 4 *Hurricane* is 65 days or 1/4 of a sacred calendar, which is also 1/9 of a Venus and 1/12 of a Mars cycle. From 4 *Hurricane* to 4 *Cyclone* is 117 days, or one Mercury revolution ($+$ 1 day), the same as 1/5 of a Venus cycle. From 4 *Sun* to 4 *Cyclone* is 182 days, or 1/2 a terrestrial revolution ($-$ 1 day). From 4 *Cyclone* to 4 *Water* is 130 days, or 1/2 a sacred calendar, which is 1/6 of a Mars cycle. From 4 *Sun* to 4 *Ocelot* is 377 days, or one Saturn cycle ($-$ 1 day). Noriega points out that all the cycles are based on multiples or submultiples of 13, the fundamental Mesoamerican calendrical number, and that 44 lunations are counted as 1300 days, or 260 $\times$ 5. (The actual number is 1299.34596.)

Raul Noriega, a Mexican jurist and anthropologist who spent a lifetime researching Mexican calendar systems to produce an extraordinarily handsome and informative book, *La Piedra del Sol,* on the Mexican calendar stone, used the Oppolzer catalogue of eclipses of the sun and moon visible in Mesoamerica from 1204 B.C. to A.D. 2250 to find that almost all the eclipses related by a number of days whose factor was 260.

The planet Mars also fits this system admirably, in that one synodic return of Mars takes 780 days, which is exactly three sacred calendar periods of 260 days.

From an analysis of a score of Mexican calendar stones Noriega shows that the Maya (as well as the Aztecs) were able to calculate the synodic revolutions of Saturn, Mercury, and Jupiter with great precision.

One of the basic mysteries of the Mayan calendar now appears to have been resolved by one of the NASA technicians responsible for the Apollo flights, Maurice Chatelain, who was born in France but has lived twenty years in California. In his *Nos Ancêtres Venus du Cosmos,* published in 1975 by Robert Laffont, Chatelain worked out the basic calendrical system of the Maya which turns out to be similar to that of the Sumerians.

Chatelain got onto the solution while puzzling over the extraordinarily high number 195,955,200,000,000 which appears on one of the 30,000 Babylonian cuneiform tablets found in Assurbanipal's Nineveh library.

Chatelain says he got the shock of his life when he realized the number was 86,400 times 2,268,000,000, and that 2,268 million was the number of days in 240 precessions of the equinox (of 25,890 years each).

In other words, some ancient astronomer had counted 240 precessions not in days but in seconds, 86,400 being the number of seconds in their day. Then Chatelain began to realize why the Mesopotamians had gone to such lengths. He was even more surprised to discover that the huge Babylonian number was an exact multiple of all the planetary revolutions and conjunctions he could check, including those of satellites and comets, correct to four points of decimal! It made the 2,268 million years, or 240 cycles of precessions of 25,890 years, the basic constant or common denominator of the life cycles of the solar system.

Chatelain then resolved the riddle of the extraordinarily high Mayan numbers by looking not for a multiple of our earth and other planetary conjunctions, but at the conjunctions of the other planets with each other.

The Mayan cycle of 942,890 days, or 2,582 years, turned out to be 130 Saturn-Jupiter conjunctions. (It also covers other cycles: 15 Neptune-Uranus, 1,555 Jupiter-Mars, 2,284 Mars-Venus, 6,522 Venus-Mercury, and 2,720 Sun-Mars.) Twice this cycle, or 5,163 years, is 260 Saturn-Jupiter conjunctions, which gives a grand cycle with the same number as there are days in the Mayan sacred year.

To see where such a cycle would lead him into the past, Chatelain took the 18,630 B.C. date which appears in the Codex Vaticanus and moving forward in increments of 5,163 years (or 260 Saturn-Jupiter conjunctions) he lit upon 13,467 B.C., 8,304 B.C., and 3,141 B.C., the last of which coincided very well with the accepted beginning of the last Maya cycle of 13 baktuns.

Chatelain saw that this grand Saturn-Jupiter cycle of 5,163 years, or 1,885,780 days, could be divided into 13 baktuns of 397.2 years or (145,060 days) a katun of 19.86 years (or 7,253 days) each katun of which was divisible into 20 tuns of 363 days. He also calculated a grander cycle of 18,720 katuns or 135,776,160 days.

Next Chatelain realized that the next figure of 34,020,000,-000 days which appears in the Mayan glyphs was 15 times the Nineveh constant of 2,268 million years, and that the even next higher number of 147,420,000,000 days in the Maya glyphs was 65 times the Nineveh constant. He also saw that 147,420 million days is 78,170 cycles of 260 Saturn-Jupiter conjunctions. It was clear to him that the Sumerians had used the same basic constant as the Maya, only multiplied by the 86,400 seconds of their day.

Furthermore, the Mesopotamians had linked their measures of time and space—in seconds of time and seconds of arc. 34,020 million days is not only the number of days in 3,600 Sumerian precessions of the equinox but 3,600 tenths of a degree—consisting of 36,000 Egyptian feet of .308 meter—is the circumference of the world in seconds of arc. The Mesopotamians had not only chosen as a unit of measure a foot that was earth-commensurate, it was also commensurate with the great Platonic year of 25,890 years. Odd would it be if the unit dispensed by Hunab Ku to the Maya were not equally earth-commeasurable. At Teotihuacan and at Palenque this ancient Middle Eastern foot fits Cinderella's shoe as neatly as it did at Cheops.

Frank Waters finds it useless to speculate on how the Mayan priest-astronomers "without telescopes, measuring apparatus, computers, and the use of fractions, could have achieved with such remarkable accuracy this immense and complex calendar system," and finds it even more incomprehensible that they could combine "the science of abstruse mathematics and astronomy with a metaphysical cosmology and mythology." The problem leads him to wonder whether

302

The Mayan palm, considered by Domingo Martinez Paradez to be the oldest continuous unit of measure, was known to the ancient Maya by the same word used for undulation: *naab.* Several Mayan palms were in use, one of which was about seven inches long.

An English radionic expert has found that every seven inches, or very close to that amount, the rotational polarity of a field of radionic energy extending from a magnetic compass reverses. This is shown by a change in the direction of rotation of a pendulum held over the horizontal plane in which the compass lies. According to astrologer Michael Heleus, this would imply that the ancient palm of nearly seven inches could have been a measure having a character intrinsically linked with the magnetic and radionic properties of the universe. Heleus suggests that the pendulum, sensing the magnetic undulation, reverses polarity at nodes whose distances are harmonic multiples of the palm, multiples whose sequence of alternation is reminiscent of the earth-commensurate palms in the ancient Greek (and Egyptian) foot and cubit.

Theoretical considerations supporting these observations are provided by D. B. Larson in *Structure of the Physical Universe.* In this work, Larson advances the hypothesis that the spacing of atoms, and indeed their production, is the result of the interplay of two opposing forces. The first, which he calls the space-time progression, moves outward from every point continually at the velocity of light, which he considers unitary. The second is rotation, which, where it exists, opposes the space-time progression, and if it exceeds that progression, creates an inward force giving rise to matter and gravitation.

"astrology, symbology and mythology could have been a shorthand to describe a galactic type of science of a different dimension from the conventional physics we use to describe earthly phenomena."

A clue as to how the Mesoamericans may have achieved such prodigious results was obtained in the 1950s by Geoffrey Hodson, the extraordinarily clairvoyant Theosophist, when he went into a semi-trance at the top of the Sun Pyramid of Teotihuacan. With closed eyes he was able to conjure pictures of the past. To Hodson it was clear that the ancient Mesoamerican priests had clairvoyant powers by means of which they could know when and where the various planets would be situated and from this knowledge deduce an accurate system of astronomy without benefit of high-powered telescopes. Such an accurate astronomy married to an accurately accumulated knowledge of the evident effects of planetary relations could have produced a valid science of astrology.

Hodson says that initiates were specially trained to detect combinations of planetary forces during astrological aspects. They could apparently feel or sense them, knowing when and where planets formed aspects like conjunctions, squares, or oppositions, which either strengthened or weakened stellar, zodiacal, or higher cosmic influences as they manifested on earth.

Hodson says the physical, astral, and mental bodies of the priests thus trained became sensitized to such a degree that they became human observatories, aided by physical recognition of the position of the planets.

The French astrologer Alexandre Volguine believes furthermore, that Mayan eyesight in those days was more powerful than today, though even with acute eyesight it would be difficult to account for how the Maya knew of 400 stars in the Seven Sisters constellation of the Pleiades, whereas today we can spot only 6 stars with the naked eye. Human senses appear to have degenerated rather than evolved under the influence of so-called civilization. Volguine says that illiterate natives in Oriental Siberia can still see the satellites of Jupiter. He adds that there is no reason to believe that the Maya were unable to see with the naked eye Uranus, Neptune, Pluto, and perhaps even the trans-Plutonian planet postulated by Harleston and others.

303

21. Astronomical Observations

All the great temples of antiquity, as Livio Stecchini has abundantly shown,* served to locate man in the cosmos, both in space and time, bringing knowledge of the heavens to the earth.

According to the Chorti priests of Guatemala, their forefathers had divided the cosmos into a quadrangle. To bring this quadrangle down to earth, they picked as geodetic points the four corners on the horizon where the sun rests at dawn and sunset of the solstices.

The *Popol Vuh* says the surface of the earth was divided into four sections corresponding to the four points of the compass, each with its own colors, fates, and gods. Bishop Landa reports that towns in Yucatan were so designed, with four principal entrances in the form of a cross; and still today in Mayaland villages are laid out in the old pattern, the sun being observed at equinox and solstice in order to establish the points at which to put up stone markers.

The Dresden Codex shows that Mayan geodesy took into consideration both the cardinal points and the intermediate solstitial points, for which they eventually built complex observatories for determining the exact moment of the solstices.

A quote from the Roys book of Chilam Balam says, "When the eleventh day of June shall come, it will be the longest day, when the thirteenth of September comes, this day and night are precisely the same length. When the twelfth day of December shall come, the day is short, but the night is long.

* In his appendix to *Secrets of the Great Pyramid,* and other writings.

When the tenth day of March comes, the day and the night will be equal in length."

The discrepancy with our September 23 and December 22 is due to the shift of one day in seventy-two years caused by the precession of the equinoxes.

Diego Duran, Toribio Motolinia, and Fernando Ixtlilxochitl describe Mexican sun priests as spending long nights in systematic observation of the heavens, registering the movements of celestial bodies. With the use of the gnomon, they obtained accurate knowledge of the equinoxes and solstices.

Motolinia says that in Tenochtitlan the festival called Tlacaxipeualiztli "took place when the sun stood in the middle of Huicholobos, which was at the equinox, and because it was a little out of line, Montezuma wished to tear it down and set it right." As part of his official duties Montezuma was required to rise regularly at midnight and offer incense to certain principal stars. Other priests watched for the appearance of certain stars at dusk, three A.M., and immediately before dawn, the time being heralded by drums and trumpets from the temples.

Zelia Nuttall demonstrated incontrovertibly, though little attention was paid her, that the ancient Mexicans not only employed carefully oriented temples and ball courts as astronomical observations, but also invented ingenious devices in and on these observatories for accurately registering the periodical appearances and disappearances of important celestial bodies: they had forked and bifurcated sticks, frets along the roofs of lined-up buildings, rows of upright sticks, and stelae carefully located several miles apart.

This circular figure with the sun symbol on the right and the star-filled sky on the left clearly shows an equal division of night and day—or the equinox.

Figure 1. This illustration from the Codex Mendoza (reproduced by Kingsborough, volume V page 101) shows a seated priest whose vision is directed toward the symbol of the nocturnal heavens—an eye-filled hemisphere in which the eyes represent stars.

Figures 2 and 3 (Borgia Codex) show open doorways in the center of which float single stars. The first doorway shows the sky at dusk or dawn, the second at night. Below the second temple is a symbol for a great star or planet. The fourth figure shows twin stars appearing in the doorway.

305

Doorways drawn in profile were the common conventional mode adopted by the native artists to represent temples. The first temple shows a single star, the second the sun, and the third an entire constellation in the form of a curved object studded with stars which is very similar to Scorpio.

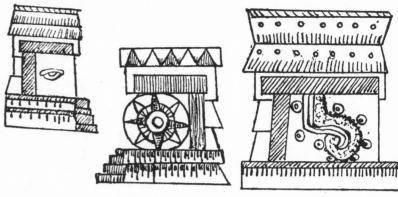

Ancient Mexican astronomers did not limit themselves to observing celestial bodies through openings in buildings. Figure 10 represents a temple on the roof and in the doorway of which stand rows of bifurcated stakes. Their purpose, says Zelia Nuttall, is revealed by figure 11, which is clearly designated as a star temple by three stars attached to the back wall. On the roof is seen a star in a bifurcated stake. Frets on the roof of the third temple indicate another method of lining up celestial bodies.

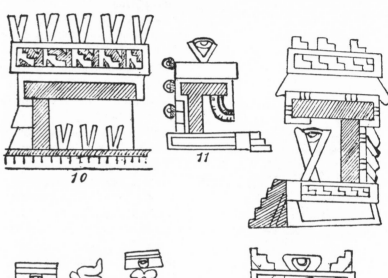

10

11

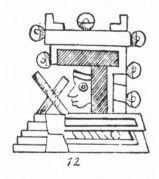

12

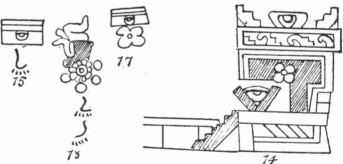

15

17

13

14

Figure 12. Here the temple walls and roof are studded with six stars, and a human face or mask is depicted peering out of the doorway through crossed sticks. Figure 14 shows a star lodged in the triangle of a forked stake erected on the summit of the temple stairway, while another large star rests on the roof exactly between the terraced corners of the edifice. On the

lintel of the temple door is represented a four-petaled flower. Proof that this was the actual sign for a particular star is furnished by figure 17, which exhibits an identical flower on the band studded with stars, denoting the nocturnal heaven. Here in figure 15 a starband is painted above a footprint directed downward, near a seated figure accompanied by a day and

year sign. Mrs. Nuttall believes this may have recorded the setting of some particular star on the date recorded. A similar footprint directed away from the temple in figure 14 suggests to Mrs. Nuttall that the doorway may have faced east, and that the footprint refers to the setting of the "Flower" star or of the adjacent constellation at a particular time of the year.

Figure 26 shows Venus atop a truncated pyramid without its winglike appendages, evidently at a different period of its revolution.

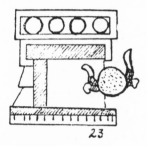

Figure 23 shows the planet Venus being observed by means of a temple.

Figure 22 shows a combination of the "Flower" star and a footprint directed downward, presumably for its setting. On top of the terrace is a curious device which resembles the drawn-up limbs of a seated human figure. It is even clearer in figure 19. Zelia Nuttall says the device serves the same purpose as a bifurcated stake, pointing out that the Nahuatl word signifying "on the knee" can be read as a homonym conveying the meaning "on the summit or head of the earth or land."

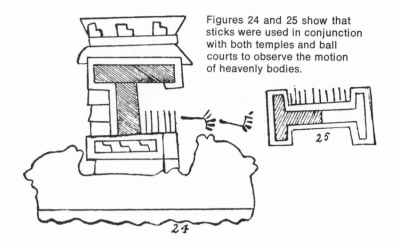

Figures 24 and 25 show that sticks were used in conjunction with both temples and ball courts to observe the motion of heavenly bodies.

Figure 27 shows Venus as the morning star at its period of greatest brilliance, a large dish with two winglike appendages. It also shows that it was observed from the center of a ball court, where it is seen rising. The fact that half the court is dark may indicate a heliacal rising of Venus at the equinox.

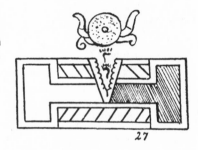

As early as the turn of the century Mrs. Nuttall found illustrations in the codices descriptive of methods used by Mesoamerican priests to observe stars and planets. The illustrations showed ancient astronomers, as in Babylonia and Egypt, observing certain stars from a dark cell or chamber through the opening doorway of the temple situated on an elevation.

Zelia Nuttall also correctly suspected that the high dome of the Caracol at Chichen Itza constituted a gnomon which would be shadowless at noon on the days the sun crossed the

The Miztec manuscript known as the Codex Nuttall.

In Florence at the turn of the century Zelia Nuttall heard from Pasquale Villari, an Italian senator and ex-minister of higher education, that while he was doing research in the Library of San Marco some two years earlier he had been accosted by a monk with a strange manuscript. This was the turbulent period of the unification of Italy, and when the Library was taken over by the state the manuscript was sold to an Englishman living in Florence who gave it to a friend in England. Determined to recover the manuscript, Zelia Nuttall searched through-out England, eventually establishing that it had been given to Sir Robert Curzon, fourteenth Baron of Zouche. Among the papers of the fif-teenth Baron, Zelia Nuttall found the manuscript where it had lain unopened for twenty-five years. It is now in the British Museum, and Zelia Nuttall's original facsimile of it, published in 1901, is available in paperback. The early history of the codex is doubtful, but it may have been among the prizes sent by Cortes to Charles V.

zenith in May and July (announcing to the populace the ad-vent of the rainy season and the beginning of a new calendar year).

Luis Arochi, author of a new book on the astronomical orientation of the Castillo at Chichen Itza, also shows in a series of remarkable photographs that the steps of the build-ing are so cunningly oriented and designed that only on the day of the vernal and autumnal equinox the sun's rays cause a great serpent (whose head is carved at the bottom of the steps) to slither up or down the stairway—up in spring and down in autumn, forming a set of seven perfect isoceles triangles patterned on the local rattlesnake, *Crotolus.*

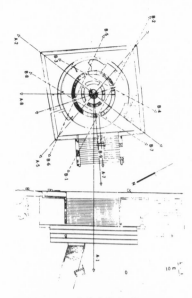

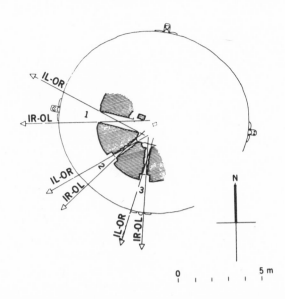

(Above and right) Anthony Aveni's diagrams showing various astronomical alignments of the Caracol building at Chichen Itza.

(Left) Arochi's picture of a great snake with isoceles markings descending the steps of the Castillo at Chichen Itza at the equinox.

Despite J. Eric Thompson, who is considered the foremost living authority on the Maya, but who disparagingly regards the Caracol as nothing more than "a two-decker wedding cake on the square carton in which it came," recent scientific investigation has shown this extraordinary building to be a sophisticatedly designed astronomical observatory and geodetic marker.

Anthony F. Aveni, an astronomer, Sharon L. Gibbs, a historian of science, both on the faculty of Colgate University in Hamilton, New York, and Horst Hartung, an architect on the faculty of the University of Guadalajara, Mexico, show that the diagonals of the main platform point to sunrise at summer solstice and sunset at the winter solstice, and that other astronomical observations could be made at different times of the year in different parts of the building by astronomer priests. In a paper presented to the forty-first International Congress of Americanists in Mexico City in 1974 they further suggested that many of the asymmetries built into the Caracol were intentionally designed to create alignments which would point to astronomical events.

Following Ricketson's hypothesis that windows functioned as astronomical sighting chambers, and that one of them might have been deliberately designed to point to sunset at the equinoxes, the trio set themselves to observe the phenomenon and were able to see that the instant of the passage of the sun across the vernal equinox occurred within ten minutes of the movement of sunset. The edge of the setting sun lined up almost perfectly with a narrow opening in the window, enabling the sunset to be viewed through a slot.

As stellar observations are especially important at the time of the solstice or zenith in order to obtain greater ac-

309

Aveni's diagrams of stellar and solar methods of observation with Mesoamerican buildings.

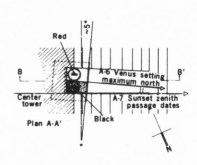

MOUND "P", MONTE ALBAN

curacy, they believe that weep holes, rectangular horizontal shafts of a width of from eight to twelve centimeters which pierce the tower at ground level both below and above the upper molding, may also have had an astronomical function. The trio found alignments for the heliacal rising of such major stars as Canopus, Castor, and Pollux, which led them to suggest that entire constellations such as the Pleiades could have been more carefully watched through the windows at important moments such as on the date of a Venus passage.

As Venus, which is exceeded in brilliance only by the sun and moon, reaches its greatest northerly and southerly extrema along the horizon at regular intervals of the calendar year, the trio suggest that the placement of the Castillo windows could have been determined by the setting position of Venus.

At Uxmal, the platform which serves as a base for the Palace of the Governor is oriented to the rising of Venus. For this, Thompson had the evidence of the elaborate Venus calendar in the Dresden Codex, believed to have been composed in the vicinity of Chichen during the Mexican period, which showed concern with the heliacal rising and setting of Venus. And the recent breakthroughs by the Hieroglyphic Section of the Institute for Mayan Studies at the Miami Museum of Science indicate that the codices contain sophisticated perpetual computer layouts for such ephemeral phenomena as the cyclical coincidence of heliacal risings of Venus in conjunction with eclipses of the sun.

Aveni also looked for slots which might point to the setting moon at its maximum northerly and southerly extremes. Every 18.6 years the full moon nearest the time of the winter solstice will be found to set at its greatest northerly extreme. This would have provided the Maya with a recurring cycle, such as the alignments at Stonehenge. The codices also contain refined data on various cycles of the moon.

Other round towers in Mayaland near Tulum, Ake, and Cozumel, also dedicated to Quetzalcoatl, are being analyzed for astronomical orientation.

310

Aveni spotted a ceremonial center on a hill five kilometers by line of sight from the governor's palace at Uxmal—first noted by Stephens as Nohpat—which lined up with a pillar and Chac-Mool to indicate the maximum southing of Venus.

311

West
Line of sunset on April 12
Stela 10

Stela 12
East

Solar alignment of the "Sundial" stele at Copan, Honduras.

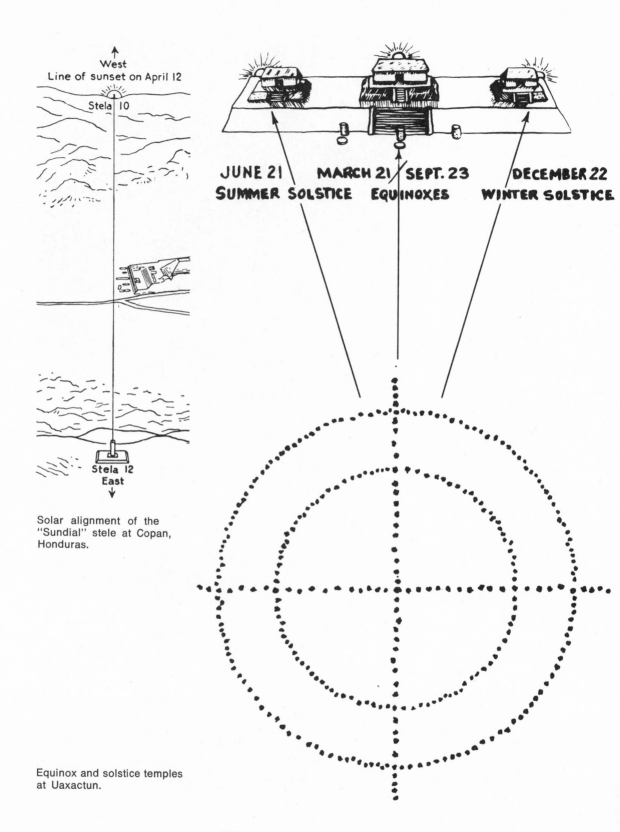

JUNE 21 / MARCH 21 / SEPT. 23 / DECEMBER 22
SUMMER SOLSTICE / EQUINOXES / WINTER SOLSTICE

Equinox and solstice temples at Uaxactun.

312

Chac-Mool.

The concave circular dish held on the stomach of the Chac-Mool first discovered by Le Plongeon, a copy of which has been placed at the top of the stairs of the so-called Temple of the Warriors at Chichen Itza, may well have been used as a receptacle for water or liquid mercury (with which the Maya were acquainted) on which to float a magnetic lodestone or compass point. The bowl could also have served as a mirror for watching the split-second transit of stars, the method still used today by the Naval Observatory in Washington, D.C., and at least 5000 years ago in the Great Pyramid of Cheops.

As the grid plans of a number of important sites in southern Mesoamerica possess orientations directed slightly east of astronomical north, close to the present compass direction, such as at Uxmal, Copan, and Ozibilchaltun, it has been suggested by Robert Furison in the *Annals of the Association of American Geographers* in 1969 that the Maya may have known the magnetic compass and used fragments of worked magnetite such as have been found and established as being pre-Columbian. There is no reason the compass, which was known in China a thousand years before Christ, could not have been brought to Yucatan by the Chinese explorers and Buddhist monks reported by Henriette Mertz to have reached Mexico in the second millennium B.C. and again in the fifth century A.D.

At Copan in Honduras a base line of 9 degrees north of west was established with a sundial to indicate sunset at the solstices and equinoxes. At Uaxactun three temples and two stelae give precise orientations of the sun's position at the solstices and equinoxes. At Xochicalco the great pyramid contains a vertical shaft down which the sun shines so as to cast a perfectly round shadow twice a year at the zenith.

Marquina and Ruiz suggest the setting of the Pleiades as a possible orientation point for the axis of the Teotihuacan and Tenayuca pyramids. Aveni says that at the time the Way of the Dead was constructed, the Pleiades would have touched the horizon point above the Cerro Colorado marker at azimuth 284° 40′, or 14° 40′ N of W.

Aveni says the Pleiades could also have served the function of "announcing" the first annual passage of the sun through the zenith of Teotihuacan, since the heliacal rising and the passage of sun through zenith occurred approximately on the same day—58 days after the vernal equinox.

The theory was supported by J. W. Dow in his *Astronomical Orientation at Teotihuacan* in *American Antiquity* in 1967. Dow suggests an east-west base line was fundamental to the layout of the city and that the Way of the Dead was oriented to it at right angles.

22. Geodetic Markers

Marker on the U.S.-Mexico border reported by Riva Palacios in 1889.

So far it has not been possible to establish precise dates when the markings could have been made. Were they inscribed as required alignment marks for the construction of the pyramids, sometime around the beginning of the Christian era, or earlier, maybe by many centuries, or much later, perhaps by observers attempting to reestablish solstitial and equinoctial lines of sight after the eighth-century fall of Teotihuacan?

When the marker at Uaxactun from which the equinoxes and the solstices could be observed was first found by American archeologist Oliver G. Ricketson in 1937, he noted it was made in the shape of a cross formed by eighty-one holes. Many years earlier a similar marker had been used by Vicente Riva Palacio to illustrate his four-volume *Mexico Atraves de los Siglos*. But no one could figure out the purpose or significance of the eighty-one holes.

During the early 1970's, searching for temple sites on the hills around the Valley of Teotihuacan, Harleston and a group of amateur archeologists found a whole system of similar stone markers which clearly lined up with the Pyramid of the Sun, and other definite markers to indicate the rising and setting sun at solstices, equinoxes, and zenith passages.

The markers indicate that various buildings of the pyramid complex were used in conjunction with markers on the hills and mountains surrounding the valley for geodetic and astronomical sightings at least as early as the fall of the Roman Empire, and presumably much earlier.

That the markers do just that was established by the researchers through repeated observation of sunrises and sunsets at Teotihuacan, where the markers line up with such fixed sighting lines as the corners of the Sun Pyramid to indicate the summer and winter solstices. Details of these discoveries and of the observed phenomena were presented at the forty-first International Congress of Americanists in Mexico City in September of 1974.

The markers, some more than a meter in diameter, are in the form of crosses in single or double circles, or in triple cloverleaves. Small holes, a centimeter wide and about two centimeters apart, were pitted into solid volcanic outcroppings or into millennial mortar floors of lime and crushed volcanic rock in what appear to be mathematically significant numbers such as 4 legs of a cross of 20, plus a center of 1, for a total of 81, or 9 times 9. The series of holes either form angles of 90 degrees, or are aligned on specific azimuth readings from true north such as 48 degrees, 60 degrees, 66 degrees, 72 degrees, 144 degrees, or 228 degrees. The astronomical and geodetic functions of some of the azimuth lines have been deciphered by the researchers; others remain a puzzle.

The most complex of the markers, a triple cloverleaf around a Cartesian coordinate cross, was found on March 9, 1974,

315

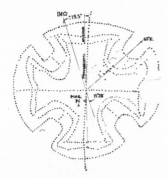

The Triple Cross.

by Alfonso Morales, an economist in hydraulic resource planning, who, like the other researchers, was anxious to accelerate archeological inquiry and the better preservation of Mexico's ancient monuments.

Morales found the marker under a loose layer of windblown earth and tourist detritus near the loggia of a patio west of the main Teotihuacan Processional axis, the so-called Way of the Dead, opposite the Pyramid of the Sun.

The cross contains 30 holes to each leg plus 1 at the center for a total of 121, or 11 squared: there are 63, or 9 × 7, holes per cloverleaf.

The north-south arm of the central cross was aligned 19.5 east of north. When the marker was shown to Harleston, he noted that one line of pitted holes indicated with special emphasis an azimuth which appeared to be almost 65 degrees.

To check this orientation with the greatest possible precision the researchers returned to the spot at noon of the vernal equinox equipped with a tripod and a pointer to center on the triple cross. They were then able to use the sun to trace a straight line across the marker without deviation from astronomical west to east, a line which was particularly accurate in 1974 because the sun happened to cross the equator at noon central standard time, which was also noon at Teotihuacan.

316

A perpendicular to this line gave the researchers a true north-south line from which it was possible to measure the azimuth marked out with holes on the mortar slab; it was precisely 65 degrees east of north.

By calculation, based on the latitude of Teotihuacan and the sun's declension, the solar azimuth on the morning of the summer solstice is 65.007 degrees.

To observe the actual occurrence of the phenomenon Harleston and Manuel Gaitan, a seventy-year-old professor of archeological restoration, who has been with the Mexican Institute of Anthropology for over thirty years, obtained permission from the institute to spend the night of June 20 in a tent on the Processional in preparation for the solstice of June 21.

During the night it rained on and off. The rainy season in the Valley of Mexico runs from June to September. But just after dawn on June 21, and shortly before sunrise, the rain stopped sufficiently for the two observers stationed by the triple cross to see the solstitial sun appear from behind the Sun Pyramid at the upper southeast corner of the third level in a way that was uniquely recognizable.

The phenomenon led the two observers to assume that another marker should exist from which sunrise could be accurately observed on the two mornings a year when the sun crosses the zenith above the Pyramid of the Sun—May 19 and

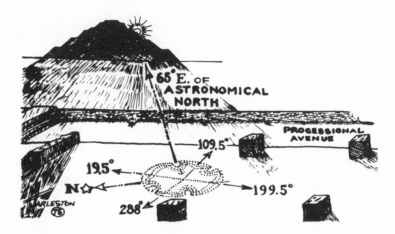

Sun at the summer solstice of June 21 as it appears behind the third level of the Sun Pyramid seen from the Triple Cross at Teotihuacan.

July 25 in 1974. Harleston calculated the spot where an observer would have to stand to be able to see across the top of the Sun Pyramid as being 14 kilometers southwest of the pyramid at an elevation of 2630 meters, forming an angle with the pyramid of 70.2 degrees east of north.

To be sure his calculations were accurate Harleston had them validated by three independent sources: by Mexico's leading geodesist, Manuel Medina Peralta, ex-director of the Geodesical School of Mexico's National University and author of *Elements of Positional Astronomy;* by Dr. Yoji Kondo, a NASA astrophysicist from Johnson Space Center in Houston, Texas; and by Dr. Paris Piçhmiçh, an astronomer from Turkey. All agreed with his findings.

Three reconnaissance trips were made to the selected area near the summit of a hill called Chiconautla (the Place of Nine) 300 meters above the Valley of Teotihuacan and 2650 meters above sea level, but the trips proved fruitless; no marker could be found. Convinced that they had somehow missed the marker, Harleston and Gaitan spent the night of July 24 (which preceded the day of the zenith sunrise) at a campsite within half a kilometer of the calculated location. Again it rained, and the dawn was foggy and drizzly, but just at sunrise the clouds across the valley lifted enough for Gaitan to photograph the appearance of the solar orb above the Pyramid of the Sun, while Harleston, cussing the weather, ascended to the summit of Chiconautla, some sixty vertical meters higher than the encampment. He was then to be thankful for the rain.

The wet shiny reflecting surface of the eroded lava outcroppings caused faint pittings of a multiangular marker to appear on the hilltop precisely at the calculated angle of 70.2 degrees and at an elevation of 2632 meters. The marker lined up perfectly with sunrise for that morning when the sun at noon stands directly over the Pyramid of the Sun at latitude 19 degrees 41 minutes.

Sunrise on May 19 and July 25, the days of the solar zenith at Teotihuacan, seen from the marker on the hill of Chiconautla.

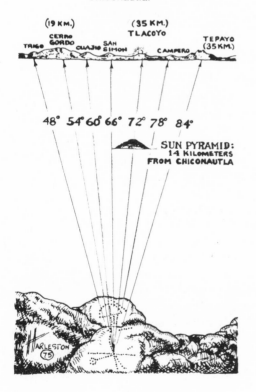

318

The marker named Uac-Kan Observatory No. 1 was located by Harleston thanks to an early morning rain that wet the surface and allowed the faint pittings to be seen. The pittings give angular directions to major mountaintops as well as alignments for the zenithal and solstitial sunrises, which strongly suggested to Harleston that the ancient Mexican geodesists used a system of 6-degree separations, the preferred Babylonian divisions.

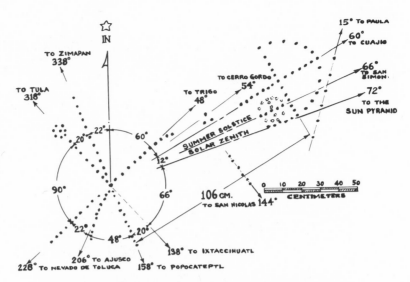

Assuming that other markers would also have been placed for sighting the summer and winter solstices, the group found two more close to the marker discovered by James Bennyhoff, an American archeologist, in 1963. Used in conjunction, the markers form a triangle which enables an observer to sight along different legs to see sunrise and sunset on both summer and winter solstices.

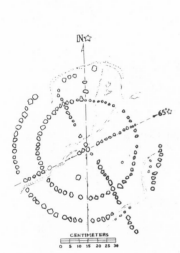

Bennyhoff marker.

In 1963, when the survey was being made of the hillsides around Teotihuacan for Millon's mapping project, archeologist James Bennyhoff, while walking the sloping southern flank of Malinalli in an area called Colorado Chico, found an almost invisible stone marker. The marker consisted of two circles and a cross; its arms were aligned on 65 degrees east of astronomical north, a fact that was not to be noticed until eleven years later. Bennyhoff's find lay dormant until its publication in 1973 as part of the introduction to the *Teotihuacan Map*.

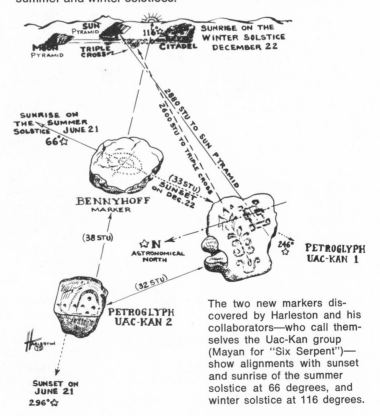

The two new markers discovered by Harleston and his collaborators—who call themselves the Uac-Kan group (Mayan for "Six Serpent")—show alignments with sunset and sunrise of the summer solstice at 66 degrees, and winter solstice at 116 degrees.

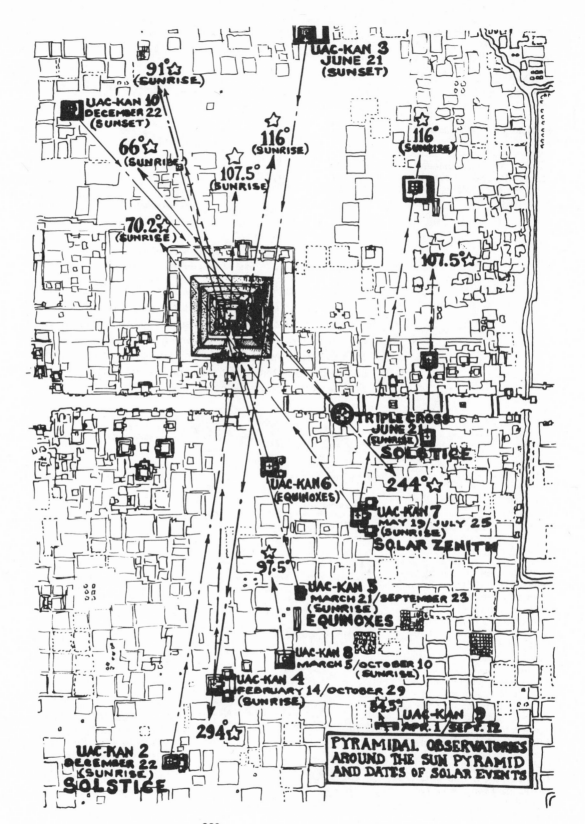

91° ☆
(SUNRISE)

UAC-KAN 3
JUNE 21
(SUNSET)

UAC-KAN 10
DECEMBER 22
(SUNSET)

116° ☆
(SUNRISE)

66° ☆
(SUNRISE)

116° ☆
(SUNRISE)

107.5° ☆
(SUNRISE)

70.2° ☆
(SUNRISE)

107.5° ☆

TRIPLE CROSS
JUNE 21
(SUNRISE)
SOLSTICE

244° ☆

UAC-KAN 6
(EQUINOXES)

UAC-KAN 7
MAY 19/JULY 25
(SUNRISE)
SOLAR ZENITH

97.5° ☆

UAC-KAN 5
MARCH 21/SEPTEMBER 23
(SUNRISE)
EQUINOXES

UAC-KAN 8
MARCH 5/OCTOBER 10
(SUNRISE)

UAC-KAN 4
FEBRUARY 14/OCTOBER 29
(SUNRISE)

61.5°
UAC-KAN 9
APR. 1/SEPT. 12

294° ☆

UAC-KAN 2
DECEMBER 22
(SUNRISE)
SOLSTICE

PYRAMIDAL OBSERVATORIES
AROUND THE SUN PYRAMID
AND DATES OF SOLAR EVENTS

Other observatories.

The Uac-Kan Observatory No. 2 was located by Dr. Matthew Wallrath as a tumulus, the ruins of an ancient pyramid 1240 meters (1170 STU) northwest of the Sun Pyramid. The alignment of 116 degrees east is across the southwest corner of the fourth body, exactly opposite to the one used for the summer solstice from the Triple Cross. This pyramid appears on the 1973 *Teotihuacan Map,* but was not identified as an observatory when the map was made.

Further investigations revealed that at least eleven other pyramids to the west and east of the Sun Pyramid could be used as observatories. All the observatories are located within a two-kilometer radius of the Sun Pyramid, and six of them are at positions for observations of the solar solstices, equinoxes, and days of zenithal crossing, six being the total number of major solar events per year. Other observatories may have been for ceremonies on February 14 and October 29, later moved to November 1, the important All Saints' Day, still a major Mexican holiday.

Further calculations led to the prediction and location of seven more observatories, including two that might have been destroyed and rebuilt as local land markers by the zealous clergy of the eighteenth century. These two markers are due east on Tepayo (U-K 11) and due south of the Sun Pyramid on Patlachique (U-K 12).

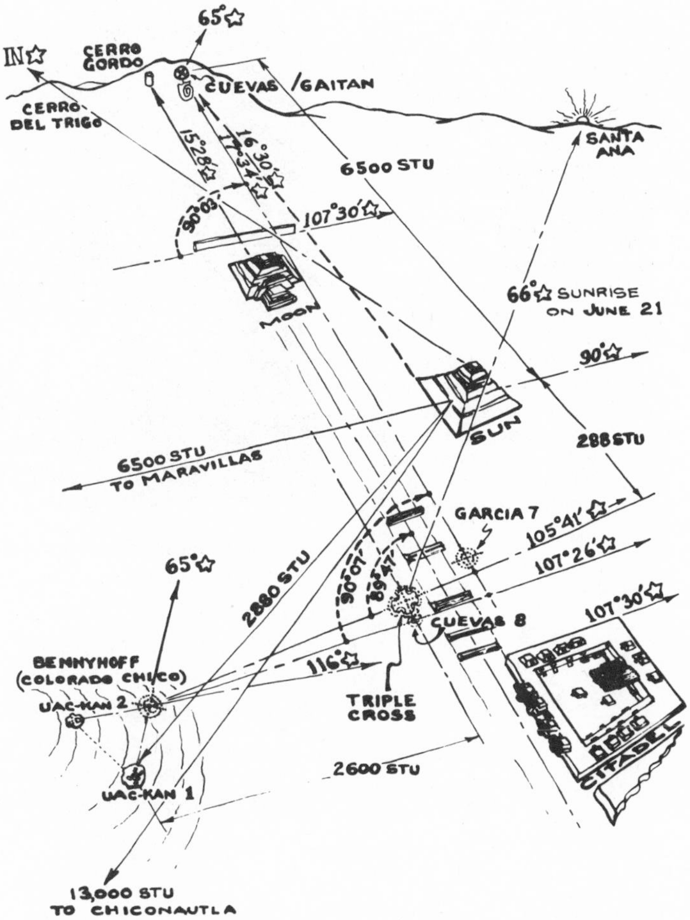

IN ☆
CERRO GORDO
65 ☆
CUEVAS / GAITAN
CERRO DEL TRIGO
15°28'
16°30'
16°34'
90°07'
107°30' ☆
6500 STU
SANTA ANA
66 ☆ SUNRISE ON JUNE 21
90° ☆
MOON
6500 STU TO MARAVILLAS
SUN
288 STU
GARCIA 7
105°41' ☆
107°26' ☆
107°30' ☆
65° ☆
2880 STU
90°07'
89°47'
CUEVAS 8
BENNYHOFF (COLORADO CHICO)
UAC-KAN 2
116° ☆
TRIPLE CROSS
CITADEL
UAC-KAN 1
2600 STU
13,000 STU TO CHICONAUTLA

Convinced that another observation post must have been located closer to the Pyramid of the Sun from which to see the solar orb appear at the winter solstice, Harleston calculated it would have to be less than two kilometers from the pyramid, at an azimuth of 117 degrees, so that the mountains would drop away from the viewer, leaving only the pyramid to act as a mountain. With Dr. Matthew Wallrath, a Ph.D. in archeology who had worked with Millon's University of Rochester mapping project, they located a pyramid marked on Millon's map at 1200 meters from the Sun Pyramid, at exactly 117 degrees, from which the solstitial sun would appear above the second body of the southwest corner of the pyramid on December 22 or 23.

Further study of the Millon map revealed a whole series of remains of pyramids at different distances and angles, east and west of the Sun Pyramid, all within two kilometers. Azimuth angles for sunrise and sunset of summer and winter solstices, as well as of equinoxes and days of the zenith, were found to pass right through certain pyramids, indicating that

321

At the summit of Cerro Maravillas, Manuel Gaitan identified a marker named U-K 14 due west of the Sun Pyramid at an elevation duplicating the Bennyhoff stone. In addition to a circle and cross, this stone has an elliptical triple oval resembling the Garcia 6 configuration, and a circle with a face similar to designs already known at Teotihuacan, but with what appear to be shallow carvings of "sun rays" (not typical of Teotihuacan) believed to be the scratching of later visitors, perhaps the Aztecs of the fourteenth century, who could not resist the temptation to add their graffiti to the original.

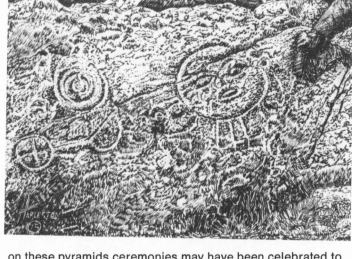

on these pyramids ceremonies may have been celebrated to mark important solar dates. From the location of many other pyramids scattered throughout the urban area it may now be possible to extrapolate the dates of other Teotihuacan celebrations marking lunar phases and stellar movements, such as the rising and setting of Sirius and the Pleiades.

From two other markers in the area southwest of the Moon Pyramid, it appears possible to sight across the third level of the Moon Pyramid and observe the maximum northward movement of the moon at the end of its nineteen-year

The valley of Teotihuacan's solar events and markers.

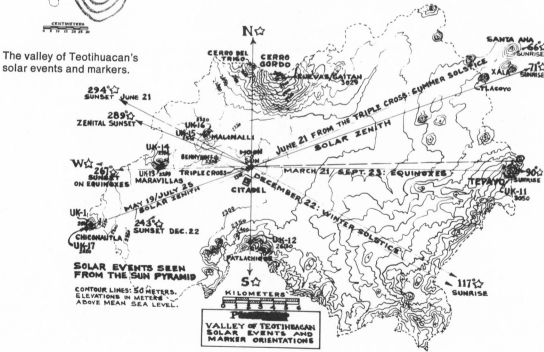

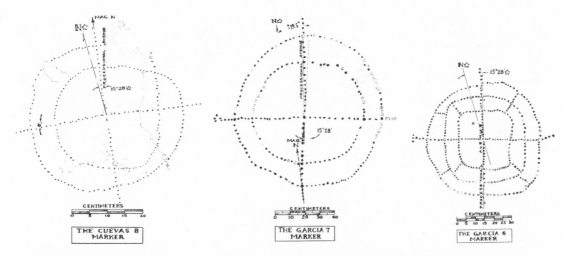

THE CUEVAS 8 MARKER

THE GARCIA 7 MARKER

THE GARCIA 6 MARKER

Garcia marker.

In 1964 Mexican archaeologist Braulio Garcia, working on the restoration of the Processional Avenue's temples at a location called Area 7 some 300 meters south of the Sun Pyramid, uncovered a fourth-century A.D. concrete floor, on which were pitted two concentric circles and a Cartesian cross. The southern arm of the cross runs 19.5 degrees east of north. Garcia also found another configuration on the floor of the patio across the street in Area 6, and his colleague Alfonso Cuevas located a third marker in Area 8, some 83 meters to the south. The data on these markers were filed in the archives, but only the Garcia 7 marker reached publication.

Metonic cycle. If this is indeed possible, the Aztec attribution of "Sun" and "Moon" to the two great pyramids may be due to a vestigial tradition that they were once used for sighting the relative movements of these celestial bodies, a function which has only now been rediscovered.

As in ancient Britain at midsummer, that is to say at the summer solstice, signals could have been sent with bonfires

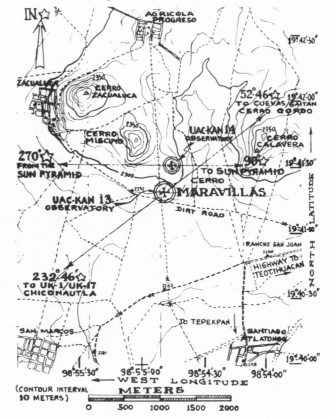

Markers on Maravillas showing angular relationships with other markers and with the Sun Pyramid.

Surrounded by petroglyph murals, the egg-shaped omphalos of Observatory U-K 13 on Cerro Maravillas lies 7½ kilometers west of the Sun Pyramid. It not only provides a point from which to observe the sunset on the equinox directly aligned with the Sun Pyramid, but also has grooves for sighting the summer solstice at 66 degrees and three circles aligned on the winter solstice at 116 degrees east. An "astronomer's chair" on the west side allows the observer to lean back and comfortably watch a star cross the zenith. The backrest of the "chair" has the sculptured head of a combined man-serpent, with eroded fangs curled downward. The horizontal grooves and vertical lines of holes cut across the back of the serpent appear to have served as marks for a sundial that could be made by standing a 35-centimeter (1/3 of a *hunab*) wooden gnomon in a hole drilled to the right of the "astronomer's chair" in the main omphalos's body.

When the sun climbs skyward on the days of the equinox, the shadows of the west side of U-K 13 begin to move southward. The inclination of the chair is such that at ten o'clock A.M. the sunlight will start to illuminate the sculptured face. Within an hour, the chair has been converted into what Harleston calls "a vertical serpent of light, flying toward heaven, with the Sun Pyramid behind it: the symbol of Quetzalcoatl, the bird-serpent, which appears one week before and disappears one week after the day of the equinox!"

As the day wanes, the sundial shadow which had followed the line of holes up the serpent's back becomes a horizontal line at three o'clock, and then a vertical line by six P.M. At sundown the direct rays cross the omphalos stone to illuminate the Sun Pyramid, seven kilometers away, clearly seen through the V notch cut in the marker.

from the top of the Sun Pyramid, point to point over great distances; and it is noteworthy that Sahagun reported that Teotihuacan, as well as being known as "the place where men became gods," was also known as "the place from which the signals are made."

Similar stone marker designs have been found at distances on a great circle as far as 100 kilometers to the south of Teotihuacan and on the Mexico-U.S. border to the north. The

Dupaix found this stone giant (the figure is twenty-seven feet long) on the floor of a cabin near Orizaba. According to archeologist Daniel C. Brinton, who describes the giant as "an ogre of horrid mien," it is a depiction of Tzontemec Mictlanteculi, "the Lord of the Realm of the Dead, He of the Falling Hair." Brinton says "falling hair" represents the slanting rays of the setting sun at the winter solstice, and that the symbols convey a specific date: the winter solstice of the year 1 fish 10 rabbit.

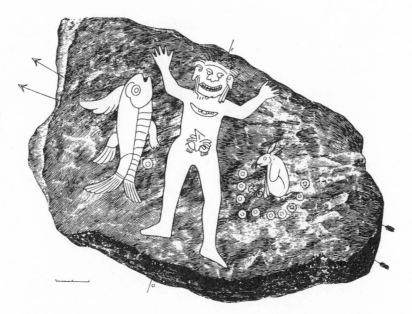

coordinates of these stones permitted the prediction and location of previously unknown markers at telescopic distances from the Sun Pyramid, apparently used for the observation of astronomical events and for the definition of earth-commensurate distances and other cosmic information.

This led Harleston to surmise that other ceremonial centers may have been built on what the English author Alfred Watkins called earthly magnetic "ley" lines at different azimuths from Teotihuacan, such as at Tupilco, 630 kilometers southeast of Teotihuacan, where a Mayan complex is presently being excavated.

Uaxactun, which was occupied by Teotihuacanos in the third century A.D., is 989 kilometers from Teotihuacan at an azimuth of 285 degrees, 30 minutes, forming a right angle to the Way of the Dead at almost 1000 kilometers.

Outside the ceremonial area at kilometric distances which appear to fit a module of 2268 of Harleston's *hunabs,* or 7800 Egyptian feet, other sites suggest that geodetic information was interlocked with the ceremonial zone's accurate display in what could be a global system of markers.

Additional information on a theoretical Teotihuacan geodesic system was presented at the Americanist Congress in Paris in September, 1976, that indicates a probable grid system that has been located by the Uac-Kan Research Group in the Valley of Tepoztlan, 85 kilometers southwest of the Sun Pyramid on the north-south alignment of 196° 30′.

23. Cosmic and Telluric Forces

John Michell, author of *The View Over Atlantis* and *City of Revelation,* is convinced that the Pyramid of the Sun at Teotihuacan, like the Great Pyramid of Cheops, is one of the fixed points in a worldwide geodetic system laid out on a vast scale with great accuracy by some former civilization with an advanced knowledge of science and what today is understood as magic. To lay out such a network of astronomical and geometrical lines across the face of the planet, says Michell, implies an advanced technology.

He believes that whoever built the system had "some remarkable power" with which to cut and raise enormous blocks of stone, vast astronomical instruments, pyramids, circles of pillars, cyclopean stone platforms, all linked together by a network of tracks and alignments, whose course from horizon to horizon was marked by stones, mounds, and earthworks, "a great scientific instrument sprawled over the entire surface of the globe."

From the evidence of old maps such as the portolanos, the Piri Reis, the Oronteus Fineus, and many others, it is clear that someone mapped this entire globe with a precision not reached again till the nineteenth century of our era. It is also apparent that they did not use Cartesian coordinates of latitude and longitude, but some system of spherical triangles, perhaps with some instrument by which they could follow earthly magnetic ley lines rather than a compass needle pointing to magnetic north.

Three Russian scientists, Nikolai Feodorovich Goncharov, Vyacheslav Moroz, and Valery Mokarov, have recently discovered evidence of faint magnetic lines which appear to run around the planet making of it a dodecahedron superimposed

Alfred Watkins of Hereford (1855–1935), discoverer of the ley system.

326

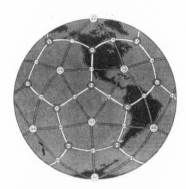

Soviet earth grid reported by Christopher Bird.

The thin lines of the grid form a dodecahedron solid with twelve pentagonal slabs. Plato has said that "the earth viewed from above resembles a ball sewn from twelve pieces of skin."

The thick lines form an icosahedron of twenty faces. The planet, therefore, appears to act energetically as if pulsating between one shape and the other.

The Soviets found that mid-oceanic ridges, core faults, and active zones occurred along the edges of these superimposed crystalline structures, and that such magnetically anomalous spots as the Bermuda Triangle fell on the nodes.

Ivan Sanderson, the professional biologist who founded the Society for the Investigation of the Unexplained, in Columbia, New Jersey, and fathered the vogue of the Bermuda Triangle, suggested nine more similar areas situated symmetrically around the globe, five above and five below the equator. To these the Soviets added the North and South Poles to obtain their dodecahedron.

on an icosahedron, as if the planet had once been a great crystal or was conditioned in its energetic nature by some crystalline core.

On a geographical map the Russians traced the seats of ancient cultures, which appeared to follow the magnetic or energetic lines of the icosahedron.

On metereological and geological maps they found that all the global centers of maximal and minimal atmospheric pressure occurred at the twenty nodes of the dodecahedral skeleton. These were the spots where hurricanes originate, or where there are gigantic vortices of ocean currents.

Christopher Bird reports that another Russian, Vitaly Kabachenko, while studying photos of the earth taken from space, found a deep-seated grid structure of the lithosphere, or upper hard core of the earth, which at times seems to "shine through." The phenomenon, says Kabachenko, appears as black streaks on the ocean, and in the sky as a barely noticeable network of nebulous streaks. Bird quotes another Soviet geologist and mineralogist, Dr. Vladimir Neiman, as suggesting a universal space-filling lattice which controls the position not only of planets and stars but of galaxies and intragalactic space. Like Wilhelm Reich, who suggested a basic ether or life force which traveled in spiral waves with matter forming where two spirals superimpose, Neiman substitutes for the idea of a primordial chaos a regulatory pulsation, with all matter—galaxies, stars, planets—being formed at the nodes.

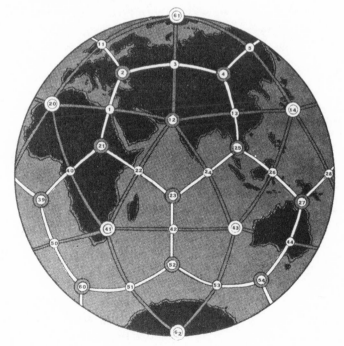

Corroborative evidence for a lattice of ley lines on the earth comes from Aimé Michel, a French writer on UFO's, who says that sightings over the planet appear to run along similar magnetic lines, lines which Air Force pilot Bruce Cathy of New Zealand in his book *Harmonic 695* has drawn as a lattice covering the globe. Similar energized lines were obtained by Buckminster Fuller as great circles which define the lowest common multiple of his vector equilibrium triangles, of which there are forty-eight to a sphere. If one of the edges of Fuller's cuboctahedron lies along the equator, the intersection of three of his great circles will define the latitude of Teotihuacan to within a quarter of a degree.

From these approaches it appears that if the planet—as Goethe and Rudolf Steiner considered it—were a living breathing entity, it would take the form of a dodechahedron-icosahedron when compressed to its most compact stage. Medially expanded, it would take the shape of Buckminster Fuller's vector-equilibrium cuboctahedron. Fully expanded, it would have the shape of a truncated tetrahedron.

The ancients apparently considered the earth to be not only living but to have a nervous system related to its magnetic field, with nodes of power similar to the acupuncture points of a human body.

These straight lines running from node to node appeared to be involved with a power which was symbolized by a serpent or a dragon; the Chinese called these lines, which ran invisibly over the whole surface of the earth, lines of dragon current. The Chinese further divided the dragon current into two kinds, negative and positive, or yin and yang, represented by a white tiger and a blue dragon, symbols very similar to the jaguar Tezcatlipoca and the plumed serpent Quetzalcoatl.

The yang, or male current, was believed to run along mountainous ridges and ranges of hills, the yin, or female, along valleys, rivers, and subterranean channels.

These powers were also symbolic of cosmic and telluric forces which became creative in wedlock—such as the sun's rays impregnating mother earth.

Michell has no doubt that the dragon current is a natural flow of force related to the earth's magnetic field, something in the nature of the orgone energy rediscovered by Wilhelm Reich, which Reich postulated to be present throughout the universe in every particle of matter, every area of space, running in definite lines, and accumulating under specific circumstances, a force on the order of Franz Anton Mesmer's animal magnetism, Karl von Reichenbach's odyle, or what has now come to be known as *pyramid power.*

Like Reich, Mesmer, and Reichenbach, the ancients concluded the dragon power to be curative, invigorating, and

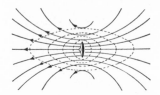

Wachsmuth illustration. Part of a series showing a living breathing earth.

Suggested method of propulsion of UFOs along magnetic grid lines.

To Michell the mathematical rules of the universe are visible to men in the form of beauty: "The secret rules of poetry and aesthetics, which we now believe to be beyond rational expression, can be demonstrated in numbers, ratio and angles of the confluent lines of terrestrial geometry." Michell elaborates: "The key numbers are those which occur prominently in several different spheres and which express the element of unity or correspondence in phenomena apparently disparate in their nature and scale. The philosophers of the ancient world discovered that the peculiar qualities of these numbers could be discerned through measurement of the visible universe. Astronomers found these in the cosmic ratios, in the relative sizes of the heavenly bodies and in the intervals that separated them; mathematicians proved their relevance to the figures of regular geometry and discovered the magic squares and numerological patterns by which their geometrical relationships were further revealed. Musicians and artists observed that these same numbers and ratios were those that produced the most perfect harmonies and touched the deepest sources of human emotion. They contained in fact the secrets of magic."

We all live within the ruins of an ancient structure whose vast size has hitherto rendered it invisible.

THE VIEW OVER ATLANTIS

John Michell

consciousness-expanding, a power which, as it passed down straight lines across the country, drew in its wake the fertilizing powers of life.

The most favored places were where two streams crossed. To find such spots, clairvoyants and dowsers were employed. Once found, temples and shrines were built on the spots, or great stones erected, linked by ley lines with other similar hot spots.

329

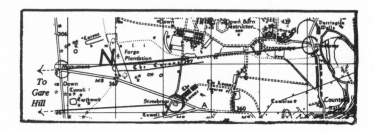

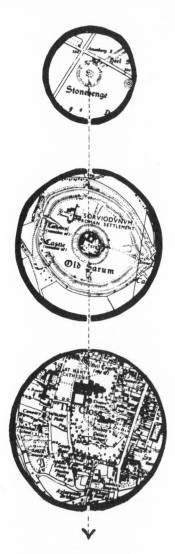

Michell says geomancers were used to detect these currents and interpret their influence on the land over which they passed, marking the course of the dragon power with alignments of mounds and stones, which then became the traditional paths of pilgrims from one holy place to the next.

According to Michell, the orientation of holy shrines and later of individual churches, including the details of their dimensions and architectural plans, was determined by these lines of current, of which the strongest spring was frequently located directly beneath the towers. At this spot the celestial influence was understood to combine with the terrestrial force to produce fusion.

Louis Charpentier, in *Les Mystères de la Cathédrale de Chartres,* says the cathedral stands on a large prehistoric mound over a buried chamber, which acts as a natural meeting place of several powerful streams of telluric current.

In *The View Over Atlantis,* Michell shows the remarkable ley-line alignment—noted by both Lockyer and Watkins— of Stonehenge, Salisbury Cathedral, and the prehistoric earth rings of Old Sarum, former site of the cathedral. The unit of measure appears to be the furlong of 220 yards.

From Stukeley's *Stonehenge.*

According to W. Y. Evans-Wentz there seem to be favored places on the earth where its magnetic and even more subtle forces are most easily felt by persons susceptible to such things. Carnac in France is said to be such a spot, as is Glastonbury in England, Iona in Scotland, and Fata in Ireland.

In ancient Britain, and once all over the world, buildings and stones were placed in landscapes according to a magic system by which the laws of mathematics and music were expressed in the geometry of the earth's surface.

Experts on geomancy such as Michell say the strength and activity of the magnetic currents is influenced by the composition of the ground over which it passes. Over firm, flat country it is said to be placid and regular; over rocky, broken land it becomes violent and disturbed, reacting with the elements that cause magnetic storms or polar lights. Near geological faults or volcanoes the magnetic flow is said to become particularly agitated because of springs of current which at these places burst through the earth's crust.

The strength and direction of the currents of the magnetic field, which is said to flow over the whole surface of the earth, are apparently influenced by such factors as the proximity and relative positions of the other bodies of the solar system, chiefly the sun and the moon, the sun imposing a daily rhythm modified by such influences as the lunar cycle, the moon exerting the same influence on the invisible magnetic flow as it does on the tides.

That is why, says Michell, the ancients were so preoccupied with lunar eclipses, which have no apparent physical influence on the earth other than on the level of magnetism.

At certain seasons the lines were believed to become animated by a current of invisible energy, reaching a peak on certain days, which could have a fertilizing effect on the land.

A dowser in the south of France, killed by the Germans during World War II, developed a machine whereby he could monitor cosmic forces which entered the soil, affected minerals, and then exited from the earth at other definite spots as telluric forces. By channeling these forces into his patients, he was able to cure humans of many varied diseases.

A young English engineer, Michael Watson, who worked on the construction of the Concorde, managed to salvage the Frenchman's notes, and claims with their help to have been able to photograph what he assumes to be the fourth state of water, or water in its plasmic state. He believes such elements as plasmic water have programmed goals which they follow like earth-encompassing genies, something close to the formative forces described by such authors as Gunther Wachsmuth, and postulated and believed in by the ancient Mesoamericans.

331

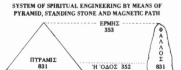

SYSTEM OF SPIRITUAL ENGINEERING BY MEANS OF
PYRAMID, STANDING STONE AND MAGNETIC PATH

From John Michell's *The View
Over Atlantis.*

Michell infers a magnetic
relation between pyramid and
obelisk, or erect stone marker,
saying that "Standing stones,
which in many parts of the
world are still regarded as the
phallic instruments of fertility,
are linked by the one mercu-
rial principle with the Great
Pyramid at the central storehouse of terrestrial current."

Michell quotes Iamblichus,
the fourth-century theurgist, on
the use of phallic stones as
markers by means of which
native geomancers directed
the flow of magnetic current to
fertilize the countryside.

"We say that the erection of
Phalli is a certain sign of
prolific power, which, through
this, is called forth to the gen-
erative energy of the world."

Michell adds that an analysis
of cabalistic numbers reveals
a definite association between
the terrestrial current and
lunar influence.

The Austrian scientist and mystic Rudolf Steiner made
numerous experiments which revealed the extent to which
planetary influences affect not only the magnetic currents of
the earth's surface but the layers of mineral ore deep below.
The minerals within the rocks, says Steiner, are never inac-
tive, but subject to regular cycles of motion in accordance
with the orbits of the particular planet to which they chiefly
respond. He says that at certain seasons they become charged
with energy which they gradually release into the soil, and
this allows seeds to germinate and stimulates vegetable
growth.

It is possible that seasonal feasts and "dragon proces-
sions" may have produced the vibrations of music and mag-
netizing effect, a sort of orgonomic injection, to increase
vitality in humans and to stimulate the growth of plants, the
plants on which the ancients survived and flourished, and
which today we poison with toxic sprays and debilitating
"fertilizers."

One of the most sacred locations where the ancients believed the most powerful telluric and cosmic forces met in a
creative intercourse was in a cave with a natural spring under
a pyramidal mound.

In 1930 a French dowser, Paul Berger, who styled himself
"a prospector at great distance," dowsed a photograph of
the Pyramid of the Sun at Teotihuacan and said he had found
the hidden entrance to yet another gallery at an approximate
depth of three meters from the base of the first level. Berger,
who said he had specialized in locating mineral deposits
while prospecting in Switzerland, Canada, and the United
States, claimed the entrance had been plugged but that
beyond the barrier a tunnel ran to the center of the pyramid,
where it opened into a room closed on all sides, except for a
small gallery on the right and another room on the left in
which he could distinguish six articles in a row which appeared to him to be of gold. Berger offered to indicate the
precise spot of the opening of the gallery so as to reduce to
a minimum the necessary work of finding it.

When the editor of *Art and Archeology,* Arthur Stanley
Riggs, tried to check on Berger's data with the Secretary of
Public Education in Mexico City, he was told by the director
of archeology, Don José Reygadas Veritz, that he had no
knowledge of any such tunnel, nor did he believe it existed.

Unaware of this dowser's report, René Millon continued to
be convinced that some sacred structure existed beneath the
bulk of the Sun Pyramid, despite the failure of either Manuel
Gamio or Eduardo Noguera to find it with their tunnels. Finally
in 1959, Millon secured enough funds from the National
Science Foundation in Washington, D.C., to organize a group

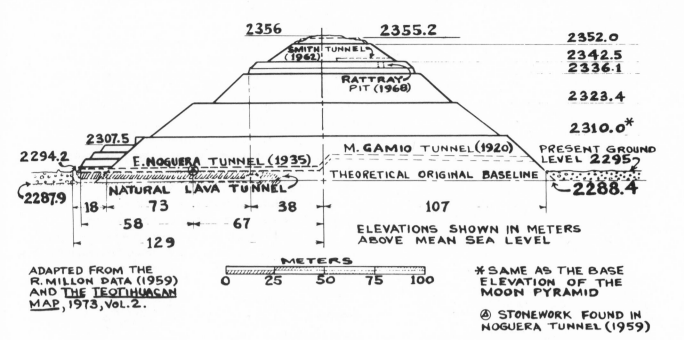

2356   2355.2   2352.0
SMITH TUNNEL (1962)   2342.5
2336.1
RATTRAY PIT (1968)   2323.4
2310.0*
2307.5   M. GAMIO TUNNEL (1920)   PRESENT GROUND LEVEL 2295
2294.2   E. NOGUERA TUNNEL (1935)   THEORETICAL ORIGINAL BASELINE
NATURAL LAVA TUNNEL   ~2288.4
2287.9   18   73   38   107
58   67
129

ELEVATIONS SHOWN IN METERS
ABOVE MEAN SEA LEVEL

ADAPTED FROM THE
R. MILLON DATA (1959)
AND THE TEOTIHUACAN
MAP, 1973, VOL. 2.

METERS
0   25   50   75   100

*SAME AS THE BASE
ELEVATION OF THE
MOON PYRAMID

Ⓐ STONEWORK FOUND IN
NOGUERA TUNNEL (1959)

The tantalizing question of what might be buried either deep within the great pyramids or underneath them was first seriously broached by Manuel Gamio in 1917, when he decided to tunnel into the base of the Pyramid of the Sun. Starting just above ground level on the east side, he pushed a tunnel about two meters high and not quite as wide horizontally toward the center at a slight upward slope.

Gamio's main purpose was to establish whether any major interior structure of stone lay within the pyramid which would indicate that it had been built in stages. Leaning toward the theory that the pyramid had been built all in one piece, Gamio found no evidence of previous structures. When the tunnel reached a hundred meters he quit, satisfied that he had proved his point.

Second thoughts on the subject were had by an engineer called Eduardo Noguera some seventeen years later; so he obtained permission to drill a tunnel from the west side of the pyramid to meet Gamio's in the center. As the entire base of the Sun Pyramid would

thus be traversed, he hoped to prove or disprove Gamio's theory. The entrance to Noguera's tunnel was slightly below present ground level, protected from rain by a masonry extension to the *adosado*, or lower structure, attached to the west facade. The tunnel ran to the center of the pyramid about 6 meters below the level of Gamio's tunnel and was offset about two meters to the north. A connecting staircase joined the two tunnels, which together ran 218 meters.

Though Noguera searched diligently, he found no signs of an earlier pyramid on which the later structure could have been superimposed, nor any internal strengthening features; so he concluded that the only way the great mound was held together was by the tensile strength of the outer skin of 15 to 20 centimeters of mortared adobe and stone.

What Noguera did find were some 35,000 pottery shards, all of the earliest period of Teotihuacan development, called by the experts Archaic, or Teotihuacan I, or Tzacualli, which indicated that the pyra-

mid had been built about the time of Christ or earlier.

If this seemed to settle the dating of the pyramid, it failed to settle the question of inner structures.

In 1962, Smith, with the help of the Peabody Museum, put a tunnel almost to the center of the east face of the fifth body of the Sun Pyramid, going west. Six years later Dr. Evelyn Rattray, working with Millon, excavated on the south side of Smith's tunnel till she ran onto a giant *talud* sloping wall, two meters high, indicating an earlier inner structure. Based on Dr. Rattray's papers, Harleston figured this wall to have had a slope up from north to south of 70.5 degrees, showing an earlier stage of construction similar to the one on the fourth level reconstructed by Batres—validating his claim of having learned to reconstruct more accurately as he approached the top of the pyramid. Since the wall was on the north side, its angular inclination could have served the same purpose as the present lower part of the fourth stage for shadow observation on or about the equinox.

to make a closer search in the tunnels for remains of earth and clay structures which might have eluded both Gamio and Noguera. Millon's group was interested in finding out what kind of fill had been used in the construction of the pyramid and in what way adobe bricks had been used.

At about fifty-five meters into Noguera's tunnel, the new investigators found evidence of adobe walls. Then, by running smaller branch tunnels north and south, near the center of the pyramid, they came across what Millon hoped they would find: the remains of what could have been a major structure, possibly a tomb of immense proportions. Here was a pyramid of much older construction, with an earth nucleus covered with adobe bricks, faced with uncut stones and cobbles, much of it destroyed. They also found evidence of what might once have been a huge pit. Millon still believed the additional blocked passages would reveal a mammoth tomb.

Hugh Harleston's Theoretical Construction Sequence of the Sun Pyramid.

If the Sun Pyramid had been built in stages, by first building the sixth level on the ground, then superimposing on it a structure equivalent to the fourth and fifth levels, the upper outlines of the pyramid could have been progressively raised, maintaining a constant outline. Harleston suggests that the 70-degree angle of the third phase was used to obtain the day of the equinox. It could thus have been repeatedly in use till it was raised to the fifth level. Harleston suggests the builders may have built the stages in four 52-year cycles, constantly maintaining the shadow devices.

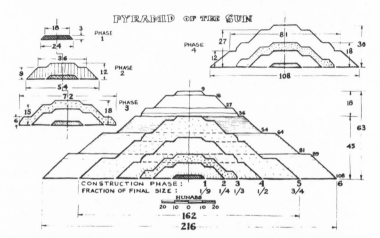

While Millon and his colleagues wrote papers on the results of these finds to be digested by the academic community and interested archeologists, a whole decade passed and nothing of interest was forthcoming for the laity. Then, in the fall of 1971, a heavy rain squall caused a deep depression at the foot of the main stairway of the Pyramid of the Sun. Examining the depression, Ernesto Taboada, locally in charge of the archeological zone, found the remains of an ancient and semi-destroyed stairway. As debris was removed, Taboada found steps that led six meters down into a pit to the entrance of a natural cave, two meters high, leading horizontally into the bedrock beneath the pyramid.

Jorge Acosta, in charge of all digs at Teotihuacan, was summoned to view the site and immediately took charge of clearing and consolidating the find. Ironically, it was he who had spotted a section of the same staircase six years earlier, but he had been obliged to cover the find for lack of funds with which to clear the pit. Now he determined to follow the cave or tunnel wherever it might lead.

As the entrance coincided with the center of the pyramid's main stairway, Acosta realized the cave entrance must have been known before the construction of the pyramid was started, which led him to surmise that its presence might even have determined the site for the construction of the pyramid.

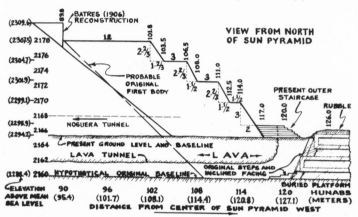

Harleston's rendering of the entrance to the cave below the Sun Pyramid beneath the *adosado*.

Entering the cave with a group of archeologists, Acosta found it to be a natural structure, two meters high and almost as wide, leading in an easterly direction. Frederick Mooser, a geologist of the Mexican University's Institute of Geology and a consultant to the Institute of Anthropology, said that in his opinion the cave was a natural formation, the result of lava flow that occurred more than a million years ago. The cave had been adapted by man for some purpose in that its walls were plastered with mud, and heavy stone slabs had been laid in the ceiling, some of them still in place.

As the group progressed along the subterranean canal by torchlight, they suddenly found themselves blocked by a wall of adobe and mortar which filled the cave with the exception of the top right-hand corner, which had been breached, apparently by vandals or by previous explorers, possibly much more recently than anyone cared to admit.

As the party advanced slowly down the tunnel, they encountered nineteen more blocking walls, all pierced. They also noted that the mortar on these walls was smoothed off between the adobe bricks only on the outer, westerly, side, evidently by masons *moving out*.

One hundred and three meters down the tunnel, the archeologists came upon an extraordinary sight: an arrangement of caves in the shape of an irregular four-leaf clover. Each chamber, which was ten to twenty meters in circumference, appeared to be of natural formation, deliberately enlarged by the hand of man.

335

Aerial view of tunnel beneath the Sun Pyramid, as drawn by Harleston from data collected in 1974 by the Uak-Kan group. Dotted lines are Batres' 1906 reconstruction. Solid lines show Harleston's hypothetical reconstruction.

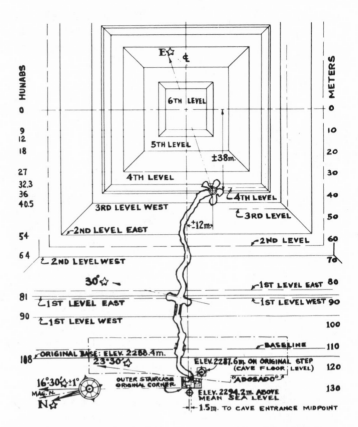

Doris Heyden, an archeologist from New Jersey who moved to Mexico after World War II to study art at the University of Mexico and marry her anthropology teacher, joined the Mexican Institute of Anthropology and History, and seized on the cave theme to write several articles and a doctoral dissertation on the *Social, Economic and Religious Symbolism of Caves in Ancient Mexico.*

Heyden first wondered whether the chamber caves beneath the Pyramid of the Sun could have been a prototype tomb, such as was found in the Temple of the Inscriptions in Palenque, placed beneath the pyramid to intentionally hide its contents from the eyes of men, a tomb long since rifled by intruders.

She then suggested that the caves could also have been for the ritual of burying children as offerings to a water deity.

Brother Motolinia describes certain offerings to Tlaloc in which four children were sacrificed and their bodies placed in a cave whose entrance was sealed until the following year when the ceremony was repeated. Sahagun tells of a rite in which the victim was flayed, and after the priest had worn the victim's skin for twenty days, it was placed in a cave "in the pyramid called Yopico." This cave was said to be at the foot of a pyramid stairway, "in an underground place . . . which had a moveable doorway."

Heyden also pointed out that there are many indications in Mexico of oracles taking place in caves. In Morelos a rock carving dating from circa 600 B.C. shows a figure in a cave with enormous speech scrolls by his mouth, indicating, says Heyden, that he is saying something of great importance.

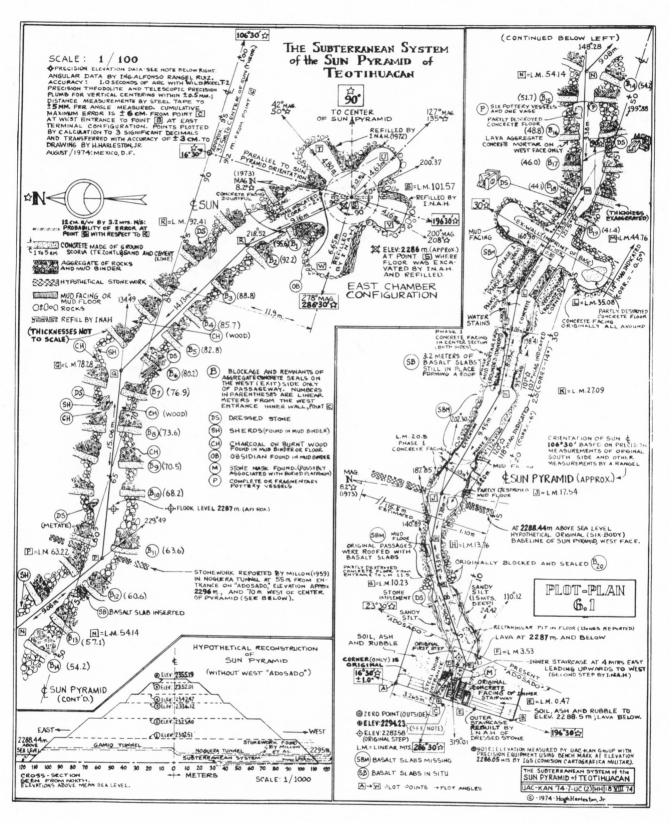

The Subterranean System of the Sun Pyramid of Teotihuacan

337

Historian George Baker's diagram of what was found at the end of the tunnel under the Sun Pyramid, indicating that at some time someone had built reinforcing walls to avoid additional cracking from earth movements; there were also indications of continual use of the chambers after the construction of the pyramid. Finger and palm marks were still visible in the millennial adobe, possibly made by violators.

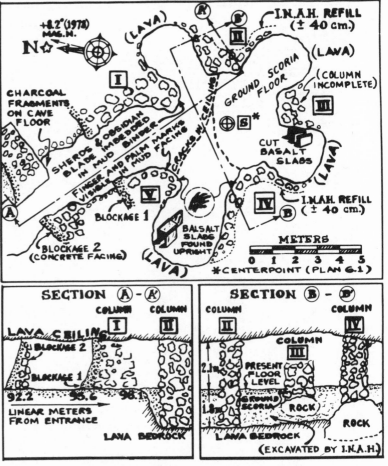

On the compacted floor the searchers reported finding numerous crudely worked vessels, together with slate disks beautifully engraved with anthropomorphic figures, one dressed in jaguar costume, another as a bird. Acosta wondered if they could have been funerary offerings, but could find no trace of skeletal material or evidence of cremation.

Bits of mirror found on the floor of the cave indicated their possible use, as at Delphi, for prophetic reasons, mirrors having been used for divination in antiquity. More interestingly, Zelia Nuttall says the priests "of the below," the personifications of Tezcatlipoca, or "Shining Mirror," employed an actual mirror of polished obsidian as an aid in pronouncing final judgment on criminals, apparently using it as a crystal ball to reach the powers beyond.

Though there was no evidence of any spring or course of water, usually associated with underground shrines, such as at Lourdes, broken pieces of interlocking segments of drainpipes made of carved rock indicated they may once have been used to channel the flow of an underground stream. A thin

338

line of vegetation stemming from beneath the pyramid, visible to Millon on his aerial maps, indicated the possibility of a former underground watercourse, which may have dwindled to a trickle.

Altogether the tunnel and cloverleafed caves presented a major and baffling discovery, the news of which the experts decided to sit on to give themselves time to conjecture on the possible uses and original function of their discovery. Caves, they knew, had from the remotest antiquity been of key importance in the religious history of Mesoamerica—a symbol of creation and of life itself.

Springs, they also knew, had been regarded as openings to the underworld and to the earth gods, the unnumbered spirits of the earth. Many of the legends spoke of gods or of extraterrestrials creating men in their present mold inside labyrinths of caves.

Zelia Nuttall maintains there were two basic rituals in ancient Mesoamerica: one by sun worshipers, with male overtones, performed on the steps of and atop the great pyramids; another, with female overtones, dedicated to the earth mother and to the powers of darkness, which took place at night and in caves.

Of the night ceremonies Nuttall says that the dangers and evils attendant on the earth cult became irretrievably associated with the female sex, so that "the votaries of Heaven naturally came to regard women as a source of temptation and degradation." Eventually, in Yucatan, says Nuttall, because of an unbridled use of pulque during the night ceremonies, the nocturnal cult of the female principle degenerated into such abominations that the incensed population actually rose in revolt, murdered the high priests, and scattered the votaries.

On the other hand, for what might have actually occurred during the sun ceremonies atop the pyramids, Geoffrey Hodson's clairvoyantly witnessed account is chillingly affective. He describes the evocation of earth forces, and of the Kundalini in particular, together with forces from the sun and from what he calls the higher planes. Hodson says he could observe the solar forces as they were made to pass rapidly down the head and spine of the officiants and others at the ceremonial to meet the ascending earth forces. These, says Hodson, combined to make a very powerful concentration of solar and planetary forces in the bodies of those present and of "associated Intelligences within and about the Great Temple of the Sun."

Hodson believes the ancient Mesoamericans considered—as indeed do modern Theosophists—that the constellations, stars, suns, and planets were governed by intelligences and

Geoffrey Hodson and the Theosophists claim that Kundalini, or the Serpent Fire, has the power of giving or transmitting Life, in a contradistinction to Prana, or vitality, which has the power of organizing Life, and Fahat, or cosmic electricity, which has the power of manipulating Life. To Theosophists, these three cosmic forces "ensoul" all substances.

Fahat, or cosmic electricity, Hodson calls the universal constructive force in all creation. Coiled in the center of the earth, it is a storehouse for solar Kundalini. When specialized and enclosed within the spinal cord of man, it is called Kundalini, or Serpent Fire, "the power that moves in a serpentine path." As the Godlike force within man, coiled at the base of the spine, it needs to be set free. When fully aroused either by Yoga or as a result of evolutionary progress, Kundalini is said to flow up an etheric canal in the spinal cord, vivifying and awakening the individual to self-conscious awareness in superphysical worlds. Kundalini is also said to give the power of astral travel.

The force opens up knowledge of the oneness of life, direct intuitive spiritual perception. It enhances the powers of clairaudience and clairvoyance, of being able to leave and return to the body at will without any break in consciousness.

Hodson says that the cerebrospinal system of man, when occultly vivified by Kundalini, resembles in many ways a TV set with superphysical broadcasts projected on the screen of the mind-brain.

The symbol of Kundalini is the caduceus, staff of the god Hermes: a rod entwined by two serpents. The winged sphere represents the freed soul of man who has awakened and learned to use his hidden powers. Hodson adds that like all the basic forces in nature, Kundalini is the manifestation of an intelligence, of an archangelic power, as shown here.

powers which the priests in Mesoamerica had learned to contact without mediation, especialy those of the sun, Venus and Mars.

Hodson thinks the colors of the priests' robes and the paintings of their temples were designed to be in mutual resonance or harmonious vibration with these superphysical forces and intelligences.

The high priest and his helpers, says Hodson, evidently knew full well of the Kundalini, the fiery serpent force in the center of the earth and in man, for they employed certain ceremonies, postures, and words of power to evoke the earth Kundalini and cause it to flow along the spines of officiants and others present.

Hodson says the chief officiant at the ceremony at the temple on the summit of the Sun Pyramid at Teotihuacan

340

seemed to be what he calls in Theosophical terms an "Initiate of the Fourth or Atlantean Root Race"—a tall man with reddish-brown complexion, very clear-cut features, large aquiline nose, eyes full of power, and a facial expression of sternness and great strength. As Hodson describes him, he wore a high feathered headdress and beautiful robes of many hues, the chief colors being red, yellow, green, and purple. His neck, arms, and legs were ornamented with jewels.

Hodson says that high in the air above Teotihuacan he observed a great circle, at least a mile in diameter, of golden Devas or angels hovering above the Sun Pyramid at a height of several thousand feet. "Their auras kept touching to form the bowl of a Deva chalice filled with solar 'wine,' a form of energy derived from a higher plane."

He says the stem of the great chalice built of intelligences and forces passed down through the temple and the pyramid into the ground while a large number of other Devas moved about high in the air above the rim of the cup, and one very great Atmic Deva supervised the proceedings, having apparently been in charge of the religion and area for many centuries.

This temple, says Hodson, was a spiritual center for the whole region, and at least three great ceremonies were regularly performed there, at sunrise, high noon, and sunset, high noon being the most important. Hodson notes that the very moment of high noon was measured by means of a vertical staff above the topmost temple, now demolished.

He says some of the people had psychic powers enabling them to see the auras of the leaders, which were brilliant and large, and that it was this direct experience which assisted in the maintenance of order throughout the land.

At the special time of the ceremony, performed when the sun was at its meridian, the summit of the pyramid seemed to become superphysically on fire, with "astro-mental flames" reaching out for a hundred yards or more above and on all sides. This, Hodson said, represented sun worship at its greatest and purest, because it was produced by the responses to invocations to the Solar Logos and the Solar Devas.

Whereas to the average citizen and even to the average scientist the sun appears to be part of a strictly mechanistic universe, to the Theosophists the sun is the visible aura of a mighty solar consciousness, part of a living, pulsing universe, an all-pervading Divine life in which we all live and move and have our being. To the Theosophists, all the entities within the Solar System, regardless of their kind, are subservient to what they call "Cosmic Vitality"; they give as a parallel the case of the human being. "Each of us," says L.

341

Gordon Plummer in his *Mathematics of the Cosmic Mind,* "is composed of myriads of subservient entities, better known among which are the cells of our bodies, which include the blood cells. Every one of these is a living organism, highly complex in itself; yet they all function within the dominance of the vitality of the man while he is alive."

The Theosophists say that just as in human bodies there is a constant circulation of vital essence via the blood and nerve fluids, so in the solar system there occurs an incessant interchange of vital essences along electromagnetic patternings, with every planet contributing to every other planet and to the sun, which, like a beating heart, revitalizes the system.

Man, they say, is an integral part of the universe which environs him, to which he must return parts of his vitality, a notion which could give meaning to the Aztec sacrificial ritual in which, while blood is shed, a spirit is freed from the body. Like the Theosophists, the Aztecs believed that vast hosts of other-dimensional entities in all degrees of development, from atoms to gods, inhabit the system, moving from body to body along the electromagnetic pathways of the universe.

Georges Ivanovitch Gurdjieff in New York in 1924.

Georges Ivanovitch Gurdjieff held that cosmic emanations in the form of matter or substance were, and are, transmitted by the planets, the solar system, the stars, and the suns of the Milky Way, on out to the ultimate principle he refers to as the "Absolute." Emanations of matter from the Absolute, upon meeting the stars, the solar system, and the planets, says Gurdjieff, change in density according to an order which corresponds to the musical notes do, si, la, and so on up the scale through different octaves.

According to the Ancient Wisdom, the Galactic Universe in its totality is a sort of living being, "an entity of such mighty power that nothing short of a universe could possibly represent it." A pretty conceit which Theosophists qualify by pointing out that the "space" of the scientist is in fact an illusion produced by our consciousness, not that it does not exist, but rather that we do not perceive it for what it truly is.

PART VI PREHISTORIC

REAPPRAISAL

24. Origins
of the Maya

Hodson's re-creation conjures up the picture of a spiritually evolved priesthood, descendants of Atlanteans, performing still vital ceremonies on the pyramids of Mesoamerica. Does such a picture fit with what is known of the Teotihuacanos, Olmecs, or Maya? Sylvanus G. Morley, who, though he died some decades ago, is still North America's leading authority on the Maya, would have one believe that Mayan civilization developed suddenly, springing fully armed like Athena from the brow of Zeus.

"The ancient Maya . . ." as he puts it, "emerged from barbarism probably during the first or second century of the Christian era." To make his point he used what he believed to be the earliest Mayan stelae erected at Tikal and Uaxactun, but failed to account for the fact that these stelae incorporate not only a developed Mayan system of writing and numerals but a calendrical system so sophisticated that it alone indicates centuries if not millennia of previous careful astronomical observation.

Opposing experts—such as the California architect Robert B. Stacy-Judd, who spent fourteen years exploring Yucatan to produce a beautifully styled book, *Atlantis, Mother of Empires*—maintain that the Mayan civilization arrived in Central America already developed, its origin having taken place elsewhere—in his opinion Atlantis, or the island of Antillia, the last large surviving segment of the Atlantean Empire, approximately what is now the Grand Bahama Bank.

As there are no historical records contemporary with the appearance of the Maya in Central America, but only the archeologists' interpretations of the buildings, stelae, sculptures, and pottery found in a fraction of what may be hun-

346

Chilam Balam de Chumayel, pag. 98

dreds or even thousands more undiscovered Mayan sites, the next best information derives from native sources, from the books concocted from memory by the Quiché and the Maya such as the books of Chilam Balam and the *Popol Vuh,* rediscovered and publicized by Brasseur de Bourbourg.

The books of Chilam Balam relate that the first inhabitants of Yucatan were the Chanes, "People of the Serpent," said to have come from the east in A.D. 219 in boats across the water with their leader Zamna, also known as Itzamna, "Serpent of the East," a healer who could cure by laying on of hands, and, like the Therapeuts, revived the dead.

The Chumael book of Chilam Balam is even more specific. It speaks of the first inhabitants of Yucatan, known as Ah-Canule, or "People of the Serpent," having come across the water from the east in boats to locate on the island of Cozumel off the coast of Yucatan. As their population grew, these Itza moved to the mainland and built cities, altogether 150, including Chichen Itza (the "Mouth of the Wells of the Itza"), Izamal, Ake, Uxmal, and Mayapan.

The *Popol Vuh* is vaguer but more poetic: "Then they came; they pulled up stakes there and left the East . . . Each of the tribes kept getting up to see the star which was herald of the sun (Venus). This sign of the dawn they carried in their hearts when they came from the East, and with the same hope they left there, from that great distance, according to what their songs now say . . ."

The history of Zodzil, by Juan Darreygosa, incorporated into one of the earliest reports from the Spanish conquerors, the *Unedited Documents Relating to the Discovery and Conquest of New Spain,* picked up the same legend: "The most ancient people who came to this land were those who populated Chichen-Itza . . . and were the first after the Flood."

Drawing of Itzamna sailing from the east, taken from one of the codices.

Reconstruction of stele found near La Venta showing an exotic Middle Eastern figure known to archeologists as "Uncle Sam."

From Bishop Landa's reports it is clear that the strangers did not come, as Morley suggests, from the *southe*ast overland, but from across the seas: "Some of the old people of Yucatan say they heard from their ancestors that this land was occupied by a race of people who came from the east and whom God had delivered by opening twelve paths through the sea."

Morley maintains the Mayan area had been inhabited from two to three thousand years earlier by Maya-speaking peoples whom he labels as nomadic, but of whom he can say no more.

Archeologists then discovered remains of another whole civilization on the east coast of Mexico, just north of the Maya, complete with hieroglyphics, calendar system, and pyramidal religious complexes which appeared to antedate Morley's "civilized" Maya by almost a thousand years. For lack of a better name, the archeologists called these people Olmecs, or the "Rubber People"—though no one knows what these people might have called themselves.

When archeologists were digging in the soil of a swamp-surrounded island about twenty miles inland from the Gulf of Mexico, close to the western border of the state of Tabasco, known as La Venta, they came upon a fourteen-foot stele, seven feet wide and three feet thick, with two figures in apparent conversation. When the mud was cleaned from the carvings, the diggers discovered a tall, handsome figure with a commanding look, high-bridged nose, and flowing beard, in conversation with a smaller man. So much did the figure resemble Uncle Sam that he was so dubbed by the astonished archeologists. The features of the figure were clearly not those of an Indian. Furthermore, the figure was wearing a long gown, elaborate headdress, and shoes with oddly upturned toes.

Fascinated by this stylistic anomaly, Constance Irwin, who pursues the riddle of ancient seafarers to the New World in her controversial book *Fair Gods and Stone Faces,* asked herself who in the world was wearing upturned pointed shoes in the first half of the first millennium B.C., the date assigned by the experts to this stele.

After considerable research she traced the upturned shoes to either the Hittites or their successors and imitators, the Phoenicians, renowned as great seafarers, who regularly wore long clinging double robes, turbans with ribbons, pointed beards, and upturned shoes.

So impressive is the evidence accumulated by scholars to the effect that the Phoenicians reached the shores of both North and South America, it is hard to understand why it continues to be shunned.

Support for a Phoenician land fall on the east coast of

At La Venta, on the east coast of Tabasco, 50 yards into the jungle, diggers came upon a huge hemispherical stone, vine-sheathed and almost unrecognizable till they dug further and revealed a colossal head eight feet high with broad nose and thick lips. Three more heads, all facing east, surfaced nearby, one of them 8 1/2 feet high and 22 feet in circumference. Later, several more were found further along the coast, many of them mutilated. One had a singularly Egyptian feature: a speaking tube that ran from a giant ear to emerge between two great stone lips through which the voice of a priest could have spoken. Nearby a huge pyramidal mound was discovered rising 100 feet above a base 300 feet square close to a colonnade with tightly fitted columns.

Mexico appeared in the form of enormous stone heads with marked Negroid features and what looked like baby caps or football helmets dug up from the subsoil of La Venta, dated to about 500 B.C. by the experts.

Pointing to other Phoenician carvings of black slaves wearing just such helmets, Constance Irwin suggests that nothing could have been more natural for Phoenician traders than to have picked up African Negroes on the west coast of Africa and sailed with them across the Atlantic to Mexico.

Further evidence of the presence of men with Negroid features accompanying bearded Semites also turned up farther west in Oaxaca.

Colossal heads in low relief found near Oaxaca.

Like the Olmecs, the earliest known settlers of Monte Alban had a hieroglyphic system of writing, a calendar, and a mathematical system of computing by bar and dot. These settlers left some extraordinary cyclopean rocks built into buildings which portray life-sized Negroid dancers with flat noses, round faces, and thick lips. Alongside them are Old Testament types with hooked noses and spatulate beards, all very un-Indian. Archeologists date these finds around 500 B.C. and attribute the ruins to the Olmecs.

Hugh Fox in his *Gods of the Cataclysm* says the association with the yogic trance is especially evident in these Monte Alban figures because the designs portrayed on the dancers' bodies are chakras, "the mystic centers connected with successful meditation."

Startlingly Semitic figures found throughout Meso-america.

Fox points to the ecstatic face of the Mochica coca-taker with its inward-turned eyes, frozen, fixed, expressionless face, and compares it to the world of yoga ecstasy.

Among the institutions and customs shared by the Phoenicians of the first millennium B.C. and the inhabitants of Central America during the same era, Constance Irwin has listed several items starting with an advanced knowledge of mathematics and astronomy (which the Phoenicians picked up from the Babylonians). In common with the Maya, the Babylonians were the only known ancient civilization that had a place value in their mathematics, the concept of zero, and the ability to express large numbers—as indicated by the cuneiform text found in Mesopotamia with the now no longer so mysterious number 195,955,200,000,000. As C. W. Ceram points out, it was not until the nineteenth century that the concept of a million became common in the West. Like the Maya, and their possible predecessors the Olmecs, the Chaldeans had records of stars going back 370,000

The Phoenicians, whose origins are vague, are known to have sailed north from the Pillars of Hercules to Britain for tin, and even farther to Scandinavia for amber. Southward, they sailed down the coast of Africa, planting colonies as close to the equator as Dakar. At one point, in the employ of the Egyptian Pharaoh Necho, in 600 B.C., they appear to have circumnavigated the entire continent of Africa—2000 years before the Portuguese next accomplished the feat. Westward the Phoenicians sailed as far as the Azores and the Canaries, jumping-off place for Columbus, where the favoring trade winds blow from the east, and the northerly equatorial current along the fortieth parallel will thrust a boat irresistibly toward the Antilles and the Mexique Bay. Diodorus Siculus wrote of a land which lay far to the west and was known to none but the Phoenicians and Carthaginians. The Tyrians, he says, at the time when they were masters of the sea, proposed to dispatch a colony to it.

At Tula, the Toltec capital, shoveling rubbish from the remains of a house, Désiré Charnay found many curios, such as huge baked bricks, filters, curved water pipes, and what appeared to be small Phoenician seals, and a vase with a bearded, robed, mustachioed Tlaloc holding a bolt of lightning.

years, while the Babylonians kept the nativity horoscopes of all children born for thousands of years, from which to calculate the effects on humans of the various planets and constellations. Like the Maya, the Babylonians measured the year in 360 and 365 days; and they estimated the period of the moon's return to within a matter of seconds. Unlike the Romans, who thought the morning and evening star were two different bodies, Lucifer and Hesperus, the Babylonians and the Maya both knew them to be the same body: Venus.

Further traits held in common by the Phoenicians and their contemporaries in Central America were hieroglyphic writing, the custom of deforming the heads of newborn children, infant sacrifice, the use of incense, phallus worship, the depiction of deities floating horizontally over the heads of mortals involved in conversation, twisted rope borders on sarcophagi and seals, pyramidal temples that rose in terraces to a truncated top where they were used as astronomical observatories, worship of the sun and the moon, to whom temples were raised, the use of gnomons to measure the sun's shadow and determine latitude, the manufacture of clay figurines depicting dwarfs, and, most astonishing, representation of the rain god Tlaloc in Central America by the figure of a white man with a handlebar mustache and long beard, holding a thunderbolt of lightning—just as did his Phoencian counterpart. (See Charnay's vases.)

When the Phoenician stronghold of Tyre fell to Nebuchadnezzar the Great in the sixth century B.C., Carthage succeeded as the wealthiest city in antiquity. Founded by the Phoenician Queen Dido in 825 B.C. near what is now the city of Tunis, Carthage became the most important outpost of Phoenician civilization in the western Mediterranean, with a population of close to a million within its walls. As an

The periplus of the Carthaginian Captain Hanno describes a flotilla of 60 ships of 50 oars and 30,000 men and women setting off in about 500 B.C. down the west coast of Africa with enough provisions to travel 3500 miles from Carthage and 2500 miles beyond the Pillars of Hercules to found new colonies as far south as Senegal and Gambia—curiously named "Chariot of the Gods."

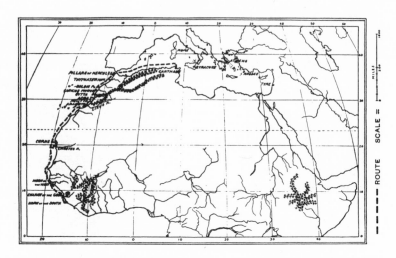

Archeologist Hugh Fox sees a profound religious link between the early Mesoamericans and the early Mesopotamians, a link that was forged by travel to the west of Phoenicians and Carthaginians. In his *Gods of the Cataclysm,* Fox has concluded that Huitzilopochtli, though an amalgam of various gods or god-qualities, is actually a Phoenician version of Zeus, or to be more exact, a Carthaginian version —a Jupiter Haman. He points out that there was human sacrifice to Zeus, including the ritual of flaying, and that in many Middle Eastern rites "worshippers were clad in the skins of animals sacrificed." He sees in Xipe Totec, the Aztec flayed God, an Adonis or Osiris or Dionysus or Baal Haman—all fertility gods. Flaying was a favorite method of torture among the Carthaginians.

outlet for this burgeoning population, and to insure its continued existence, Carthage sent out colonists to sail past the pillars of Melkarth (as they called them) down the coast of Africa, carrying their knowledge and their cults.

From that latitude these Carthaginians, like their Phoenician predecessors, could well have sailed to the New World and made landfalls in Yucatan, Tabasco, or Chiapas, giving substance to the tale of Votan. For the return journey to the Mediterranean, as is recounted in the *Odyssey of Votan,* the Gulf Stream would have swirled them clockwise around the Atlantic, eastward along the 39th parallel, to where the prevailing westerlies would drive a ship to the Azores, and home to Africa and Europe. On Corvo, the northwesternmost island of the Azores, just over a thousand miles from the shores of North America, a cache of Carthaginian coins was found dating from the fourth and the third centuries B.C. In 1975, stones were found on the Atlantic coast near Cape Cod inscribed in a southern Iberian alphabet attributed to Hanno and dated between 480 and 475 B.C.

Nor does the tale of travel to the West stop there. After the Phoenicians and the Carthaginians, Greeks, Romans, Irish, Welsh, and all manner of Scandinavians left tales and evidence of travel to the Americas. Books with information on these voyages fill several shelves in the stacks of the Library of Congress, some with specific studies like those of Professor Cyrus Gordon, others, popular summaries, such as Charles Michael Boland's *They All Discovered America.*

There is equally intriguing evidence of travel to America across the Pacific from the west. As an explanation for the abundance of Indians in Mexico with pronounced Chinese features, Henriette Mertz in her book *Pale Ink* tells of two Chinese expeditions to America, one in the fifth century A.D.

According to Fox, whereas Judaism developed away from human sacrifice, toward surrogate animal and then cereal and then symbolic sacrifice, "the Aztecs caught up the Canaanite religion in its most primitive phase and developed it almost solely along its cannibalistic/human sacrifice lines." He points out that the Phoenicians were the great child-sacrificers, and that in the Old Testament the gods were only appeased by blood sacrifice. Wherever the Phoenicians went they left behind a heritage of blood and sacrifice.

To the Phoenician mind, says Fox, whether in Syria, Palestine or North Africa "the whole sacrificial system was based on an attempt to prevent another—and final—Great Cataclysm."

Fox found Tanit-Baal-Haman, the god-goddess, at the very top of the Aztec Pantheon, and saw her as the Aztec version of Kali, the great Indian mother-goddess, destroyer-creator, and the simultaneous beginning and end of the whole.

To Fox, the benign, benevolent life-giving *mater magna,* mother of heaven and earth, may have become a malevolent destructive force as the result of some great cataclysm. It is clear to him that when the Mayas killed a victim and offered his heart to Venus, the Evening Star, they were offering it to the Phoenician Venus, Tanit, out of fear. He adds that the Hopi were Phoenicians, or strongly influenced by the Phoenicians, and that the Olmecs were black African Phoenicians or escaped Phoenician slaves.

Summing up, he puts the rhetorical question: "If this whole religion was Phoenician, as it certainly seems to be, and if the oldest memory of Aztec theological sources reached back to Teotihuacan, then didn't that make Teotihuacan a Phoenician colony? And the original Quetzalcoatl a Phoenician priest?"

and another much earlier in the twenty-third century B.C., both of which are in the Chinese records.

The fifth-century expedition is described by Hwui Shan, a Buddist monk who reported on the travels of five Buddhist missionaries to a country far to the east called "Fu-sang," which Henriette Mertz and several other modern historians identified as Mexico, overall from Los Angeles to Yucatan, and specifically around Chichen Itza. Fu-sang was so named by the Chinese because of its trees, which looked like bamboo but produced an edible fruit, pear-shaped, and reddish in color, which could be preserved for a year without spoiling. At the beginning of the Christian era, corn in Mexico was only about three inches long, wider at the base, like a pear, with reddish kernels.

Hwui Shan describes finding a civilized people in Fu-sang who knew writing, which they did on paper made from a plant, and who, though they had no iron, had plenty of gold and silver. According to Mertz, this fifth-century visit to Mexico changed the entire course of Mexican history. In Hwui Shan's story, a Chinese nobleman of the first rank was called "Tui-lu," and the Mayan books of Chilam Balam tell of a leader who came from the west, from Tulupan, who had the title of "Tutul Xiu." Mertz describes Tutul Xiu as a Chinese Quetzalcoatl who contributed to the Mexicans Oriental knowledge of the calendar, astronomy, metallurgy, agriculture, jade carving, and the compass.

The earlier report of Chinese travel to America, known as the *Classic of Mountains and Seas,* is the record of a series of journeys about the globe compiled in 2250 B.C. at the request of the Emperor Shan by a man called Yu, his minister of public works, who later became emperor himself. The Chinese travels describe mountains and rivers across the Pacific, or the "Great Eastern Sea." This classic Chinese periplus, known as the Shan Hai King, or oldest Chinese geographical work, though severely truncated, miraculously survived the repeated burning of Chinese libraries and the emasculation of less interested or accurate Chinese historians, and Dr. Mertz believes it "will be found to be the most astounding ancient document detailing geographical phenomena that has ever been written."

The periplus tells of great rocky mountain ranges beyond the sea and names and describes a series of peaks stretching 2200 miles from Manitoba in Canada to Mazatlan in Mexico. With great pains Mertz has followed the record of the Chinese peregrination, whose geographical details described in vivid language are as recognizable today as when they were noted in the third millennium B.C.

As she puts it, "We can do no more than to stand with

353

bowed heads before the intrepid Chinese who mapped those jagged snow-capped peaks over 4000 years ago."

At about the same period, the Japanese appear to have explored the west coast of South America. Both Japanese and Chinese histories abound in stories concerning boat-loads of thousands of people sailing out across the Pacific Ocean in search of a promised land. From careful analysis of pottery on the Ecuadorian coast, which compares very closely with Japanese pottery of 2500 B.C., Betty J. Meggars and her husband, Clifford Evans, were led to the conclusion that the Japanese had reached Ecquador thousands of years ago.

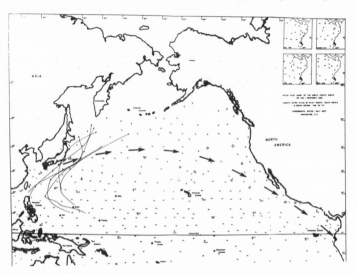

Route taken by Japanese to reach Ecuador before the Christian era, from Betty J. Meggers.

These reports of voyages to the Americas from both east and west take the story back to the third millennium B.C., but much earlier remains of buildings, often extremely sophisticated, have been found in North, Central, and South America, and various authors have hypothesized advanced civilizations which long preceded the Mayan and the Olmec. However, as there are no known historical records for such early periods, and no sure system for dating the remains, these stories float in a limbo between fact and fiction.

Their cumulative evidence, however, is too evocative to be ignored.

25. Prehistoric Mexico

One indication that a far earlier civilization existed in the Valley of Mexico than was reached by Manuel Gamio's spades comes from the tantalizing discoveries made in the Mexican highlands by a Scotsman, William Niven. As a mining engineer working for a Mexican corporation, Niven described coming upon the remains of two separate prehistoric civilizations at depths of from six to thirty feet below the present level of the Valley of Mexico. These discoveries, made between 1910 and 1930, have hardly been considered by the "scientific world," partly because they fit into none of the preconceived notions, and partly because they were used by an even more unorthodox author, James Churchward, to validate his, to them, even wilder hypothesis—the existence of a vast continent in the Pacific Ocean which he called Mu, mother, says he, of several colonial civilizations which spread around the globe.

Churchward's efforts, though very popular with aficionados of Atlantean and Lemurian tales, and often prophetically exact in certain details, have, because of Churchward's unsupported and highly improbable notions, been thrown out by an establishment which may have discarded, along with Churchward's Lemurian bath water, some living, screaming babies.

Being befriended by fellow Freemason Churchward was of no greater help to William Niven than it had been to Le Plongeon, except that with the thousands of copies of Churchward's books sold around the world Niven was rescued from oblivion. When he died in 1937, his obit in the *American Historical Review* listed him merely as a professor who had been engaged for several years in mineralogical research, an

Churchward's rendering of prehistoric North America with part of his great continent of Mu in the Pacific.

1 FOOT OF EARTH

9 FEET OF BOULDERS, GRAVEL, SAND WITH BROKEN POTTERY

← FIRST PAVEMENT

6 FEET OF SMALL BOULDERS, GRAVEL AND SAND

← SECOND PAVEMENT

14 FEET OF SMALL BOULDERS, GRAVEL, SAND

← VOLCANIC ASHES

←BURIED CITY

←THIRD PAVEMENT

Niven's Mexican Buried Cities
Now 7000 feet above level of sea. Mountains 5000 feet higher intervening

In the several strata clearly revealed by the pits, Niven says he found traces of what he describes as three well-preserved concrete floors or pavements at depths from about 6 to 25 feet. Above the first pavement there was a deposit of small boulders, pebbles, and sand, covered with a foot-thick coating of rich valley soil. Everywhere in the first layer of debris, Niven found fragments of broken pottery, small clay figures, diorite beads, spear- and arrowheads, spindle whorls, and other artifacts, mostly broken.

honorary life member of the American Museum of Natural History and various other such scientific societies who had become involved in Mexican archeology, nothing more. Nothing to indicate he might have made the most controversial archeological discovery of the Western world.

Actually, Niven had been exploring in Mexico since 1889. While digging among the ancient ruined cities in the unknown and uninhabited portion of the state of Guerrero, southwest of Mexico City in the Acapulco area, he began to receive periodic visits from local Indians who came to him with terra-cotta figurines and other objects for sale. Though the Indians pretended to have found these objects at the pyramids of the Sun and Moon at San Juan Teotihuacan, Niven realized that the source of the artifacts must be nearer; with a bribe of five pesos ($2.50 at that time) he managed to discover the actual spot.

Between Texcoco and Haluepantla, hamlets just north of Mexico City, he came across hundreds, if not thousands, of pits dug into the sand, clay, and tepetate used for material by the builders of Mexico City for more than three hundred years. Exploring these pits, which Niven says cover an area of about ten by twenty miles in the northwest corner of the Valley of Mexico, he came across vast layers of what appeared to be very ancient ruins, whole prehistoric cities lying as deep as thirty feet below the plain, which appeared to have been overwhelmed by a series of cataclysmic tidal waves, perhaps at several-thousand-year intervals, which,

356

In 1920 William Niven (in light suit) was exploring a passageway in the Pyramid of the Moon with an enthusiastic Sunday archeologist, Charles Beeching, a bridge-building civil engineer from Boston, Massachusetts, when the latter fell into a well-like hole. Beeching described the event in a letter to his daughter Mariana Beeching de Prieto, a writer of children's books now living in Miami, Florida. "I fell feet first through a hole and tumbled into blackness. One moment I was walking along a dim corridor, the next I was plunged from Aztec into a pre-Aztec or Teotihuacanic era. My undignified drop turned out to be a valuable archaeological discovery. I had fallen into the chamber of an ancient race. As soon as I could collect myself I let out a yell. Niven was within earshot. The only escape from the chamber was through a narrow opening which I myself had punctured in the roof. Niven lowered a rope and hauled me bruised and shaky out of the place.

"While waiting for rescue, my eyes became accustomed to the darkness . . . in the corners of the stone-walled rooms there were heaps of images, tablets and pieces of pottery."

From Beeching's report it appears that passageways, wells, and hidden chambers, such as were reported by Ewing and Latrobe, still existed in 1920 before they were obliterated by a massive restoration of the Moon Pyramid.

as Niven described them, had left telltale strata of boulders, sand, and pebbles. By their depth beneath the surface, Niven estimated the oldest remains might go as far back as 50,000 years.

Four to six feet below the first pavement, Niven says he encountered a second "concrete floor," but in the intervening space failed to find a single piece of pottery or other trace to indicate that humans had once lived there. Beneath the second pavement, he describes coming upon what he considered "the great find of my many years' work in Mexican archeology."

Niven discerned, beneath a well-defined layer of ashes from two to three feet thick, analyzed as being of volcanic origin, traces of innumerable buildings, large, but regular in size, the remains of a vast city which appeared uniformly at the same level throughout more than a hundred clay pits. In one of the houses—most of which were crushed and ruined, filled with ashes and debris—he says he found an arched wooden door which had turned to stone. The walls of this house were bound together with white cement, harder than the stone itself. In one

357

Niven believes the figure of a Chinaman, which he found thirty feet from the surface in a pit which he had dug at San Miguel Amantla, near Haluepantla, nineteen miles from the national palace in Mexico City, had been buried thousands of years earlier. Niven says the oblique eye slits, padded coat, flowing trousers, and slippers make the statuette clearly Chinese. He explains the lack of a queue by pointing out that the Chinese did not have the queue till they were conquered by Tartar hordes from the north in the seventh century. The statuette is seven inches high, of friable clay, which on the outside has turned to stone. It is three and a half inches wide at the chest and one and a half inches through the abdomen. The ears are ringed; the skull cap has a button in the center like the caps of mandarins of the empire.

uncrushed room, about thirty feet square, full of volcanic ash, with a flat roof of concrete and stone, Niven says he came across many artifacts and human bones, which "crumbled to the touch like slaked lime." According to his detailed report, a complete goldsmith's outfit was still on the floor with some two hundred models of figures and idols molded in clay turned to stone, each model thickly coated with iron oxide, bright and yellow, presumably there to prevent the molten metals adhering to the patterns while in the casting pot.

Niven says the ornaments were unlike any found in Palenque or Mitla or anywhere between. The work was fine, beautifully polished, demonstrating an advanced degree of civilization. On the walls Niven found paintings in red, blue, yellow, green, and black, which he says compared favorably with the best he had seen from Greek, Etruscan, or Egyptian works of a similar sort. The ground color of the wall was a pale blue; six inches down from the fourteen-foot ceiling a frieze painted in dark red and black ran around the room, glazed with some native wax which had perfectly preserved the color and pattern, which depicted the life of some person, apparently a shepherd, from birth to death.

Beneath the floor Niven found a tomb three feet deep, lined with cement, in which were seventy-five pieces of bone, all that was left of a skeleton. A large fragment of the skull contained the blade of a hammered copper axe, which appeared to have been the cause of death, for it had not been removed. Niven also found in the tomb 125 small terra-cotta idols, manikins, images, and dishes, some with features strongly Phoenician or Semitic, one sitting crosslegged with a hollow movable head set on its neck by a cleverly devised truncated tenon fitted into a mortise at the base of the skull.

Less than three miles away Niven found an ancient riverbed in the sands and gravel of which he says were thousands of terra-cotta and clay figures with faces representing "all the races of southern Asia."

Then, in 1921, in the course of excavations at Santiago Ahuizoctla, a hamlet contiguous to Amantla, about five miles northwest of Mexico City, Niven came across a discovery so startling he says it opened up for him a whole new field of archeological research. At a depth of twelve feet Niven described coming across the first of a series of stone tablets with very unusual pictographs. Systematically exploring other clay pits and tepetate quarries within an area of twenty square miles, he claimed he was able to unearth during the course of the next two years 975 more tablets. In the end he says he found more than 2600. Though there was nothing in these tablets by which he could determine their exact

Niven's showcase number 6 containing a portion of his collection of carved stones from the Valley of Mexico. When William Niven died in Austin, Texas, in 1937, the New York *Times* described him as a distinguished mineralogist and archeologist who had discovered buried prehistoric cities beneath the Valley of Mexico. He was also noted as the discoverer of four new minerals including cytrialite, thorogon, and nivenite. According to the *Times*, Niven donated to the Mexican government the best of the relics he found in Mexico, keeping for himself some, which he sold to finance further archeological expeditions. With what was left over there were enough pieces to establish in Mexico City a private museum of 30,000 exhibits.

or even approximate age, Niven deduced from the depth at which they were buried and the accumulation of debris on top of them that they were over 12,000 years old and more likely closer to 50,000.

The tablets, which Niven carefully numbered in the order in which he found them, had no particular shape. They appeared to be water-worn stones with smooth surfaces on which the figures had been carved, often to conform with the shape of the stone, much like the so-called Cabrera stones found almost contemporaneously in Peru, which depict strange human beings with four-fingered hands in combat with dinosaurs, though such prehistoric creatures were

In the 1920s the American Museum of Natural History in New York was given a collection of artifacts by a man who informed the curator that many of them had been bought from Niven. In 1976 the curator of Mexican archeology, Gordon F. Eckholm, said the museum still possessed a collection of objects from Guerrero sold to them by Niven, but that he did not know what had become "of the famous Niven tablets."

Stone carving of men fighting dinosaurs, part of a collection of twenty thousand such stones recently found in Peru by Dr. Cabrera, who believes them to be over fifty thousand years old. The collection includes an anatomical library accurately showing man's inner organs and an extraordinarily sophisticated series of heart transplants.

thought to have been extinct many millennia before the appearance of man on the planet.

When Niven showed tracings of the tablets to "informed professors both American and foreign," including Sylvanus G. Morley, he was told the symbols were unlike anything they had ever seen. No prominent archeologist was able to decipher a single one of the tablets. So Niven went to the not inconsiderable trouble of making tracings of each and every tablet, which he sent to his old friend James Churchward for comment. And so Pandora's box was opened.

Churchward said he was not the least surprised that none of the archeologists could decipher the tablets. He, on the other hand, recognized in Niven's tablets symbols and designs similar to the ones he had been shown on tablets in a monastery in Tibet known as the Naacal tablets, which, Churchward said, contained "Sacred Inspired Writings" originating in the lost continent of Mu, which had sunk into the Pacific Ocean about 12,000 years ago at about the same time the last remnant of Atlantis had gone down in the Atlantic.

On closer study, Churchward said that Niven's Mexican tablets confirmed data he had derived from the Tibetan Naacal tablets, filling in many missing gaps.

From the intimate links in the content of Niven's tablets, Churchward concluded that they were the work of members of a colony of Mu which had been established in the Valley of Mexico, thousands of years before the birth of Christ.

This priestly brotherhood, said Churchward, had been sent out from Mu to teach the sacred writings, which contained the religion and science of the mother country, to colonists in southeast Asia. From there they had moved to India, where eventually the brothers had taken refuge from persecution in the mountain fastness of Tibet.

Designs found on Niven's Mexican tablets which Churchward said confirmed data he had obtained from Naacal tablets in India. According to Churchward the figures represent the "Four Great Primary Forces of Nature."

According to the tablets, as interpreted by Churchward, they took the history of man back 200,000 years. Archeologists threw up their hands; they not only refused to countenance Churchward but decided on a similar treatment for Niven. Undismayed, Churchward incorporated Niven's data to bolster his own thesis.

Churchward's books on Mu received a new impetus in the Aquarian age when the Paperback Library of New York reprinted his five books, plus one of explanation and support entitled *Understanding Mu*, by Hans Stefan Steffanson.

Then in 1970 Paperback Library went further: they published a thin volume, *Mu Revealed*, by Tony Earll, in which the author described recent excavations at Niven's site by a Professor Reesdon Hurdlop, who reported the discovery of a stone sarcophagus under the floor of a small temple found by Niven. The sarcophagus was said to contain sixty-nine scrolls or leaves of papyrus bearing strange writings.

Professor Hurdlop was described as well known in archeological circles for his work at Johore Lama, the site of the

361

One of the reasons Niven may have failed to receive the attention he deserved was his discovery of indications of both Masonic and phallic worship in the figurines he unearthed, both of which were subject to being glossed over. In lava fields dated at over ten thousand years, Niven found figurines with one hand pressed to the lips and the other resting on a muscle or against the head—gestures which he recognized as being similar to those still practiced in his day by Masons. Nor was Niven shy about pointing out that "these miniature figures, both masculine and feminine, in these secret mysteries, show the genital organs in a perfectly nude condition as if such rites had some relationship with those of phallicism."

Niven further noted that the female figures "reveal

ancient city of Singapura, and at Kota Tinggi, where he followed up the work started by the late Dr. Gerald Brosseau Gardner, who discovered the original site; and he was said to have been advised in his work by Sir Richard Windstedt, British general adviser in Johore at that time.

By 1964, wrote Earll, the scrolls had been deciphered sufficiently to reveal that they held the intimate details of life on the continent of Mu (which the scrolls called Muror) over a period of years prior to its destruction; and Professor Hurdlop dated the scrolls at 20,000 to 25,000 B.C. The scroll writings, which purported to be the diary of a young priest called Kland, were said to include descriptions of homes and families, temples, transport, wars, elections, crimes and punishments, household accounts, and personal letters.

Though Professor Hurdlop had considered Churchward's discoveries deserving of further investigation, "little did he realize," wrote Earll, "that this was going to lead to one of the greatest discoveries of our time, comparable to Schliemann's discovery of Troy and Evans' work on the Minoan civilization."

Earll says he followed Hurdlop to Mexico from India via Egypt and England, where they talked with directors of the Marquina-Jolicoeur Institute in London in preparation for an expedition to dig at Niven's old site in Mexico, apparently the first to do so. The rest of Earll's book describes how the scrolls were worked on with probes and tweezers, opened a fragment at time, and the broken fragments pieced together. Carbon-dated at 23,000 years, the text, says Earll, was translated with the help of Dr. Eward Stich of Boston.

Unfortunately, Tony Earll turned out to be an anagram of "Not Really," who in real life is Dr. Raymond Buckland, a Canadian of Weirs Beach, New Hampshire, now deep into witchcraft. Professor Reesdon Hurdlop never made the dig near Niven's site, and never found a sarcophagus with the diary of a priest called Kland written on ancient papyrus. He is an anagram for Rednose Rudolph, the reindeer. So: *caveat* the *emptor* of quickie paperbacks, and let him beware of taking on faith the unqualified data of the precursors and followers of Erich von Däniken. There is no indication whatsoever on the covers—front or back, or anywhere between them—that Earll's work, which advertises itself as "the archaeological discovery that rewrites earth's history," is spurious. And that's the world we live in, not much better than the sixteenth century, when the Jesuits pirated important works such as those of Paracelsus to replace them with bowdlerized editions, spreading the notion that Paracelsus was a phony, a notion which lasted till the present century

the pudendum or vulva with every detail; and here is something more wonderful, there is an object which seems to be falling, which at first appears to represent a small timbrel, but on closer inspection is seen to be the representation of a drop of semen oozing from the feminine organ of generation."

Niven adds that in the Jonuta work of relief (number 26 in the gallery of monoliths in Mexico's Museum of Archeology) the symbols of the male organ of generation, which are portrayed in the manner of projecting cloves around the head of the priest of the temple, are evidently "ejecting semen."

when a couple of Swiss researchers finally produced a sounder version of his works.

Was Churchward a phony? Did he invent the Naacal tablets? And what of Niven's tablets?

At last some serious attention is being paid to Niven by Robert Wicks of the University of Washington in Seattle, who is preparing a book on Niven and his tablets. In correspondence with leading academicians in the field of Mexican antiquities, Wicks has managed to obtain their admission that negligence of Niven's work may have been an error.

In due course not only Niven but Churchward may be revalidated, as have been Mesmer and Paracelsus, who for centuries were treated with vituperative denigration. More digs on Niven's sites and a closer look at Mu may be in order, for beneath the ancient myths, as Humboldt and Brasseur averred, some history may surface yet.

26. Churchward: Fantasy or Fact

Colonel James Churchward (1850–1936), of an old Devonshire family, was educated at Oxford and Sandhurst Military College: he served in India with the Royal Engineers and as colonel of a regiment of Lancers. When his marriage broke up he resigned his commission to become a tea planter and amateur painter, an exponent of the proverb: *"Les aventures arrivent aux aventuriers."*

After many adventures in many lands he settled in the United States, where he became renowned as an angler and a teller of tall stories.

Above medium height, sturdy, with an aquiline nose, the eye of a hawk, and a firm mouth which constantly broke into a smile, he is described as a man of affairs and culture, cordial and candid, a great lady killer, who, though charming, had a "thirty-third-degree efficiency in the art of making enemies."

After working as a civil engineer with the railroads and traveling to sell his own patented inventions, he made a killing in the steel business organizing the Churchward International Steel Corporation and

On the basis of his interpretation of the Niven tablets, Churchward rewrote the text of his book *The Lost Continent of Mu* and dedicated it to Niven. In the book he describes the land of Mu as having been a large continent between America and Asia, its center lying somewhat south of the equator. Its area he bases on remains still above water, on rocky islands scattered over the Pacific, where there are still great cyclopean walls, stone-lined canals, paved roads, and enormous monoliths and statues such as those discovered on Easter Island.

Churchward saw Mu as having been about 6000 miles from east to west, and about 3000 north to south, a vast stretch of rolling country, extending from Hawaii to the Fijis, divided into three land areas separated by narrow seas.

He describes it—whether intuitively or on the basis of actual information—as a beautiful tropical country, with vast plains covered with rich grazing grasses and tilled fields, shaded by luxurious growths of tropical vegetation, a true Garden of Eden, teeming with gay and happy life, over which 64 million human beings reigned supreme, grouped into ten tribes, a white or olive-skinned race with large soft dark eyes and straight black hair, a yellow-skinned, a brown, and a black people, each distinct, but all under one government, builders of great temples and palaces of stone, navigators who took their ships around the world leaving inscriptions and legends from China to the Middle East, in both directions.

Churchward says that, according to the tablets, when a colony had advanced enough to govern itself it was turned into a colonial empire; one branch of colonization ran from Mu to Central America, thence to Atlantis, thence to the developing a nickel-chrome-venadium alloy, excellent for armor-plating. But he soon tangled with the magnates of steel and high finance who quickly disposed of him. Churchward accused the large mills of having "milked me dry of all I could show them, stolen my patents, tried to kill me by dumping tons of white hot steel on me, and were in cahoots with the Navy Department and fellows in there, to unload my steel on Uncle Sam at fabulous prices."

His attorney, Percy Tate Griffith, who at first considered the statement preposterous, later said: "Events proved that far more of it was true than I was willing to credit, and much that even the suspicious Colonel had not visioned."

Churchward claimed to have learned the truth about the dirty dealing in the steel industry from highly placed friends in Masonry. Churchward's brother Albert, a medical doctor and inventor, was a prolific writer on Freemasonry and its relation to primitive mankind.

As a comeback from his debacle in the steel business, Churchward turned to the story of Mu, bringing out *The Lost Continent of Mu* in 1930, *The Children of Mu* in 1931, *The Sacred Symbols of Mu* in 1933, and *Cosmic Forces as They Were Taught in Mu,* in 1934.

In the late 1930s his attorney, Percy Griffith, wrote a fourteen chapter, two hundred page biography of Churchward in which he set himself to validate much of Churchward's career, intimating that Churchward had solid data on which to base his fabulous tales of Mu. Unfortunately, only six chapters of the biography were salvaged by Griffith's daughter Joan, and the mystery of Churchward's sources remains to be revealed.

Mediterranean and Asia Minor; another branch ran from the west coast of North America down the east coast of South America, traceable as far as Argentina.

Before Mu went down, a great civilization existed in South America, in the area of Tiahuanaco, says Churchward, adding that the Inca are not a prehistoric people but a mixture of Quichés who emigrated to Peru from Guatemala, settling among the local Aymaras.

Among the tablets Churchward was shown in Tibet, he says some described an extended history of Atlantis; one included a map two feet square showing Atlantis with the contour of the lands around the Atlantic Ocean, vastly different from today, Atlantis being not an island but joined to America, Europe, and Africa, at a time "when great monsters roamed the earth and seas were filled with monstrous forms."

The tablets, says Churchward, also tell of Osiris being born in Atlantis, whence he traveled 20,000 years before Christ to Mu to become a master, so as to return to Atlantis to eliminate the "extravagances, superstitions, misconceptions and inventions that had crept into the Atlantean religion." Osiris is reported as having reinstalled in Atlantis an original religion of love and simplicity, of which he became high priest. From Atlantis, says Churchward, the Osirian religion was carried to Egypt by Toth about 16,000 years ago, a religion, Churchward says, which reportedly contained word for word and sentence for sentence the same teachings as those of Jesus, and from which Moses fathered his doctrine of monotheism.

In the other direction, westward from Mu, several lines of colonization are described; the best known ran from Burma to India to Babylon and upper Egypt, thus resolving the apparent conflict in legends about Egypt having been settled by strangers arriving from both east and west.

Churchward says lower Egypt was settled by colonists from Mu, via Mayax and Atlantis, both of which lay to the west, whereas the upper Egyptians came to Egypt from Mu, via Burma and India, which lie to the east.

The latter, as described by Le Plongeon, were known as the Nagas. Hindu records tell of the central parts of India (the Deccan) being first colonized by a white race who came to India via Burma from a motherland one moon's journey toward the rising sun, east of Burma, where now are the Polynesian islands. Churchward dates this migration as having taken place more than 15,000 years ago. The same Nagas are credited with starting the civilization of Babylonia, whose recently discovered cuneiform tablets contain religious concepts identical with those reported in the Naacal tablets.

In support of the theory that numerous Pacific island groups form the last remnants of a once large continent, Stacy-Judd says the natives of Easter Island in the Pacific, 2000 miles west of Chile, state that their ancestors did not come from Lemuria but that they *are* Lemurianas living on a peak of a Lemurian holy mountain, the only portion of Lemuria remaining above the water.

Comparison of Easter Island glyphs (right columns) with those of the Indus valley.

Easter Island is known as one of the world's geodetic navels, or omphali. Barbieri says that a few years after the catastrophe which destroyed civilization on the island, missionaries found wooden tablets with hieroglyphs similar to ones found in Mohenjo Daro by the Hungarian Guillaume de Hevesy, and also to the archaic Chinese characters of the epoch of Chang as described by Dr. Hervé Geldren. One of the tablets was translated by W. J. Thompson in 1886 as saying "This (little island) was once part of a great continent of land, crossed with many roads . . ."

There are some twenty such tablets with Easter Island script scattered among the museums of the world.

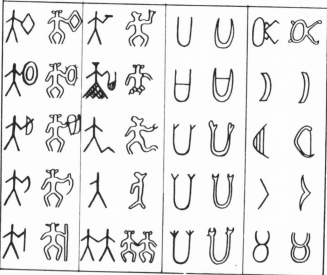

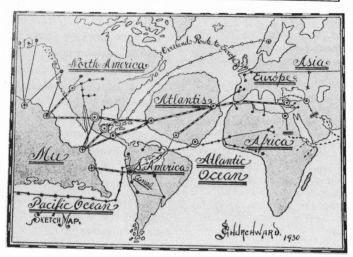

Churchward's rendering of communications from Mu through North and South America to the Mediterranean via Atlantis.

Amazon Canal.

This canal, and the Amazon Sea, are shown on a map of South America which Churchward says he found on a tablet in a monastery in Western Tibet on his last trip there. He says the date of the map was marked by the position of certain stars in certain constellations, and that astronomers told him it was twenty-five thousand years ago when these stars were in the positions given.

*＊ I-I-I- Ancient S A
— Present S A
∻ From Ancient Oriental

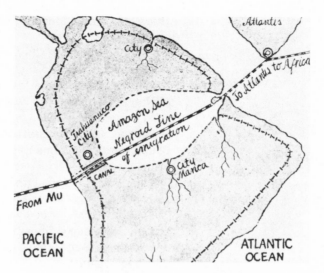

Churchward says that when he compared the writings of the old civilizations with the legends of Mu, he established to his satisfaction that the civilizations of the early Greeks, Chaldeans, Babylonians, Persians, Egyptians, and Hindus all derived from the civilization of Mu.

As for the Israelites, he says that when they were captives in Babylon, they were able to study in the colleges of the Chaldi (or Chaldeans) where they learned the cosmic sciences. "The Chaldi," says Churchward, "were open and free to all who wished to come to them for learning. There was no expense to the student, and the slave was as welcome as the prince. Directly the threshold of the Chaldi was passed, everyone was on an equality. They were symbolically at the feet of the Heavenly Father, and became in fact brothers in truth."

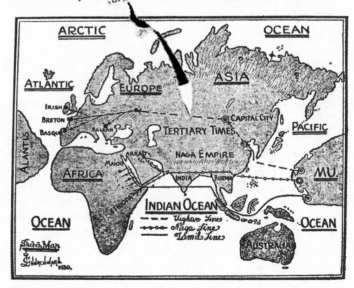

Westward lines of communication from Mu, according to Churchward.

These Israelites, although in bondage, attended the Chaldi and became Masters."

A secondary line in Churchward's scheme ran from Mu to the Malay islands and thence to southern India, called Dravida, and from India to Africa, where they settled south of Nubia, becoming the ancestors of the Ethiopians.

To the northwest of Mu the predecessors of the Japanese became a colonial empire; and on the mainland of Asia, says Churchward, was formed the largest and most important colonial empire ever derived from Mu, the great Uighur Empire, which stretched from the Pacific to Moscow, with outposts in Europe as far as the Atlantic, where the British Isles, at that time, 17,000 years ago, were still attached to Europe. This colony, whose southern borders were formed by Cochin China, Burma, India, and part of Persia, was said to have been destroyed partly before the cataclysm which ended Mu and partly afterward; its history, to Churchward, is the story of the Aryan races.

The Great Uighur Empire, which Churchward believes to have existed in the Tertiary Era, stretching from the Pacific to what is now the British Isles.

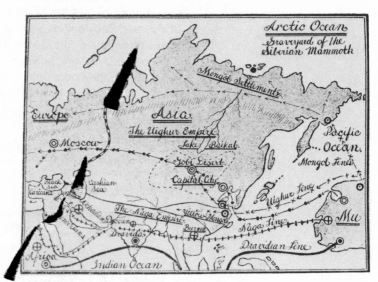

To the various colonies and colonial empires, says Churchward, the sacred writings of Mu were carried by a body of trained masters known as Naacals, who formed colleges in each country where priest-teachers could be taught religion and the sciences, the priesthoods in turn teaching the people.

As reconstructed by Churchward, the religion of Mu was without dogma, taught in the simplest and most easily understood language that the most unschooled mind could grasp. Confusion, he says, set in only after the collapse of Mu, when bigotry and impossible theologies were developed. "At various times in the history of man, unscrupulous priesthoods have caused the downfall of religion by introducing into it vicious systems of theology made up of inventions, extravagances, and immorality as well as false translations from the Sacred Writings from which all religions sprung, for the purpose of inspiring superstitious fears, to ensnare people body and soul into slavery to the priesthood." Having accomplished this, says Churchward, it did not take long for the priesthoods to acquire wealth and to become all powerful.

The Vedas, says Churchward, were stolen from the Naacal writings and changed by the Brahmins to be foisted on the world as sublime thoughts of their own, whereas the Brahminical theology became, as it was intended, a breeder of superstition and awe, dragging the nation down from a pinnacle of civilization to the lowest rung of the ladder.

The priesthood in Egypt, says Churchward, caused a "cataclysmic wave of false gods, idolatry and spiritual degradation to sweep over the land."

Churchward maintains that the Naacal tablets he was shown in Tibet contain religious concepts and a cosmology of a very high order. He says the civilization which produced the tablets was in no way primitive, even though some of the workmanship of the tablets appears crude. According to his interpretation, their knowledge of the cosmic forces of "energy" was remarkable, and the tablets were the exposition of the knowledge of a profound science, "which is only dawning on the scientific world of today, and which has not been learned and mastered by modern man."

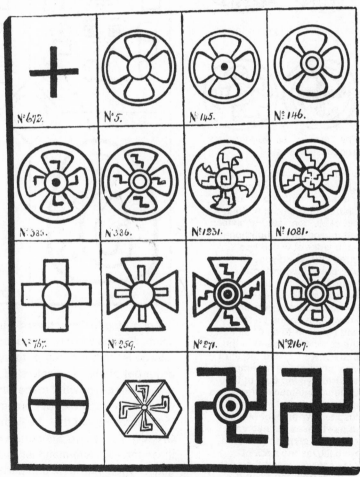

Group 6.

Ancient symbols of the Sacred Four.

Churchward's interpretation of the Four Forces proceeding from the source.

And the Four Forces within the absolute.

Rays proceeding from the Four Forces.

The Four Forces working from east to west.

A group of four tablets which Churchward says symbolize the dual principle of creation. Churchward says the alphabet of Mu consisted of sixteen letters and many diphthongs, each letter of which had three different glyphs to express it. According to Churchward, the first was the hieratic letter, which also carried a hidden meaning known only to the priests, and not even to all of them; the second was used in the body of words; and the third was an adjective for emphasis. He says the bulk of the tablets contained extracts and sentences from the Sacred Inspired Writings of Mu, and in most cases the esoteric or temple glyphs were used. He believes the ancient Mexicans obtained their cosmogony from the Sacred Writings of Mu, the fountainhead.

Churchward's interpretation of the Naacal and the Niven tablets indicates a much earlier awareness of where man had come from, why he was on earth, and how the universe is governed and controlled.

The tablets, says Churchward, tell of how originally the universe was all soul or spirit.

The principal symbol of the tablets was the sun—a monotheistic or collective symbol of the Creator; later it was given many attributes, each of which was also symbolized, though it was stressed that these attributes were only powers of the One Supreme.

According to Churchward's interpretation of the tablets, two cosmic forces were required for creation; thereafter, the first four gods were the four primary forces which evolved law and order out of chaos, creators of all that is physical throughout the universe—or what in the Christian and Moslem worlds would be termed the four archangels. Churchward adds that Pythagoras taught that the number four referred to the Great Creative Forces. In Steinerian or anthroposophical terms, these forces could manifest as the force fields behind hydrogen, oxygen, nitrogen, and carbon.

Later in the history of man, according to Churchward's analysis, the disembodied souls of men were added to the list

The raising and collapsing of mountains by the action of great subterranean gas belts, which, according to Churchward, occurred in more recent times than geologists are ready to accept.

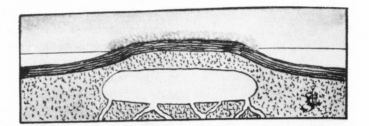

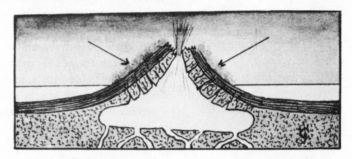

Churchward's depiction of a mountain rising from a plain.

of gods. The formulator of this theology, says Churchward, knew that man at his creation was given cosmic forces under the control of the soul, and that when the soul leaves the material body it carries the cosmic forces with it, eventually back to the originating power.

Churchward claims the symbols of Mu reveal an origin of Freemasonry far older than in Egypt 5000 years ago. He also claims the sacred writings of the Naacals, which contain many Masonic symbols, evidently going back to Mu, perhaps

371

as far back as 70,000 years, constitute the first known religious teachings, of which the present Masonic doctrines are but fragments outlining a monotheistic religion of All-in-One, with love for the Creator as Heavenly Father, and love for mankind as brothers, handed down from generation to generation since the collapse of Mu 12,000 years ago. Ever since, says Churchward, man has lived many lives in many places, not always of this world, with between each life a veil of darkness breached only in some daydream or casual thought of previous circumstances, all of which in the end will be revealed.

Churchward's most improbable explanation for the evident tidal wave which swept across the Valley of Mexico, a mere 5000 feet above the sea, is to suggest that the valley was once *at* sea level and that vast mountain ranges were pushed up by the explosion of subterranean gases in a relatively recent period, not more than 12,000 years ago. He suggests a similar explanation for the abundant evidence indicating that Tiahuanaco in the Bolivian Andes, now at 9000 feet, was also once at sea level, ignoring H. S. Bellamy's theory that the waters of the oceans once reached up to these levels when held by the attracting force of earth satellites which preceded our moon and which caused cataclysmic tidal waves when these satellites disintegrated onto the earth, releasing enormous girdles of water accumulated around the equator. Though each suggestion seems farfetched, either, and especially Bellamy's, is at least an attempt to explain remarkable evidence for which geologists cannot provide explanations.

This story of Mu does give a background to the influx of peoples to Central America and fill some gaps in a rational way, but as no one other than Churchward appears to have reported on the Naacal tablets, and as he produces

Illustration from H. S. Bellamy showing level of oceans on Andean Altiplano as held by his postulated satellite predecessor of Luna.

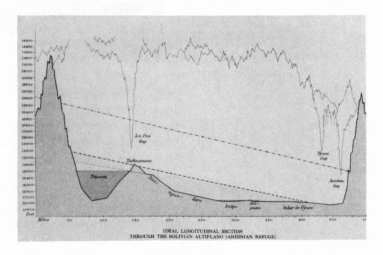

IDEAL LONGITUDINAL SECTION
THROUGH THE BOLIVIAN ALTIPLANO (ANDINIAN REFUGE)

illustrations of only very few—and none of these in photographs—his word can only be taken by those who wish to believe him.

It might therefore seem foolhardy to dwell on the geo-. logical possibilities of a sunken continent in the Pacific were it not for a great deal of solid data recently put forward by a group of Soviet academicians. Soviet author N. F. Zhirov, who lucidly marshaled the data in his scholarly *Atlantis,* fully subscribes to the opinion of V. V. Belousov, who writes in *The Geological Structure of Oceans:* "It may be asserted that very recently, partially even in the age of man, the Pacific Ocean grew considerably at the expense of great chunks of continents which, together with their young ranges of mountains, were inundated by it. The summits of these mountains are to be seen in the island garlands of East Asia."

Zhirov also quotes from an interesting paper read by George H. Cronwell at the 10th World Pacific Congress on the discovery of coal on Rapa Island (Rapaiti, southwest of Mangareva Island) which "provides irrefutable testimony of the fact that there was a continent on that part of fhe ocean." The flora on the island likewise dates back to remote antiquity. On the basis of these discoveries, which, Zhirov says, passed virtually unnoticed, Cronwell assumed the existence of a vast submerged land area in and south of the region of Polynesia.

A comparison of island and continental lava led R. Furon to surmise in *Sur des trilobites dragues à 4255 de profondeur par le "Talisman"* that the Hawaiian Islands were once part of a Pacific continent. "We believe," says Zhirov, "that in the not very distant past the submarine Hawaiian ridge was a large land area—Hawaiis; perhaps the sinking of its remains was witnessed by man—let us recall the Polynesian legend of a happy motherland named Hawaiki about whose location there are the most diverse guesses." Zhirov adds that at one time Hawaiis may have been a chain of islands or even a large land mass over which man (possibly Mesolithic and Neolithic pre-Ainu and Mongoloid tribes) migrated from Asia to America and southward to Polynesia.

North of New Guinea there is also the vast submarine Carolina plateau, over which are islands of the same name. This region is the home of an enigmatic Megalithic culture about whose origin and people there is little trustworthy data. The cradle of this culture, says Zhirov, was on Ponape with its remains of a huge mysterious port carved into basalt cliffs, Nanmatal, sometimes called the Venice of the Pacific. This port of the western Pacific is now virtually

Solar-year part of the great
calendar at Tiahuanaco,
Bolivia, from H. S. Bellamy.

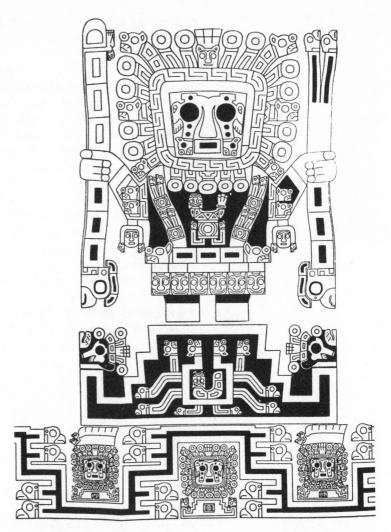

inaccessible to archeological and oceanographic investigation because of U.S. naval and air bases—possibly the
cause of such detailed interest by the Soviets in a lost
continent of Mu.

27. Cayce's Mesoamerica

Edgar Cayce (1877–1945), America's "Sleeping Prophet" was a medical diagnostician by clairvoyance whose 30,000 "readings" while entranced gave detailed medical and spiritual advice to thousands of individuals, often thousands of miles away from Cayce's office. The stenographic records of these "readings" are now at the Association of Research and Enlightenment in Virginia Beach, Va., along with hundreds of affidavits from satisfied patients and physicians who followed Edgar Cayce's prescriptions.

As a psychic observer, Cayce also described geological changes in the remote past of this planet, and calmly prophesied catastrophes for the future, believing, as he did, in endless cycles of life in which spiritual entities occupy one body after another.

From Cayce's description of the "past lives" of his patients, going back several millenia, it has been possible to create or recreate a picture, sometimes hodge-podge, sometimes lucidly rational, of what might have occured on this planet, for which there is little historical data but for which recent geological and archaeological research has adduced some startling verification.

There is one strange source corroborating Mu. In the voluminous "readings" given by America's foremost psychic, Edgar Cayce, over a period of a quarter of a century, he describes in broad strokes and fine lines the same sinking of two great continents, Mu in the Pacific, Atlantis in the Atlantic; he also outlines an inspired religion very similar to that exhumed by Churchward from the Mexican tablets of Niven.

Cayce's data is extracted from "past life" readings of several hundred individuals whose incarnations in Atlantis, Mu, and their various colonies he describes in such fascinating detail that, as the Italians say, *"se non è vero è ben trovato."*

Mu, which Cayce calls short for Lemuria, he describes as a continent covering a large area of the southern Pacific which sank beneath the sea even before the end of Atlantis. The arrival of fleeing Lemurians to the Yucatan peninsula, says Cayce, had its part in changing the civilization already established there by the Atlanteans, though it was the Atlantean civilization which was the most powerful influence in shaping the earliest culture in Yucatan. According to Cayce, at the time of the final destruction of Atlantis much of the land area of Yucatan also sank and was covered by the sea so that the land assumed its present outline.

Again it might seem idle to pursue such tenuous leads as the psychic readings of Cayce were it not that many of the same eminent Soviet geologists quoted by N. F. Zhirov support the thesis that a large continental body sank into the Atlantic in relatively recent times. Furthermore, the University of Miami's top geologist, Cesare Emiliani, is categoric, on the basis of corings in the Gulf of Mexico, in his description of the flooding of Yucatan about 12,000 years ago. He says that at the end of the last great ice age a flood of icy water poured down the valley of the Mississippi to raise the waters of the Gulf of Mexico some 130 feet. Pointing to Antillia on the map, he is quite specific: "That's where the last of Plato's Atlantis could have been submerged."

The lost continent of Atlantis, which Cayce places just about where Plato placed it in the Atlantic, went down, says Cayce, in three successive disasters. The readings claim that many lands have risen from or collapsed into the seas in a series of cataclysms over hundreds of thousands of years, shifting the poles repeatedly, causing tropical areas to freeze while frozen ones became warm and fertile.

Antillia (B) and Atlantis (A).

No definite date is mentioned for the first destruction of Atlantis, though 50,722 B.C. is given as the time of a meeting held to discuss how to rid the earth of a menacing horde of prehistoric beasts; the first destruction is presumed to have occurred not too long thereafter.

The readings tell of a few Atlanteans leaving before the first destruction, going to South and Central America, Egypt, and to what are now Spain and Portugal as places of refuge.

Cayce describes a struggle on Atlantis between two main groups, the "Sons of the Law of One," who believed their bodies to be a temple to the living God, with whom they could communicate by meditation, and the "Sons of Belial," who opposed the Law of One, using their creative forces for self-aggrandizement and the control of others. Cayce attributes the

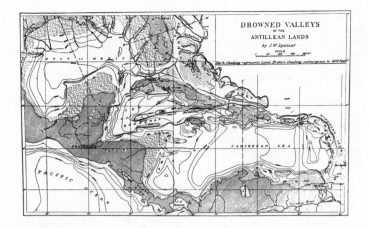

J. W. Spencer's map showing coastal areas of the Caribbean islands, Florida, and Yucatan that were above water before the flooding of the Mississippi, estimated by geologists to have occurred at the end of the last ice age about 12,000 years ago.

catastrophes which overcame Atlantis partly to the noxious thought forms of the Sons of Belial and partly to misjudgment by the others in the use of power.

In the first destruction of Atlantis, a large portion of the area of the Sargasso Sea is said to have gone under, inundating a huge land mass that "would be considered a large continent." The breakup apparently produced large islands "with intervening canals, ravines, gulfs, bays and streams."

Prior to the breakup, Cayce speaks of the earth's rotation about the sun being different, revolving around Arcturus and the Pleiades. As the earth's axis shifted, people rose up and there were great movements toward the south during which the enormous animals which threatened to overrun the earth were fortuitously destroyed by the changing of the poles.

The second period of disturbance is given by Cayce as "some twenty-eight thousand years before Christ." In this catastrophe he tells how representatives of Atlantis fled the land and settled in what is now Yucatan. According to the readings, they fled in airships as well as water craft.

Elsewhere Cayce describes aircraft "lifted by gases," and pleasure vehicles "that pass along close to the earth," as well as craft that traveled on and under the water.

To power these craft at a distance, Cayce describes a mysterious cylindrical glasslike stone placed in an oval building where it could be activated by the sun's rays to produce phenomenal energy, which the Atlanteans had apparently learned to broadcast.

Cayce says that knowledge of how to construct such a "mighty firestone" was taken to Yucatan, where it was preserved, the records of the manner of the construction of the stone being secreted in three places in the earth: "in the sunken portion of Atlantis, or Poseidia, where a portion of the temples may yet be discovered, under the slime of ages of the sea water—near what is known as Bimini . . . And in the

Controversial part of the so-called Bimini Wall believed by some first-rank European geologists to be a man-moved megalithic structure, but which Florida geologists believe to be a natural formation of beach-rock. Now in about eighteen feet of water, it appears from recent corings by geologists to have been above water some eight thousand years ago.

temple records that were in Egypt . . . Also the records that were carried to what is now Yucatan."

Much of Cayce's evidence is either corroborated or complemented by the research of Robert B. Stacy-Judd, who belives that the people of the Cro-Magnon invasion of Europe in 23,000 B.C. were also Atlanteans, and that another large wave came about 14,000 B.C. He says the Cro-Magnons were a tall well-built people with long skulls, fine foreheads, of light brown or red complexion, "one of the finest peoples, mentally and physically, that the world has ever known."

According to Stacy-Judd, the Cro-Magnons brought with them to Europe a mixed bag of assets, including the art of pyramid building, witchcraft, the cult of the phallus, and wor-

Teobert Maler obtained this depiction of an Atlantean cataclysm from a bas-relief in a remote and, at that time, unknown spot deep in the jungle of Yucatan. The relief shows a volcano erupting, a pyramidal temple crumbling, land sinking, men drowning, and a survivor fleeing by boat. The original of the photograph is in the possession of Robert B. Stacy-Judd, who suggests that when, between 200 and 500 B.C., the last of a great Atlantean empire vanished beneath the waves of the Atlantic Ocean, the remnant of her highly cultured people, last of the root Atlanteans, fled hurriedly to Yucatan and Central America, bringing with them—among numerous other expressions of a great civilization—the highly developed art of symmetrical pyramid building, and were thereafter known as the Maya.

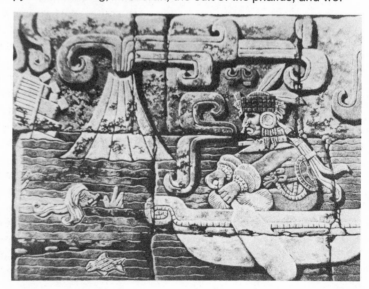

ship of Osiris. He says that all the ancient races of Europe, with the exception of the Negro, claim that their ancestors arrived in boats from a land which sank beneath the waters toward the setting sun or west, and that with each successive subsidence of the disintegrating Atlantis, escaping hordes invaded the shores of the Mediterranean, slowly pushing their way eastward toward the fertile lands of Egypt, already settled by colonists of their own mother country.

To Cayce, the escape from Atlantis was not a random scattering but an organized movement to colonize lands that were carefully chosen. Several readings indicate there were already inhabitants in the Yucatan area when the Atlanteans first arrived, though these were less developed than the newcomers.

Cayce refers to considerable temple activity in Yucatan by the refugee Atlanteans, with temples set up to propagate the original faith and to preserve the "knowledge that would make for a unifying of the understandings as to the relationships of man to the creative forces." From Cayce's readings it appears that the Atlantean civilization was well advanced and that their art reappeared in Yucatan as a full-blown accomplishment.

The Canary Islands as depicted by Churchward.

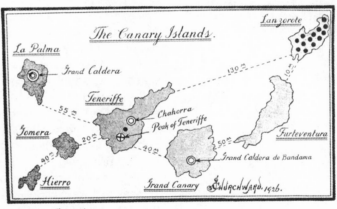

Stacy-Judd believes that fleeing Atlanteans became the Cro-Magnons who settled on the Canary Islands. Humboldt and Bonpland searched for remains of ancient Atlantis among the extinct volcanoes of the Canaries.

379

Plato described the capital of Atlantis as being divided into alternate zones of land and water.

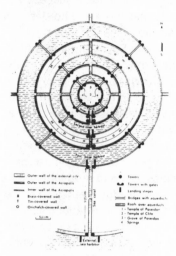

Plan of the Atlantean capital as it appears in Soviet geologist N. F. Zhirov's book *Atlantis*.

Cayce tells of a leader named Iltar with a group of followers, "members of the worship of the One," who came westward and entered what is now a portion of Yucatan to develop their civilization as it had been on Atlantis. He says the first temples that were erected by Iltar and his followers were destroyed at the period of the final collapse of Atlantis, when there were great physical changes also in the contours of Yucatan. In one of his readings he adds that these temples built by the Atlanteans in Yucatan were being rediscovered in the 1930s, saying that many of the second and third civilizations may never be discovered because to do so "would destroy the present civilization in Mexico."

Corroborating Le Plongeon, Cayce says that ruins of temples still stand in Yucatan which contain secrets pertaining to the occult. As for the temple of Iltar, he says it is located on a portion of the land that now rests beneath the waters, but may yet rise again.

Cayce categorized the two types of remains from Atlantis as "stones that were circular" and "altars upon which there were the cleanings of the bodies of individuals." The readings state that the altars were not for human sacrifice. Instead, the bodies of those to be "cleansed" were placed on the altars so that such undesirable qualities as hate, malice, and self-indulgence could be removed "through the rise of initiates from the sources of the light."

The altars apparently served as focal points for spiritual forces brought from "the source of light," the cleansing being accomplished through a sort of spiritual healing.

Partly corroborating Le Plongeon, Cayce says small numbers of Egyptians also came to Yucatan, where they prepared "The Temple Beautiful" in which song and music were used to make "for losing even the association with the body" except for the body's vibrations which "make for light, then become color, then become tone, then become activity . . ."

380

With the music, there was dance which "enabled those with the disturbing forces and influences to become more erect, upright in body, in thought, in activity . . . being in the world, yet not of the world . . ."

Cayce says the "children of the Law of One" could concentrate their thoughts for the use of the universal forces, with the guidance of what today would be called the saints. Through concentration of the group mind, they were able to reach a higher level of consciousness which brought them into a fourth-dimensional consciousness, an out-of-body experience.

Stacy-Judd's romanticized version of the collapse of Atlantis. And Edgar Cayce's description of the events told in the strangely archaic language which issued from him when he fell into a trance.

The records in Egypt, says Cayce, contain "A record of Atlantis from the beginnings of those periods when the Spirit took form or began the encasements in that land, and the development of the peoples throughout their sojourn, with the record of the first destruction and the changes that took place in the land, with the record of the sojournings of peoples to the varied activities in other lands, and a record of the meetings of all the nations or lands for the activities in the destructions that became necessary with the final destruction of Atlantis and the buildings of the pyramids of initiation." According to Cayce, the Great Pyramid of Gizeh in Egypt was completed around 10,000 B.C. to be used as a temple of initiation for the White Brotherhood.

He speaks of the Atlanteans being able to transpose "those materials that did not pertain to themselves bodily, by that ability lying within each to be transposed in thought and body." He suggests that Atlanteans were not only able to move matter about the universe, but could move themselves in consciousness beyond the earth plane.

He speaks of the "full consciousness of the ability to communicate with or to be aware of the relationships of the Creative Forces and the uses of same in material environs," adding that during the age of Atlantis and Lemuria (or Mu) this brought destruction to man because of selfish use.

As for the Lost Tribes of Israel, Cayce confirms that a portion of them came into the southernmost portion of the United States, mixing with the refugees from Mu, then moved on to Mexico and Yucatan, but mostly to the central part near what is now Mexico City. He says they came much later than settlers from Atantis or Mu, but did add their influence, as re-recorded by the Mormons, to the cultural melange that had been gathering in Central America for thousands of years. He says they too came by boat, setting sail during those periods

Barbiero's Atlantis in Antarctica, with shifted pole.

By some ardent fan, Atlantis has been placed almost everywhere on the globe. It has even been placed in Antarctica in the area bathed by the Weddell Sea. In the book *Una Civiltà sotto Ghiaccio,* Italian author Flavio Barbiero maintains—with some cogent evidence—that the earth was struck by an asteroid or comet about 12,000 years ago, just about when Plato said that Atlantis sank. The ensuing cataclysm, says Barbiero, shifted the poles and caused Antarctica to be shrouded in a mile-thick mantle of ice. The same event, says Barbiero, caused the melting of the great Wisconsin icecap and the melting of the icecaps over parts of Scandinavia, Russia, Germany, Britain, and the Alps.

Taking as historic fact Plato's description of the sinking of Atlantis in a single night under the action of earthquakes and tidal waves, and as scientific evidence the carcasses of mammoths congealed with springtime food in their stomachs, Barbiero suggests that the cataclysm would have had to be sudden.

Barbiero postulates that a vast civilization with a high technology and a fleet of great trading ships flourished in Antarctica before the catastrophe; he believes the survivors from this civilization got away in ships to create colonies elsewhere. According to Barbiero, neolithic culture was not a civilized advance but a regression of Atlantean survivors who landed in various areas, gradually losing their original know-how. Barbiero believes that sophisticated Atlantean artifacts will be found beneath the icecap of Antarctica.

A preface to Barbiero's book by the director of the Italian Polar Geographic Institute, Silvio Zavatti, attests to the seriousness with which the thesis was received.

when there was the breaking up of the Tribes of Israel, and while "the rest were enslaved in the Persian land."

Several tests of the veracity of Cayce's prophecies have already turned in his favor. His prophecy about the recovery of the Quamran papers is quite breathtaking.

Though all of this is highly speculative material, hardly the makings of history, the data adduced by Churchward, Niven, and Cayce makes so much more sense and resolves so many apparent incongruities in what passes for history and prehistory that it should perhaps be pigeonholed rather than discarded a priori.

More tests are in the making. Between now and 1998, Cayce envisages another shifting of the poles with great upheavals. The earth, says Cayce, will be broken in many places, which he lists for the benefit of those who wish to listen to his

382

Barbiero's ancient Atlantean Continent.

Barbiero maintains that 15,000 years ago the seas were 130 meters lower and that the missing water was heaped up on what is now Europe and the northern part of the United States in the form of 80 million cubic kilometers of ice.

He rests his thesis primarily on the evidence of geologists that a large celestial body precipitated into the North Atlantic 10 to 12,000 years ago, and quotes Austrian geologist Otto H. Much to the effect that the body which weighed 2 billion tons landed near Florida, breaking into two large fragments. According to Much, this event occurred on June 5 of 8496 B.C. at 2000 hours local time.

Barbiero further maintains that because of the pull of the moon, the earth cannot maintain its axis of rotation constant to the ecliptic. He says the moon's pull makes the earth's tilt vary from 15 to 20 degrees over a period of about 20,000 years, causing more or less ice on the poles and glaciations that occur in cycles. Ten to twelve thousand years ago, says Barbiero, the earth was tilted no more than 4 to 5 degrees from the ecliptic.

Professor Cesare Emiliani, head of the Department of Geology at the University of Miami, has worked out a graph from deep-sea core samplings taken in the Gulf of Mexico which indicate glaciation and deglaciation in cycles of about 20,000 years over the past 700,000 years, with the last major deglaciation occurring in 11,600 B.C. when ice water pouring down the Mississippi Valley from the melting Wisconsin icecap caused the waters of the Caribbean to rise about 130 feet, at precisely the date given by Plato. Emiliani postulates that the ensuing flooding of low-lying coastal areas, many of which were inhabited by man, gave rise to the deluge stories common to many traditions.

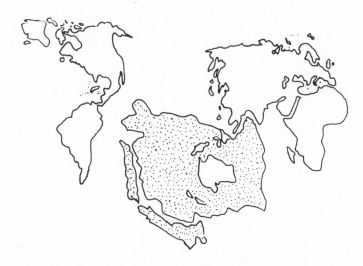

warnings. If any more of the events he has predicted come to pass, a closer look may be given to Cayce's descriptions of events purported to have occurred on this planet in remote antiquity. And an even closer look may be given to his descriptions of the spiritual religion of the Atlanteans, remnants of which were passed on to Yucatan and Central America for the avowed purpose of finding a better way to handle man's affairs upon this planet.

28. Therapeutic Theater

From the first reports of the Spaniards in Mexico it was evident that the stepped pyramids they encountered had been used for religious rituals but had long since degenerated into monuments of senseless slaughter. The Spaniards also found that the stadiumlike ball courts of the Indians appeared to have once had astronomical and cosmic overtones.

Edmond Bordeaux Szekely, philosopher, psychologist, and author of many books on ancient cultures, whose brilliantly intuitive work on Mexico is described in the prestigious *Handbook of Latin American Studies* as a "compendium of misinformation with unsubstantiated conclusions to explain Toltec, Aztec, and Maya cosmology," has, in fact, delved deep into the philosophy of ancient Mexico to produce a convincing analysis of the pyramid and ball-court rituals which indicates they were originally designed by initiate priests for religious dramas to convey to large audiences religious truths of cosmic import.

A Sanskrit and Aramaic philologist, whose Transylvanian forefather, Csoma de Kőrös, compiled the first grammar of the Tibetan language, Szekely claims to have deciphered the hermetic symbolism of the ancient Mesoamericans to show that their pictographs incorporate a philosophy of life similar to the world picture of the Sumerians and Persians, which interpreted the realities of the universe and gave expression to the strange forces within and surrounding man.

The predecessors of the Aztecs, says Szekely, believed that everything in the cosmos, including life and human consciousness, was brought about by a struggle between the two cosmic principles of Life and Death: a system similar to that of Zoroaster, or Zarathustra, in which Ormuzd, or Ahura Mazda,

Edmond Bordeaux Szekely.

The Life and Death sides of a single deity as they appear in an Aztec codex, with the symbols for the Aztec days of the month.

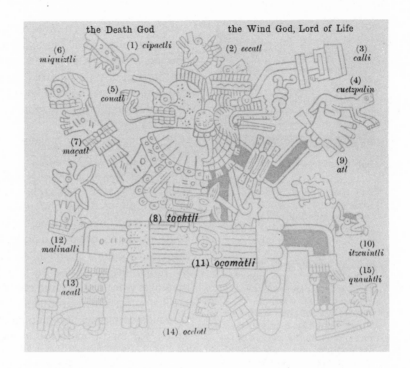

the Death God   the Wind God, Lord of Life

(6) miquiztli

(1) cipactli

(2) eecatl

(3) calli

(5) conatl

(4) cuetzpalin

(7) maçatl

(9) atl

(8) tochtli

(12) malinalli

(10) itzcuintli

(11) oçomàtli

(15) quauhtli

(13) acatl

(14) ocelotl

the holy spirit of Light, and Ahriman, the evil spirit of Darkness, waged war for man's soul—a war that constituted the history of the world.

In Mesoamerica, says Szekely, the spirit of Light and Life was symbolized by the plumed serpent Quetzalcoatl; his opponent, the spirit of Darkness and Death, by the jaguar or tiger called Tezcatlipoca.

At the center of this struggle, man, created free, could partake of either Life or Death, could make himself accessible to the influences of either good or evil. By his actions man could render service to, and thus strengthen, one or the other protagonist.

Aztec Tezcatlipoca.

Aztec depiction of Quetzalcoatl.

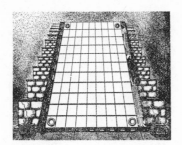

Ball Courts.

Both Brinton and Troncoso observed that the game of ball was intended by the Mesoamericans to represent the idea of the perpetual motion of the heavenly bodies. Tezcatlipoca, Lord of the Shining Mirror, Lord of the Nocturnal Heaven, was reflected in a myriad of mirrors each night throughout Mesoamerica. His priests, who called themselves "sons of the night," were associated with the divination of human destiny, which was linked with the movement of the stars.

Nuttall draws attention to the fact that the courts were called *tlach-tli,* which literally means "the looking place" or observatory, and the *tezca-tlachtli* is the obsidian mirror-observatory. The double tau-shaped courtyard or enclosure surrounded by a high wall with battlements, which at night was employed for observation, was employed by day for the national game of ball by figures depicted with obsidian mirrors.

Mexican astronomers extensively used black obsidian mirrors as an aid to astronomical observation by means of reflection. Nuttall says that besides mirrors on the summits of temples and mountains, the codices depict square columns, placed on an elevation, faced with a broad band of polished obsidian. The latter, says Nuttall, if properly oriented, would have served as an admirable means of registering the periodic return of

To dramatize the struggle for man's soul between the forces of "good" and "evil," the ancient Mesoamerican priests, according to Szekely, devised a religious ritual to be enacted on the steps of the great pyramids, a ritual that was not mere pageant, but combined a knowledge of the science of the time, of astronomy, philosophy, psychology, and of social organization.

All the pyramids in Mesoamerica so far discovered, says Szekely, contain symbols of the two cosmic principles of Life and Death: in Mexico, Yucatan, Guatemala, and Honduras all the stepped pyramids leading to the sky contain representations of the plumed serpent and of the jaguar.

Later the ritual was transferred to the flat surface of a ball court, gradually degenerating into a mere display of athletic prowess or bloody sacrifice. As Szekely reconstructs the original ritual, largely on the basis of the extant codices, the pyramids were divided into eleven horizontal levels and nine vertical ones, which produced ninety-nine squares. Larger pyramids consisted of multiples of this basic system, a pattern which was then transferred to the flat ball courts.

	1	2	3	4	5	6	7	8	9	
·‖					a					11
‖				c		b				10
∶			f		e		d			9
∶		k		j		h		g		8
∶|										7
·|					M					6
			K		J		H		G		5
∶			F		E		D			4
∶				C		B				3
∶					A					2
·										1
	·	· ·	· · ·	· · · ·	——	·	· ·	· · ·	· · · ·	

A. Grass — Malinalli — Life
B. Feathered Serpent-Quetzalcoatl-Creator
C. Adobe House — Calli — Preserver
D. Flower — Xochitl — Joy
E. Dog — Itzcuintli — Love
F. Deer — Mazatl — Peace
G. Sun — Ollin — Movement and Power
H. Lizard — Cuetzpallin — Fertility
J. Eagle — Cuauhtli — Air and Wisdom
K. Water — Atl — Source of Life
M. Man

a. Skull — Miquiztli — Death
b. Crocodile — Cipactli — Idleness
c. Vulture — Cozcaquautli — Spoiler
d. Reed — Acatl — Emptiness
e. Jaguar — Ocelotl — Hatred
f. Monkey — Ozomatli — Inferior Man
g. Rabbit — Tochtli — Weakness
h. Flint — Tecpatl — Barrenness
j. Windstorm — Ehecatl — Violence and Ignorance
k. Rainstorm — Quiahuitl — Violence and Destruction

planets, stars and constellations to certain positions; they would have been reflected on the polished surface, as in a frame. Thus the obsidian mirror became the symbol of Mexican Star Cult adherents. Small mirrors of polished pyrite—used to concentrate rays of the sun to light sacred fires at noon on the days of the vernal equinox and summer solstice—were the symbol of the Sun Cult.

TLA **MAN**

Father Duran's depiction of various masks and costumes worn by Mexican dancers for rituals, the original purpose of which was lost.

(Facing page)
Szekely's arrangement of players on the pyramid steps.

As with Protagoras, who proclaimed that man was the measure of all things, so in ancient Mexico man stood at the center of the pyramid (on the sixth horizontal and fifth vertical position) represented by a priest wearing a human mask. Szekely shows that in the codices the numbers representing the rising steps were written horizontally and those representing the squares were written vertically. On the various squares stood the twenty basic characters of the religious drama, ten representing the forces of Life, ten representing the forces of Death, each wearing an appropriate mask symbolizing the force or power represented. Szekely says the masks, which are still worn by dancers at festivals in central and south Mexico, are survivals of these ancient pyramid rites, whose original significance has long been lost.

The object of the drama, in which actions had deep symbolic meaning, similar to the rituals of Freemasonry, was for man, at the center of the stage, to rise toward the summit of the pyramid, aided by the forces of Life embattled against the forces of Death, which tended to drive him down and off the bottom rung of the pyramid.

If man could triumph over the forces of Death and destruction so as to reach the summit of the pyramid, the spiritual part of him could then triumph over the force of gravity and he would become transfigured into the light of Quetzalcoatl, the evening star.

The pyramids, says Szekely, were invariably designed in such a way as to have a level which formed an angle with the motions of Venus. In this game, man's ceasing to be subject to planetary gravity meant a true return to the stars, a reunion with the cosmic ocean of life.

According to Laurette Sejourné, when the internal war in the human heart was resolved by reconciliation of the two opposite forces symbolized by water and fire, man "could bud and flower" from fleshly matter into spirit, finally freeing himself from duality—a shedding of man's earthly clothing to free his spirit from his mortal body.

To Sejourné, Teotihuacan was the place where the serpent learned miraculously to fly, that is, "where the individual, through inner growth, attained the category of a celestial being."

From the scant remains of two palaces within the Citadel area, recently excavated and measured by Drucker, he suggests that there may have been two rulers at Teotihuacan, one the head of the rite of the feathered serpent, or Quetzalcoatl, who lived in one palace, and a second ruler, presumably identified with Tezcatlipoca, who lived in what Drucker euphemistically calls the "other" palace.

In Szekely's analysis, if man were brought downscale and forced off the bottom of the pyramid, he would be devoured by jaguars and disintegrated, losing his individuality and having to start another cosmic cycle.

Like the Persians, says Szekely, the Mesoamericans believed that at death a body disintegrated and returned to "the reign of gravity"—the entropy of modern science. But each birth of an individual or organism was considered by the Persians to be a triumph of Life over Death. In Mesoamerica, Quetzalcoatl was considered the germ, the cause of germination in a seed, of the birth of an animal or a child, of the production of ever more abundant life. He was the Attis, Adonis, Thammuz, Bacchus, Dionysus, Osiris, and quite possibly the Pan of the Western World.

Quetzalcoatl was also seen as a unifying symbol which could achieve the union of opposites: of heaven and earth, morning and evening star, matter and spirit, light and darkness, male and female, good and evil, which, in their separate forms were Quetzalcoatl and Tezcatlipoca. The conflict between them, says Indianist Frank Waters, and their reconciliation, were what gave movement and life to man and the universe.

Out of the interplay of these opposing forces rose the world of being, change, and movement, conceived as the continuous transformation of one force into the other.

In Szekely's reconstruction of the ritual on the Mexican pyramids, a priest, wearing the mask of man, or *tla,* as the Aztecs called him, would go up or down the steps, depending on whether his thoughts and actions supported the forces of Life or Death. If his thoughts and actions had favored Tezcatlipoca, he would go downscale; if they had favored Quetzalcoatl, he would move upscale. On the face of the pyramid, man could only move slantwise, like the rays of the sun, because it was believed that Ollin, the sun, was the source of all movement, and thus of the power behind both Quetzalcoatl and Tezcatlipoca.

According to Szekely's reconstruction, the deathly priests

of Tezcatlipoca occupied the higher steps of the pyramid, attempting to force man down, whereas the life-giving forces of Quetzalcoatl occupied the lower steps, hoping to raise man higher.

Coatl, the serpent, represented energy moving in spirals—the Kundalini of the Tantras or the wavelengths of modern science, which views the entire universe, from the smallest vibration in the atom to the longest wavelength in the supergalaxies, as fluctuating within a gamut of a mere 144–151 octaves.

Moving and undulant, the serpent in Mesoamerica symbolized life, power, planets, suns, solar systems, galaxies, ultragalaxies, and infinite cosmic space. The plumes, says Szekely, were an added symbol of the levity with which birds can overcome gravity better than other creatures. When the plumes were depicted folded within the circle formed by the snake's body, they signified matter in its latent form, potential, as it was before the creation of stars and solar systems. If the plumes were fanned out from the serpent, they represented the universe in manifestation, with all its created worlds, each plume symbolizing a basic element in the strength of nature—fire, earth, water, air.

Depicted with its tail in its mouth, the serpent represented infinity, eternity, no beginning, and no end. The symbolism was comparable to that of the Hindu cosmic cycles of Brahma. When Brahma sleeps the material universe is nonexistent. When Brahma wakes, all of creation comes into existence. When, after eons, Brahma sleeps again, the planets, solar systems, and all the energies of the cosmos revert to nothing.

The power of gravity and disintegration was represented by the jaguar Tezcatlipoca, who brought everything back to the kingdom of Death.

As with Goethe, the ideal of the Mesoamericans was the triumph of levity over gravity. The pyramids were the symbols of this triumph, of the ascension of man from the kingdom of Tezcatlipoca in dark caves under the earth, step by step, up to the light and wisdom of Quetzalcoatl, high above the earth.

In a ritual which expressed the cosmic life of man living in a universe governed by the absolute laws of Karma, every good move tended to free man from the slavery of gravity, leading him to levity, from which the jaguar could no longer hold him back.

To Irene Nicholson it was clear that the bloody ritual sacrifices of the Aztecs were a distortion of what must have once been an extraordinary vision of the place of man and of organic life in the universe.

She sees Quetzalcoatl as the wind god representing spirit freed from matter, yet in his totality as a composite figure

The lively world of Quetzalcoatl in Szekely's interpretation of ten of the Aztec
day-signs.

THE WORLD OF QUETZALCOATL

SYMBOL	AZTEC NAME	ENGLISH NAME	SYMBOLIC MEANING
	MALINALLI	GRASS	LIFE
	COATL	FEATHERED SERPENT	CREATOR
	CALLI	HOUSE	PRESERVER
	XOCHITL	FLOWER	JOY
	ITZCUINTLI	DOG	LOVE
	MAZATL	DEER	PEACE
	OLLIN	SUN	POWER
	CUETZPALLIN	LIZARD	FERTILITY
	CUAUHTLI	EAGLE	AIR
	ATL	RAIN	WATER

"describing the many orders of matter in creation; a kind of ladder with man at the center, but extending downward into animal, water and mineral, and upward to the planets, the life-giving sun, and the god creators."

On the lowest rung of the pyramid, the first Quetzalcoatl supporter of man, according to Szekely, was what the Aztecs called *malinalli,* or grass, because grass grows on the surface of the earth where the basic life-giving elements of air, water, earth and sun are united. Grass also revives perennially, so it was considered the source of renewed vitality, a giver of sustenance to all creatures, which permitted them to take the first step in the conquest of gravity.

In opposition to grass, on the top level of the pyramid stood a skull or death's-head, representing disintegration and the return to gravity. Man was depicted as seesawing between these parameters.

The second negative or downward force was represented by the crocodile, known to the Aztecs as *cipactli,* a creature which lounges in the sun, creating nothing. On the other hand, because life has both the aspects of creation and preservation, a small adobe house, known as *calli* to the Aztecs, represented the values of conservation, of planting, of watering gardens, of painting pictures, of building new things, of preventing deterioration, deterioration being symbolized by a vulture, quick to spot death and corruption.

A stylized flower, *xochitl,* was considered gaily positive: its color, shape, fragrance, and the lovely effect it had on humans, representing joy. Its reverse was the cane, representing vacuity.

Disinterested love and devoted affection were symbolized by the dog, *itzcuintli.* In Mexico, where there were few domestic animals before the arrival of the Spaniards—no cows, horses, donkeys, or mules—the dog was man's most constant companion, the only possession which accompanied a Toltec to the next world.

In opposition to the dog was *ocelotl,* the meanest of killers, enemy to all animals, obliged to make a kill every day to survive.

To symbolize peace, the Mesoamericans had *mazatl,* the deer, an animal which eats only plants and vegetation, never attacks other animals, is pacific, inoffensive, and the ideal of a tranquil life.

For inferior humanity the symbol was a monkey, for weakness a rabbit, for fertility a lizard or newt, because it was also considered alchemically close to the basic elements of earth, water, air, fire. For sterility the Aztecs chose the flintstone; for wisdom, because of its high point of view and its airiness—Quetzalcoatl's favorite element—Mesoamericans chose

The ten Aztec day-signs of the deadly world of Tezcatlipoca, according to Szekely.

SYMBOL	AZTEC NAME	ENGLISH NAME	SYMBOLIC MEANING
	MIQUIZTLI	SKULL	DEATH
	CIPACTLI	CROCODILE	IDLENESS
	COZCAQUAUHTLI	VULTURE	SPOILER
	ACATL	CANE	EMPTINESS
	OCELOTL	JAGUAR	HATRED
	OZOMATLI	MONKEY	INFERIOR MAN
	TOCHTLI	RABBIT	WEAKNESS
	TECPATL	FLINT	STERILITY
	EHECATL	WINDSTORM	VIOLENCE
	QUIAHUITL	RAINSTORM	EMOTION

the eagle. Violence and ignorance were symbolized by the pointlessly destructive force of *ehecatl,* the hurricane. Water, considered the font of life, was symbolized by three drops of. water; its opposite, a devastating torrential rain, by *quiahuitl,* the monsoon. Such is Szekely's interpretation of the ancient symbols. With just ten positive ones the Mesoamericans were able to represent the Life powers of vitality, creativity, conservation, gaiety, love, peace, power, fertility, wisdom, and eternal life; on the negative side stood the ten deadly forces of sloth, corruption, vacuity, hatred, inferiority, weakness, sterility, violence, and ignorant destructiveness.

The purpose of each ritual on the pyramid steps was to drum into the audience what was considered an essential moral: the fact that as man faces each and every problem in life, the result depends entirely on his own thoughts and actions; it is up to him whether he rises toward the stars or slips to the underworld. The audience was shown that with freedom of choice man has responsibility for his own actions, that a man's past actions affect his future, and that man, subject to the inviolable laws of the universe, determines his destiny by his thoughts and actions, by his positive or negative output. Man can create more abundance, or more destruction, he can be full of appreciative joy, or empty as a reed. He can love or hate. He can have fertility, wisdom, and the font of life, or sloth, corruption, and death.

Szekely reconstructs the ritual in which a high priest, positioned on a platform on the summit of the pyramid, announced to the accompaniment of drumbeats to the crowd below the movement of each character from square to square on the pyramid steps, drums and voice being loud enough for an audience a mile away to participate in the ritual. Zelia Nuttall describes two kinds of drums: a large *huehuetl,* which emitted a loud, deep tone heard for miles, and a smaller portable drum suspended from the neck, which emitted a shrill piercing note employed as a signal.

At the opening of the drama, man would be in the center of the field; his object was to rise to the eleventh level and to avoid being pushed below the first. The ritual, says Szekely, was an actual trial of man for his good and evil deeds. Whereas today a man is judged for a crime by a judge and jury according to a labyrinthine code of laws, in Mesoamerica man was judged by the sum of his past deeds, good or evil, as searched out by two high priests, one looking for his deeds in support of Quetzalcoatl, the other for his deeds in support of Tezcatlipoca. If a man had watered a tree, mended a wall, or saved a bird, he got points for the Quetzalcoatl team; if he had killed, maimed, or hated, he got points for Tezcatlipoca.

For each point, a man was entitled to a small round object,

or *pelota*, originally made of stone and then of rubber, with a hole in the center so it could be strung on a thong. The *pelotas* were given to the players on the team with which he had cooperated.

In the ritual, when a masked player was reduced to a single ball he would have to retire from the game and could no longer help man either up or down. If a man had cooperated very little with the forces of Tezcatlipoca, that team would have few *pelotas* and would be forced to disappear from the stage, allowing the man to rise rapidly to the top.

With such a clear-cut world picture of Karmic law, it was easy for a man to harmonize his acts. Szekely says that during every moment of his experience the early Aztec, Toltec, Mayan, and presumably Teotihuacano would ask himself if what he was doing was in harmony with the positive, constructive principles of Quetzalcoatl or with the negative, destructive principles of Tezcatlipoca.

With just twenty symbols, says Szekely, it was easier for the priests of Mesoamerica to instill a moral code into society than it is for a modern judge to handle contemporary man with thousands of volumes of codified law.

Szekely's depiction of the horizontal ball game of King Netzahualcoyotl.

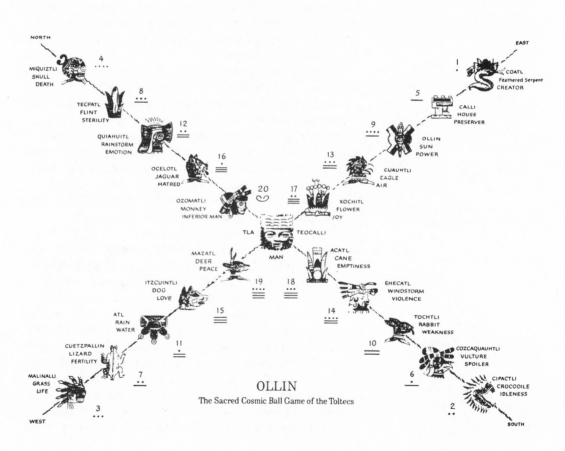

OLLIN

The Sacred Cosmic Ball Game of the Toltecs

Order in which the ball had to be moved to the winning goal at the center of the horizontal ball game, according to Szekely.

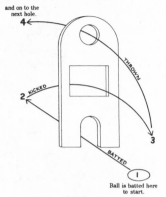

In Szekely's reconstruction of the game, the player had to bat, kick, and throw the ball through the apertures in a stone marker.

As Frank Waters put it: "The tonalamatl may thus be seen as a four-sided pyramidal structure of twenty day-signs arranged in five terraces of four steps each, symbolically showing the process of creation—the birth of spirit in matter, death to the world of forms, and the ascent of the spirit to a higher plane as was exemplified by Quetzalcoatl."

An interpretation of the Mayan procession of days as symbolizing man's cycle of birth, death, and resurrection is also given in Irene Nicholson's *Mexican and Central American Mythology.*

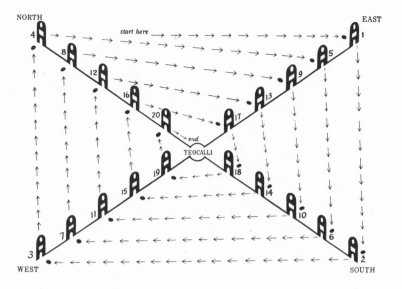

In due course the pyramid ritual was transferred to a level court that retained the pyramid format only when seen from a bird's-eye view: a cross with a central point, symbolizing the rays of the sun. In this ritual man still stood in the central position, symbolizing his fundamental unity with the creator. Here man was like a pawn on a checkerboard moved backward or forward by the force of his own past actions.

In different areas the ritual varied, says Szekely, until King Netzahualcoyotl, poet, philosopher, and lawgiver, compared by Szekely to King Solomon, synthesized the four games of Teotihuacan, Monte Alban, Tula, and Tenayuca into a single new game. In Netzahualcoyotl's game the twenty classical symbols were erected on the ball court in the form of stone stelae with three separate holes through which a ball had to be batted, kicked, and thrown.

Played with a rubber ball, the game was the evident prototype of several of our modern games, a mixture of croquet, baseball, soccer, and basketball, with scoring similar to golf, depending on the number of strokes it took to finish. This game, says Szekely, constituted "one of the most advanced judicial systems in the history of man." It took into account not simply the crime committed, but the entire past history of the person accused.

Whenever a person violated the law, a priest would go to his home and neighborhood, talk to his friends, neighbors, and family, and objectively collect accounts of his good and bad deeds. With sixty holes in the game to contend with, sixty good deeds could get the accused to the center of the field safely into the *teocalli,* "home of the gods." Anything less would bring him punishment, no matter how well he played.

395

Ball court in Copan as it is
estimated by archeologist
Proskouriakoff to have
existed in A.D. 600.

The beauty of the game, as described by Szekely, is the
emphasis placed by law on the pursuit of good deeds rather
than the punishment of evil, with an extra incentive for keeping physically fit in case of a trial.

Eventually the game degenerated into a spectacle, with
professional ballplayers touring the country to give exhibi-
tions of their skills and engender a fever for gambling.

Sometime earlier it may have been an even more sensa-
tional exhibition of paraphysical prowess.

Stephan Schwartz, author of *Psychic Archeology,* and Dr.
Lindsay Jacob, a psychiatrist in Pittsburgh, both students of
the Cayce readings as well as of the archeology of Mayaland,
surmise from the reliefs on the walls of Chichen Itza that
there may have been more to the game of Tlachtali than described by conventional archeologists. They suggest that the
original ball in play may have been of a substance more subtle than rubber, a sort of plasma on the order of a static
electric thunderball, or orgone, requiring a high degree of
initiation to move around the court and pass through a ring
high on the wall, possibly by means of such developed talents as those described by Carlos Castañeda in his qua-
trilogy on the metaphysical feats of the Yaqui bruja. Failure to
control such a fireball could have resulted in an out-of-body
experience, which, carried to excess, might have left the body
fulminated.

Archeologists concur that the game had deadly implica-

Aztec depiction of the
Pleiades according to
Sahagun.

The big dipper in an Aztec
codex.

Ball-game arenas among
the constellations, according
to Szekely.

tions and that the losers could forfeit their lives as easily as
they did on the pyramids. This too could have been a corruption of the original sport.

Several researchers have linked the ball courts with maps
of the heavens. According to Livio Stecchini, the great ball
court at Chichen Itza displays on its walls a cylindrical mercator projection of the path of the planets around the zodiac,
a 14-degree swath 7 degrees above and below the ecliptic
along which the planets move, a sort of ball court for the
gods, in which to dribble the planets.

Other researchers have suggested the ball courts dramatize a bigger game, the game of life in the entire universe,
symbolizing the various levels at which spirit creates and
handles matter. They suggest that the ring through which the
ball must pass may have represented the spot in the heavens
whence travelers came to this planet from their previous cosmic home.

Whereas the pyramid ritual appears to have been a dramatization of man's earthly struggle between the poles of spirituality and materiality, between gravity and levity, the ballcourt games may have dramatized the space adventures described by modern science-fiction writers—the exploits of
spirits operating bodies, robots, and spacecraft to and from
planets orbiting various stars in various galaxies—exploits
which appear less fictional since man has landed on the
moon, and since UFOs have been validated by tenured
academics.

L. Ron Hubbard, originator of Dianetics and Scientology,
produced fine data on such "space games" by regressing
individuals in reverie back on the time track to remote periods
during which they described invasions of this planet by
extraterrestrials. Hubbard added to this data from his
own out-of-body exploration of the universe and from his
own travel along the track of time. In the early 1950s

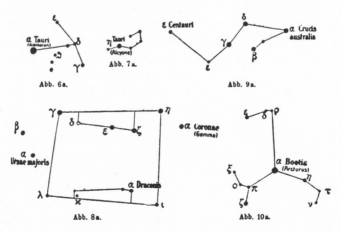

397

he used the electropsychometer—a galvanometer refined by Olin Mathieson—much like the standard lie detector, only more sensitive, and calibrated for longer trips, to probe the Jungian memories of the race going back thousands and thousands of years.

Delicate movements of the electropsychometer's needle subtly and fleetingly reflect the thought patterns of the subject, enabling the questioner to probe for memories heavily charged with emotion. These, when contacted and reviewed by the subject, appear to run in almost endless chains, revealing three-dimensional dramatic scenarios with full color, sound, and sensation, set in the most exotic surroundings, scattered through time and space. By this technique, any subject can become a potential Edgar Cayce, capable of projecting his point of view throughout the cosmos, a technique which enabled Hubbard to produce one of his more unorthodox but startling books: *A History of Man.*

In the "space opera" of the twilight world between science and fiction there is said to flourish a group of extraterrestrials known as the Brotherhood of the Serpent, familiar in terms of Mayan history. They are described as members of a Great White Brotherhood who arrived on earth from bases they had established on Mars and the moon during the Atlantean and Lemurian periods to set up mystery schools to teach humans how to free themselves from mortal coils. These Serpent People are described as a pro-evolutionary group, on whose instructions the original pyramids in Egypt and Central America are said to have been built.

G. I. Gurdjieff in his *Beelzebub's Tales to His Grandson* claims that the beings responsible for the occult school in which he was instructed in Central Asia—the ones who developed the Sufi movement—also had a base on Mars.

Psychics have described certain temples in Atlantis as being used by priests to encase spirits in human bodies so they might better learn to care for them, a process which apparently degenerated into a state of identification with the body in which they forgot who they were: a condition only to be remedied by other initiate priests who could get them out of their bodies to recognize the game—through initiation.

From the accumulated data on the rites of initiation in the mystery schools, it is clear that the initiate was led to see and be and know without a body, facing certain out-of-body terrors as illusions that could be handled by postulate and will. Initiation was a rebirth to the world of levity and the realization that no harm can befall a spirit other than that which it does to itself, mostly by willing harm to others, or by restricting, for the perverse enjoyment of the sensation, its own unlimited powers. Once initiated, a person could be in this world but no longer of it, see it as an entrancing game in which a player can be trapped by believing he is a body, or by agreeing he must hurt when the body hurts, or die when the body dies, despite the fact that such a notion is easily disproved by a hypnotist in twenty minutes, when pain can be seen to be a subjective imposition on the body, and that one can be and see without the bonds of space and time.

Any Indian taking peyote can tell you that all are one, and each is but a point of view. Out of body, anyone can see, and be, like Edgar Cayce, a thousand or a million miles away.

Frank Waters, in his *The Book of the Hopi,* says the Hopis still claim that the Maya were helped by extraterrestrials or interstellar people. He says the Cochines also claim to have come from outer space and to have helped the Maya.

Dogon tribesmen in central west Africa have reported contact with blue-skinned men, purportedly extraterrestrials from Sirius—a fascinating subject dealt with in great detail by Robert K. G. Temple in his *The Sirius Mystery.* All over the world and throughout history there have been reports of blue-skinned men who are somehow related to the star Sirius. There were blue-skinned gods in the Vedas, blue-skinned men of northern Japan and the Marianas, blue-skinned men of Wales.

Sirius is a blue-white star, bigger and hotter than our sun, thirty-four times as bright, with eight times the mass. In occult literature, it is said to act as a cosmic throat center for this area of the galaxy, whereas the Pleiades act as the heart.

Lao Russell, wife of the extraordinary mystic writer Walter Russell (described as a modern Leonardo da Vinci), says she was in touch with a group who said that Sirians had come to Atlantis about 20,000 years ago and left important records which, with the sinking of Atlantis, were entrusted to Phoenicians who took them to Brazil, where they remained sealed in a cave in the cliffs marked by great Phoenician petroglyphs.

Sensitives say the Serpent People are due to return to earth in 2011 to help create a world government. But all is not so simple. In opposition to the Brotherhood of the Serpents, the grand opera of space has its heavies: members of the "Marcab Confederation." Marcab, or Markab, is a star in the constellation Pegasus. It is located in the same general direction as the stars belonging to the group reconstructed in a three-dimensional model by Marjory Fish from Betty Hill's hypnotically described star maps of the area seen while aboard a space ship.

Those spacemen are said to be monitoring this planet

preparatory to manifesting themselves en masse, and to be sending ahead scouts in human bodies to prepare the way.

Some individuals, when regressed or out of body, describe the Marcabs as having been in existence some 200,000 years, operating meat bodies and androids, or robots modeled to look like human beings, but who have lost the power to crawl out of their present condition. In this semi-degenerate state they can apparently only try to control others and drag them to their level.

Subscribers to the Marcab-Serpent People theory envisage a struggle between extraterrestrials for the souls, minds, and bodies of terrestrials, with the Marcabs using control methods to keep humans ignorant and enslaved while the Serpent People use initiatory methods to help humans recover the knowledge of their true spiritual identity.

Identity with a body can lead to easy blackmail by a controller who wishes to enslave an individual simply by guaranteeing the requirements of shelter, food, sex, and security. Hence the various attempted routes of escape via fasting, abstinence, free love, and vagabondage. Hubbard's remedy is to recover the certainty of one's spiritual essence and and learn to operate, successfully and at will, with or without a body.

Ball, hole, and body games seem to predominate in this particular corner of the universe.

Much of the violent history and pre-history of this planet could rationally be accounted for by such a hypothetical conflict between the Marcab-type "controllers" and the Serpent People "liberators," or the roles could be reversed.

For those who find it hard to postulate the existence, even in space, of friend and foe on the Quetzalcoatl and Tezcatlipoca order, it is suggested that a cosmic game, just

400

like any earthly game, requires levels of "friend" and "foe," stacked in alternating harmonics, otherwise the layers will coalesce until eventually everyone will be on one side—and the game will end.

As Hubbard points out, to have a game you must have barriers and delimitations—arbitrary limits. One can hardly kick a goal where there are no goalposts. To have surprise and variety, there must be something one does not know, or temporarily hides from oneself. To have a contest there must be opponents. To have a winner, someone must suffer defeat. Thus games can lead to falls, and harder falls to forgetting it's a game and who invented it.

If all this sounds grossly farfetched, far from the point of a pyramid, it is no further than the substance of all myth and of most organized religion: it is the perennial subject of great art and literature; it is as much the source of *The Magic Flute* as of *A Midsummer Night's Dream.*

But whereas in Renaissance England the Ancient Wisdom was still preserved hermetically in the Temple and the Inns of Court to be dramatized for the Globe in Shakespeare's plays, elsewhere on the planet the prospect was less brilliant. In Spain and New Spain, with rack and pillar and stake, the Holy Office cast itself to eradicate the vestiges of wisdom, and those reflections of the game of life still dramatized upon the local temples—on the pyramids and ball courts of Mexico and Mesoamerica.

Bibliography

Acosta, Jorge R.

El Palacio del Quetzalpapalotl. Mexico: Instituto Nacional de Antropologia e Historia, 1964.

———

Esplendor del Mexico Antiguo. Mexico: Centro de Investigaciones Antropologicas de Mexico, 1959.

———

Exploraciones en Palenque 1967. Mexico: I.N.A.H., 1968.

———

Guia Oficiel de Teotihuacan. Mexico: I.N.A.H., 1965.

———

Thirteen Masterpieces of Mexican Archaeology. Mexico: Editoriales cultura y polis, 1938.

Adamson, David G.

The Ruins of Time. New York: Praeger, 1975.

Aguilar, Francisco de

Relación Breve de la Conquista de la Nueva España. Mexico: J. Porrua, 1954.

Alaman, Lucas

Historia de Mexico. Mexico: Carlos Pereyra, 1942.

Almaraz, Ramon

"Report on Teotihuacan" in *Archives de la Commision Scientifique du Mexique.* Paris: Imprimerie Impériale, 1865–1867.

Alva Ixtlilxuchitl, Fernando de

Horribles crueltades de los conquistadores de México. Mexico: A. Valdis, 1829.

———

Obras historicas. Edited by Alfredo Chavero. 2 vols. Mexico: Editora Nacional, 1952.

Alvarado Tezozomoc, Fernando

Cronica Mexicana. Mexico: Universidad nacional autonoma, 1943.

Alvarez Lopez, José

Física y Creacionismo. La Plata, Argentina: Almafuerte, 1960.

Anonymous Conquistador (companion of Hernan Cortes)

Narrative of Some Things of New Spain. Boston: Milford House, 1972.

Aranzabal, Fernando

"Preguntas Sin Respuesta de los que Descubrieron la Gruta Subterránea Bajo la Pirámide de Sol." *Excelsior.* Mexico: July 25, 1974.

Arochi, Luis E.

La Pirámide de Kukulcan. Mexico: Orion, 1976.

Aubin, J. M. A.

Memoire sur la Peinture Didactique. Paris: Imprimerie Nationale, 1885.

Aveni, Anthony F. et al.

Archeoastronomy in Pre-Columbian America. Austin: University of Texas, 1975.

Aveni, Anthony F. and Aden Meinel

Catalogue of Emission Lines in Astrophysical Objects. Tucson: Optical Sciences Center and Steward Observatory, 1968.

Baker, G. T. III, Hugh Harleston, Jr., Alfonso Rangel, Matthew Wallrath, Manuel Gaitan and Alfonso Morales.
"The Subterranean System of the Sun Pyramid at Teotihuacan: A Physical Description and Hypothetical Reconstruction." *XLI International Congress of Americanists.* Mexico City: September 3, 1974.

Baker, G. T. III
A Non-Euclidian Geometry. (MSS) Mexico: 1972.

Bancroft, Hubert Howe
The Early American Chroniclers. San Francisco: A. L. Bancroft, 1883.

——
History of Central America. San Francisco: The History, 1890.

——
Mexico. San Francisco: A. L. Bancroft, 1883–1888.

——
The Native Races of the Pacific States of North America. San Francisco: A. L. Bancroft, 1882.

Baradère, H. Abbé
Antiquités Mexicaines. Paris: Bureau des Antiquités Mexicaines, J. Didot l'aîné, 1834.

Barbiero, Flavio
Una Civiltà Sotto Ghiaccio. Milan: Nord, 1974.

Barrero, Vasquez and Sylvanus Morley
The Maya Chronicles. Washington: Carnegie Institute, 1949.

Batres, Leopoldo
A historic guide of the City of Mexico. Mexico: Mundial, 1935.

——
Anthropologie Mexicaine: ostéologie, 1898. "La Europea." Mexico: J. Aguilar Verra, 1900.

——
Antigüedades mejicanas falsificadores. Mexico: F. S. Soria, 1910.

——
Archaeological explorations in Escalerillas Street, City of Mexico. Mexico: J. Aguilar Vera, 1902.

——
Antropologia Mexicana. Mexico: Gobierno federal en el ex-arzobispado, 1890.

——
Arqueologia mexicana. Mexico: Gobierno federal en el ex-arzobispado, 1888 (1891).

——
Critica científica de la devastacion de los monumentos arqueologicas de Teotihuacán. Mexico: Artistica, 1922.

——
Diverse letters in the Archives of the I.N.A.H. Mexico: 1906–1908.

——
El nacimiento del General Porfirio Diáz. Mexico: 1925.

——
Exploración Arqueólogica del oriente del valle de Mexico. Mexico: Gante, 1903.

——
Exploraciónes en Huexotla, Texcoco y El Gavilan. Mexico: J. I. Guerrero, 1904.

——
Explorations of Mount Alban, Oaxaca. Mexico: Gante St. Press, 1902.

——
IV Halpilli: ciclo ó periodo de 13 años: piedra del aqua. Mexico: Gobierno federal en el ex-arzobispado, 1894.

——
La isla de sacrificios. Mexico: Tipografia economica, 1910.

——
La lápida arqueológica de Tepatlaxco-Orizaba. Mexico: F. S. Soria, 1905.

——
Recordatorio del General Diaz. Mexico: 1925.

——
The Ruins of Teotihuacan, or the Sacred City of the Toltecs. Mexico: Hull, 1906.

——
Teotihuacán, memoria que presenta Leo. Batres. Mexico: F. S. Soria, 1906.

——
Teotihuacán: o la ciudad sagrada de los Toltecas. Mexico: Talleres de la Escuela N de artes y oficios, 1889.

——
Visita a los monumentos arqueológicos de "la Quemada," Zacatecas. Mexico: F. Diaz de Leon, 1903.

Beals, Carleton
The Coming Struggle for Latin America. Philadelphia: Lippincott, 1938.

——
Porfirio Diaz, Dictator of Mexico. Philadelphia: Lippincott, 1932.

Bellamy, H. S.	Works.
Bellini, Giuseppi	*Due classici ispano-americani.* Milano: la Goliardica, 1962.
Belousov V. V.	*The Geological Structure of the Oceans.* Moscow: 1942.
———	*The Geological Structure and Development of Ocean Hollowing.* Moscow: 1955.
Benitez, Fernando	*The Century after Cortes.* Chicago: University of Chicago Press, 1965.
Benzoni, Girolamo	*La historia del mondo.* Venice: Rampazetto, 1565.
Bernal, Ignacio	*Exploraciones en Cuilapan de Guerrero, 1902–1954.* Mexico: I.N.A.H., 1958.
———	*Introducción a la arqueológia.* Mexico: Fondo Cultura Economica, 1952.
———	*Mesoamérica.* Mexico: 1953.
———	*Mexican Wall-paintings of the Maya and Aztec periods.* London: Collins, 1963.
———	*Mexico Before Cortes.* Garden City, N.Y.: Doubleday, 1963.
———	*The Olmec World.* Berkeley: University of California Press, 1969.
———	*Tenochtitlan en una isla.* Mexico: I.N.A.T., 1959.
———	*Teotihuacan.* Mexico: I.N.A.H., 1963.
Bird, Christopher and Peter Tompkins	*The Secret Life of Plants.* New York: Harper & Row, 1973.
Blasio, José Luis	*Maximiliano intimo.* Paris: Veuve de C. Bouvet, 1905.
Blom, Franz Ferdinand	*The Conquest of Yucatan.* Boston: Houghton Mifflin, 1936.
Blomberg, Rolf	*Latitude 0°.* Stockholm: Geber, 1960.
Boas, Franz	*Anniversary Volume.* New York: G. E. Stechert, 1906.
Boland, Charles M.	*They All Discovered America.* New York: Doubleday, 1961.
Bossi, Luigi	*Histoire de Christophe Colombe.* Paris: A. Boulland, 1825.
Boturini Benaducci, Lorenzo	*Idea de una nueva historia general de la america septentrional.* Mexico: I. Escalante, 1871.
Bowditch, Charles Pickering	*Mexican and Central American Antiquities, Calendar Systems and History.* Washington: U.S. Government Printing Office, 1904.
———	*The Numeration, Calendar Systems and Astronomical Knowledge of the Mayas.* Cambridge: Cambridge University Press, 1910.
———	*On the Age of Maya Ruins.* New York: Putnam, 1901.
———	*The Temple of the Cross of the Foliated Cross and of the sun at Palenque.* Cambridge: Cambridge University Press, 1906.
———	*Was the beginning of the Maya month numbered zero (or twenty) or one?* Cambridge: Cambridge University Press, 1901.
Brasseur de Bourbourg, Charles Etienne	*Essai historique sur les sources de la philologie Mexicaine.* Paris: 1858.
———	*Histoire des Nations Civilisées du Mexique et de l'Amérique Centrale.* Paris: A. Bertrand, 1857–1859.
———	*Histoire primitive du Mexique dans les monuments egyptiens.* Paris: 1864.
———	*Lettre à M. Leon de Rosny sur la découverte de documents relatifs à la haute antiquité américaine.* Paris: Amyot, 1869.
———	*Lettres pour servir d'introduction à L'histoire primitive des nations civilisées de l'Amérique Septentrionale. Addressées a M. le duc de Valmy.* Mexico: M. Murguia, 1851.
———	*Manuscrit Troano.* Paris: Imprimerie Impériale, 1869–1870.
———	*Monuments anciens du Mexique.* Paris: A. Bertrand, 1866.

———	*Quatre Lettres sur Mexique.* Paris: Maisonneuve, 1868.
———	*Recherches sur les ruines de Palenque etc. avec dessins de M. de Waldeck.* Paris: A. Bertrand, 1866.
———	*S'il existe des sources de l'histoire primitive du Mexique dans les monuments egyptiens et de l'histoire primitive de l'Ancien Monde dans les monuments américaines.* Paris: Maisonneuve, 1864.
———	*Des Sources de l'histoire primitive du Mexique et l'amérique centrale.* Paris: A. Durand, 1864.
———	*Somaire des voyages scientifiques et des travaux de géographie, d'histoire, d'archéologie et de philologie américaine.* St. Cloud: Madame veuve Belin, 1862.
———	*Voyage sur Isthme de Tehuantepec.* Paris: A Bertrand, 1861.
———	*Popol Vuh.* Paris: A. Bertrand, 1861.
Brinton, Daniel G.	*The Books of Chilan Balam.* Philadelphia: Stern, 1882.
———	*Essays of an Americanist.* Philadelphia: Porter and Coates, 1890.
———	*Maya Chronicles.* Philadelphia: D. G. Brinton, 1882.
Brunhouse, Robert L.	*In Search of the Maya.* Albuquerque: University of New Mexico Press, 1973.
———	*Sylvanus Morley and the World of the Ancient Mayas.* Norman: University of Oklahoma Press, 1971.
Bry, Theodor de	*America.* Frankfort: 1599.
Bullock, William	*Six Months Residence and Travels in Mexico.* London: John Murray, 1824.
Burland, Cottie Arthur and Werner Forman	*Feathered Serpent and Smoking Mirror.* New York: Putnam, 1975.
Burland, Cottie Arthur	*Montezuma, Lord of the Aztecs.* London: Weidenfeld and Nicholson, 1973.
———	*The Selden roll.* Berlin: Verlag Gebr. Mann, 1955.
Cabrera, Paul Felix	*Description of an Ancient City Discovered near Palenque.* Translation of del Rio. London: 1822.
Calderon, Hector M.	*La Ciencia Matematica de los Mayas.* Mexico: Editorial Orion, 1966.
———	*Clave fonética de los Jeroglífigos Mayas.* Mexico: Editorial Orion, 1962.
Calderon de la Barca, Frances E.	*Life in Mexico During a Residence of Two Years in That Country.* New York: Dutton, 1931.
Camelo Aredondo, Rosa de Lourdes	*Historiografía de la matanza de Cholula.* Mexico: 1963.
Campbell, John	*The Spanish Empire in America.* Folkestone, England: Daissons of Pall Mall, 1972.
Carli, Giovanni conte	*Lettres Américaines.* Paris: Buisson, 1788.
Carlson, Hohn B.	"Did the Olmec Possess a Magnetic Lodestone Compass? An Analysis of a Hematite Artifact from San Lorenzo, Veracruz Mexico." *XLI International Congress of Americanists.* Mexico City: September, 1974.
Carmichael, Elizabeth	*The British and the Maya.* London: Trustees of the British Museum, 1973.
Carnac, Pierre	*Les Conquerants du Pacifique.* Paris: Robert Laffont, 1975.
Carrillo, Julian	*Pre-Sonido 13.* San Luis Potosi: Escuela Industrial Militar, 1930.
———	*Sonido 13.* Mexico: Talleres Graficos de la Nacion, 1948.
Casas, Bartolomé de las	*Obras Escogidas.* Madrid: Atlas, 1957–1958.
———	*Thirty Propositions.* (In Spanish) Spain: 1522.
Caso, Alfonso	*Los Calendarios Prehispanicos.* Mexico: Instituto de Investigaciones Historicas, UNAM, 1967.

————	*Contribución de las culturas indigenas de Mexico a la cultura mundial.* Mexico: Sec. de educación publica, 1946.
————	*Culturas mixteca y zapoteca.* Mexico: Encuadernables el Nacional, 1942.
————	*Exploraciones en Mitla.* Mexico: Talleras graficos de la Ofi. de Puls. y prop. de la S., 1936.
————	*Las exploraciones en Monte Alban temporada 1931–1932.* Mexico: Mundial, 1832.
————	*Exploraciones en Oaxaca.* Mexico: Editorial Cultura, 1938.
————	"Las Medidas del Calendarion Azteca." *Revista de Estudios Historicos.* Vol. 2, No. 4. Mexico: Edition Cultura, 1928.
	El Puebla del Sol. Mexico: Fondo Cultura Economica, 1963.
————	*The Religion of the Aztecs.* Mexico: Central News, 1937.
————	*Thirteen Masterpieces of Mexican Archaeology.* Mexico: Editoriales Cultura y polis, 1938.
————	
Caso, Antonio	"Glifos Teotihuacanos." *Revista Mexicana de Estudios Antropologicas.* No. 15. Mexico: 1958–1959.
Castañeda, Francisco de	*Official Report to Philip II, 1580.* Translated by Zelia Nuttall. Cambridge, Mass.: Peabody Museum, 1926.
Casteñeda, Lenor, Warden, Fracy, St. Pries	*Relation des Trois Expeditions du Capitain Dupaix, 1805–1807.* Paris: 1834.
Castillo F., Victor M.	"Unidades Nahuas de Medida." *Estudios de Cultura Nahuatl.* Vol. 10. Mexico City: 1972.
Catherwood, Frederick	*Views of Ancient Monuments in Central America, Chiapas and Yucatan.* New York: Bartlett and Welford, 1844.
Cathie, Bruce L.	*Harmonic 33.* Wellington: Auckland Reed, 1968.
Cayce, Edgar	*Readings on Atlantis.* Selected by the A.R.E. Foundation. Virginia Beach: 1975.
————	*Edgar Cayce on Atlantis.* New York: Paperback Library, 1968.
Chakravorty, K. R.	"Appraisal of Scientific and Philosophical Concepts in Ancient India in the Light of the Theory of the Universal Wave." *Technology.* Vol. 5, No. 1. 1974.
Charnay, Désiré	*America Pintoresca.* Barcelona: Montauer y Simon, 1884.
————	*Les Anciennes Villes du Nouveau Monde.* Paris: Hachette, 1885.
————	*Cités et Ruines Américaines, Mitla, Palenque, Izamal, Chichen-Itza, Uxmal.* Paris: Gide, 1863.
————	*Codex Ramirez.* Paris: E. Roux, 1903.
————	*Hernando Cortes.* Paris: Hachette, 1896.
————	*Les Explorations de Téobert Maler.* Paris: Société des Américanistes, 1904.
————	*Le Mexique 1858–1861: Souvenirs et impressions du voyage.* Paris: E. Dentu, 1863.
————	*Notes d'histoire et d'archeologie Mexicaines.* Paris: Société des Americanistes, 1903.
————	*Les Ruines de Tuloom d'après John L. Stephens.* Paris: Société des Americanistes, 1906.
————	*A Travers les forêts vierges: aventures d'une famille en voyage.* Paris: Hachette, 1890.
————	*Viaje á Yucatan á finis de 1886.* Mérida: Revista de Merida, 1888.
Charpentier, Louis	*Les Mystères de la Cathédrale de Chartres.* Paris: Robert Laffont, 1966.
Chatelain, Maurice	*Nos Ancêtres Venus du Cosmos.* Paris: Robert Laffont, 1975.

Chavero, Alfredo	*Historia Antigua y de la conquista.* Barcelona: Espasa, 1888.
———	(Unsigned Article.) *Mexico través de los Siglos.* Mexico City: Ballesco, 1887–1889.
Chimalpahin Quauhtlehaunitzin, Domingo Francisco de San Anton Munos	*Das Memorial Breve acerca de la fundacion de la ciudad de Culhuacan und weitere ausgewahlte Teile aus den "Diferentes historias originales."* Stuttgart: W. Kohlhammer, 1958.
Churchward, Albert	*The Arcana of Freemasonry.* London: Allen and Unwin, 1915.
———	*The Origin and Evolution of Freemasonry.* London: Allen and Unwin, 1920.
———	*The Signs and Symbols of Primordial Man.* New York: Dutton, 1910.
Churchward, James	*Cosmic Forces as They Were Taught in Mu.* New York: Baker and Taylor, 1934.
———	*The Children of Mu.* New York: Washburn, 1931.
———	*The Lost Continent of Mu.* New York: Paperback Library, 1959.
———	*The Sacred Symbols of Mu.* New York: Washburn, 1938.
———	*The Lost Continent of Mu, Motherland of Man.* New York: W. E. Rudge, 1926.
Ciampi, Ignazio	*Il Gemelli.* Rome: Stab tip, di Marco L. Aureli, 1859.
Clavijero, Francisco Javier	*Historia Antigua de Mexico.* Mexico: Editorial Porrua S.A., 1945.
CODICES	*Codex Aubin.* Manuscripto Azteca de la Biblioteca real de Berlin. Oficina tip de la Secretaria de formento, 1902.
———	*Codex Boturini.* Tira de la Peregrinación Azteca. Mexico: Libreriá Anticuaria G. M. Echarriz, 1940.
———	*Codex Chimalpopocatl.* Anales de Cuauhtitlan. Mexico: I. Escalante, 1885.
———	*Codex Mendoza.* London: Waterlow, 1938.
———	*Codex Nuttall.* Ed. by Zelia Nuttall. New York: Dover, 1975.
———	*Codex Troano.* Mexico: Libreria Donceles No. 12.
Coe, Michael D.	*America's First Civilization.* New York: American Heritage, 1968.
———	*The Jaguar's Children.* New York: Museum of Primitive Art, 1965.
———	*Map of San Lorenzo.* New Haven: Yale University Press, 1968.
———	*The Maya.* London: Thames and Hudson, 1966.
———	*The Maya Scribe and his World.* New York: Grolier Club, 1973.
———	*Mexico.* New York: Praeger, 1962.
Cogulludo, Diego Lopez de	*Historia de Yucatan.* Madrid: 1688.
Cole, J. H.	*Determination of the Exact Size and Orientation of the Great Pyramid of Giza.* Cairo: Government Press, 1925.
Collin, Rodney	*The Theory of Celestial Influence.* London: Stuart and Watkins, 1968.
Cortes, Hernan	*Five Letters, 1519–1526.* New York: Norton, 1962.
———	*Letters from Mexico.* New York: Grossman, 1971.
———	*The Conquest of Mexico.* Philadelphia: David Hogan, 1801.
Coto, Thomas	*Vocabularia de la lengua Cakchiquel.* London: W. E. Gates, 1913.
Cruz, Laudacio de la	*Teotihuacán, una Sinfonia.* Mexico: Editorial Orion, 1968.
Culbert, T. Patrick	*The Lost Civilization: The Story of The Classic Maya.* New York: Harper & Row, 1974.
Deuel, Leo	*Conquistadors Without Swords.* New York: St. Martin, 1967.
Diaz Bolio, José	*La Serpiente Emplumada.* Merida: Registro de Cultura Yucateca, 1955.
Diaz del Castillo, Bernal	*The Bernal Diáz Chronicles.* Garden City, N.Y.: Doubleday, 1956.
Diaz Solis, Lucila	*La Flor Calendrica de Los Mayas.* Merida: C.E.D.A.M., 1966–1968.

Donnelly, Ignatius	*Atlantis: The Antedeluvian World.* New York: Gramercy, 1949.
Dow, J. W.	"Astronomical Orientation at Teotihuacan." *American Antiquity.* 1967.
Drewitt, R. Bruce	"Data Bearing on Urban Planning at Teotihuacan." *American Anthropological Association Current Research Report.* Toronto: 1969.
Drewitt, R. Bruce and René Millon	*The Pyramid of the Sun at Teotihuacan.* Philadelphia: American Philosophical Society, 1965.
Drucker, R. David	*Renovating a Reconstruction: The Ciudadela at Teotihuacan, Mexico.* Doctoral Thesis. University of Rochester, 1974.
Dupaix, Guillermo	*Antiquités Mexicaines.* Paris: Bureau des Antiquités Mexicaines, J. Didot l'aîné, 1934.
———	*Expediciones acerca de los antiguos monumentos de la Nueva España.* Madrid: J. Porrua Turanzas, 1969.
Duran, Diego	*Historia de las Indias de Nueva-Espana.* Mexico: Editora Nacional, 1951.
Dusaert, Louis Edouard Joseph	*La Carie Américaine en civilisation de l'antique Egypte d'après les documents de M. l'Abbé Brasseur de Bourbourg.* Paris: Didier, 1882.
Earll, Tony	*Mu Revealed.* New York: Warner Paperback, 1975.
Emerson, J. N.	"Intuitive Archaeology: A Developing Approach." *AAA Symposium: Parapsychology and Anthropology.* Mexico City: November 23, 1974.
Evans-Wentz, Walter	*Tibetan Book of the Dead.* London, New York: Oxford University Press, 1968.
Fauché, Hippolyte	*Le Ramayana, Poeme Sanscrit de Valmiki.* Paris: A. Lacroix, Verboekhoven, 1864.
Fehrenbach, T. R.	*Fire and Blood; A History of Mexico.* New York: Macmillan, 1973.
Fernandez, Justino	*Coatlicue.* Mexico City: Instituto de Investigaciones Esteticas, 1959.
Fisher, Lillian Estelle	*The Background of the Revolution for Mexican Independence.* New York: Russell & Russell, 1971.
Förstemann, Ernst Wilhelm	*Commentary on the Maya Manuscript in the Royal Public Library of Dresden.* Trans. A. M. Parker. Cambridge, Mass.: The Museum, 1906.
Fox, Hugh	*Gods of the Cataclysm.* New York: Harper's Magazine Press, 1976.
Friederichstal, Emmanuel de	*Les Monuments de Yucatan.* Paris: Eres nouvelles, 1841.
Fuller, R. Buckminster	*Synergetics.* New York: Macmillan, 1975.
Fuson, Robert H.	"Orientation of Mayan Ceremonial Centers" in *Annals of the Association of American Geographics.* 1969. p. 494.
Gage, Thomas	*A New Survey of the West Indies.* New York: R. M. McBride, 1929.
———	*Travels in the New World.* Ed. by J. Eric S. Thompson. Norman: University of Oklahoma Press, 1958.
Gaitan, Manuel, Alfonso Morales, Hugh Harleston, Jr., and George Baker, III	"La Triple Cruz Astronómica de Teotihuacan." (Grupo Uac-Kan) *XLI International Congress of Americanists.* Mexico City: September 5, 1974.
Galindo, Juan	*The Ruins of Copan in Central America.* Proceedings of the American Antiquarian Society. Vol. 2. 1835. pp. 543–550.
Gamio, Manuel	*La Poblacion del Valle de Teotihuacan.* 3 vols. Mexico: Secretaria de Fomento, 1922.
———	*Introducción, Sintesis y Conclusiones de la obra Población del Valle de Teotihuacán.* Mexico: S.E.P., Direccion de Talleres Graficos, 1972.
Gann, Thomas W. Francis	*Mexico, from the Earliest Times to the Conquest.* London: L. Dickson, 1936.
Garcia Cubas, Antonio	*Ensayo de un Estudio Comparativo Entre Las Piramides Egipcias y Mexicanas.* Mexico: I. Escalante, 1871.

409

Gardiner, Clinton Harvey	*Naval Power in the Conquest of Mexico.* New York: Greenwood Press, 1969.
Gemelli Careri, Giovanni	*Giro del Mondo.* 8 vols. Venice: G. Malachin, 1719.
───	*Mexico à la fin du XVII siècle.* Paris: Calmann-Levy, 1968.
Gendrop, Paul	*Arte Prehispánico en Mesoamérica.* México: Editorial Trillas, 1970.
Gómara, Francisco López de	*Historia de la Conquista de Mexico.* Mexico: Editorial Pedro Robredo, 1943.
Gordon, Cyrus	*Before Columbus.* New York: Crown, 1971.
───	*Riddles of History.* New York: Crown, 1974.
Graham, Ian	*The Art of Maya Hieroglyphic Writing.* Cambridge: Harvard University Press, 1971.
───	*Corpus of Maya Hieroglyphic Inscriptions.* Cambridge: Peabody Museum, 1975.
Gurdjieff, G. I.	*All and Everything.* London: Routledge & Kegan Paul, 1950.
───	*Meetings with Remarkable Men.* London: Routledge & Kegan Paul, 1963.
Hagar, Stansbury	*The Celestial Plan of Teotihuacán.* Mexico: Museo de Arqueologia, Historia y Etnologia, 1912.
───	*Elements of the Maya and Mexican Zodiacs.* Vienna: A Hartleben, 1909.
───	*The Zodiacal Temples of Uxmal.* Reprinted from *Popular Astronomy.* Vol. 29. 1921.
Hall, Manly P.	Works.
Hanke, Lewis	*Aristotle and the American Indians.* Chicago: Regnery, 1959.
Harleston, Hugh, Jr.	"A Mathematical Analysis of Teotihuacán." Mexico City: *XLI International Congress of Americanists.* October 3, 1974.
Haslip, Joan	*The Crown of Mexico.* New York: Holt, Rhinehart & Winston, 1971.
Herschel, Sir John	*Popular Lectures on Scientific Subjects.* London: W. H. Allen, 1880.
Hodson, Geoffrey	*The Kingdom of the Gods.* Madras, India: Theosophical Publishing House, 1953.
───	*The Science of Seership.* London: Rider, 1929.
───	*Some Experiments in Four Dimensional Vision.* London: Rider, 1933.
Holmes, William Henry	*Archeological Studies Among the Ancient Cities of Mexico.* Chicago: 1895–1897.
Hubbard, L. Ron	Works.
Humboldt, Alexander	*Atlas Geographique et Physique du Royaume de la Nouvelle Espagne.* Paris: G. Dufour, 1812.
───	*Cosmos; A Sketch of a Physical Description of the Universe.* New York: Harper & Row, 1844.
───	*Cristobal Colón y el Descubrimiento de America.* Madrid: Viuda de Hernando, 1892.
───	*Essai Politique sur l'île de Cuba.* Paris: J. Smith, 1826.
───	*Examen Critique de l'historie de la Geographie du Nouveau Continent.* Paris: Gide, 1836–1839.
───	*A Geognostical Essay on the Superposition of Rocks in Both Hemispheres.* London: Longmans, 1823.
───	*Personal Narrative of Travels to the Equinoctial Regions of America during the Years 1799–1804.* London: Bell, Daldy, 1870.
───	*Researches, Concerning the Institutions & Monuments of the Ancient Inhabitants of America.* London: Longmans, 1814.
───	*Views on Nature: or, Contemplation on the Sublime Phenomena of Creation.* London: Bell, 1896.

	Vues des Cordilleres et Monuments des Peuples Indigenes de l'Amerique. Paris: F. Schoell, 1810.
Hunter, C. Bruce	*A Guide to Ancient Maya Ruins.* Norman: University of Oklahoma Press, 1974.
Innes, Hammond	*The Conquistadors.* London: Collins, 1969.
Irwin, Constance	*Fair Gods and Stone Faces.* New York: St. Martin, 1963.
Iturbide, Agustin de	*Memoires Autographes de Don Augustin Iturbide, Emperor of Mexico.* Paris: Bossange Frères, 1824.
Jimenez Gomez, José	*Aztec Calendar (An Explanation).* Mexico City: 1954.
Jimenez Moreno, Wigberto	*Tula y los Toltecas.* Mexico: Revista Mexicana de Estudios Antropologicos, 1940.
Jomard, Edmé François	*Description Génerale de Memphis et des Pyramides.* Paris: Imprimorie Royal, 1829.
Joseph, Jorge	*Mexico, Cuna de la Civilizacion Universal.* Mexico: Casa Ramirez Editores, 1965.
Keratry, Emile, comte de	*L'empereur Maximilian.* Leipzig: Duncker et Humblot, 1867.
Kingsborough, Edward King, Viscount	*Antiquities of Mexico.* 9 vols. Illustrated by A. Aglio. London: 1830–1848.
Knorozov, I. V.	*La Antiqua Escritura de los Pueblos de América Central.* Mexico: Fondo de Cultura, 1954.
	A Brief Summary of the Studies of the Ancient Maya Hieroglyphic *writing in the Soviet Union.* Moscow: Academy of Science, 1955.
	La Escritura de los Antiguos Mayas. Moscow: 1955.
Kubler, George	*The Art and Architecture of Ancient America.* London: Penguin, 1961.
	The Iconography of the Art of Teotihuacan. Washington: Dumbarton Oaks, 1967.
Landa, Diego de	*Relacion de las Cosas.* (MS) Madrid: 1566. *Landa's Relacion de las Cosas de Yucatan.* Trans. with notes by Alfred M. Tozzer. Cambridge: The Museum, 1941.
	Relation des Choses de Yucatan. Trans. Brasseur de Bourbourg. Paris: A. Durand, 1864.
	Yucatan Before and After Conquest. Baltimore: Maya Society, 1937.
Larrainzar, Manuel	*Dictamen Presentado a la Sociedad de Geografia y Estadistica de Mexico.* Mexico: J. Cumplido, 1865.
Larson, Dewey B.	*Beyond Newton.* Portland, Oregon: North Pacific Pub., 1964.
	The Case Against the Nuclear Atom. Portland, Oregon: N. Pacific Pub., 1963.
	New Light on Space and Time. Portland, Oregon: North Pacific Pub., 1965.
	Quasars and Pulsars. Portland, Oregon: North Pacific Pub., 1971.
	The Structure of the Physical Universe. Portland, Oregon: privately published, 1959.
Latrobe, Charles Joseph	*The Rambler in Mexico.* London: Seeley & Burnside, 1836.
Leduc, Alberto	*Diccionario de Geografiá Historia y Biografia Mexicana.* Mexico: V de C. Bouret, 1910.
Leon y Gama, Antonio de	*Descripcion Historica y Cronologica de las Piedras.* Mexico: Zuniga y Ontiveros, 1792.
	Saggio Dell'astronomia Cronologia e Mitologia Degli Antichi Messicani. Rome: Solomoni, 1804.
Léon-Portilla, Miguel	*Aztec Thought and Culture.* Trans. J. Eruory Davis Norman: University of Oklahoma Press, 1963.

——	*The Broken Spears.* Boston: Beacon, 1962.
——	*Imagen del Mexico Antiguo.* Buenos Aires: Editorial Universitaria, 1963.
——	*De Teotihuacán a los Aztecas.* Mexico: Instituto de Investigaciones Historicas, 1971.
——	*Pre-Columbian Literatures of Mexico.* Norman: University of Oklahoma Press, 1969.
Leonard, Irving Albert	*Don Carlos de Sigüenza y Gongora, a Mexican Sarvant of the Seventeenth Century.* Berkeley: University of California Press, 1929.
——	*Ensayo Bibliografico de Don Carlos de Siqüenza.* Mexico City: La Secretaria de Relaciones exteriores, 1929.
Le Plongeon, Alice	*Here and There in Yucatan.* New York: J. W. Bouton, 1886.
——	*The Monuments of Mayach and their Historical Teachings.* Albany Institute (Read 12/22/1896): n.p., 1897?
——	*Notes on Yucatan.* Proceedings of the American Antiquarian Society. Worcester: 1879.
——	*Queen Moo's Talisman: the Fall of the Empire.* London: Kegan Paul, 1902.
Le Plongeon, Augustus	*Archaeological Communication on Yucatan.* American Antiquarian Society. Worcester: 1878.
——	*La religion de Jesus comparada con las enseñanzas de la Iglesia: o, La vida de Jesus autentica del M.R.P. Fr. Pedro Gual. ante el tribunal de la razon y de la ciencia.* Boston: White, 1867.
——	*Letter from Dr. Augustus Le Plongeon.* American Antiquarian Society. Worcester: 1879.
——	*Los misterios sagrados entre los mayas y quichés hace 11.500 anos.* Barcelona: Biblioteca Orientalista, 1931.
——	*Manual de fotografia.* New York: Scovill, 1873.
——	*Mayapan and Maya Inscriptions.* American Antiquarian Society. Worcester: 1882.
——	*Queen Moo and the Egyptian Sphinx.* London: Kegan Paul, 1896.
——	*Sacred Mysteries among the Mayas and the Quiches, 11,500 years ago.* New York: R. Macoy, 1886.
——	*Scarlet book of Free Masonry.* New York: Redding, 1880.
——	*Vestiges of the Mayas, or, Facts Tending to Prove that Communications and Intimate Relations must have Existed.* New York: J. Polhemus, 1881.
Lighthall, William D.	*The Origin of the Maya Civilization.* Ottawa: Royal Society, 1933.
Linne, Sigwald	*Archeological Researches at Teotihuacan, Mexico.* Stockholm: Victor Pettersons, 1934.
——	*Mexican Highland Cultures.* Stockholm: Ethnographical Museum of Sweden, 1942.
Lockyer, Joseph Norman	*The Dawn of Astronomy.* London: Macmillan, 1894.
——	*The Early Temple and the Pyramid Builders.* Washington: Smithsonian Institute, 1893.
——	*Surveying for Archeologists.* London: Macmillan, 1909.
Lorenzo, José L.	*Materiales para la Arqueologia de Teotihuacán.* Mexico: I.N.A.H., 1968.
Luyties, Otto G.	*Egyptian Visits to America.* New York: Noonan & Skelly, 1922.
Macias Villada, Mario	*Los Calendarios Indígenas Americanos.* Chapingo: Private, 1955.
MacShane, Frank, ed.	*Impressions of Latin America.* New York: Morrow, 1963.
Madariaga, Salvador de	*Hernan Cortes.* Buenos Aires: Editorial Sud-Americano, 1948.

Magaloni Duarte, Ignacio   *Educadores del Mundo.* Mexico: B. Costa-Amic., 1969.

Makemson, Maude   *The Maya Correlation Problem.* Poughkeepsie: Vassar College Observatory, 1946.

Marquina, Ignacio   *Arquitectura Prehispanica.* Mexico City: I.N.A.H., 1951.

Martin, Perry   *Maximilian in Mexico.* London: Constable, 1914.

Martinez Paredes, Domingo   *Hunab Ku.* Mexico: Editorial Orion, 1964.

———   *El Idioma Maya Hablado y Escrito.* Mexico: Editorial Orion, 1967.

———   *El Popol Vuh Tiene Razon.* Mexico: Editorial Orion, 1968.

Matos Moctezuma, Eduardo   *México Prehispánico y Colonial.* Mexico: Editorial Grijalba, 1967.

Maudslay, Alfred Percival   *Archaeology.* London: Porter & Dulau, 1889–1902.

Maudslay, Anna Cary   *A Glimpse at Guatemala.* London: Murray, 1899.

Mayer, William   *Early Travellers in Mexico.* New York: Heinemann, 1961.

Medina Peralta, Manuel   *Manual elemental de astronomia de posicion.* Mexico: Talleres grafcos de la nacion, 1942.

Meggers, Betty Jane   *Ecuador.* New York: Praeger, 1966.

Meggers, B. J.,   *Early Formative Period of Coastal Ecuador.* Washington Smithsonian
   C. Evans, and E. Estrada   Institution, 1965.

Mercer, Henry C.   *The Hill Caves of Yucatan.* Norman: University of Oklahoma, 1975.

Mertz, Henriette   *Pale Ink.* Chicago: Swallow Press, 1972.

———   *The Wine Dark Sea.* Chicago: Mertz, 1964.

Mesmer, Anton   Works.

Michell, John F.   *City of Revelation.* London: Garnstone Press, 1972.

———   *The Earth Spirit.* London: Thames & Hudson, 1975.

———   *The Flying Saucer Vision.* London: Sidgwick & Jackson, 1967.

———   *The View over Atlantis.* New York: Ballantine, 1973.

Millon, René   "The Beginnings of Teotihuacan." *Am. Antiquity.* Vol. 26, No. 1. July, 1960.

———   "Extension y Poblacion de la Ciudad de Teotihuacan en sus Diferentes Periodos." *Onceava Mesa Redonda.* Mexico: 1967.

———   "Teotihuacan." *Scientific American.* Vol. 216, No. 6. June, 1967.

———   "New Data on Teotihuacan I in Teotihuacan." *Boletin del Centro de Investigaciones Antropologicos de Mexico.* Mexico: 1957.

———   "The Pyramid of the Sun at Teotihuacan: 1959 Investigations." Translations of American Philosophical Society, Vol. 55 Part VI. Philadelphia: 1965.

———   "The Teotihuacan Mapping Project." *Am. Antiquity.* 1964.

———   "Teotihuacan: Completion of Map of Giant Ancient City in the Valley of Mexico." *Science.* Vol. 170, pp. 1077–1082.

———   *"Urbanization at Teotihuacan: The Teotihuacan Mapping Project."* XXXVII International Congress of Americanists. Argentina: 1968.

Millon, René,   *The Teotihuacan Map.* Vol. 1. Austin: University of Texas Press,
   B. Drewitt, and   1973.
   G. L. Cowgill

Mitchell, Hugh   "Definiciones de Términos Topográficos." Canal Zone: *Interamerican Geodetic Survey,* 1952.

Mitchell, J. L.   *The Conquest of the Maya.* London: Jarrold, 1934.

Molina Montes, Augusto   *Consideraciones Sobre la Restauracion Arquitectonica en Arqueología.* Mexico: Tesis I & II, 1974.

Monges Lopez, Ricardo   "La Medición del Tiempo Según Los Mayas." *Naturaleza.* Vol. 5, No. 2. Mexico: April, 1974. pp. 78–84.

Mooser, Federico   "Geologia, Naturaleza y Desarrollo del Valle de Teotihuacan." *Materiales Para la Arqueologia de Teotihuacan.* Vol. 17, Investigaciones. Mexico: I.N.A.H., 1968.

413

Morley, Sylvanus G.	*The Ancient Maya.* Stanford: Stanford University Press, 1946.
———	*An Introduction to the Study of the Maya Hieroglyphs.* New York: Dover, 1975.
———	*In Search of Maya Glyphs.* Santa Fe: Museum of New Mexico Press, 1970.
Motolinia, Fray Toribio de Benavente	*Historia de los Indios de la Nueva Espana.* Mexico: 1941.
———	*Memoriales.* Mexico: Instituto de Investigaciones Historicas, 1971.
Muller, E. Florence	*Historia Antigua del Valle de Morelos.* Mexico: 1949.
Muses, Charles Arthur	*Illumination on Jacob Boehme.* New York: Kings Crown Press, 1951.
———	*Esoteric Teachings of the Tibetan Tantra.* Lauzanne: Falcons Wing Press, 1961.
———	*Consciousness and Reality.* New York: Outerbridge and Lazard, 1972.
Nebel, Carl	*Voyage Pittoresque.* Paris: M. Moench, 1836.
Newham, C. A.	*The Astronomical Significance of Stonehenge.* Leeds: Blackburn, 1972.
Nezahualcoyotl, King of Texcoco	*The Zopancuica of Nezahualcoyotl.* compiled, ed. by R. J. Sontas in English. Washington: 1944.
Nicholson, Irene	*The Conquest of Mexico: a Collection of Contemporary Material.* New York: Grossman, 1968.
———	*The Liberators.* New York: Praeger, 1969.
———	*Mexican and Central American Mythology.* London: Paul Hamlyn, 1967.
Niven, William	*Illustrated Catalog of Minerals.* New Jersey: Privately Printed, 1888.
Noguera, Eduardo	"La Cultura Mayance del Vieje Imperio." *Mexico Prehispanico.* Mexico: 1946.
Noriega, Raul	*Esplendor de Mexico Antiguo.* Mexico: Centro de Investigaciones Anthro., 1959.
———	"Interpretacion Matematico-Astronomica de la Piedra del Sol." *XLI International Congress of Americanists.* Mexico: 1974.
Norman, Benjamin M.	*Rambles in Yucatan.* Philadelphia: Carey and Hart, 1849.
Northrop, F. S. C.	*The Meeting of East and West.* New York: Macmillan, 1962.
Novo, Salvador	"Teotihuacan: The City of the Gods." *Pensee.* Vol. 3, No. 1. Portland: 1967.
Nunez de la Vega, Francisco	*Constituciones Diocesianos del Opispado de Chiappa.* Rome: Caietana Zenobi, 1702.
Nunnari, Filippo	*Un Viaggiatore Calabrese della fine del Secolo XVII.* Messina: Mazzini, 1901.
Nuttall, Zelia	*Astronomical Methods of the Ancient Mexicans.* New York: 1906.
———	*The Aztecs and their Predecessors in the Valley of Mexico.* Philadelphia: 1926.
———	*Codex Magliabecchi.* Berkeley University of California, 1903.
———	*The Fundamental Principles of Old & New World Civilizations.* Cambridge, Mass.: 1901.
———	*The Gardens of Ancient Mexico.* Smithsonian Institution Annual Report. Washington: 1925.
———	*Note on the Ancient Mexican System.* Dresden: B. Schulze, 1894.
———	*The Periodical Adjustments of the Ancient Mexican Calender.* New Era, 1904.
O'Conner, Richard	*The Cactus Throne.* New York: Putnam, 1971.
Ordonez y Aguiar, Ramon	*Descripcion de la ciudad palencana.* Brasseur De Bourbourg Collection.

———	*Historia de la creacion del cielo y de la Tierra*. Mexico: Nicolas Leon Museo Nacional, 1907.
Orozco y Berra, Manuel	*Historia antigua y de las culturos aborigenes de Mexico*. Mexico: Editiones Fuente Cultural, 1880.
———	*Los conquistadores de Mexico*. Mexico: P. Robredo, 1938.
———	*Historia de la dominacion Española en Mexico*. Mexico: Antigua Libreria Roberdo, de J. Porrua e hijos, 1938.
Palacios, Enrique Juan	*El Calendario y Los Jeroglificos cronograficos Mayas*. Mexico: Editorial Cultura, 1933.
Parker, Franklin D.	*José Cecilio del Valle and the Establishment of the Central American Confederation and the Central American Republic*. Honduras: La University, 1954.
———	*Travels in Central America 1821–1840*. Gainsville: University of Florida Press, 1970.
Pauw, Cornelius de	*Recherches philosophiques sur les Americains*. Berlin: G. J. Decker, Imp. du Roi, 1770.
Peñafiel, Antonio	*Teotihuacan*. Mexico: La Secretaria de Fomento, 1900.
Perez, Juan	*A Short Maya-Spanish Dictionary*. Seattle: Copy Mart, 1970.
Peterson, Frederick	*Ancient Mexico*. London: Ruskin House, 1959.
Plato	*Critias–Timaeus*. London: Methuen, 1929.
Plummer, Gordon	*Mathematics of the Cosmic Mind*. Theosophical, 1970.
Prescott, Wm. Hickling	*Mexico, and the Life of the Conqueror Hernan Cortes*. New York: P. F. Collier, 1902.
———	*History of the Conquest of Mexico*. New York: Harper & Row, 1843.
Price, Christine	*Heirs of the Ancient Maya*. New York: Scribner, 1972.
Proskouriakoff, Tatiana A.	*An Album of Maya Architecture*. Norman: University of Oklahoma Press, 1963.
Rangel Ruiz, Alfonso	*Datos de Orientacion de Teotihuacan y Marcadores Cerro Gordo/ Colorado Chico*. Mexico: Apuntes, Libreta de Campo, 1965.
Rattray, Evelyn Childs	"Some Clarifications on the Early Teotihuacan Ceramic Sequence." *XLI International Congress of Americanists*. Mexico: 1974.
Recinos, Adrian	*Annals of the Cakchiquels*. Norman: University of Oklahoma Press, 1953.
Reed, Alma M.	*The Ancient Past of Mexico*. New York: Crown, 1966.
Reed, Nelson	*The Caste War of Yucatan*. Stanford: Stanford University Press, 1964.
Reich, Wilhelm	Works.
Reygadas Vertiz, José	"Las Ultimas Excavaciones en la Zona Arqueologica de Teoti-huacan." *XX International Congress of Americanists*. Mexico: 1922.
———	"Nota Preliminar Sobre las Actuales Excavaciones en Teotihuacan." *Revista Mexicana de Estudios Prehistoricos*. Mexico: 1928.
Rico Gonzales, Victor	*Historiadores Mexicanos del Siglo XVIII*. Mexico: Mexico Auto-nomade, 1949.
Rio, Antonio del	*Description of the Ruins of an Ancient City Discovered near Palenque*. Trans. P. Felix Cobrera. London: H. Berthoud, 1822.
Riva Palacio, Vincente	*Mexico a Traves de los Siglos*. Mexico: Ballesca, 1887–1889.
Rivera Cambas, Manuel	*Los Gobernates de Mexico*. Mexico: J. M. Aguilar Ortiz, 1872–1873.
———	*Mexico Pintoresco, Artistico y Monumental*. Mexico: Gustavo G. Velasquez, 1872.
Robertson, William	*History of America*. London: Straham, 1777.
Ross, Parmentier	*Glimpses of a Friendship*. In *Pioneers of American Anthropology*. Seattle: University of Washington Press, 1966.
Ruiz, Eduardo	*Don Carlos de Sigüenza y Gongora*. Mexico: Vargas Rea, 1950.

Saenz, Cesar A. *Quetalcoatl.* Mexico: I.N.A.H., 1962.

Sahagun, Fray Bernardino de *Historia General de las Cosas de Nueva España.* 5 vols. Mexico: Ed. Robrero, 1969.

Salisbury, Stephen, Jr. *The Mayas, the sources of their history.* Worcester, Mass.: Privately printed, 1877.

———— *Dr. Le Plongeon in Yucatan; His account of discoveries.* Worcester, Mass.: Privately printed, 1877.

———— *The Mexican calendar stone,* by Philipp J. J. Valenti, Ph.D. (from the German). Terra cotta figure from Isla Mujeres, northeast coast of Yucatan. *Archeological communication on Yucatan,* by Dr. Augustus Le Plongeon. *Notes on Yucatan,* by Mrs. Alice D. Le Plongeon. Composed and arranged by Stephen Salisbury, Jr. Worcester, Mass.: C. Hamilton, 1879.

———— "The Mayas, the Sources of their History." Proceedings of the American Antiquarian Society. 1876, 1877.

Sanchez, George I. *Arithmetic in Maya.* Austin, Texas: Privately printed, 1961.

Sanderson, Ivan Works.

Santa Anna, Antonio Lopez de *Mi historia militar y politica, 1810–1874.* Mexico: Vda. de C. Bouret, 1905.

Santesson, Hans Stefan *Understanding Mu.* New York: Warner paperback, 1970.

Satterthwaite, L. *Concepts and Structures of Maya Calendrical Arithmetic.* Philadelphia: Museum of the University of Pennsylvania, 1947.

Saville, Marshall *Bibliographical Notes on Uxmal.* New York: 1921.

Schlemmer, Alfred E. "Some Special Aspects of Technological Forecasting." Primer Simposium de Pronosticos Tecnologicos, *XI Convencion Nacional de Ingenieros Quimicos.* Mexico: October 22, 1971.

Schondube, Otto *Teotihuacan, Ciudad de Los Dios.* Mexico: Imagen de Mexico, 1971.

Schwartz, Stephan *Psychic Archeology.* New York: Grossett & Dunlap, 1977.

Sejourné, Laurette *Arquitectura y pintura en Teotihuacan.* Mexico: Siglo XXI Editores, 1966.

———— *El Universo de Quetzalcóatl.* Mexico: Fondo de Cultura Economica, 1962.

———— *Pensiamento y religión en el Mexico Antiguo.* Mexico: Fondo de Cultura Económica, 1957.

Seler, Eduard *Mexican and Central American Antiquities. Twenty-four Papers.* Trans. under the supervision of Charles P. Bowditch. Washington: Smithsonian Institution, 1904.

Sigüenza y Gongora, Carlos de *Obras, con una biografía escrita por Francisco Perez Salazar.* Mexico: Sociedad de bibliofilas Mexicanos, 1928.

———— *Libra Astronomica y filosofica.* Mexico: University Centro de Estudios Filosoficos, 1959.

Skinner, James Ralston *Key to the Hebrew-Egyptian Mystery in the Source of Measures.* Philadelphia: McKay, 1876.

Soustelle, Jacques *Daily Life of the Aztecs.* New York: Macmillan, 1955.

———— *The Four Suns.* New York: Grossman, 1971.

———— *Mexico.* London: The Cresent Press, 1969.

Spence, Lewis *Atlantis in America.* London: Benn, 1925,

———— *The Gods of Mexico.* London: Unwin, 1923.

———— *The Civilization of Ancient Mexico.* Cambridge: Cambridge University Press, 1912.

———— *Arcane Secrets and Occult Lore of Mexico.* London: Rider, 1950.

Spinden, Herbert J. *Ancient Civilizations of Mexico & Central America.* New York: American Museum of Natural History, 1917.

Stacy-Judd, Robert B.	*Atlantis, Mother of Empires.* Santa Monica, Cal.: De Vorss, 1973.
Stearn, Jess	*The Sleeping Prophet.* London: Muller, 1968.
Stecchini, Livio C.	Appendix, *Secrets of the Great Pyramid.* New York. Harper & Row, 1971.
———	"A History of Measures." *American Behavioral Scientist.* IV. 1961.
Steiner, Rudolph	Works.
Stephens, John Lloyd	*Incidents of Travel in Central America, Chiapas and Yucatan.* New York: Harper & Row, 1843.
———	*Incidents of Travel in Egypt, Arabia, Petraea and the Holy Land.* New York: Harper & Row, 1851.
———	*Incidents of Travel in Yucatan.* New York: Harper & Row, 1847.
Stevenson, William Bennet	*Historical & Descriptive Narrative of 20 years Residence in South America.* London: Hurst, Robinson, 1825.
Sutton, Ann	*Among the Maya Ruins.* New York: Rand-McNally, 1967.
Szèkely, Edmond Bordeaux	*The Essene Book of Creation.* San Diego: First Christians Church, 1968.
———	*La filosofia del Mexico antiguo.* Baja California: Ediciones de la Academia de Filosofia, 1954.
———	*How the Great Pan Died; The Origin of Christianity.* San Diego: Academy Books, 1968.
———	*The Soul of Ancient Mexico.* San Diego: Academy Books, 1968.
Taylor, John	*The Great Pyramid: Why Was It Built and Who Built It?* London: Longmans, 1864.
Teeple, John Edgar	*Mayan Astronomy.* Washington: Carnegie Institute, 1931.
Temple, Robert K. G.	*The Sirius Mystery.* London: Sidgwick & Jackson, 1976.
Thomas, Cyrus	*A Study of the Manuscript of Troano.* Washington: U.S. Government Printing Office, 1882.
Thompson, Edward H.	*People of the Serpent.* Boston: Houghton Mifflin, 1932.
Thompson, J. Eric S.	*Maya Archaeologist.* Norman: University of Oklahoma Press, 1963.
———	*Maya Hierogliphic Writing.* Norman: University of Oklahoma Press, 1960.
———	*The Rise and Fall of Maya Civilization.* Norman: University of Oklahoma Press, 1954.
Tolstoy, Ivan	*The Pulse of a Planet.* New York: New American Library, 1971.
Tompkins, Peter and Christopher Bird	*The Secret Life of Plants.* New York: Harper & Row, 1973.
Tompkins, Peter	*Secrets of the Great Pyramid.* New York: Harper & Row, 1971.
Tomson, Robert	*An Englishman and the Mexican Inquisition.* Mexico: G. R. G. Conway, 1927.
Torquemada, Juan de	*Monarquia Indiana.* Mexico: S. Chavez Hayhoe, 1943–1944.
Tozzer, Alfred	*Stephens, Prescott, Bancroft and Others.* Mexico: El Colegio de Mexico, 1941.
———	*Zelia Nuttall.* Washington: 1933. Reprinted from *American Anthropologist.* Vol. 35, No. 3.
Tudor, Henry	*Narrative of a Tour in North America.* London: J. Duncan, 1834.
Vaillant, George	*Aztecs of Mexico.* New York: Doubleday, 1941.
Van Sinderen, Adrian	*A Journey into Neolithic Times.* New York: 1947.
Veytia, Mariano	*Los Calendarios Mexicanos.* Mexico: Museo Nacional, 1907.
———	*Historia Antigua de Mexico.* Mexico: J. Ojede, 1836.
Villacorta Calderon, José A. and Carlos A.	*Codices Mayas.* Guatemala: Tipografia Nacional, 1930.

Volguine, Alexandre — *Astrology of the Mayas and Aztecs.* Sharples, England: Pythagorean Publications, 1969.

Von Hagen, Victor — *F. Catherwood, Architect-Explorer of two Worlds.* Barre, Mass.: Barre Publishers, 1967.

——— *Frederick Catherwood, Architect.* New York: Oxford University Press, 1950.

——— *Maya Explorer, John Lloyd Stephens.* Norman: University of Oklahoma Press, 1947.

——— *Search for the Maya.* Farnborough: Saxon House, 1973.

——— "Waldeck, Fantastic Archeologist." *Natural History.* December, 1946.

Waldeck, Frederic — *Le Sacrifice Gladiatorial.* Paris: E. Mauclerc, 1872.

——— *Voyage Pittoresque et Archeologique.* Paris: 1838.

Wallrath, Matthew — *Excavations in Tehuantepel Region of Mexico.* Philadelphia: American Philosophical Society, 1967.

Waters, Frank — *The Book of the Hopi.* New York: Ballantine, 1963.

——— *Mexico Mystique.* Chicago: Sage Books, 1975.

——— *Pumpkin Seed Point.* Chicago: Sage Books, 1969.

Watkins, Alfred — *The Old Straight Track.* London: Garnstone Press, 1970.

Watts, Alan — *The Book.* New York: Pantheon, 1966.

——— *The Way of Zen.* New York: New American Library, 1959.

Wauchope, Robert — *Handbook of Middle American Indians.* 12 vols. Austin: University of Texas, 1964.

Weaver, Muriel Porter — *The Aztecs, Maya & Their Predecessors: Archeology in Mesoamerica.* Seminar Press, 1972.

Wicke, Charles — *Olmec.* Tucson: University of Arizona Press, 1971.

Wilcox, Elizabeth G. — *Mu–Fact or Fiction.* New York: Pageant, 1963.

Wilcox, Thomas — *The Cosmic Papers of Thomas Wilcox.* Los Angeles: Published privately, 1957.

Wilkins, Harold T. — *Mysteries of Ancient South America.* New Jersey: Citadel, 1956.

Willard, T. A. — *City of the Sacred Well.* New York: Century, 1926.

——— *The Lost Empire of the Itzaes & Mayas.* Glendale, Cal.: A. H. Clark, 1935.

Wolf, Eric — *Sons of the Shaking Earth.* Chicago: University of Chicago Press, 1959.

Wood, Herman G. — *Ideal Meteorology.* Dorchester, Mass.: H. G. Wood, 1908.

Woodroffe, Sir John G. — *The Serpent Power.* Madras: Ganesh, 1924.

Wuthenau, Alexander von — *Pre-Columbian Terra-Cottas.* London: Methuen, 1970.

——— *Unexpected Faces in Ancient America.* New York: Crown, 1975.

Zavala, Lorenzo de — *Ensayo Historico de las Revoluciones de Mexico.* Mexico: Hacienda Dep. Editorial, 1918.

Zhirov, Nikolay Feodorovich — *Atlantis.* Moscow: Progress Publishers, 1970.

Index

Chavero, Alfredo, 149, 158
checkerboard in Mayan mathematics, 286
Cheops, Great Pyramid of, 33, 55; dimensions, 125, 216–217, 241; King's Chamber, 77; numbers in unraveling secrets, 256; as perennial clock, 252; pi proportion in, 125; sacred cubit, 244; vs. Sun Pyramid, 253
Chichen Itza: attack by sublevados, 165–166; bought by Thompson, 178; building reconstruction, 175; Caracol, 104, 308–309; Castillo, 103; Cenote, 179, 180–181; Charnay at, 149, 160; gymnasium, 105, 167; Le Plongeon's mausoleum tableaux analysis, 172; monjas, 105; nunnery, 161; Thompson's dredging at, 180–181
Chilam Balam, 102, 114, 347; quoted, 304–305; Russian translation, 292
Chimalpahin, Quauhtlehuanitzin, 20, 34
Chimalpopoca Codex, 115, 116
chinampas, 46, 47
Chinese, travels eastward, 353-354
Cholula, Great Pyramid of, 33, 57–58; massacre at, 4, 6
Chonay, Padré Dionisio-José, 79
chronology: Atlantis, 175–176; Mayan, 102
chumay (measure), 255
church, baroque, 156
Churchward, James, 283; on four forces, 370; and Le Plongeon, 174–175; *The Lost Continent of Mu,* 364; and Niven's find, 360, 362; report of Mesoamerican origins, 364–372
cientificos, 146–147, 148; end of, 203, 205, 206
cipactli, 391
circle: Mayan names for, 173; pattern of numbers, 257; symbolism, 173; for time and space, 257–258
Citadel at Teotihuacan, 213; in calendric ritual, 259–261; calendric system, 258–263; Gamio's excavations, 211–217; Hagar's perception of, 221; measure, 253; mound, 154, 214; pyramids, 212–217; reflecting pools as seismic monitors, 272
civil war, 125, 127, 208

clairvoyance, Maya, 167
Clavigero, Francisco Javier, 121, 164; *Storia Antica,* 50
Cleito vs. Coatlicue, 68
Cleveland, Grover, 176
clock, pyramid as, 252
coatl (serpent), 388
Coatlicue (earth goddess), 67–69
Codex, 51; Cortesianus, 171; Grolier, 295; Madrid, 297; Magliabecchiano, 73; Mendoza, 305; Nuttall, 308; Porrua, 288; Sanchez, 207; Vaticanus, 302; *see also* Dresden Codex; Troana Codex; Tro-Cortesianus Codex
Coe, Dr. Michael D., 295; on Mesoamerican calendar, 289
Cogulludo, Diego Lopez de, *Historia de Yucatan,* 20
Coh, prince, 172
Cole, J. H., 217
Collin, Rodney, *The Theory of Celestial Influence,* 120
Commission for the Study of Mexican Antiquities, 127
compass, magnetic, 313
conquistadores, 3–11
Copal, sundial stele, 312
Copan: altar, 97; Maudslay at, 163; Stephens and Catherwood at, 96–97
Corral, Ramon, 208
Cortes, Hernan, 19; at battle of Otumba, 71; Bullock on, 63, 71–72; and conquest of Mexico, 3–11; and founding of Mexico City, 14; at pyramids, 71–72; reward for service, 14; at Veracruz, 63
Cortes, Don Martin, 18
cosmogony, Maya, 282–283
cosmos, polarity, 284
Coto, Thomas, 255
Council of the Indies, 19
Cowgill, George L., 230
Crabtree, William, 291
Criollos, and Grito de Dolores, 58
Cro-Magnons, Stacey-Judd on, 378–379
Cronwell, George H., 373
crops, Mesoamerica, 32, 232
cubit (measure), 253; vs. hunab, 251; Mayan, 255; sacred, 244
cuc (measure), 255
Cuevas, Alfonso, 316
Cuevas, Mariano, 50
Cuevas–Gaitan marker, 322
Cuicuilco, excavation at, 207
Curzon, Sir Robert, 308

Darreygosa, Juan, *Unedited Documents Relating to the Discovery and Conquest of New Spain,* 347
de Bry, Theodore, 15
del Rio, Don Andres Manuel, 47
del Rio, Don Antonio, 80; *Description of the Ancient City Discovered Near Palenque,* 87
del Rio, Don Manuel, 67
Denon, Dominique, *Egypt Illustrated,* 125
de Pauw, Cornelius: on Mexican calendar, 42; *Recherches Philosophiques sur les Américains,* 41
de Prieto, Mariana Beeching, 357
Diaz, del Castillo, Bernal, 8; on Aztec priests, 11; on Montezuma, 9
Diaz, Felix, 147
Diaz, Porfirio, 128, 139, 145, 204, 208, 210; as Batres benefactor, 185, 190, 192; as dictator, 146, 148; exile, 202–206; portrait, 138; recruiting method, 145; visit to Teotihuacan, 198–199
Dido, queen, 351
diligencia, 127, 149
dinosaur in fight with men, carving of, 360
Diodorus Siculus, 351
divination: geomancy, 331; of Yucatan Indians, 166
dodecahedron–icosohedron, 326–327, 328
Donnelly, Ignatius, 176
Dow, J. W. A., *Astronomical Orientation at Teotihuacan,* 313
Dozal, Pedro, 242
dragon power, 328–329
Dresden Codex, 292, 304; astronomical data, 295; decipherment, 294; Venus calendar, 310; *see also* Codex
Drewitt, R. Bruce, 230
Drucker, David R., 388; on Teotihuacan calendric system, 259, 261
Duke, Dr. Douglas, 295
Dupaix, Guillermo: *Antiquités Mexicaines,* 87; at Palenque, 83–87; petroglyphs, 315
Duran, Diego, 19, 255–256, 305
dwarf, pyramid of, 99
dwellings, *see* buildings
Dyan-Chohans, 173

Earll, Tony, *Mu Revealed,* 360–362